PREHISTORY

Part I of Volume I of the *History* records the development of mankind from the Palaeolithic and Mesolithic ages to the time less than 10,000 years ago when man began the cultivation of plants and the domestication of animals. Jacquetta Hawkes describes man's physical and mental evolution and the environmental stimuli that spurred these changes. She offers provocative queries into the possibility of a common racial memory as she details the emergence of religion, art, and a material culture among primitive man. Her story, fully illustrated with plates, drawings, and maps, follows mankind from his African cradle through Asia, Europe, and on to the New World, to a time when Neolithic communities could live a settled life, develop crafts, and assume their advance into the beginnings of civilization.

"Miss Hawkes writes so well that even her descriptions of stone tool types are a pleasure to read . . . interesting and instructive"

—National History Magazine

"A great, ambitious work"—Houston Post

Other MENTOR Books Published in
Cooperation with UNESCO

HISTORY OF MANKIND: Cultural and Scientific Development Volume One, Part II, The Beginnings of Civilization by Sir Leonard Woolley

The second part of this UNESCO history describes the dawn of culture in the Bronze Age and goes up to the splendid civilizations of Mesopotamia and the Nile at the end of the 13th century B.C.
(#MY633—$1.25)

THE EVOLUTION OF SCIENCE: Readings in the History of Mankind edited by Guy Metraux and François Crouzet

Essays from the *Journal of World History,* a UNESCO publication, by leading scholars including V. Gordon Childe, Bertrand Gille, Francois Russo, Clyde Kluckhohn. (#MQ505—95¢)

THE NINETEENTH CENTURY WORLD: Readings in the History of Mankind edited by Guy Metraux and François Crouzet

Essays on the nineteenth century from UNESCO's *Journal of World History,* by such scholars as R. R. Palmer, Werner Conze, Henri Gouhier, and others. (#MQ506—95¢)

HISTORY OF MANKIND

Cultural and Scientific Development

Volume I, Part 1

PREHISTORY

by Jacquetta Hawkes

A MENTOR BOOK

Published by The New American Library, New York and Toronto
The New English Library Limited, London

Published as a MENTOR BOOK
By Arrangement with George Allen and Unwin, Ltd.

FIRST PRINTING, AUGUST, 1965

Prepared under the auspices and with the financial assistance of the United Nations Educational, Scientific and Cultural Organization and published for the International Commission for a History of the Scientific and Cultural Development of Mankind

Consultant for Volume I, Part 1
Professor A. G. Bandi
(University of Berne, Switzerland)

A hardcover edition of *History of Mankind*, containing Volume I, Parts 1 and 2, is available in the United States from Harper & Row, Publishers, Inc.

MENTOR BOOKS are published *in the United States* by The New American Library, Inc., 1301 Avenue of the Americas, New York, New York 10019, *in Canada* by The New American Library of Canada Limited, 295 King Street East, Toronto 2, Ontario, *in the United Kingdom* by The New English Library Limited, Barnard's Inn, Holborn, London, E.C. 1, England

PRINTED IN THE UNITED STATES OF AMERICA

FOREWORD

Director-General of UNESCO

At a time when man is preparing to launch out from this planet into space, it is well that History should hold him in contemplation of his trajectory through the ages.

Never before, indeed, has he shown so searching a curiosity about his past or such jealous care to preserve its vestiges. It is as though in some mysterious way a balance were now maintained in his thought between the exploration of space and that of time, the extroversion of the one being offset by the inwardness of the other.

Be that as it may, never more than now, when man finds himself hurtling at vertiginous speed towards a wondrous future, has there been a great need for the function of memory to ensure for mankind the appropriation of its creative actuality. If consciousness were not thus rooted in such reflection on its own process of becoming, many of the inventions we hail as conquests and advances would be no more than the uncontrollable workings of an alienated destiny.

To evoke this retrospective awareness is the first thing that this work which we now have the honour of introducing to the public sets out to do; it is an attempt to sum up the heritage of civilization to which we owe our present élan.

The ambition to write a universal history is a very old one indeed. Many have tried their hand at it before, particularly in the classical epochs—not without merit, nor without success. The present work belongs to that noble line of great syntheses which seek to present to man the sum total of his memories as a coherent whole.

It has the same twofold ambition, to embrace the past in its entirety and to sum up all that we know about that past. And

v

it adopts the same intellectual approach—that of the interpretative as opposed to the descriptive historian—reducing events to their significance in a universal frame of reference, explicit or implicit.

However, this *History of Mankind* parts company with its predecessors on several essential points. In the first place, it deliberately confines itself to shedding light on one of mankind's many aspects, its *cultural and scientific development*.

In so doing it departs from the traditional approaches to the study of history, which, as we know, attach decisive importance to political, economic and even military factors. It offers itself as a corrective to the ordinary view of man's past. And those who initiated the enterprise may well have thought at first that this was, in itself, sufficiently useful and original for them to dispense with any further aim.

Admittedly, it rests with the science of history to decide objectively, *a posteriori* and according to the case, on the relative importance of the different elements and factors in particular situations. To that extent the approach deliberately adopted in this history may well be said to be an *a priori* postulate. This is the very postulate on which UNESCO itself is based, namely, the conviction that international relations, in their ultimate reality, are determined not merely by political and economic factors and considerations but spring as well, perhaps even more surely, from the capabilities and demands of the mind.

Nevertheless, even from the strictly scientific point of view, this History, deliberately partial though it be, may well claim that, in restoring to the achievements of culture and science their full reality and significance, it has made an essential contribution to that sum of factual knowledge and right understanding which a complete history aspires to offer.

But the originality of the enterprise does not stop there. In point of fact, that is where it begins. For the facts of which this History treats are no ordinary ones. To put them back in their proper place is not merely to fill a long-standing gap and thus complete the sum, restoring its balance to the whole. It is to discover a new dimension of the historical object, perceptible only when approached from a particular intellectual angle.

Cultural or scientific facts, whatever their subject-matter, means, cause, pretext or circumstances, are essentially thoughts of man about man.

This is obvious in the cultural sphere, every value being a human ideal. But it is no less true of science; for apart from the fact that truth, too, is a value, the essence of science is not knowledge, but the method by which knowledge is gained, the rule the mind prescribes itself in order to attain it; and every rule is a form of reflection and self-discipline; that is, doubled consciousness.

Thus, the history of what has no doubt been too simply described here as 'the cultural and scientific development of mankind' is, strictly speaking, the story of how, through the ages, men—individually and collectively—have conceived of humanity. Or, to be more correct, have conceived of *their* humanity, that is, the universal aspect of their experience. In short, the subject of this work is the gradual development, in its most expressive manifestations, of the consciousness of the universal in man.

As will be seen, great care is taken to describe the exchange and influences which link the different foci of civilization across space or time. We are shown how this web of reciprocal influences is becoming more closely woven as spatial communications grow more numerous and rapid and relations in time more intensive.[1] Indeed by no means the least interesting feature of this work is the stress it lays upon this still too little known aspect of historical reality in which the 'intellectual and moral solidarity of mankind' referred to in the Preamble to UNESCO's Constitution can really be seen at work.

Yet even this is not the decisive discovery. That lies not so much in the evidence of interrelation between the many and varied civilizations as in the fact, manifest in all forms of culture and science, that every civilization implies, produces or invokes an image of man in terms of the universal.

This immanence of the universal in every cultural and scientific experience is what gives its essential character to the spiritual solidarity of mankind. And it is in this form that that solidarity can serve as the foundation for the true peace described in UNESCO's Constitution, whereas the effect of

---

[1] Even in time, relations are reversible—not, of course, through any real causation, but owing to the perpetual reappraisal of the significance of events that takes place in the course of man's constantly renewed, and renewing, retrospection.

intercultural relations upon the interplay of the forces conducive, in a given situation, to peace is, as well we know, extremely complex and indirect, and therefore contingent. In fact it is because the object of this History, as already pointed out, is the development of the consciousness of this solidarity that UNESCO regards such an undertaking as both vital and necessary.

But straightway we are faced with another fact, no less rich in implications. In the actual experience of science and culture, sense and style, which constitute the universal element, remain indissolubly bound up with the singular act of invention or creation from which they derive. It may truly be said both of science and of culture, regarded as experiences, that 'the more one concentrates on the particular, the more universal one becomes'. And it is only by repeating the various operations of the act of creation, reduced to their objective characteristics—which make up what we call method—or by subjective communion with the mental atmosphere of that act—which is what we call intuition—that another person can understand and assimilate this sense and style.

It follows that for a history which aims to keep in constant touch with experience and restore it in its contingent truth, scientific and cultural facts have significance only for certain individuals, namely those who are capable of applying these methods and of exercising this intuition which give access to the secrets of creativeness in its unique aspects. However, to possess this ability, there is no doubt that one must belong to the particular context of civilization in which such unique phenomena occur. Accordingly a concrete history of science and culture can only be written from a plurality of viewpoints corresponding to the variety of civilizations.

To acknowledge the fact that there is more than one civilization is not to deny in any way the continuity or solidarity of human development. On the contrary, the study of the interrelations, across time and space, of ideas, values and techniques restores this sense of continuity and solidarity, which have never before been so definitely and convincingly established as in this History. Similarly, to be aware of the originality of the works and symbols which make up each civilization is not to gainsay the universality of the human mind. As we have seen, true universality is no more than a dimension of this consciousness of a sense or style, which opens out to the potential totality of mankind only by rooting itself in the particularity of its initial emergence.

The classical rationalism of the West conceived the history of the human mind as a process of development in which all scientific and cultural facts are arranged in order with reference to a single, constant subject that is universal by nature. There is no need to plunge into a philosophical discussion on ontological humanism in order to expose this myth. It would be only too easy, now of all times, to show how into this allegedly universal subject has been projected, out of pride or sheer naïveté, the subjectivity, in more or less sublimated form, of certain personalities eminently representative of their epoch, civilization or race.

The work you are about to read represents the first attempt to compose a universal history of the human mind from the varying standpoints of memory and thought that characterize the different contemporary cultures.

But in doing so, its main purpose was not to banish all subjectivity of interpretation. Indeed, such a pretension could not be entertained in a history which seeks to assess the significance of events and which takes as its starting points the positions adopted by the various cultures. For there is a kind of subjectivity, co-substantial, as it were, with culture, which causes the perspective opened by each culture on the universal in man to be a projection of that culture's humanity in its own particular circumstances. The originality of this attempt at a universal history lies in its having taken for its frame of reference the multiplicity of contemporary cultural perspectives and projections. For the first time an attempt has been made to present, with respect to the history of consciousness, the sum total of the knowledge which the various contemporary societies and cultures possess and a synthesis of the conceptions which they entertain. For the first time an attempt has been made to offer a history of human thought which is the product of the thought of mankind in every aspect of its present complexion. A universal history indeed, and doubly so—in both its object and its subject.

This aspiration, which is the essence of the whole undertaking, has determined the choice of method.

The History is the work, not of a team with a homogeneous

cultural background, but of an International Commission which, by its very composition and even more by the spirit pervading it, embraces all the varied cultural traditions and modern ideologies which form the spiritual framework of our present-day world. What is more, the International Commission made it a rule that the contributions of the many scholars whose services it enlisted be submitted to the scrutiny of the National Commissions which, in the Member States of UNESCO, group together persons particularly qualified to represent the fields of education, science and culture. Subject always to the overriding considerations of scientific truth, the observations received in the course of these extensive consultations were scrupulously taken into account in drawing up the final text. Never before has what I may call the decentralization of viewpoints and interpretations been carried so far in the science of history.

Accordingly the work is also an act; for this historical study is itself a cultural achievement calculated to influence, by its spirit and its methods, the present trend of culture. And that, no doubt, is its ultimate end. For just as the awareness of mankind's intellectual and moral solidarity to which it leads stems less from the discovery of the interrelations of the past than from the effort of synthesis by which mankind seeks to apprehend the whole compass of its scientific and cultural heritage, so the essential feature of this effort is not so much the complete restitution of the object which it is designed to achieve as the fact that the whole of the subject as it exists today is taking part in it and thus affirms its own unity in the process of achieving it.

In this humanism, whose universality springs not from a unique abstract nature but is being gradually evolved, on the basis of a freely acknowledged diversity, through actual contact and a continuous effort at understanding and co-operation, UNESCO recognizes both its own *raison d'être* and its guiding principle. The unity of mankind, we believe, has to be patiently built up, through mutual respect for the cultures which diversify it without dividing it, and by the establishment of more and more centres of science which spread man's technological power throughout the world, fostering equality of opportunity for progress and for the genuine preservation of his dignity.

Such, then, are the principal ideas and essential features of this work; they are, at the same time, the very reasons which led UNESCO, as the educational, scientific and cultural organization of the United Nations, to conceive the project and assist in its execution.

The author of this History is not UNESCO; it is the International Commission which, since 1950, has directed this venture in complete intellectual independence. It is to the Commission, therefore, and to it alone, that the full credit for this work is due. And at the same time—allow me to state—it also bears the sole responsibility for its scientific worth.

UNESCO is, however, proud to have organized this work and to have made possible its accomplishment by providing the necessary funds, administrative machinery and international background. In that sense this great venture, without precedent in many respects, is also in some measure its work, too.

It is, therefore, my pleasant duty to express the Organization's gratitude to all those who have, to whatever degree, participated in this undertaking and contributed to its success. Above all its thanks are due to the distinguished members of the International Commission and to its eminent Chairman, Professor Paulo E. de Berrêdo Carneiro, who for thirteen years have given unsparingly of the wealth of their knowledge and talents, with a devotion and selflessness equalled only by the nobility of their thought. In this concept of scientific and cultural development in which consciousness is an act and all reflection a creation, it may be said without fear of exaggeration that, in presenting this vast panorama of the past history of the human mind, such as never was before, they have made a powerful contribution towards the advent of a consciousness of civilization on a scale encompassing the whole of mankind. With all my admiration, I wish to express to them UNESCO'S gratitude.

RENÉ MAHEU
Director-General

UNITED NATIONS EDUCATIONAL, SCIENTIFIC
AND CULTURAL ORGANIZATION

Paris, 1962.

PREFACE

PROFESSOR PAULO E. DE BERRÊDO CARNEIRO
*President of the International Commission
for a History of the Scientific and Cultural Development
of Mankind*

Among the great tasks assigned to UNESCO by its Constitution is the duty to promote and encourage mutual knowledge and understanding throughout the world. While many of the divergencies which divide peoples date from a distant past, an analysis of their historical antecedents discloses links which draw them nearer to one another, brings to light their contributions to a common patrimony of humanity, reveals the ebb and flow of cultural exchanges and emphasizes their increasing tendency to become integrated into an international community,

Beyond differences of race, climate, economic structure and systems of ideas, history shows the fundamental identity of the various human groups, making it possible to discern, in many cases, profound analogies among the transformations they have undergone from the Palaeolithic era down to the present time. If we consider the human species as a whole, we perceive that the course of its evolution has been accomplished from one region and one people to another by way of a series of oscillations, greater or lesser in extent, longer or shorter in duration. The different civilizations which have arisen in the course of the ages correspond to distinct phases and patterns of this general movement. Almost every one of them is to be found somewhere in the world of today. Contemporary society appears as a mosaic in which the most widely-differing cultures adjoin and confront each other.

It was, I think, in order to know them better and to strengthen their solidarity that UNESCO took the initiative of entrusting to historians, men of science and of letters, recruited from all parts of the world, the task of preparing and publishing this work. This, at least, is how I have understood the mandate of the International Commission over which I have the honour to preside. Our task was not to draw up a philosophy of history in the light of the economic, intellectual and moral laws which may govern social development, but to describe, from a universal standpoint, the contribution of each age, each region, each people to the scientific and cultural ascent of humanity.

In the official reports which I have presented since 1951 to the General Conference of UNESCO, will be found a detailed account of the steps taken in implementing this project which originated in a resolution submitted to the second session of the General Conference held in Mexico City in 1947. The idea had been put forward in 1946 by Dr Julian Huxley, then Executive Secretary of the Preparatory Commission for UNESCO:

'The chief task before the Humanities today would seem to be to help in constructing a history of the development of the human mind, notably in its highest cultural achievements. For this task, the help of art critics and artists will be needed as well as of art historians; of anthropologists and students of comparative religion as well as of divines and theologians; of archaeologists as well as of classical scholars; of poets and creative men of letters as well as of professors of literature; as well as the whole-hearted support of the historians. Throughout, of course, the development of culture in the various regions of the Orient must receive equal attention to that paid to its Western growth. Once more, UNESCO can help by being true to its many-sidedness, and by bringing men together from all these various fields to help in one or other facet of this huge work.' (UNESCO: *Its Purpose and Its Philosophy* [London, 1946]).

Several preparatory meetings were held and preliminary studies made in 1947 and 1948 with the participation of Professors Carl J. Burckhardt, Lucien Febvre, Joseph Needham, Georges Salles, Taha Hussein, and UNESCO officials, among whom Dr Julian Huxley, then Director-General, Mr Jean Thomas and Professor Pierre Auger. In 1949, Professors Lucien Febvre and Miguel Ozorio de Almeida were asked to prepare general reports on the basis of which the General Conference, at its fourth session, recommended that the work should proceed immediately.

In the same year a committee of experts was to draft the plan to be submitted to the General Conference for the elaboration of a scientific and cultural history of mankind. It included the following scholars: R. Ciasca, L. Febvre, M. Florkin, J. Needham, J. Piaget, P. Rivet and R. Shryock. In opening the proceedings, Dr Jaime Torres-Bodet, at that time Director-General, evoked the spirit in which he considered the work should be accomplished:

'Through UNESCO, humanity must come to realize its common past and understand the significance of the sum total of endeavour, invention and enlightenment which have gone to make up the heritage we seek to serve today. If we can regard this moment in the world's history as UNESCO'S hour, it is thanks to the slow and often unnoticed growth of an outlook shared by all men, which is now beginning to take shape as the outlook of Mankind. . . .'

'We seek only to draw up the table of the major cultural events which have shaped Man's existence and slowly brought civilization into being. . . .'

'The important thing is to embark on it with the will to succeed and in a spirit of serene and dispassionate objectivity. . . .'

'Nevertheless, by publishing today a synthesis of our present knowledge of *humanity's scientific and cultural history,* UNESCO, far from lulling the critical spirit to sleep, will spur it to new and eager research. It is my profound conviction that there is nothing in the nature or the present state of historical science precluding the making of such a synthesis; indeed all circumstances invite us to it.'

In accordance with a resolution of the General Conference of 1950, consultations were held with the International Council of Scientific Unions (ICSU) and the International Council for Philosophy and Humanistic Studies (CIPSH) as to the appointment of an international commission to undertake, on behalf of UNESCO, full responsibility for the preparation and execution of the work. The following experts nominated by these two councils were invited by the Director-General to become active members of the Commission: Professors Homi Bhabha (University of Bombay), Carl J. Burckhardt (Switzerland), Paulo E. de Berrêdo Carneiro (University of Brazil), Julian Huxley, FRS (United Kingdom), Charles Morazé (University of Paris), Mario Praz (University of Rome), Ralph E. Turner (Yale University), Silvio Zavala (University of Mexico) and Constantine K. Zurayk (University of Damascus).

The International Commission met for the first time in December 1950 and again in March 1951 in Paris. It decided during these two meetings to invite a number of distinguished persons to become Corresponding Members, and to set up an Editorial Committee, under the chairmanship of Professor Ralph E. Turner, with Professors Constantine K. Zurayk and Charles Morazé as members. The Commission did me the honour of electing me as its President, with Dr Julian Huxley and Professor Carl J. Burckhardt as Vice-Presidents. A Bureau was created comprising the President, the Vice-Presidents and the Chairman of the Editorial Committee. Dr Armando Cortesao, a member of the Department of Cultural Activities of UNESCO, initially responsible for the secretariat of the Commission, was unanimously elected Secretary-General. In 1952 he was succeeded by Dr Guy S. Métraux.

Between 1952 and 1954 new members were added to the International Commission to enlarge its geographical, cultural and philosophical representation. The following scholars were appointed in agreement with the Director-General of UNESCO: Professors E. J. Dijksterhuis (Netherlands), Jacques Freymond (Switzerland), Mahmud Husain (Pakistan), Hu-Shih (China), Erik Lönnroth (Sweden), R. C. Majumdar (India), Percy E. Schramm (Federal Republic of Germany), Ali A. Siassi (Iran), and J. Pérez Villanueva (Spain).

As early as 1952 the International Commission approached scholars of countries which, at the time, were not members of UNESCO but which represented important cultural areas. Invitations were sent to national academies of sciences and arts, but met with no response. It was only in 1955 that the International Commission was able to welcome as new members historians and scientists from the Union of Soviet Socialist Republics and the People's Republics of Czechoslovakia, Hungary and Poland.

Since 1954, the Bureau, acting as delegate of the International Commission with additional responsibilities placed on it by the General Assembly, has been enlarged to comprise the President and six Vice-Presidents as follows: Sir Julian Huxley (United Kingdom), Professor R. C. Majumdar (India), Professor Ralph E. Turner (United States of America), Professor Gaston Wiet (France), Professor Silvio Zavala (Mexico), and Professor A. A. Zvorikine (Union of Soviet Socialist Republics). Professor Louis Gottschalk (United States of America) was unanimously elected as a further Vice-President in 1961.

The first publication which the International Commission initiated, on the proposal of Professor Charles Morazé, was a quarterly review, the *Journal of World History*. Professor Lucien Febvre was the Editor until his death in 1956, when it came under the supervision of the Bureau, with Dr François Crouzet and Dr Guy S. Métraux as its editorial staff.

The main function of the *Journal of World History* has been to provide the International Commission with material for the final compilation of the History—documentary or bibliographical details about problems which have so far remained obscure; translations of documents which may have appeared desirable; contributions to the History itself. This review has also enabled scholars in all countries to take part in an exchange of views on questions of interpretation and the actual presentation of the History.

The *Journal of World History* represents a considerable contribution on the part of the International Commission to historical knowledge and towards a better understanding of historical processes. Composed of articles of the highest scientific quality which bear the signature of scholars from every country and which express the most diverse ideological trends, it foreshadows to some extent the great work for which it has furnished basic materials.

The preparation of the History was examined in detail during the first and second meetings of the International Commission. Several courses of action presented themselves: the Commission could draft the final text, or it could be entrusted to a single editor, or to independent authors. It was decided that, while the Commission would retain the full authority conferred upon it by the General Conference of UNESCO, the wisest course would be to select individual author-editors for each of the six volumes. The author-editors would be fully responsible for the text, but they would work under the supervision of, and in collaboration with, the Editorial Committee and the Commission; they would benefit by the assistance of scholars, designated by them, to deal with certain chapters; and, if necessary, sections could be referred to specialists.

On the recommendation of the Editorial Committee, author-editors for five of the six volumes were at this time appointed. For Volume I, Parts 1 and 2, Jacquetta Hawkes and Henri Frankfort, both of the United Kingdom. On the death of Professor Frankfort in 1954, the late Sir Leonard Woolley (United Kingdom) was appointed to write the second part of this volume. For Volume III, René Grousset (France), with two co-authors, Vadime Elisséeff and Philippe Wolff (France). Professor Gaston Wiet (France) took over the author-editorship of this third volume in 1953 on the death of Professor Grousset. For Volume IV, Louis Gottschalk (United States of America); for Volume V, Jorge Basadre (Peru), who afterwards resigned and was replaced later by Professor Charles Morazé (France); and for Volume VI, K. Zachariah (India), who was succeeded in 1956 by Dr Caroline F. Ware (United States of America), H.E. Dr K. M. Panikkar (India), and the late Dr J. M. Romein (Neitherlands).

In 1953 the late Professor Luigi Pareti (Italy) was appointed author-editor of Volume II, with Professors Paolo Brezzi and Luciano Petech of Italy as assistants.

By the spring of 1952 a first draft plan of the History was in circulation. Through the active interest of the author-editors, the members of the International Commission, and scholars consulted throughout the world on the initiative of the International Commission, this plan was slowly revised to constitute a general guide for the elaboration of the six volumes.

At a meeting of the International Commission in February 1954 it was decided, on my proposal, to include in its membership the author-editors of the six volumes and the editor of the *Journal of World History*. This measure was designed to

enable those primarily responsible for the text of the volumes
to take part in discussions and so to make a more effective
contribution to the direction of the activities of the International Commission. In addition it was decided that one
single body—the Bureau of the Commission—should be made
entirely responsible for the co-ordination of the Commission's
work. To ensure the unity of style and presentation essential to
a work of such high intellectual standing and covering so wide
a field, Professor Ralph E. Turner was entrusted with the task
of editing the English texts.

In the course of the execution of its programme the International Commission benefited by the co-operation of
UNESCO and of the General Conference which, at several of
its sessions, had the opportunity to examine the work plans
prepared for the History, and on two occasions took decisions
which markedly influenced our work. The Ninth General Conference held in New Delhi in 1956 recommended that the texts
of all volumes be submitted to the National Commissions set
up in the Member States. The objective was to assist the International Commission in obtaining for each volume additional
critical materials to enable the author-editors to revise and to
perfect their texts. While not all National Commissions responded, the comments which were received proved most useful. All the author-editors have conscientiously noted the
criticisms received and have taken them into account, wherever possible, when revising their texts. Furthermore, the
International Commission has sought the advice of experts on
several points.

Again at the invitation of the General Conference, following
its tenth meeting held in Paris in 1958, the International Commission decided to appoint a number of historians to advise
the Bureau and the author-editors on possible modifications of
the text of each volume of the History, in the light of comments and criticisms received, and to suggest editorial notes
on controversial issues. This step had become necessary as
Professor Turner's illness had prevented him from accom-
plishing the editorial work. In pursuance of this policy, and in
agreement with the members of the Bureau and with the
author-editors, I selected a number of eminent historians, of
different nationalities, particularly qualified to act as special
consultants. Thus, at the end of each chapter of all volumes
the reader will find grouped together editorial notes and biblio-

graphical references that will provide him with summaries of historical opinions on those questions which can be variously interpreted.

The International Commission plans to issue a supplement to Volume VI, *The Twentieth Century*. While the first part treats of the History of our age in the same way as the history of previous periods was considered in all the volumes, this second tome will be devoted to an open debate on the main trends in scientific and cultural development at mid-century.

The six volumes include line drawings prepared by Mrs Stella Robinson at the request of the author-editors, photographic plates assembled by the Secretariat of the International Commission in co-operation with the author-editors and their assistants, and maps drawn specially by the Swiss firm, Hallwag, A.G.

At the time of publication I must recall with gratitude and regret the memory of those scholars whom the International Commission had the misfortune to lose in the course of its work and who contributed so much to the achievement of its task: Professors René Grousset, Henri Frankfort and K. Zachariah, Sir Leonard Woolley, Professors Luigi Pareti, Lucien Febvre, and J. M. Romein.

I must hereby express, on behalf of the International Commission, my gratitude to the General Conference of UNESCO which made this project possible, to the Director-Generals, Messrs. Julian Huxley, Jaime Torres-Bodet, Luther Evans, Vittorino Veronese and René Maheu, and to the Secretariat of UNESCO which, through ten years, has extended assistance and guidance on every possible occasion.

The International Commission is greatly indebted to the author-editors who, often under difficult circumstances, fulfilled their task with the highest competence and devotion; to its Vice-Presidents, who constitute the Bureau, for assuming with me full responsibility for every phase of the execution of this project; and in particular to Professor Ralph E. Turner, Chairman of the Editorial Committee, for the elaboration of the general plan of the History and for his whole-hearted dedication to the success of the work to which he brought his own personal outlook of an integrated world history. I am particularly happy to acknowledge herewith the co-operation of the Corresponding Members, the consultants, and the translators, whose work proved invaluable for the completion of this project.

The International Commission benefited throughout its work by the advice of the offical Observers of the International Council of Scientific Unions, Professor R. J. Forbes; of the International Council for Philosophy and Humanistic Studies, Sir Ronald Syme; and of the International Social Sciences Council, Professor F. H. Lawson.

Lastly, I would like on behalf of the International Commission to thank the Secretary-General, Dr Guy S. Métraux, and his staff for their active and faithful collaboration which has contributed so much to the success of this scientific and cultural history of mankind.

ACKNOWLEDGEMENTS

The UNESCO International Commission, the authors and the publishers wish to thank all those who have kindly given permission for the reproduction of the plates in this book. Acknowledgements are made under each illustration and abbreviated as follows:

Commission of the French Republic for Education, Science and Culture CESC

Commissioners of Public Works in Ireland PWI

Denver Museum of Natural History, Colorado DM

Professor Roman Ghirshman GHIRSHMAN

K. Kenyon, *Digging up Jericho* (Benn) KENYON

Musée de l'Homme, Paris L'HOMME

Musée du Louvre, Paris LOUVRE

Ostasiatiska Museet, Stockholm OM

Professor F. Schachermeyr and Verlag W. Kohlhammer, Stuttgart SCHACHERMEYR

Thames & Hudson, *The Dawn of Civilisation* TH

Valletta Museum, Malta VALLETTA

A. R. Willcox, *Rock Painting of the Drakensberg* (Parrish) WILLCOX

ACKNOWLEDGMENTS

The UNESCO International Commission, the author and the publishers wish to express their gratitude to the following for the reproduction of the photographs used in this book. The numbers are those under each illustration and appear as follows:

Copyright of the French Republic for the National Science and Cultural Center.

Commissariat of India Stockholm Ireland, Paris.

Central Museum of Natural History, Colombo, etc.

Professor Ronald Callaghan, Paris, France.

Professor Dayrie, agranomie ghandy, Léniton.

Alexandre Thronne, Paris, France, etc.

Musée del Louvre, Paris, France.

Professor A. Kroen, Stockport, U.S.

Professor P. Schaefer, Bern, Switzerland, Kunstmuseum.

Stuttgart technical area.

Theresa Rudolph, The Drawing Company, etc.

Vatican Museum Bible, Switzerland.

Prof. Victor Beck, Holland of the American Museum, etc.

Vatican.

CONTENTS

Section One: The Palaeolithic and Mesolithic

LIST OF ILLUSTRATIONS

FIGURES

MAPS

LIST OF CHARTS

INTERNATIONAL COMMISSION FOR A HISTORY OF THE SCIENTIFIC AND CULTURAL DEVELOPMENT OF MANKIND

MEMBERS

H.E. Professor Paulo E. de Berrêdo Carneiro	*Brazil*	PRESIDENT
Professor Louis Gottschalk	*United States of America*	Vice-President
Sir Julian Huxley, FRS	*United Kingdom*	Vice-President
Professor R. C. Majumdar	*India*	Vice-President
Professor Ralph E. Turner	*United States of America*	Vice-President Editor
Professor Gaston Wiet	*France*	Vice-President
Professor Silvio Zavala	*Mexico*	Vice-President
Professor A. A. Zvorikine	*Union of Soviet Socialist Republics*	Vice-President
Dr Jorge Basadre	*Peru*	
Professor Eduard J. Dijksterhuis	*Netherlands*	

Canada
Professor Wilfrid Cantwell Smith

Chile
Dr Ricardo Donoso

China
Professor Tso-ping Tung
H.E. M. Chang Chi-yun

Colombia
Professor German Arciniegas
Professor Luis Martinez Delgado

Cuba
H.E. Dr J. Remos y Rubio

Denmark
Dr Kaj Birket-Smith

Egypt
Professor Aziz S. Atiya

France
Monseigner Blanchet
Professor Julien Cain
Professor J. B. Duroselle
Professor C. Lévi-Strauss

Federal Republic of Germany
Dr Georg Eckert
Dr Hermann Heimpel
Dr Ludwig Dehio

Honduras
H.E. Prof. Rafael Heliodoro Valle

India
Professor J. N. Banerjea
Dr Humayun Kabir
H.E. Sir Sarvepalli Radhakrishnan
Professor K. A. Nilakanta Sastri

Indonesia
Dr S. T. Alisjahbana
Professor M. Sardjito

Iran
Professor Ali-Asghar Hekmat

Iraq
Dr Abdul Aziz al-Duri

Israel
Professor B. Mazar

Italy
Professor Domenico Demarco
Professor Giacomo Devoto
R. P. Antonio Messineo

Japan
Professor Shigeki Kaizuka
Professor Suketoshi Yajima
Dr Seeichi Iwao
Professor Daisetso Suzuki

Lebanon
Emir Maurice Chehab
H.E. Dr Charles Malik

Mexico
Dr Alfonso Caso
Professor Samuel Ramos
Professor Manuel Sandoval Vallarta
Professor Daniel Cosio Villegas

Nepal
Professor Gókal Chand

Netherlands
Professor Dr R. Hooykaas
Dr Maria Rooseboom

New Zealand
Dr J. C. Beaglehole

Norway
Professor Alf Sommerfelt

Pakistan
Dr A. Halim
Dr I. H. Qureshi
Dr S. Suhrawardy

Philippines
Professor Gabriel
Bernardo

Senegal
H.E. M. L. S. Senghor

Spain
Professor Claudio Sanchez
Albornoz
Professor Antonio Garcia
Bellido
M. Ciriaco Pérez
Bustamante
M. F. Cantera
Professor Emilio Garcia
Gomez
Duke of Maura
Professor R. Menendez
Pidal
Professor José Pijoan

Sweden
Professor Axel Boëthius

Switzerland
Dr Werner Kaegi
Professor Jean Piaget

Syria
H.E. Khalil Mardam Bey

Thailand
Prince Dhani Nivat

Turkey
H.E. Mehmed Fouad
Köprülü

Union of South Africa
Professor A. N. Pelzer

*Union of Soviet Socialist
Republics*
Professor A. V.
Artsikhovski
Professor N. A.
Figourovsky
Professor Guber
Professor B. Kedrov
Professor D. V. Sarabianov
Professor N. A. Sidorova
Professor Vinogradov
Professor V. P. Zoubov

United Kingdom
Sir Ernest Barker
Dr Joseph Needham
Bertrand Russell

United States of America
Professor Eugene
Anderson
Professor Salo W. Baron
Professor Norman Brown
Professor J. K. Fairbank
Professor Harold Fisher
Professor G. Stanton Ford
Professor R. H. Gabriel
Professor Oscar Halecki
Dr C. W. de Kiewiet
Professor A. L. Kroeber
Professor Martin R. P.
McGuire
Professor H. W. Schneider
Professor Richard Shryock
Professor John A. Wilson

Uruguay
Professor Carlos M. Rama

Venezuela
H.E. C. Parra-Perez
Professor Mariano Picon
Salas

NOTE ON
THE EDITORIAL TREATMENT
OF VOLUME I, PART 1

The original text of Jacquetta Hawkes was submitted to all the National Commissions of UNESCO and to a number of specialists selected by the International Commission for a History of the Scientific and Cultural Development of Mankind.

All the comments which were made available to the International Commission on the original text were communicated to the author-editor, who used them widely in revising the manuscript. The final revised text was entrusted to Professor H. G. Bandi, of the University of Berne, Switzerland, who was asked to prepare notes on major points at issue in order to complement the information in the manuscript or to summarize the thought of various schools on disputed questions.

Professor Bandi, in preparing the notes (translated by Ann E. Keep), utilized the comments of the following scholars:

Dr D. C. Baramki, American University, Beirut.

Professor R. M. Berndt, University of Western Australia, on behalf of the Australian National Advisory Committee for UNESCO.

Professor K. Birket-Smith, University of Copenhagen, Corresponding Member of the International Commission.

The late Professor A. C. Blanc, Director of the Institute of Palaeontology, Rome, on behalf of the Italian National Commission for UNESCO.

The late Professor F. S. Bodenheimer, Corresponding Member of the International Commission, Hebrew University.

Dr P. Bosch-Gimpera, Secretary-General, International Union of Anthropology and Ethnography, Mexico, D.F.

Professor J. G. D. Clark, Peabody Museum, Harvard University, Cambridge, Mass.

Dr H. B. Collins, Bureau of American Ethnology, The Smithsonian Institution, on behalf of the United States National Commission for UNESCO.

Professor C. S. Coon, University of Pennsylvania.

Professor G. F. Debetz, Institute of Ethnography, Moscow, on behalf of the Commission of the USSR for UNESCO.

Professor W. Koppers, University of Vienna, on behalf of the Austrian Commission of UNESCO.

Professor P. Martinez del Rio, University of Mexico.

Professor S. Mizuno, Kyoto University, on behalf of the Japanese National Commission for UNESCO.

Dr J. Neustupný, Department of Prehistory, National Museum, Prague, on behalf of the Czechoslovak Commission for Co-operation with UNESCO.

Professor C. A. Nordman, Helsinki, on behalf of the Finnish National Commission for UNESCO.

Professor Luis Pericot García, University of Barcelona.

Professor H. D. Sankalia, Deccan College, Poona.

Professor A. Sommerfelt, Corresponding Member of the International Commission, on behalf of the Norwegian National Commission for UNESCO.

Dr W. C. Sturtevant, Bureau of American Ethnology, Smithsonian Institution, on behalf of the United States National Commission for UNESCO.

Professor André Varagnac, Conservateur en Chef du Musée des Antiquités Nationales, on behalf of the Commission of the French Republic for Education, Science and Culture.

Professor John A. Wilson, Corresponding Member of the International Commission, Oriental Institute, University of Chicago.

In addition, the comments and suggestions of the following scholars were made available to the International Commission through the National Commissions for UNESCO in their respective countries:

Professor M. Almagro Bach (Spain), the University of Madrid.

Professor K. Jazdzewski and Maria Chmielewska (Poland), the University of Lodz.

Dr B. Klima (Czechoslovakia), Institute of Archaeology, Prague.

Dr Björn Kurten (Finland).

Professor M. I. Nestor (Rumania), the University of Bucharest.

Professor S. Paranavitane (Ceylon), the University of Ceylon.

Dr F. H. H. Roberts (United States of America), Bureau of American Ethnology, The Smithsonian Institution.

Professor M. Sauramo (Finland).

Professor L. Sawicki (Poland), Centre of Palaeolithic Studies of the Polish Academy of Sciences.

Professor M. Senyürek (Turkey), the University of Ankara.

Dr R. S. Solecki (United States of America), Division of Archaeology, United States National Museum.

Dr T. D. Stewart (United States of America), United States National Museum.

The Academy of Sciences of Bulgaria, on behalf of the National Commission for UNESCO, the Indian National Commission for UNESCO, Members of the Faculty of the Hebrew University on behalf of the Israel National Commission for UNESCO, the Afghanistan National Commission for UNESCO and the Ministry of Education, Pakistan, sent observations which the International Commission acknowledges herewith most gratefully.

GUY S. MÉTRAUX,
Secretary-General.

Paris, March 1962

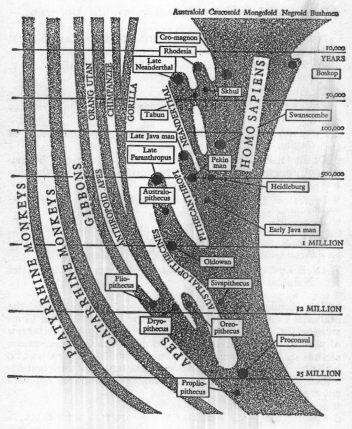

CHART I. *The Evolution of Man*

INTRODUCTION

I

THE opening of any full history of man must be its Book of Genesis, the story of man's creation. It will be its task to show the emergence, that is to say the gradual creation, of the being whose noble achievements and fearful abominations are to be the subject of the main work. The creature who has now changed the whole face of the habitable earth will be seen coming up out of Africa only a little better equipped than the apes that were his poor cousins. His intelligence and his physical adaptability enabled him to spread throughout the earth, to endure its extremes of heat and cold, to fit himself into earth's forests, plains and hills, but at first in what small numbers and with what little power. The mark which he could make upon a virgin planet, so abounding in other forms of life, was hardly greater than that made by a rabbit running through a hay-field.

It is appropriate, however, that the Book of Genesis, the opening section of our *History of Mankind,* should carry him a little farther forward than this. For very many thousands of years after man was fully man in his physical and mental capacities, his way of life, his culture, remained that of the natural world. He was still a hunter among other hunters, a food gatherer among innumerable other species that picked up their food from the natural products of the earth. It was not until he began the cultivation of plants and the domestication of animals to serve his needs that his life as well as his person became fully human. This part of the History will therefore carry man on to the time less than ten thousand years ago when he began to establish himself as a farmer in certain favoured regions of the Old World. Here is the proper point at which to hand on the story to those who can tell how once man had achieved the agricultural way of life which is still the basis of our existence, his mental powers could flourish and put out the astonishingly rich and various fruits of human civilization.

All later parts of the *History of Mankind* will be introduced by some account of how the content of the particular phase with which they are concerned, the products, practices, thoughts and deeds of its men, are to be related with what went before. These introductions will, in short, describe the inheritance of the new age from the one before. Here, at the beginning of it all, the position is rather different, for in looking back we do not see a stretch of human history leading up to our point of continuation, but instead an immense vista of natural history. A tremendous perspective of landscape and living forms, but not a glimmer of science or culture.

Yet after all the position is not so very different. The inheritance which the Prehistoric Age received from the Prehuman Age was immense and powerful. It was the whole body of man and the environment in which he was to live, that basic inheritance which all later ages could take for granted. It is in fact not only the basic inheritance but the most enduring. While civilizations have come and gone we still are born to the identical equipment of body and limbs already shaped a hundred thousand years or more ago— yes, down to our scratching nails and that tendency to long canine teeth. As for our environment, though we have vastly changed its surface and have learnt how to pass its barriers, the shapes formed by oceans and continents, mountain ranges, great rivers, together with the climatic zones of the world still powerfully affect our lives and determine the pattern of our communities great and small.

Whatever view one takes of the means and meaning of evolution, it must now be impossible to doubt that it took place. It is still possible to doubt the orthodox view that the sole agency of change and development in life was natural selection working together with sudden spurts, or mutations, in the organisms; it is possible to believe that these factors only affected the fringes of some process too tremendous for us, its mere products, to comprehend. It may be, too, that the nature of the 'time' in which the process took place is something equally beyond our full comprehension. But the fact that the human stock grew from a creature that walked upright and was ancestral to ourselves and the great apes cannot be denied. Nor that this creature in turn sprang from keen-eyed, deft-footed tarsiers and they again from the little tree shrews that, biding their time, peeped through the shiny leaves at the great dinosaurs and other condemned reptiles of the Cretaceous Age. From there it is no more than a mental stone's throw back by way of the amphibians and fishes to life itself generating between Sun and Earth.

What it will prove most important to remember is that our species did not only inherit from the past its bodily equipment, dominated by its subtly elaborated brain, but also highly charged emotional centres and all the strange ancient furniture of the unconscious mind. Man emerged bringing with him hate, fear and anger, together with love and the joy of life in their simple animal form. He also brought the social heritage of family affection and group loyalty. Today some of us believe (while others do not) that among the most elusive and yet the most precious heirlooms of all were shadowy, deep-seated memories of the experience of the evolving animal line during the vast stretches of its history, memories which enrich and unite modern men by throwing up from the unconscious the images and ideas that inspire our arts and help to make them universally evocative.

Memory of this kind, if it exists, not only unites all men at a very profound level of their being through their common response to its images, but also can serve to make us aware of our old kinship with all life and all being—that blessed and also truthful sense of oneness of which our intellect, if granted too much power, quickly deprives us.

There can be no question, whatever construction we put upon them, that these mental and emotional inheritances which man received from the prehuman past were to provide a most potent force in the creation of culture. We shall find them giving colour and form to all aspects of human life other than the purely rational and intellectual.

As for the counterpoint to man in history—the natural environment—the problem of inheritance is complicated by the fact that it is less stable. We shall find that by the time, near the beginning of the Pleistocene, when human beings can first be recognized, the geographical structure of the earth as we know it was already roughly established. There were to be many minor changes in sea-level affecting the coastlines, but the main land and sea masses and all the mountain and hill formations were already there. What was unstable was climate, a part of the physical inheritance which affects human life at least as much as the configuration of the land.

All through the Old Stone or Palaeolithic Age, which corresponds in terms of human culture with the Pleistocene of geologists, world climate was violently affected by intermittent phases of great cold when glaciers and ice-sheets spread down from the polar ice-caps and from high mountain ranges. Not only did the ice itself make vast regions virtually uninhabitable, but its presence caused wide shifts in the rain belts and other climatic zones. Such great climatic changes inevitably affected the regions where the Palaeolithic hunters could live: they must also have had some influence on the fate of the different species of men who were then competing for dominance.

The climate continued to fluctuate sharply long after the final triumph over their rivals of men of modern type. During the Late, or Upper, Palaeolithic Age when they were developing what may be called high hunting cultures, there were considerable variations in the intensity of the last glaciation, and afterwards there was the more drastic change that went with the final (from our point of view) retreat of the ice.

Thus for by far the greater part of the time to be covered by the opening section of the History there was no stable environmental inheritance from the past. But by about 5000 B C, when the first agricultural communities were already extending in Asia, the climate, the distribution of vegetation and all the related factors had settled to approximately their present condition. When true civilization at last began, not only was *Homo sapiens* and the agricultural basis of his existence finally established, but the natural environment which was to form the background of all subsequent history had already assumed the form which we ourselves have inherited.

II

For many years it was held to be most likely that the earliest human species originated in Asia, probably in some region along the southern slopes of the Himalayas, but it is now very generally agreed that the African continent was the birthplace of mankind. The opening of a human history must, therefore, begin by showing how creatures whose human and simian characteristics very nearly balanced lived in Africa, probably late in the Pliocene, and there gave rise to the earliest beings that can be identified as men both from their bodily characters and from their ability roughly to shape stone and wood to suit their purposes. Here we have the dawn of culture, the beginning of that vast and varied creation—material and mental or spiritual—which the mind of man has achieved in its efforts to resist, to master, to understand, to enjoy and to embellish the thoughtless natural world in which he finds himself.

It will appear that it was quite soon after the emergence of man and the beginning of tool-making that some of the human stock moved into eastern Asia and there established a new centre for physical and cultural development. In fact we shall find that from very early times there were to be two great cultural traditions, one cradled in eastern Asia, the other in Africa. Both traditions (with their many different branches) met along an extensive frontier which included India and Europe: as so often in later history this meeting of contrasting traditions proved stimulating to beneficial development and change. Such encounters shake communities of men into a realization that there can be methods of manufacture, ways of thinking and feeling, other than those they have always assumed to be right and inevitable. So, with or without violence, the cultures borrow, blend, and sometimes set off in new directions.

From the latter part of the last Ice Age, let us say after about forty thousand years ago, the old pattern of the opposition and interaction of broadly differing types of humanity gave way to the development, and cultural and racial diversification, of a single human species, that of *Homo sapiens*. From that time we have not been seriously threatened by any species other than our own.

The beginning of this period, the Upper Palaeolithic Age, marks the beginning of the acceleration in the cultural development of mankind that has continued ever since. Further sudden accelerations were to come with the adoption of farming and, so far as technological advance is concerned, with the industrial revolution, but this was the first plunge forward. It seems that the impetus may perhaps have come from the fairly rapid advancement among the Palaeolithic hunters of the possibilities of coherent speech. Whatever opinion is accepted about the origins of language, no one can question the immense importance of the ability to give verbal shape to images and ideas resulting from the experience of life, and so to give them a new coherence and a new permanence. As the invention of granaries made it possible to store corn instead of living from hand to mouth, and as the invention of money made it possible to accumulate the fruits of work and use them for fresh enterprise, so the invention of conceptual speech made it possible to save the fruits of experience and use them for the formulation of new thoughts and theories. All alike are a form of banking, a way of making the past serve the future.

The acceleration of progress shows itself most clearly in the development of all kinds of specialized tools to serve the particular purposes of hunters, fishers, fowlers, bone carvers and carpenters. The development of a splendid visual art in Europe suggests that it must also have had powerful imaginative manifestations; probably as well as learning how to paint, carve and engrave these most gifted hunting peoples also achieved altogether new heights of imaginative expression through dancing and poetry.

The overall historical result of such increase in the speed and complexity of cultural change was bound to be that for the first time the evolution of culture far outstripped its diffusion. Until now change had been so immensely slow that traditions could spread over half the globe, providing a universal culture to which we are only beginning to return today. Thus the most characteristic Lower Palaeolithic tool, known as a hand-axe, was made in identical forms in England, Kenya, South Africa and India. But with the Upper Palaeolithic we at once find local cultures differing sharply from one another; it is no longer possible to point to any worldwide cultural product. It seems safe to assume that with this definition of distinct ways of making things and, presumably, of behaving, went an altogether new sense of community. Men must have become aware of belonging to one people and being opposed to others. History suggests that already members of groups not one's own would have been held to be inferior, evil and dangerous people; indeed, hardly fit to be called *Homo sapiens*.

Although it was probably no more true in the late Pleistocene than it is today that cultural groups corresponded at all exactly with racial ones, this was in fact the time when the major races of mankind emerged and were established. Divided from one another in part by the facts of geography and in part by the events of prehistory, perhaps with slightly differing biological inheritances from the remote past, the main racial groups became further differentiated as they responded to the sharply contrasting environments against which they had to struggle. So by twenty thousand years ago there were apparent those differences in appearance and perhaps in temperament, and incipient differences in the traditions of how it was best to live, which still enrich, plague and divide us today.

The end of the Pleistocene was also the age which saw the first human settlement of America. Some of the easternmost Mongolian people crossed into what was to be known as the

New World, apparently by way of the Bering Straits, and so pushed slowly southward through the continent.

After the end of the Upper Palaeolithic Age, characterized by a rapid advance in man's technical skill, by the differentiation of races and their spread throughout the world, history must be mainly concerned first with the efforts of the hunting peoples to adapt themselves to the spread of forests that in vast regions followed the end of the last glacial phase, and then with the adoption of pastoralism and agriculture which began not very long after the fall of the high hunting cultures. While in many parts of the world, Europe among them, the hunters merely played the passive role of adjusting their habits to forest conditions, in some regions of south-west Asia men were inspired to counter-attack against nature and make the momentous revolution in human history that accompanied the domestication of cattle, pigs, sheep and goats and the cultivation of wheat and barley. From this time, some eight to ten thousand years ago, the historical attention is bound to be focused on the spread of this new economy which was to be the basis of all future civilizations. By 5000 B C there were peasant communities—the first permanently settled communities of history—in Palestine, Iraq and Iran, and soon they were extending eastward as far as India and west and south to Egypt and the eastern Mediterranean. To some territories, such as Europe, the new way of life spread very slowly, the hunting people remaining undisturbed for thousands of years. To many others it never spread at all until modern times. So from this time onward men were to be divided not only by differences of race and tradition, but by violent distinctions of cultural attainment.

This Neolithic or New Stone Age saw an increase in the growth of local cultures, already conspicuous at the end of Palaeolithic times. Hunters must always range over wide territories, and movement had been easy in much of the Old World during late Pleistocene times when open steppe or tundra conditions prevailed. Now there were farming settlements where generation might follow generation in one village or farmstead and where quite small communities were so nearly self-sufficient as to need little contact with the outside world. In some areas, too, dense forests muffled with undergrowth made barriers between one stretch of habitable countryside and the next such as had not existed before. So there developed a patchwork of small cultures, each with its distinctive products. This era of human history was equally unlike the past when the immense slowness of change allowed a uniform culture to prevail from London to Madras, and the future when the immense speed of communications has had the same effect.

It was perhaps the heyday of local colour, for within a few thousand years of the growth of settled peasantries, the favoured lands of the great river valleys of the Tigris and Euphrates, the Nile and the Indus were supporting the development of cities. Villages where cultivators lived together for mutual protection and convenience grew into places where highly skilled and specialized artisans, merchants, administrators, priests and kings gave society an altogether new complexity. The trade and conquest that were a part of this aggrandizement tended to break down the boundaries of the regional cultures and impose instead the larger pattern of commerce and imperialism.

III

When thinking of the contribution made by this earliest period of human history to those which are to follow, we are inclined, perhaps, to take too much for granted. After all, men might well have lived either in solitary pairs, or in groups in which the individual psyche was as completely fused with its fellows as is the body of a single starling in a wheeling flock; they might regularly have made their homes in underground tunnels or in the tree-tops and have concentrated all effort on howling to the moon. It is, in fact, quite astonishing how quickly, once cultural development was under way, men began to adopt the general habits that they still follow today. We are right to marvel at the enormous variety of human life, yet we should also remember these essential conformities. Early in our history it became usual to inhabit houses built on the ground, to wear ornaments and some clothes, to cook food, to live in family groups with wider social allegiances that might lead to warfare, to work and to play and to give all remaining social energy to religion and the arts.

Thus in addition to the basic contributions of the bodily and mental equipment of man, and his knowledge of how to control animals and plants to make them support a stable society, this age before civilization handed on many traits, of both material and mental culture, to the earliest civilizations. Many of them are with us still, forming some of the universal assumptions of humanity.

In the realm of material culture men had long mastered

the mechanics of fire-making, the spear-thrower and bow, and had already gone far with the crafts of weaving and the making of ceramics, with carpentry, masonry and the design of tools for cutting, piercing, hammering and smoothing; also (less happily) with weapons for cutting, piercing and hammering.

In the arts it is astonishing to realize that in the very first known manifestation of the artistic impulse in man, nearly all the existing forms of visual art were already practised. The Palaeolithic artists of western Europe understood outline drawing, engraving, polychrome painting, modelling and carving both in relief and in the round. As far as we can judge from what was written down later, the verbal arts must also have early assumed a fair variety of forms. There were probably both lyric and epic poetry, prose narrative, and partly legendary ancestral history. Music, with its technical and theoretical difficulties, may have lagged behind, but dancing, the most social of the arts, was certainly used as a means of expression by the close-knit, emotional and intuitive communities of prehistoric times.

In any primitive society it is impossible to consider the arts apart from religion, or religion apart from social morality. Man's sharpening self-consciousness gave him a sense of isolation from the rest of life, and almost all his activities other than those necessary to keep him alive were directed to establishing a harmonious, satisfying and effective relationship with the external world. Perhaps no contribution made by prehistoric man to his successors is more important than the body of magico-religious attitudes, beliefs and customs that grew up as a part of this mental traffic with the universe.

It is a process of immense subtlety, this traffic, and one still as far beyond our full comprehension as the mystery of existence itself. There is no doubt, however, that man's religious outlook always in large part reflected what he found within himself. It was a kind of mirror image of his own soul. Thus when self-consciousness gave at least some awareness of an entity feeling, thinking, willing, acting, man conceived the idea of a soul responsible for these functions; then, looking outwards, he saw comparable souls or spirits present in all things, animate and inanimate, and possessing a terrible power over man himself. There is no doubt either that he projected emotionally charged desires, such as the desire for fertility in animals, crops and his own family, into personified spirits—in this instance into the fertility goddess or great mother worshipped from Palaeolithic times until today. These reflections of the inner man into the outer world were naturally exalted and refined as humanity itself was exalted and refined. Thus the simpler forms of animism in which things and places are imbued with spirits satisfied minds still almost merged in a tribal consciousness, while the concept of high gods went with a heightening of individuality in man. Similarly in the more primitive stage morality is related to religious practice mainly in so far as the individual, by provoking the spirits, may bring harm to the community.

Even these several suggestions concerning the religious impulse in early man are far too simple, for many other factors are involved. Thus we have to remember that beyond conscious desires and conscious ideas concerning the existence of the soul, man carried unknowingly the impulses of his unconscious mind and these too were projected into the outer world of spirits and divinities. Then, at the opposite extreme from his unconscious mind, man's young, untried intellect made valiant efforts to order and rationalize all his imaginative projections and so devised stories concerning the origin of spirits, gods and men and their relationships one with another that became a part of the body of belief. Finally, we do not know what intuitions of higher levels of being actually present in our universe even the simplest of men may not find within himself. In short, the religious inheritance of the ancient civilizations from the prehistoric past was of a complexity beyond any definition. That it was of compelling importance is well symbolized by the fact that from the first temples dominated the architecture of the cities as the priests and kings dominated their society.

Belief in the existence of a spirit world affecting the human was bound to lead to attempts to establish intermediaries. Even in primitive societies, including those of the Palaeolithic hunters, we find medicine men, shamans, seers and artists who in one way or another can interpret the ways of the spirits to men and the wishes of men to the spirits. These specially gifted men were probably the first privileged individuals in human communities, and are undoubtedly the forerunners of the priests and divine kings who came to power with urban civilization. Clearly, then, these figures were originally raised up out of the hearts and minds of the peoples that supported them. They were a part of organic social growth. This is a fact which must discredit the politically inspired view that the priests and kings of the ancient civilizations contrived in some way to foist themselves as economic parasites upon a helpless population and to exploit their simplicity with conscious cunning. Whatever they later became, the men of holy or magic powers which the Prehistoric Age passed on to civilization were of the people and for the people.

It is evident that by the fourth millennium, when what had been peasant settlements were beginning to show the graces, complexities and evils of cities, many trends in the future history of mankind had already been determined. Historically it was already certain that the first centres of civilization would lie in western Asia and round the eastern Mediterranean. It was already likely that lands lying near these centres would fairly rapidly acquire civilization, others more distant would acquire it gradually, while others again, either geographically isolated or with hostile climates, would remain unaffected natural 'reserves' where the old hunting life would survive for thousands of years.

It was already decided that civilization should rest on domesticated animals and plants, and the main breeds of these animals and plants were established as a living inheritance. Very many of the crafts that were to keep men busy until the industrial revolution had already made progress, and all the fine arts were in existence. It was already determined that man was to be a social being and a religious being, and that the first great ones of civilized society would receive their authority as intermediaries between man and unseen powers present in the external world. It was also certain that man would carry indefinitely into the future an unconscious mind whose contents would do much to give form and colour to his culture, and in particular to his imaginative creations in whatever field.

Anyone who today looks back at the history of his species may well feel that time has set a vast gulf between the cities of Iraq and Egypt and New York, London and Moscow, yet even so he cannot fail to see what tremendous achievements lay between their foundation and those days of primeval savagery when men went as hunters armed with a few rough weapons in lieu of horns and teeth. The enormous longueurs of prehistory may make our minds yawn, yet momentous, irreversible events took place during those uncalendared ages. They did much to determine the pattern of the ancient civilizations, and they affect us still.

SECTION ONE

THE PALAEOLITHIC
AND MESOLITHIC

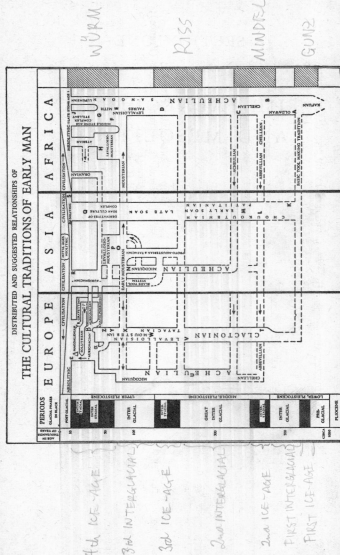

PERIODS, CULTURES AND FOSSIL HOMINIDS, PRINCIPALLY OF THE PLEISTOCENE AGE.

Key to letters representing fossil hominids:

A, Makapan Limeworks (S. Africa);
B, Sterkfontein (S. Africa);
C, Ternifine (Algeria);
D, Kanjera (Kenya);
E, Saldanha (S. Africa);
F, Florisbad (S. Africa);
G, Broken Hill (N. Rhodesia)
  and Eyasi (Tanganyika);
H, Haua Pteah (Cyrenaica);
I, Singa (Sudan), Boskop and
  Matjes River (S. Africa);
J, Fish Hook (S. Africa);
K, Sangiran (Java);
L, Choukoutien (near Pekin);
M, Trinil (Java);
N, Galilee;
O, Tabun, Mt Carmel;

P, Skhul Cave, Mt Carmel;
Q, Ngandong, Solo River (Java);
R, Hotu Cave (Iran);
S, Wadjak (Java);
T, Heidelberg (Germany);
U, Swanacombe (Kent, England);
V, Steinheim (Germany);
W, Fontechevade (France);
X, Ehringedorf (Germany);
Y, Gibraltar;
Z, La Chapelle-aux-Sainte (France);
α Chatelperron and Combe Capelle (France);
β Cro-Magnen (France);
γ Predmost (Czechoslovakia);
δ Chancelade (France);
ε Cheddar and Aveline's Hole (Somerset),
  Whaley (Derbyshire, England)

The remains from A and B belong to *Australopithesus*; those from K, L, M and possibly C and T to the *Pithecanthropus* group of men; those from Y and Z to the Neanderthal group; those from E, G, H, N, O, P, Q, V and X are neanderthaloids showing various degrees of affinity to *Homo sapiens*; remains from D, F, I, J, R and—are referable to *Homo sapiens*.

CHAPTER I

THE NATURAL STAGE

OUR species, *Homo sapiens,* emerged into full humanity during the Pleistocene Age, the last major period of geological time. It is no mere egotistical prejudice which makes us, through the mouths of our geologists, proclaim this age as being an abnormal one. To begin with it is exceptionally short, less than a million years compared with the tens of millions of earlier ages. This may be due to the fact that it is so close to us in time and so well recorded geologically that we are looking at it out of perspective; nevertheless, the geographical, climatic and biological changes do appear to be sufficiently great to justify its recognition as a distinct period.

We are on safer ground in saying that it is unusual in the large extent of land surface exposed above the oceans, in the size of its great upland regions and the height of its mountain ranges. In this respect, in which it appears merely as the climax of the whole Cenozoic, or Recent, geological era, it is an age of unusual geographical interest and variety, a time of great grandeur and contrast of scenery. For several hundred million years before the Cenozoic era the continental plains were normally broken only by low, rounded hills, and contrasts in climate, in vegetation and animal life were less numerous and sudden.

Above all the Pleistocene is abnormal in its violent and extensive glaciations. Indeed, it is as a glacial epoch that it has been recognized as a period of its own to be distinguished from the Pliocene and other Cenozoic periods. At the height of the greatest of the glacial phases very nearly one-third of the land surface of the earth was under ice sheets or glaciers. There had been no conditions anywhere approaching this for the previous two hundred million years; nothing like it, that is to say, since Permian times when our planet did pass through another glacial phase, though one probably far less intense and widespread in its effects.

We are still living under the exceptional conditions of the Pleistocene period. Although it is usual to separate the ten thousand or so years that have passed since the last retreat of the ice as the Holocene, or Wholly Recent, period, our present times can equally well be seen as still belonging to an age of mountain building and glaciation. Not only are we living among the highlands uplifted during the Pleistocene and earlier periods of the Cenozoic era, but we are living in times of considerable disturbance in the earth's crust. The storm that built the Alps and Himalayas, the Rocky Mountains and the Andes is dying down, certainly, but the earthquakes and volcanic eruptions which yearly destroy human life and property are a part of its weakening convulsions.

As for glaciation, although only about one-tenth of the land surface is now ice-covered compared with a third during the periods of its greatest extent, it is exceptional for the earth to carry any ice-caps whatever. Taking the long view of the geologists one can say that normally the poles of our planet have been free of permanent ice, with temperate conditions extending far into the Arctic Circle. Even during the Pleistocene period certain of the inter-glacial spells were warmer than the present; and as these spells lasted up to a quarter of a million years, it is impossible to judge whether the time of periodic freezing is over or whether the whole of human civilization has happened to fall within the early millennia of an interglacial phase similar to those of the Pleistocene.

Thus although we may have been well justified in distinguishing the Pleistocene as a full geological period, there is no doubt that in giving the same recognition to the Holocene our geologists were expressing our human bias. If we had not felt that the time of human ascendency demanded an age of its own, the last ten thousand years would not have been detached from the million preceding them.

In order to understand the physical world mankind was to inherit it is necessary to look back over the whole seventy million years of the Cenozoic. This, the era of recent life, not only, as its name indicates, saw the evolution of most of the animal species of the present day including man himself, but also the modelling of the dominant features of the continents which were to have so important an influence on human history. The events of the Cenozoic era shaped the modern world.

The end of the previous era, the Cretaceous Age when the great reptiles seemed destined to remain in the ascendency, had been a time of mountain building when the

Rockies and the Andes were first folded, but they were eroded away during the Eocene and Oligocene Ages which cover the first forty million years of the Cenozoic. Their re-elevation towards their present grand and craggy heights occupied the second half of the Cenozoic, culminating in the Pleistocene Age itself. The uplift of these great American ranges was accompanied by widespread volcanic activity which was at its most intense during the Miocene Age.

The history of the Alps and Himalayas, that colossal spine of Europe and Asia, is a little different and even more dramatic. During the previous era the zone which now supports the loftiest peaks in the world (and probably the loftiest peaks there have ever been on earth) was a long narrow trough filled by the Sea of Tethys. As early as the Cretaceous Age two or three folds along the line of this basin made a small beginning of the Alps, but the first great thrust did not come until Eocene times. The Tethys basin persisted until the Oligocene Age when violent pressure from the south made great folds buckle up into the air along the line of the ancient northern edge of Tethys. This paroxysm was repeated in the last ages of the Cenozoic, the Pliocene and Pleistocene, and the once vast ocean of Tethys shrank to form the Mediterranean as we know it.

While the geographical setting against which human history was to be enacted was taking shape during the successive ages of the Cenozoic, so too were the bodily forms and habits of the animals man was to know, including all those species which were to be of such immense importance to him as his domestic slaves. The disappearance of the great reptiles at the end of the previous era and the rise of the mammals in this one has not been fully explained; geological changes seem hardly enough to account for so tremendous a revolution in the pattern of life. Certainly, however, it happened; in the earlier half of the Cenozoic the mammals achieved great variety and strength. Many of them, notably the elephants, titanotheres and rhinoceroses, had almost as great a physical exuberance as the reptiles before them, carrying strange excesses of tusk, fang and horn. One of the rhinoceroses attained a length of twenty-five feet and stood eighteen feet at the shoulder, the largest warm-blooded creature ever to have imposed its bulk upon the earth. This monster was still flourishing in the Miocene Age, the period when, as we shall see, the family of the primates, from which man was to emerge, began the most vigorous phase of its evolution.

One very significant trend marks the whole course of

evolution during this so-called Age of the Mammals: the trend towards larger brains. Though much better provided than the huge, witless dinosaurs, the early mammals had much smaller brains in relation to their body size than have most modern species. That is certainly one of the reasons why so many of the groups of animals which shot up to achieve such spectacular bodily forms during this age had vanished or left only a few scattered survivors long before its end. From this point of view man and the primates merely continued a movement generally characteristic of the mammals in Cenozoic times.

Of the animals which were fated to be domesticated by man and therefore to share in his dominance of the modern world, the family of the Bovidae is by far the most important, including as it does cattle, sheep and goats. It also includes the bison, musk-ox and antelopes which were to be of importance to man during the hunting stages of his history. The Bovidae were an Old World group, the earliest known representatives emerging only in the Miocene Age but diversifying very fast during the succeeding Pliocene and attaining approximately their present forms during the Pleistocene period. It was during this last phase that a few of them, notably the bison and musk-ox, made their way from Asia into North America. In contrast with this family, whose lasting significance in human affairs cannot be exaggerated, the horses and camels were both New World groups, appearing as little beasts no more than a foot high early in the Cenozoic era. The modern type of horse had evolved from the original three- and four-toed species of *Eohippus* by the beginning of the Pleistocene, but then unaccountably died out in North America at the time of the last glaciation; as it had in the meantime spread into Eurasia (reversing the route of the bovids), the horse was able to complete its migration round the world when reintroduced into its homeland by the Spanish conquerors. The history of the camel was very much the same except that it survived in America rather later, while recent attempts to reintroduce it have been unsuccessful.

As for the dogs, the first species to enter the service of man, the foxes, jackals and wolves[1] from which the domestic forms were to be bred, had established their identity by the mid-Cenozoic times.

Most of the species of the modern flora and fauna of our planet had evolved by the end of the Pleistocene period. But although most of the living forms we know were already present in this period, very many ancient species died out during its successive glacial phases, while certain cold-loving animals like the famous woolly rhinoceros and mammoth became extinct after the last retreat of the ice. No doubt many of these failures were caused by the glaciations, some 'old-fashioned' species having become too inflexible to be able to migrate before the advancing ice and make the adaptation necessary for survival. Nevertheless there seems very little doubt that some animals were pushed towards extinction by man himself, for well before the end of Pleistocene times our Palaeolithic forebears had, as we shall see, become formidable hunters whose weapons, traps and organized drives were already far more deadly than the natural armature of the beasts. Evidence for this theory is provided by differences which have been noticed between the Old World and America. In the continents of the Old World, where our kind were slowly increasing their skill as hunters during the whole Pleistocene Age, extinctions occur evenly spread throughout its course; in America, on the other hand, we find species disappearing in much larger numbers during and after the last glaciation, the time when man first penetrated the New World. It seems, then, that already by fifty thousand years ago, man was beginning to make a mark in the world out of natural proportion to his still very modest numbers.

Before we can advance to a discussion of the emergence of man and these early phases of his history when he began to make the power of his intelligence felt, it is necessary to consider the climatic background, and particularly that of the Pleistocene period with its violent fluctuations.

While, as has been shown, the flora and fauna give the whole Cenozoic era its unity, the climatic conditions show no such continuity. The era began with some drop in average temperature, but already half-way through its first period, the Eocene, the earth was returning towards the warmth of the previous, Mesozoic, era, though it was never fully recovered. During the later Eocene and the Oligocene times much of Europe and of North America was clothed with sub-tropical forest such as now only flourishes in moist lowlands and low latitudes; palms and alligators, for example, are representative of the conditions at that time in the state of Dakota. Temperate forest dominated by giant redwoods with deciduous trees such as elm and beech could grow as far north as Alaska, Greenland, Spitzbergen and northern Siberia.

Not only was the climate much warmer and milder, but it was far more uniform than it is today; on land surfaces which seldom rose above the gentle, rounded hills, there could be none of the rain-drenched slopes or lee-side deserts created by mountain ranges.

During the Miocene Age a slight cooling was already apparent, with the temperate and sub-tropical belts contracting towards the equator, and this became more pronounced in the Pliocene before culminating in the devastating freezes of the Pleistocene Age. We have seen that these later phases of the Cenozoic were marked by titanic upheavals of the earth's crust, and there seems no question that the newly formed mountains contributed to the development of glacial conditions. Comparable upheavals preceded the Permian glaciation of two hundred million years before. Glaciers forming at high altitudes, and fed by the increased precipitation encouraged by mountain ranges, would flow downwards to form piedmont glaciers on the slopes, which would in turn spread and compact into extensive ice-sheets, often growing thick enough to coalesce with the mountain ice-sheets on the summits and so bury entire ranges. Once this ice-building process has begun, it gains an impetus of its own: thick ice drops the mean temperature and through adding to land height further increases the snowfall necessary to nourish the glaciers; furthermore, the surface of the ice-sheets throws back far more of the sun's heat than does a land surface, thus losing it to the earth. It has been calculated that while ice-free country loses no more than 20 per cent of solar radiation in this way, an ice-sheet will reflect as much as 80 per cent back into space.

Nevertheless, the folding of the Alps, Himalayas, Rockies and other great mountain masses cannot alone account for the Pleistocene glaciations. This is sufficiently proved by their intermittence. The irregularities in the rate of mountain building do not correspond in any way with the warm intervals which divided the period into several distinct glacial periods. It would seem, too, that the rate of fluctuation is far too rapid to be caused by earth movement. Many different theories have been advanced and still find support, but there is now a fairly wide acceptance of the view that the second main factor causing the glaciations was reductions in the amount of solar radiation reaching the earth's surface.

There is no evidence other than the glaciers for a decline in the amount of solar heat reaching the earth at this time; but as minor fluctuations have been recorded in recent times, it is quite possible that the Pleistocene may have been subjected to major ones. Thus in all probability the spells of intense cold which played so great a part during the time of man's emergence and first steps towards culture were due to a combination of uplifts in the earth's crust with temporary (and unexplained) weakening in the heat of the sun's rays at the earth's surface.[2]

Whether or not this dual explanation of the Pleistocene glaciations is the correct one, they played so important a part in human development throughout the world that it is absolutely necessary to look at them in some detail, studying not only the glaciated areas but also the regions beyond them where the climatic changes that went with variations in temperature were as significant if less spectacular. It seems legitimate to begin with the European region as this is where research began and where knowledge is still very much greater than it is in Asia. In America, where research is rapidly overtaking the European start, the facts are of far less importance to us as man himself arrived on the scene at so late a date. Africa is of the utmost interest but, as it was hardly affected by actual glaciation, its turn must come later.

The exact point in the geological record at which to open the Pleistocene period has been disputed. Here it is assumed to begin with the first indications of glaciation and by the appearance of the modern horse (*Equus*), the elephants, camels and men. As for its subdivision, the Lower Pleistocene is held to last until the end of the first inter-glacial, the Middle until the end of the third glaciation, while the Upper Pleistocene covers the last interglacial and glacial phases.

The recognition that the drop in temperature of Pleistocene times was not continuous but divided into several glaciations separated by periods of warmer climate was first made in Europe. There four cold phases were detected which, under the Alpine titles of Gunz, Mindel, Riss and Würm, have become a classic system providing a basis of comparison for the rest of the world. The third, Riss, glaciation was probably the most extensive of all, and certainly greater than the last. The Würm glaciation, however, had four distinct maxima with slightly warmer conditions intervening. In many regions, as will appear, evidence for the earliest, Gunz, glaciation is exiguous or still lacking, but in general there is no doubt that the fourfold glaciation was a world-wide phenomenon affecting both northern and southern hemispheres and causing a shift in the rain belts that brought corresponding wet phases to lower latitudes. Thus wherever they were living the men who were building up their Palaeolithic cultures during the Pleistocene Age were affected by this periodic freezing of their planet, often being forced into slow migrations and

See table P. 58.

sometimes finding wide areas habitable which under warmer conditions would be dry or desert.

In every glaciation the pattern of the ice formation was much the same though various in extent. In Europe the main ice-sheet started in the Scandinavian mountains and spread asymmetrically, with a much greater reach to the east where the southern edge reached 48°N, and farther north met the Siberian ice-sheet; on the west it pushed some two hundred miles across the North Sea bed (then dry or with shallow waters) before converging with the British glaciers. It is possible that this blocking of the North Sea diverted the Rhine to the west where it formed the valley which has since become the Straits of Dover.

Owing to its asymmetrical growth, the centre and thickest part of the Scandinavian ice-sheet crept eastward from the mountain crests until it stood over the region of the present Gulf of Bothnia. At this point it accumulated to the thickness of ten thousand feet, while at its greatest extent it covered well over two million square miles. This was only one ice-sheet out of many; it is not difficult to see how the locking up of so vast a bulk of water would reduce the volume of the oceans throughout the world, even while in some areas the tremendous weight of ice temporarily depressed the land surfaces on which it rested.

To the south of this ice-sheet with its vast almost unbroken stretches of dazzling white the other highlands of Europe generated their own glaciers which spread out more or less widely from their summits; thus the Pyrenees, Apennines and Carpathians carried considerable glaciers, while the Alps, where both height and precipitation were greater, came near to being cloaked by a true mountain ice-sheet. This Alpine ice covered eleven thousand square miles and attained the astonishing thickness of fifteen thousand feet. As for Britain, it formed a smaller version of Scandinavia with glaciers centred on the mountainous areas of Scotland, northern England, Wales and Ireland. During the later glaciations the British ice-sheet met the Scandinavian roughly along the eastern coasts of the island from the Orkneys to East Anglia; during the Gunz and Mindel glaciations, however, the Scandinavian ice-sheet had greater thrusting power and invaded eastern, and even central, England.

In northern Germany and other parts of central Europe glaciations corresponding to the last three of the Alpine system have been identified (and named the Elster, Saale and Warthe); there is little doubt that an earlier (pre-Elster) cold period must have existed there, but proof of it is still insufficient. The situation is very much the same in European Russia, with three glacial phases recognized and a more ancient one inferred.

Like northern Europe, northern Asia supported vast ice-sheets; one, extending from the Urals to the present islands of Novaya and Severnaya Zembla and down to the Byrranga mountains of the Taimyr Peninsula and the Putoranas, at its greatest (probably during the third glacial period) covered as much as 1,600,000 square miles. However, because the snow precipitation was less, it was very much thinner than the Scandinavian ice-sheet; it never seems to have reached more than 2,300 feet, a thickness which left its mountain ranges partially uncovered. Other mountainous regions of Siberia, the Central Siberian Plateau, the Baikal and Altai mountains, had their own glacial centres, and the mountains of north-eastern Siberia nourished a complex system of ice-cap, piedmont and valley glaciers.

In general, although the wastes of Siberia have hardly encouraged modern man to devote much time to the study of their glacial history, there seems no reason to doubt that the sequence of events was much the same as in northern Europe, although considerable difference in precipitation may have caused regional divergencies. It seems certain, however, that there as farther west the last (Würm) glaciation was less severe and extensive than the third.

On the more southern half of the Asiatic continent information is sometimes even scantier. Indeed here we have one of the few patches of the earth's crust not yet fully penetrated by *Homo sapiens;* there are ranges in its vast highland core which have hardly been explored, much less geologically studied. The exceptional height and mass of its mountains naturally caused the formation of glaciers in much lower latitudes than would otherwise have been affected. In the Caucasus, where at present only two cold phases have been distinguished, glaciers stretched unbroken for four hundred miles. In the main mountain mass where the three mighty prongs of the Himalayas, the K'unlun Shan and the T'ien Shan mountains unite in the Pamirs and then extend westward as the Hindu Kush, from three to four glaciations are now recognized. In the Pamirs the glaciations were intense, though limited to valley and piedmont glaciers with no true mountain ice-sheet; in the Himalayas four glaciations have been established, but as the last two probably both correspond with the Würm, the earliest of the Alpine sequence is either absent or unrecognized. In Kashmir and the Punjab, where careful studies have been made, three Pleistocene phases can be distinguished, of which the older and middle may be identified with the first and second glacials and interglacials in the Himalayas and the latest with the third and fourth.

If this patchwork account of the Old World is fitted together, it will be seen that in each of the Pleistocene glaciations, ice-sheets covered great parts of the northern territories of Europe and Asia down to about latitude 50°–60° though with considerable breaks; farther south the mountain ranges and plateaux which emboss the continents from Switzerland to China formed their own icy islands, large or small, where precipitation was sometimes enough to build thick ice-sheets which buried the mountain that gave them birth, sometimes only sufficient to fill the valleys and cover the slopes with glaciers. We can now turn to North America to find very much the same glacial events, although there they could have no effect on human history until towards their end.

Just as in Europe a vast ice-sheet building up from the Scandinavian mountains spread until it coalesced with the smaller one born of the British uplands, so in North America an eastern ice-sheet (the Laurentide) originating in the mountains of Baffin and Ellesmere Islands, coastal Labrador and east Quebec thrust westward until it met a smaller one (the Cordilleran) formed by precipitation on the western ranges. At its largest the Laurentide sheet covered more than four and three-quarter million square miles, probably extending far enough eastward to join with the Greenland ice. Along its western edge where it met its neighbour along the eastern side of the Rockies and jammed the valley glaciers, ice must have piled into huge and probably unstable masses. The Cordilleran ice-sheet was itself at its most extensive and thick in the region of British Columbia.

The fourfold division of Ice Ages has now been recognized in North America as in Europe; they have been named the Nebraskan, Kansan, Illinoian and Wisconsin, and seem to correspond quite closely with the Alpine system. Like the Würm glaciation the Wisconsin has been subdivided, the Iowan marking its climax and the Tazewell, Cary and Mankato (or Valders) representing minor readvances of the ice. From Cary times the retreat of the ice towards its present limits was fairly rapid. As in Europe, the second interglacial was the longest and the third the shortest (about one hundred and twenty thousand years); in none of them was the climate very much warmer than at present. Alaska was glaciated only in its mountain regions so that the coast of the Bering Sea remained passable during the final glaciation, and soon after the Iowan climax a corridor opened along the east side of the Rockies on the former line of the earlier junction of the Laurentide and Cordilleran ice-sheets. Thus a route was open from the easy line of access across the Bering Straits from Siberia; the straits themselves, which even today are no more than fifty miles wide and very shallow, would disappear with an increase in land level relative to the sea of only one hundred and fifty feet. Such a shift would link Alaska with Siberia by a broad plain offering grazing as good as the long grass of the present Alaskan Plain. That animals such as the mammoth, bison and antelope entered America in later Pleistocene times by a land-bridge of this kind is certain.

While in the northern hemisphere the continents were weighted down by many million square miles of ice, in the southern the drops in temperature which we have attributed to the lessening of solar heat must have led to a considerable spread of sea ice, but the glacial history of this ocean hemisphere passed with little trace and is of almost no concern in the development of man. There was a growth of glaciers in the Andes and in the mountains of New Zealand and Australia.

What are of very great significance for this development are the changes of climate which were the counterpart of the Ice Ages in regions of lower latitude not directly affected by glaciation. The existence of the ice-fields caused a shift in the belt of rain-bearing westerlies, the cyclonic storms, of some fifteen degrees towards the south in the northern hemisphere and towards the north in the southern hemisphere. So it was that Africa, the Mediterranean, Asia Minor, central Asia and north China, the south-west of the United States, and southern South America experienced 'pluvial' periods corresponding with the glaciations of higher latitudes. The reality of these shifts in the rain belt is shown mainly in the swelling of rivers, in a rise in existing lake levels and the filling up of basins now dry, and in the spread of vegetation in many areas now desert. Thus the Caspian and Aral Seas were united as were the Black Sea and the Sea of Azov; at some fifteen hundred feet above its present level, the Dead Sea attained a length of two hundred miles. In northern Africa there were lakes in the Fayum and Kharga basins, now dry depressions, and many more and larger lakes in Kenya and Abyssinia. Although there was a marked increase in rainfall in the Sahara and Kalahari deserts and much of the northern part of the Sahara area was able to support vegetation and animal life, desert tracts remained throughout the pluvial periods.[3] In the dry parts of North America there were lakes in basins such as the Bonneville, now completely parched. Australia, too, was to some extent affected by pluvial conditions; Lake Eyre, for example, attained ten times its present size.

Glaciation had one other result which influenced the life of man and his fellow-creatures, and in particular their migrations. The volume of water locked up in glaciers and ice-sheets can lower the ocean levels of the world. It has been calculated that at the height of the greatest glaciation of Pleistocene times the sea-level may have fallen up to four hundred feet, while during the last (Würm) glaciation it fell by well over two hundred. Should the present remaining ice-caps melt (as they show some signs of doing) the oceans might rise by as much as one hundred and sixty-five feet, though it would probably be less.

Such considerable falls in sea-level during the Ice Ages undoubtedly led to the emergence of land-bridges between areas now isolated, enabling men and animals to move freely between them. A bridge linking Alaska with Siberia has already been mentioned; others may have united Japan with the mainland of Siberia, Tasmania and New Guinea with Australia, while Borneo, Java and Sumatra are all likely to have been made one with Malaya by the exposure of the Sunda Shelf. There is archaeological and zoological evidence (p. 126) to suggest that the Celebes and Philippines were linked with the Asiatic mainland not through the Sunda Shelf group, but northward through Formosa. Among many other lesser effects of lowered sea-levels was the emergence of a land-bridge between England and western Europe; this probably took place during each Ice Age, the last severance having occurred some eight thousand years ago.

Looking back to the million years of the Pleistocene, then, we can see the whole surface of our planet swept by a slow climatic pulse. Four times colossal ice-caps with their slow, hardly visible flow crept farther and farther southward, while every considerable mountain mass, some of them still being lifted up to greater heights, supported its own glacial system, and the great rain belts converged towards the Equator, bringing grass and other vegetation in their wake. Four times, after holding their own for thousands of years, the ice-sheets and glaciers began to weaken, and year by year contracted, advancing less far each winter and retreating farther every summer. As they dwindled they left behind them the massive banks and ridges of moraine, the wide spreads of clay and gravel, the spreads of wind-borne loess, the smooth, planed faces of striated rock which were their legacy to the lands man was to inherit and to cultivate.

With each of these climatic pulsations we have also to envisage a world-wide migration of plant and animal life. If the period was too short for the evolution of new species, those which had come into being during the earlier Cenozoic era were obliged to shift territories with the ebb and flow of the ice. Such instability of environment made a stern test, and very many of the less adaptable species, failing to meet it, became extinct. One among the mammals, the most adaptable of all, may have been profoundly affected by the forced migrations that made him move to and fro between Europe and Africa, between northern Asia and the south. During the million years of the Pleistocene, man had become possessed of the rudiments of culture,[4] and the challenge of new surroundings and encounters with strangers of his own species with habits and equipment differing from his own may have done much to stimulate his growing mental powers.

This chapter on the natural background of human history must be concluded by an account of the last retreat of the ice and the establishment of the present geographic and climatic conditions which, though they are still in fact slowly fluctuating, appear, to our naturally short-term view, to make the stable background to our modern world. The pattern of tundra and forest, of grassland and rain forest or jungle, the courses of the cyclonic storms and the monsoons, the direction of tides and currents, have played a leading part in influencing the distribution of civilizations, the movements of men, the material basis and some part of the nature of the cultures which, taken all together, form the subject of this history.

The ice, as we have seen, retreated gradually after the climax of the last glaciation, and this retreat was interrupted by several halts or small readvances. In northern Europe, where the sequence has been most carefully studied, there were four of these checks, of which the first, the Brandenburgian, was the most considerable. It was followed by the Pomeranian, the Scanian and the Bothnian, each being named after the region where the edge of the ice-sheets stood at the time of the check or advance. There appears to have been a similar sequence of events in North America, but it has not yet been proved whether it synchronized exactly with the European. During the whole period marked by these colder spells our planet was still in the grip of the last Ice Age with a climate which in the present temperate regions varied from sub-arctic to arctic while the rain belt crossed northern Africa and south-west Asia. After the Bothnian advance, however, which can be dated to about 10,000 to 8000 B C, there was a steady rise in average temperatures during the pre-Boreal phase, followed by a more rapid and striking one during the succeeding Boreal and Atlantic climatic periods. In Atlantic times the dry continental climate of the Boreal gave way to moister conditions in Europe with westerlies bringing much greater humidity from the ocean; within it falls the period known as the climatic optimum, lasting from about 4000 to 2000 B C, when the average temperature was several degrees warmer than at the present day and the arctic ice-caps seem to have dwindled almost to vanishing point. There is clear evidence for this exceptional rise in temperature in regions as far apart as the Bering and Magellan Straits and New Zealand, although the degree of humidity varied with the position in relation to the rain-bearing ocean winds. Unquestionably then, this brief warm spell, as much as the glaciations themselves, was of world-wide extent and is therefore likely to have been due to an increase in solar radiation.

During Boreal times the present temperate zones began to be more heavily forested, conifers spreading where before there had been birch or the dwarf vegetation of the tundra; with the warm, moist Atlantic conditions the great deciduous forests of oak, elm, lime and other broad-leaved trees attained their greatest density and extent, while the coniferous forests retreated before them towards the north. With the slight worsening of climate which occured during the later sub-Boreal and sub-Atlantic times (we are still enjoying a sub-Atlantic climate), the deciduous forests had already passed their heyday even before our own species began its onslaught upon them to win arable and pasture land for the new farming economy.

The natural conditions of the Boreal and Atlantic phases are of special concern because it was during these millennia, from 7000 to 2500 B C, that man was exchanging the hunting life that he had shared with so many other mammals for the need to dominate nature that went with his initiation as a farmer. Indeed, well before the close of Atlantic times he had advanced to full civilization in south-west Asia, northwest India and the Nile valley, while farming had spread westward throughout Europe and eastward (intermittently) to northern China. In this context it must be remembered that while 4000–2000 B C has been recognized as the climatic optimum in the temperate zone, this is a biased assessment of a period that brought harsh conditions to some areas in drier latitudes as the rain belt shifted northward. It is probable that while the desiccation of northern Africa and southwest Asia had already gone far enough during Boreal times to begin to drive animal and human populations towards the valleys and moister uplands, this general trend was complicated by local variations. In north Africa, for instance, there is evidence for a temporarily wetter phase particularly affecting the west and south Sahara round about the fourth millennium B C.

During the whole of the glacial retreat there was wide fluctuation in the relative height of land and sea. At first the release of a great volume of water caused the sea-level to rise throughout the world but this was followed, much more locally, by a rising of land surfaces as the earth's crust responded gradually to its release from the weight of ice. These two contrary forces caused fluctuations in levels varying widely from one area to another, even within relatively small regions. They are recorded today in many parts of the world in raised beaches and submerged forests or other drowned land surfaces. The series of ups and downs has been most exactly studied in the Baltic where, after the release of an ice-dammed lake corresponding with the Scanian advance, the water rose above the present level to form the Yoldia Sea. Recovery of the land during pre-Boreal and Boreal times resulted in the formation of the Ancylus lake, with Denmark and the southern part of the Scandinavian peninsula united to cut it off from the North Sea. In the Atlantic period further melting and other factors led to another rise in relative sea-levels in the Littorina Sea which can be dated from about 5000–2000 B C. Since then the levels have adjusted themselves gradually to those of the present Baltic.

By the beginning of the Atlantic period all the major climatic and geographical changes resulting from the vast reduction in earth's burden of ice had taken place; there were to be many more small changes, but broadly the amazing variety of scene and condition which man was to exploit on the surface of his planet was already established. The jungle was there for the pygmy, the ice-floes for the Eskimo, and between these two extremes easier conditions offered the possibility of high civilization. We can follow the main pattern as a series of zones encircling the earth on either side of the Equator, although owing to the clustering of the continents in the northern hemisphere and the watery nature of the southern, most attention must be focused on the north. If climate were determined entirely by the sun, these belts would follow one another with steady uniformity, and would correspond more or less exactly on either side of the Equator. Happily, however, we have inherited an earth on which land surfaces are quite unevenly distributed and of uneven height and with its waters and atmosphere stirred by currents both vigorous and various. These powerful agents of irregularity combine to create a physical climate diverging widely from what would have been determined by solar radiation alone. Thus, for example, the warm, mild and moist peninsula of Cornwall is on the same latitude as the near-tundra conditions of northern Newfoundland on the one hand and the Gobi desert on the other.

So cutting across the broad zones there are oceanic and littoral climates, continental and mountain climates. Again, all these variables, with the added one of soil, have a strong influence on vegetation, so that the correspondence between the broad climatic and vegetational zones is very erratic, particularly in those humanly all-important latitudes between the extremes of heat and cold.

Nevertheless, the ancient conception of five great zones has its validity, and it is worth recognizing the Torrid zone round the equatorial girth of our planet (in fact the hottest latitude is $10°$N), followed by the pair of Temperate zones lying between the Tropics of Cancer and Capricorn and the Arctic Circles, and the pair of Frigid zones capping the globe beyond the Arctic Circles. If to this solar climatic system we add the factors of the enormous overgrown size and lofty mountain core of the Eurasiatic continents and the dominant winds, we shall gain some understanding of the main pattern of climate and vegetation against which human history has been played (Map I).

The wind systems, then, must be examined before the zones themselves are traversed. The essential distinction is between the latitudes dominated by the trade winds and those dominated by the westerlies and the cyclonic storms. The equatorial belt itself is generally calm and windless, the territory of the doldrums, but from $10°$ to $30°$ to the north of it the north-east trades blow steadily, while from $0°$ to $25°$ to the south the south-east trades take charge. Within these two vast zones, therefore, the east coasts of the continents, particularly if they are bold or mountain-lined, tend to be well watered while the west coasts and even the central areas are dry or desert. This is the explanation of the deserts that run right to the coast in South Africa (the Kalahari) and central Chile, and of the aridity of Western Australia. The most striking exception is in India, where a south-west monsoon supervenes to bring abundant moisture to the west coast.

To the north and south of the trades lie the latitudes of the westerlies, where the rule is reversed and west coasts tend to be wet and east ones dry. Indeed, as the westerlies carry the cyclonic storms, they are far wetter than the trades, and such high or mountainous coasts as those of British Columbia, Ireland and southern Chile have some of the highest rainfalls found outside the tropics. The contrast between the wetness of the southern Andes and the desert of the northern makes the clearest possible demonstration of the contrary influence of trades and westerlies.

Having taken account of the main factors other than the sun which control climate we are ready to examine the zones in order, generalizing so far as is permissible about their climates and vegetation and the opportunities these offer to man and beast. Beginning at the centre, we find in the equatorial belt itself a region little disturbed by winds and with practically no seasonal variation, where the power of the sun is absolute. The tropical rain forests grow tall and sombre, for intense heat and heavy rain encourage the growth of gigantic trees whose branches, bound with creepers, fuse into vast platforms of vegetation where monkeys, birds and snakes can flourish in an upper treescape of their own; below in the dim green twilight only insects find ideal conditions. There are no large animals, and the human history of the Congo and Amazon basins, the west coast of central Africa, Sumatra and Borneo is sufficient proof that the rain forests do nothing to encourage man to activity, of either body or mind.

On either side of the equatorial zone, these forests tend to give way to jungle of a less impenetrable kind. The heat is still tropical, but the humidity less; grass and shrubs mingle with the trees and the sunlight is not altogether shut out. Many of the ancient and less adaptable species of animal such as the elephant, hippopotamus and the great apes have managed to survive in small numbers in these regions where competition is not too great. Man has lived among these jungles sometimes in ease but seldom with much cultural distinction.

In the succeeding zones park conditions prevail in highland regions and savannah on the plains. In the southern zone conditions of this type occur in parts of Brazil, Uruguay and Paraguay, then in Angola, the Rhodesias and Bechuanaland. One might justifiably include in this category the partly grass-covered alluvial plains of eastern Australia. In the northern zone they occupy much of Venezuela and Guiana and are found at their most characteristic in Africa in the vast belt that crosses the Sudan and Abyssinia. This kind of

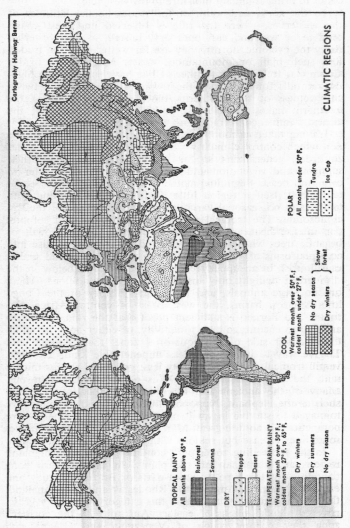

Cartography Hallwag Berne

CLIMATIC REGIONS

TROPICAL RAINY
All months above 65° F.

Rainforest

Savanna

DRY

Steppe

Desert

TEMPERATE WARM RAINY
Warmest month over 50° F.;
coldest month 27° F. to 65° F.

Dry winters

Dry summers

No dry season

COOL
Warmest month over 50° F.;
coldest month under 27° F.

No dry season ⎱ Snow
Dry winters ⎰ forest

POLAR
All months under 50° F.

Tundra

Ice Cap

MAP I

country, at least before man invented the sporting rifle, often supported mammalian life at its finest and most spectacular.

To the north of this open and fairly dry region, rainfall dwindles to almost nothing in the tropical deserts which stretch across Africa and Arabia from the Atlantic to the Red Sea; in the southern hemisphere tropical desert is prevalent only in central Australia, in the Kalahari area of South Africa and in a strip of the South American coast. Nearly continuous with the belt of African and Arabian desert, but mountainous and in colder latitudes to the north, are the almost equally immense though more broken continental deserts of central Asia where the winter climate is intensely cold. A comparable desert covers much of New Mexico and Arizona and parts of California, Colorado and Utah in the south-west of the United States. These continental deserts owe their aridity not to lying in latitudes of great heat but to their distance from rain-bearing ocean winds, and often to lying in the lee of mountain ranges which catch the precipitation and form these desert 'rain shadows'. While the tropical deserts are normally quite uninhabitable by man or beast except where there are underground water supplies, the continental deserts often carry enough scrub and tough grasses to be able to nourish sparse flocks and herds.

North of the deserts the pattern for a time becomes more broken. A narrow belt of what is now poor grassland follows the southern shore of the Mediterranean, through Palestine (with a westward extension back into Asia Minor), Syria and Mesopotamia to run along the Asiatic littoral north of the Red Sea, and so on to widen out with the Indus valley. The beasts which in a natural state grazed this poor pasture verging on the desert were the wild ass and camel. On the many limestone uplands adjoining, however, such as the Iranian plateau, where more park-like conditions prevail, wild sheep were native. Here, too, grew the wild grasses ancestral to our cultivated cereals. This strip of grassland and limestone park country is of extraordinary importance in the history of man.

Much of this territory can be accepted as sub-tropical, as is also the otherwise very different neighbouring region of the Mediterranean basin. Although they have nearly all been cleared by the many great peoples that have flourished round this most famous inland sea, evergreen forests once covered much of the area with its many peninsulas and islands. Trees such as the ilex, bay and olive with their deep roots and leaves designed to reduce evaporation are able to withstand the hot and dry summers which disturb an otherwise moderate climate. These Mediterranean lands (which have a near counterpart in a small region round the Cape in South Africa and in California) are ideally suited to man, supporting in abundance the fruit, flowers, oil, nuts and domestic animals —to say nothing of the vines—that bring him most delight.

Moving northward from the sub-tropical to the temperate zone we also enter what since Boreal times has been the course of the westerlies, bearers of cyclonic storms, those spiralling disturbances that travel round the globe bringing violent, changeable weather with rain and veering winds. In the northern hemisphere they sweep over North America from British Columbia to New England, storm across the Atlantic and then onwards right across Europe and Asia from Ireland to Japan. In the southern hemisphere their course lies mainly across the oceans, but they cross South America (in the region of the northern Argentine and Uruguay), Tasmania and New Zealand.

The broad pathways of the cyclonic storms support different kinds of vegetation determined mainly by the position in relation to the oceans, by mountain barriers and by soil. In western Europe as in the eastern United States and central Canada, there is a natural covering of deciduous forest, found again in Chile, Tasmania and New Zealand. Farther from coastal moisture and on the light, loose soils inimical to dense forest, there are the natural grasslands such as those of the mid-western prairies in the United States and the great open passage-way of the steppes running from central Europe far eastward through southern Russia as far as the Altai mountains. In between these sharply contrasting realms of grassland and forest there may be intermediate regions of parkland.

The natural condition of this part of the temperate zone has been revolutionized by man. Much of the grassland which was once the home of flocks of wild horse and cattle (in America the bison) is now given over to wheat, while the deciduous forests, where the pig was most at home, have been cleared and devoted to mixed farming, including the herds of domestic cattle whose ancestors were native to the grasslands.

Moving beyond these very broken regions in the northern hemisphere we are once again in the latitudes of more uniform climatic zones. First is the great gloomy belt of the coniferous forests occupying the northern part of the temperate zone where pine, spruce and fir cloak so much of Canadian North America and of Eurasia from northern Scandinavia to the Bering Strait. Here, although man ceaselessly attacks the forests for lumber, he has not done much more to change the natural vegetation and animal life, for summers in these latitudes are too short for agriculture except of a very specialized kind.

Beyond the sub-arctic forests even the tough conifers die out before the arctic cold, and we reach the extensive belt of tundra that follows the northern coasts of Canada and Eurasia. Here marshy soil which even in the short summer thaws only on the surface, nourishes mosses and, in its more favourable stretches, arctic birch and dwarf willow. Reindeer, caribou, musk-ox and other cold-loving animals that once ranged far to the south beyond the Pleistocene ice-sheets, retreated with the ice and now browse the mosses of these desolate lands.

While the southern hemisphere has no land surfaces to support sub-arctic forests and only a few exiguous patches such as Graham's Land which might qualify as tundra, both poles alike are crowned by ice-caps, which, as we have seen, are the survival of the Pleistocene glaciation and are not a geologically normal feature of our planet. The Arctic supports polar bears, seal, walrus and great quantities of migrant birds rendering human life just possible. The much larger Antarctic, lying so remote from the great continents, was inhabited until recently only by seals and penguins and a few other sea birds; even now its human population is limited to a few observant scientists.

Here then, in rough outline are the principal climatic zones that band our earth from the Equator towards the poles; it is a survey which ignores countless local regional differences that have had a powerful influence on the cultural tone and well-being of human populations. Nevertheless, it gives some idea of the main controls which environment exercised on the development of man, here offering him opportunities, there imposing burdensome handicaps. Environment does not determine cultures or the fortune of peoples; that is a view that can be held only by those whose rigid minds habitually ignore everything that cannot be pinned down by natural laws. One cannot even be sure of the outcome of opportunity and handicap: for example, the inhabitants of tropical jungles seem to have found the necessities of life so abundant and easily won that they made no effort to advance their culture, while on the other hand the energetic enterprise of many hard-pressed mountain peoples is well known.

Without erring towards determinism, however, no one can deny the idea of natural conditions as a limiting factor of high importance. It is not by chance that nearly all the crucial achievements in the history of ancient civilizations took place within the temperate zone of the northern hemisphere. While the growth of art, religion, science and philosophy cannot be absolutely prohibited by an environment as that of, say, lime-hating plants may be, nevertheless there are many settings in which it is never likely to reach its highest development.

NOTES TO CHAPTER I

1. The origin of the dog domesticated during the Mesolithic has not yet been fully proven. Its ancestry must be traced back among *Canidae* in the narrower sense (genus *canis* s. str.), wolves and jackals. According to Boessneck 'there are the greatest difficulties in defining the different forms within this genus and in establishing the connections between the different species. Opinions vary on the extent to which the larger-sized Nordic wolves and jackals proper were related to the dog. The most likely ancestors of the domesticated dog of today are the smaller wolf-like forms of the south, such as the *Canis pallipes* Sykes in particular, which also from the standpoint of animal psychology are best adapted to domestication'. See J. Boessneck, 'Herkunft und Frühgeschichte unserer mitteleuropäischen landwirtschaftlichen Nutztiere', *Züchtungskunde*, Vol. 30, 7 (1958), p. 293.

2. Professor Martinez del Rio considers that it must nevertheless be borne in mind that there is neither proof of, nor general support for, the hypothesis that 'insolation' (= the amount of solar radiation reaction upon the surface, in the broad sense) is the cause of glaciation. See H. Shapley, *Climatic Change: Evidence, Causes and Effects* (Cambridge, Mass., 1953).

3. Professor D. C. Baramki suggests that the existence of deserts during the pluvial periods may be explained by the fact that the 'lift' immediately north of the equatorial belt contributed greatly towards the desiccation which produced the Sahara, Kalahari and Arabian deserts. See F. E. Zeuner, *Dating the Past. An Introduction to Geochronology* (London, 1958), pp. 265–71.

4. 'Culture' is a complex word that has been variously defined. Two anthropologists have suggested that culture is 'the sum total of learned behavior patterns which are, therefore, not the result of biological inheritance' (Hoebel), or that 'culture consists in all transmitted social learning' (Kluckhohn).

    See A. L. Kroeber and C. Kluckhohn, 'Culture: A Critical Review of Concepts and Definitions', Peabody Museum of American Archaeology and Ethnology, Harvard University, *Papers*, XLVII (1952).

CHAPTER II

THE EVOLUTION OF MAN

As we follow the history of man, we shall find the centres of interest, the fresh growing points, swinging from continent to continent. Often after a period of such eminence or initiative, the region may lapse into relative unimportance, only to come to the fore again at a later time. There is now not very much doubt that the continent which has the first claim to pre-eminence is Africa.[1] Although it is too soon for final judgement, recently gathered evidence suggests that the earliest hominids emerged there, the earliest tool-making men, and perhaps, though by no means so probably, the earliest representatives of our own species, *Homo sapiens.*

Man, the unique animal with whose subsequent achievements and failures these volumes are concerned, belongs to the order of the Primates, which he shares with the tree shrews, lemurs, tarsiers, monkeys and apes. To follow his emergence, then, we shall be following the main line of Primate evolution from the tree shrew up to the super-family of the Hominoidae, to which man is assigned together with his nearest surviving kin, the anthropoid apes—chimpanzee, gorilla, orang-utan and gibbon. Although in following such an evolutionary line we legitimately illustrate it by surviving examples of its various stages, it has to be remembered that in fact although the modern species—such as the tarsiers, for example—may keep many primitive traits, they too have developed over the vast spans of time involved and may show specialized features not found in their early ancestors. Another factor which makes the tracing of such a direct line through fossil forms extremely difficult is the frequency in evolutionary history with which a genus, family or species may branch off, run parallel with others for a time, and then become extinct. Again and again we shall find uncertainty as to whether a particular fossil primate is on the ancestral line of the modern apes or man or whether it represents one of these unsuccessful offshoots. Primate evolution shows several general trends. One is the modification of the limbs to fit them for tree-climbing, and later, among the hominids, for walking upright on the ground. The others, shown in the all-important development of the skull, are the enlargement of the brain (including an increase in the space devoted to the sense of sight, and a decrease in that for smell); the gradual advancement of the eyes from the side to the front of the head (allowing stereoscopic vision) and their enclosure in bone sockets; the shortening of the snout, and the forward movement of the opening for the passage of the spinal cord and blood vessels into the brain—the *foramen magnum*—from the extreme back of the skull to a more central position below it. This last development was made necessary by the assumption of an upright stance and the consequent balancing of the head directly upon the spinal column. A rather surprising fact firmly established only in recent years is that among the early men, or hominids, the evolution of the limbs for walking and standing upright and for free manipulation preceded and outstripped the evolution of the brain and skull. The interplay between the freeing of the hand by the assumption of an upright carriage, the development of acute, stereoscopic vision and the growth of mental capacity presents a vital aspect of primate evolution which will be more fully discussed in Chapter IV.

Our knowledge of these general trends derives from a scatter of fossil finds from many regions of the Old World. These are already considerable in number and rapidly increasing, yet they are still haphazard, greatly affected by the varying intensity of research in different areas—and in many instances extremely fragmentary. Moreover, a complete unity of study can hardly be obtained; there is certain to be some degree of insularity even among palaeontologists. Thus, as is recognized to have been true in the case of *Pithecanthropus* and *Sinanthropus,* the recognition of distinct species and genera is sometimes due as much to differences between the knowledge and opinions of their modern interpreters as to differences between the bodily forms of the ancient primates themselves. Yet in spite of all shortcomings, and in spite of one or two major issues still in dispute, a coherent picture is beginning to emerge (Chart on p. 44).

The earliest known primates were already widespread in the Eocene period, near the dawn of the Cenozoic era. Their fossil remains, which have come to light in North America, France and southern England, relate one branch to the present-day lemurs of Madagascar, and another to the East Indian tarsiers. They were descended from little shrew-like

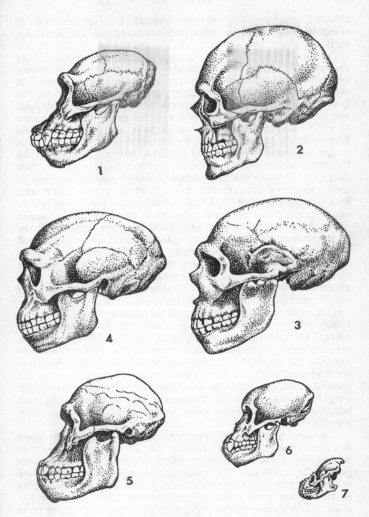

FIG. 1. *Primate evolution. 1: Modern chimpanzee; 2: Modern man; 3: Neanderthal man; 4: Peking man; 5: Australopithecus; 6: Proconsul Africanus; 7: Adapis parisiensis, an ancient lemur.*

arboreal creatures which were making a livelihood out of insect-hunting when the great reptiles were still dominant on earth.

During the succeeding Oligocene period the emergence of the apes in Africa had already begun with *Parapithecus,* a very small species whose teeth have some points in common with those of the great apes. *Parapithecus* was followed by the gibbon-like *Propliopithecus,* and the evolutionary ground was now prepared for the great expansion and diversification of the apes which was such a remarkable feature of the Miocene period in Africa.

Among the early apes (or perhaps, better, proto-apes) of this time which were either our direct ancestors or had not diverged far from the human stem, was *Proconsul,* a generalized species of monkey-like agility, which could climb and leap among the trees, but which might also run on all fours on the ground and perhaps occasionally raise itself to scamper on its hind legs. In many important respects, specifically in its somewhat lighter build, smaller canines and absence of the 'simian shelf' on the lower jaw, *Proconsul* was more human in appearance than are the modern apes. It was, in fact, still so generalized that it could conceivably have been ancestral to both apes and men, although it is more probable that it should be placed near the base of the simian stem. For at that time, some thirty-five million years ago, the family of the Pongidae, which was to produce our nearest animal kin, the gibbon, orang-utan, gorilla and chimpanzee, was beginning to diverge from that of the Hominidae. Remaining for the most part tree-dwellers (though the chimpanzee and gorilla have taken to living most of their lives on the ground, they are still forest-bound) the apes developed the long hands and arms, and retained the opposable big toe, adapted to an existence spent swinging and running from branch to branch.

The new primates did not long remain confined to their African cradleland, but before the end of the Miocene period had spread into other parts of the Old World. One genus, *Dryopithecus,* was widespread in Eurasia, while another, *Pliopithecus,* showing affinities with the gibbons, seems to have been quite common in southern Europe before the close of Miocene times. Although the balance of present evidence suggests that Africa remained the evolutionary centre for the higher apes, the rival claims of southern Asia cannot be ignored. The Siwalik hills of India have yielded quantities of the fossil remains of large primates belonging to numerous genera. Many are species of *Dryopithe-*

cus, and of these some groups, it has been argued, might be ancestral to the Pongidae, while others could be trending in the human direction. One Pliocene species from Siwalik, *Ramapithecus brevirostris* (like so many others, known only from a jaw bone) has been seen as bridging the anatomical gap between the anthropoid apes of this period and the Australopithecines soon to be described.

One of the apes native to southern Europe demands special mention because of the ambitious claims made for it. The Pontian beds of Italy in which this *Oreopithecus* has come to light are assigned to the early Pliocene by all geologists save some of the French who prefer to call them Miocene. The previously scrappy fossils of *Oreopithecus* have now been reinforced by an almost complete specimen and some authorities see in it a fully evolved hominid, the earliest man known to us and an ancestor of *Homo sapiens*. This claim has been further developed to suggest that the division of the Hominoidae into the Pongidae and Hominidae took place earlier than was thought. Quite apart from the argument supported here, that the true men should be recognized by an ability to make tools rather than by any anatomical definition, other interpretations of the *Oreopithecus* fossils are possible. One is that this Italian genus represents a third branch of the Hominoidae which forked off at the same time as those of the apes and men but died out in early Pliocene times.

For the next crucial step in human evolution we return to Africa, and the Australopithecines (Fig. 2). As their name shows, these beings have been regarded as apes rather than men, but it has long been accepted that they possess a number of features bringing them closer to man than any other ape. Now that it begins to appear that they were capable of shaping stone tools, it may be necessary to promote them to a place among the true hominids. The plentiful fossil remains of *Australopithecus* which have been excavated, chiefly from stalagmitic deposits in limestone caves and fissures in the Transvaal and Bechuanaland, all date from the first to the second pluvial periods of the Pleistocene Age and are therefore too late to be ancestral to man. On the other hand they come so near to fulfilling all the scientific requirements for our Pliocene ancestors that they are generally considered to represent a persistent branch of such an ancestral stock that survived almost unchanged among the dolomite hills of South Africa long after their more progressive cousins had advanced to tool-making and were spreading triumphant-

FIG. 2. *Chimpanzee and reconstruction of an* Australopithecus
       *showing modification of pelvic girdle (after Singer
       et al.).*

ly throughout the Old World. In looking at the Australopithecines, then, we are seeing creatures that must closely
have resembled our still missing Pliocene forebears.

They were small, rather slightly built beings, about the
size of modern pygmies; although their feet were probably
more flexible than our own, they seem normally to have
walked upright, with the skull balanced above the spine very
much in the human fashion. The back-bone, long bones, pel-
vis, and *foramen magnum* at the base of the skull, all indicate this upright carriage. The head borne in so human a
manner, however, had a strongly apelike aspect, with low
forehead, eyes deepset below prominent brows, flat nose and
protruding muzzle. On the other hand the teeth of *Australopithecus*, in their cusps, in the moderate size of the canines
and in the parabolic plan on which they are set, are much
more human than simian. Furthermore their brains, though
only in one instance absolutely larger than those of modern
apes, are considerably bigger relative to their body size.

The characteristics described are common to the sub-family, but the known specimens of Australophithecines can be divided into two groups, differing slightly both in age and anatomy. The older type, living during the latter part of the first African pluvial and into the succeeding interpluvial, was, as might be expected, the more human in appearance; the original Taungs (Bechuanaland) example belongs to this group and others have been identified at Makapansgat and Sterkfontein. The more recent type, living during the first interpluvial period and possibly on into the second pluvial, was taller, rather more heavily built (*Australopithecus robustus* or *Paranthropus robustus*) and generally slightly more apelike. The Australopithecines were, in short, trending away from the original ancestral human line in much the same direction as the Pongidae, although their evolution in this direction did not go as far and could not include any of those traits which the apes developed as an adaptation to the arboreal life.

For all the Australopithecines had left the forests and their edges to live in dry, open savannah broken by rocky outcrops. Some appear, also, to have taken to flesh-eating, enjoying a mixed, perhaps omnivorous diet like that of baboons. It may be that they were like the baboons again in hunting in groups. Possibly they were scavengers.

It is commonly agreed that the surest way to distinguish the earliest men from their fellow animals was in the possession of sufficient will-power, foresight and skill for the manufacture of tools. Had these creatures, with their almost equal balance between human and simian characters, taken this first step towards the creation of culture? It begins to look as though the answer may be yes. As we shall see, it is certainly true that equally ancient and related hominids were tool-makers. In the limestone fissures and caves where most of the *Australopithecus* fossils were discovered there were also many other animal remains, including the skulls of baboons broken in a manner which suggested to some observers that they had been clubbed. In none of the early excavations, however, were any stone artifacts or other deliberately shaped tools found in association with *Australopithecus*. Some interpreted this evidence as showing that the little ape-men, though incapable of tool-making, used natural sticks and stones as weapons. Others were sceptical of the significance of the baboon skulls, and moreover were inclined to think that the caves and fissures were the dens of carnivores and that the Australopithecines were there not as hunters but as hunted, perhaps dragged to their lairs by sabre-toothed cats. Yet it was certain that stone tools were being made at this time (p. 118), and so it had to be assumed that a higher breed of hominid, a tool-maker and therefore deserving the name of man, was living contemporaneously with *Australopithecus,* having passed him by on the evolutionary road.

In 1956–57 the picture was changed by further discoveries made at Sterkfontein. In a brecciated layer in the cave, overlying the abundant *Australopithecus* fossils but itself containing some probably Australopithecine teeth, were considerable numbers of pebble tools of the Oldowan type (p. 118). The obvious way to interpret this discovery is to accept the fact that in spite of his small brain *Australopithecus* was indeed capable of making tools, and that in this part of South Africa, at least, he was the possessor of the Oldowan pebble culture. It remains puzzling that no implements were found in the main fossil bed at Sterkfontein or at the other Australopithecine sites. One explanation put forward is that the cave was first inhabited by carnivores, which were responsible for bringing in the plentiful remains of *Australopithecus,* while the tool- and teeth-yielding horizon represents a later occupation of the cave by the ape-man himself. Such a sequence of events is excessively hard to swallow—but it is not quite impossible. Other authorities again deny that the large teeth found in the tool-bearing stratum are Australopithecine.

In 1959 a complete human skull together with a tibia was found in the horizon in Oldoway (or Olduvai) Gorge, Tanganyika, which probably dates from the very beginning of the Middle Pleistocene (although it has also been assigned to the late Villafranchian period at the end of the Lower Pleistocene). That is to say this human being was living at least half a million years ago. What makes the find of such outstanding importance is that the skull (and no doubt the rest of the skeleton) was lying in a horizon where it appears to have been associated with pebble tools and waste flakes, a hammer-stone, and the remains of food which included birds, frogs, fish, lizards, rats, and mice, as well as the young of some of the gigantic animal species which existed in the region at that time—such as pigs, sheep, cattle and giraffe. Although it is tempting to assume that this individual made the pebble tools associated with his remains, the usual troublesome possibility remains that he may have been the prey of the actual tool-makers. Further evidence on this point may come from yet more recent finds in the immediate vicinity.

This Oldoway man shows a mixture of characteristics. In a general way he has much in common with the Australopithecines, and in particular he resembles them in the pattern of the molar teeth and in the fact that while these molars are huge the canines and incisors are relatively small. Both show the molars worn flat. On the other hand the Oldoway man has a very long face in which the cheek bones are like those of *Homo,* he has huge frontal sinuses but no heavy brow ridge or frontal torus. The forehead is very low but the cranium rises towards the back so that the brain capacity is likely to prove to be very considerably greater than that of *Australopithecus.* A feature unique among known hominids, he has a sagittal crest on the crown of the head like a lighter version of that found in the gorilla. Presumably this must be associated with the muscles needed for the extraordinarily heavy jaws which have earned him the nickname of the Nutcracker man.

The finder has given Oldoway man the name of *Zinjanthropus boisei,* but some anatomists may question whether it would not be more correct to recognize him as belonging to the genus *Paranthropus.* All are prepared to agree that he belongs to the same sub-family of the Australopithecinae. Again, while the finder has boldly claimed that '*Zinjanthropus*' is half-way between *Australopithecus* and *Homo* and therefore on the direct line of our ancestry, other opinion may incline to see in him yet another of the unsuccessful 'dead end' branches that grow from every evolutionary tree.

It is always possible, too, that although Oldoway man is supposedly the oldest pebble-tool maker yet known* (for the tool-bearing horizon at Sterkfontein is later) implements of this same type, which are remarkably widespread in Africa, may have been made by a variety of hominids. Indeed there may have been as many human species in the continent at this period as there were of the apes in Miocene times. Two jaws found at Swartkrans in the Transvaal are claimed to represent another hominid (*Telanthropus*). The jaw found in Lower Pleistocene beds at Kanam, Kenya, was once identified as belonging to an advanced type of pebble-tool maker, but its genuine antiquity is so doubtful that it cannot be given much weight for the present.

It is likely to prove that, once begun, tool-making spread rapidly, and that its beginning was due to the assumption, perhaps by a number of different human species, of the upright stance. Walking upright has biological and mechanical disadvantages, and for survival would probably have had to be compensated for by the use of tools and weapons. This in turn

---

* Remains of a yet older hominid, apparently with a larger brain capacity, were found at Oldoway in 1961.

would have led to a relatively rapid selection in favour of braininess and so speeded the evolution of our kind.

At this point we have to face what is now the one really crucial dispute in our reconstruction of human evolution. How soon did the pre-*sapiens* stock, that is to say the line which was to lead to *Homo sapiens*, part from that of the other hominids? In the past some authorities have held that this happened very early, and that the *Pithecanthropi*, represented by Java and Peking man, who were to dominate Asia from early Middle Pleistocene times, were a collateral branch, quite distinct from the ancestral line of the pre-*sapiens*, which developed the extreme forms of massive brow ridge and other distinctive features in Asia alone. Others see the *Pithecanthropi* as representing a long stage in the evolution of *Homo sapiens* and as a stock widespread throughout the Old World. This would include in it, for example, '*Atlanthropus*', the hand-axe-making man of north Africa (p. 96). Indeed the extremists in this direction believe that *Homo sapiens* began to emerge as a distinct species only during the last interglacial age—and even that he was a descendant of Neanderthal man. Adherents of the first view have put a heavy weight of argument on the at present rather slender fossil evidence for the existence of men of pre-*sapiens* type quite early in Pleistocene times (pp. 101–103), while supporters of the second do their best so to belittle it as to be able to set it aside.

By suggesting that pebble-tool makers in what was to be a progressive cultural area were of so primitive and 'non-sapient' a breed, the discovery of '*Zinjanthropus*' may be said to have given some encouragement to the second 'late emergent' point of view. On the other hand, as has been said, it is possible that Oldoway man was only an unsuccessful side-branch and that there were biologically more progressive breeds already in existence.

A still more recent discovery (1961) is a skull from the overlying Chellean horizon in the Oldoway Gorge. This hominid seems to be basically of Pithecanthropic type, but has a higher forehead and other features said to point towards Steinheim man—recognized as belonging already to the genus *Homo*.

Thus it has become clear that the main stages of evolution are represented first by early Australopithecines, then by progressive *Pithecanthropi* and finally by *Homo* in its various species. Moreover, it can be claimed that hominids representing these three stages were dominant in the Lower, Middle and Upper Pleistocene periods respectively. Yet it still remains uncertain how early the more progressive 'pre-*sapiens*' element began to diverge from the Pithecanthropic line; it is always possible for what is going to prove a dominant strain to remain in the background for a time—as was true of the earliest mammals. There may have been a long period of overlap, as is indeed suggested by the evidence soon to be given for the existence of the genus *Homo* in Middle Pleistocene times.

This account will therefore follow a course between the two extreme points of view defined above. It will treat the remains of the *Pithecanthropi* and Neanderthal men separately from those of the supposed pre-*sapiens* types leading on to *Homo sapiens*. One will be referred to as the Palaeoanthropic and the other as the Neoanthropic wing. While it is no longer possible to accept these terms as standing for distinct branches of humanity, they are still convenient adjectives for distinguishing between the two wings of the broad front of human evolution. That they do represent two valid evolutionary tendencies is brought home when during the last glaciation men of fully modern type were in conflict with the Neanderthalers.

The Neoanthropic trend towards *Homo sapiens,* then, is marked by the development of large cerebral hemispheres with the corresponding high vault and full rounded back to the skull, flat mouth, small canines and a prominent chin. Another less conspicuous feature is the broadening of the back of the palate until the teeth are set in a half-oval, parabolic form, in contrast with the parallel-sided rectangular palate developed by the apes. This trend also saw the maintenance and further development of the relatively light skeleton, straight long bones and upright carriage already found in the Australopithecines. The tendency on the opposite—Palaeoanthropic—wing was for an increase in the volume of the brain without the growth of a lofty skull vault; the chin remained receding and the jaw very prominent, and the canines tended to be large. Certain features evolved strongly in the same direction as among the Pongidae, particularly the massive bar of bone above the eyes, and the heavy jaw.

We can now look more closely at the principal early representatives of the lowbrow wing of advancing mankind—the *Pithecanthropi* of eastern Asia. They have one great advantage over their cousins for students of our origins: they have left quite abundant remains behind them. Whereas the skeletal evidence for earlier Pleistocene *Homo* is exiguous and their existence too often has to be inferred from their tools and from the appearance of their descendants, and by inference from later events, the fossil record of the East Indian and Asiatic stock is well established. For some time after their discovery, it was usual to assign types represented by Java man and Peking man to different genera, but an accumulation of finds has led to their being united into the single genus, *Pithecanthropus*.

The most ancient of the Java fossils came from the Djetis deposits, dating from the mid-Pleistocene period. Their excavator claimed that the remains of four individuals which he discovered represented two distinct species within the genus *Pithecanthropus*, and a third belonging to a different genus. He named them *P. modjokertensis, P. dubius* and *Meganthropus palaeojavanicus*. The most famous of the Java men, found in 1890, some fifty years before the Djetis bed specimens, came from the Trinil beds which are rather more recent, having formed in Upper mid-Pleistocene times. Probably *Pithecanthropus erectus*, as he is named, was living in Java during the first half of the second interglacial phase. In most features he very nearly resembles the *Pithecanthropi* from the Djetis beds, and it is probably right to regard all three as belonging to a single species, the difference being no more than racial. As we shall see, the breed long continued to inhabit the region. *Meganthropus*, at present represented only by a jaw, has many features in common with the most massive of the *robustus* branch of the Australopithecines; it has given rise to a widespread belief in the existence of an early man of gigantic stature; this, however, is no more than legendary—the jaw is massive, but the African evidence shows that the individual to which it belonged need not have been of exceptional bodily size.

The *Pithecanthropi* of Java had skulls with very low vaults and an exceedingly heavy brow ridge, running unbroken across the forehead above their eyes; the chin was undeveloped, and the teeth, although set on a parabolic plan approaching that of the modern type, included slightly projecting canines. The thigh-bone found at Trinil proves this species to have walked upright as the name *erectus* indicates. The brain capacity of from 750 to 900 cubic centimetres falls between the average of the modern apes and man but reaches the lowest limit of *Homo sapiens*. Volumes of less than 1,000 cubic centimetres are common among living Vedda.

Pithecanthropus erectus was from the first recognized as a true hominid even though there is no sign of his having been a tool-maker. The rightness of this inclusion within the human pale is, however, fully borne out by his near kinsman and near contemporary *Pithecanthropus pekinensis* (Fig. 3) whose remains have been found in some numbers (though many were lost again in the Sino-Japanese war) in the Choukoutien caves near Peking. This most remarkable assemblage of mid-Pleistocene fossils shows the Asiatic stock to have been very similar to the Javanese in many simian features, although the brow ridge tended to be lighter between the eyes and the canine teeth smaller. More important, the vault of the skull was appreciably more raised, giving a brain capacity of round about 1,000 centimetres which falls just within the modern human range. There was, however, a remarkable degree of variation in brain size, the largest having a volume of as much as 1,300 cubic centimetres.

Most significant of all, the cave deposits proved the ancient human inhabitants to have been capable of chipping rough tools (p. 127) as well as maintaining fires for warmth and protection. The Choukoutien tools show beyond doubt that although these Far Eastern species of *Pithecanthropus* had many ape-like characteristics, and almost certainly belonged to a branch of humanity which had already diverged from the main stream leading to *Homo sapiens* and was to die out before the end of the Pleistocene Age, they were true men, capable of manufacture. The Choukoutien skulls are suggestive of the correlation to be expected between increase in the size of the new brain or cerebrum and the capacity to create culture.

Considering the abundance of the skeletal material from Java and Peking, it is surprising how few other fossil remains of early Palaeoanthropic men have as yet been discovered in the rest of the world. Proof that human beings of this kind were living in Europe contemporaneously with the Djetis bed men of Java and the cave-dwellers of Choukoutien is, however, provided by the lower jaw discovered in the Mauer sands near Heidelberg, also dating from the first, Gunz-Mindel, interglacial phase. This jaw is exceptionally massive and entirely without any projecting chin, yet the teeth are humanly set, and small in relation to the heavy bone structure, while the canines are not prominent. There is no doubt that this man who hunted the Neckar valley, perhaps as much as five hundred thousand years ago, belonged to the Pithecanthropic stock; as he represents a rather more evolved variant he is usually allowed a distinct species of his own, *Homo heidelbergensis*. The Mauer jaw has already a look of the later Neanderthal forms of man, and it may well be that the Heidelberg stock was directly ancestral to the Neanderthal.

Three lower jaws with receding chins and other features in common with Heidelberg man have been found in association with Acheulian implements at Ternifine, Algeria. While it seems that Ternifine man (rather unhappily named *Atlanthropus*) also belongs to the general Pithecanthropic stock, it is impossible to suggest any more precise affinities until a braincase has come to light.

FIG. 3. Pithecanthropus pekinensis *(Peking man): a reconstruction (after R. Carrington).*

Before returning to the central theme of this chapter, the emergence and spread of our own species, it is necessary to follow to its end in total extinction this Palaeoanthropic wing of the human advance, and first to clarify the terminology to be employed. The general term Palaeoanthropic has already been explained as standing here for all species of men, whether directly related or examples of parallel evolution, having a number of features diverging from those evolved in *Homo sapiens* and generally resembling those evolved in the apes. In the later part of the Pleistocene, that is to say during the last interglacial and glacial periods, when dealing with the latest members of the Palaeoanthropic stock, we shall refer to them all as Neanderthaloid. The fully evolved Neanderthal man (*Homo neanderthalensis*) was a well-defined species dominant in Europe and adjacent areas of Africa and Asia; the Neanderthaloids may not have been directly related to him, for we shall see that they possessed important differences especially in bodily form, but as descendants of *Pithecanthropi* and other members of the ancient Palaeoanthropic men evolving in the same direction as the Neanderthal species itself, they can all conveniently be called Neanderthaloid.

The first two individuals to be considered come from Germany, and while they have strong enough simian features to fall within the Palaeoanthropic type, they show a further development of the progressive evolution away from the early Pithecanthropic form already visible in Heidelberg man. The earlier fossil comes from Steinheim near Stuttgart and is probably a little less than two hundred thousand years old, dating from the early third (Riss) Glacial Age. The skull shows the long forehead, pronounced torus and prognathous face of the *Pithecanthropi* but all in milder form; the back of the skull is rounded and well filled out in contrast with the flattened and angular Pithecanthropic occiput. In spite of this more capacious back to the head Steinheim man seems to have had a brain volume no greater than 1,000 cubic centimetres. The second fossil man, from Ehringsdorf near Weimar, lived during the second half of the last interglacial period, about one hundred and twenty thousand years ago. This skull has a high forehead and vault giving a brain capacity of 1,450 cubic centimetres, slightly above the modern average; on the other hand it still shows the Palaeoanthropic characters of heavy brow ridges and receding chin.

Both these ancient men who were inhabiting Germany before the onset of the final, Würm, glaciation have been classified as 'Neanderthaloids close to *Homo sapiens*'. So, too, have certain of the individuals interred at the Skhul cave on the western foot of Mount Carmel in Palestine. This group of caves so near the gateway from Asia to the west is of high interest both for its men and their cultures (p. 138). While certain of the Skhul skulls show a form as advanced as that of Ehringsdorf together with a protruding chin bone that brings them yet closer to ourselves, others from the same site and the skeleton of a woman from the adjoining cave of the Tabun approach very closely to the full Neanderthal type. These facts, together with the mixed cultural tradition evident in the Carmel caves, have been used to support a claim for a hybrid population there. Recent study of the various skeletons in the light of genetical knowledge seems to reinforce this interpretation. Whether this is true, or whether these Palestinians happened to be a very variable stock ranging widely between the Neoanthropic and Palaeoanthropic tendencies, the warning against too absolute a division between the two is clear enough.

It is now widely held that the extreme Neanderthal and
Neanderthaloid breeds of man disappeared without direct
issue during the last glaciation. This extreme Neanderthaler
was a very peculiar species indeed, and one which one would
not expect to be thriving in Europe, Asia and north Africa
until as late as forty thousand years ago. The explanation now
generally accepted is that this highly specialized species evolved
from less specialized forms such as Ehringsdorf man, developing farther and farther away from *Homo sapiens* in a re-
gression which made them increasingly ape-like both in face
and in bodily form. A surprisingly large number of remains of
the typical *Homo neanderthalensis* have now been unearthed,
very commonly from cave deposits. The Neanderthal skull
itself, coming from a valley of that name near Düsseldorf in
Germany, was found in 1856 (three years before the publication of Darwin's *Origin of Species*) and as early as 1848
another specimen had already been discovered, though without comprehension, in a Gibraltar cave; other important early
finds were from Spy in Belgium (two individuals, associated
with mammoth, woolly rhinoceros and other fauna typical of
the last glaciation) and from La Chapelle-aux-Saints in south-
west France, where the body was exceptionally well preserved
and appeared to have been ritually buried (p. 290). Since then
Neanderthal remains have been found at Krapina in Croatia
(as many as twenty individuals represented), the Channel Islands, two sites in Italy and several in Palestine, Spain, the
Crimea, in western Asia, and at Rabat and Tangier in north
Africa (see Map IV, p. 136). These remarkably numerous and
widespread fossils prove the fully developed Neanderthal man
to have been a homogeneous species with its own distinctive
characteristics. They would not, to our eyes, have seemed
attractive ones. The skull, though large, with a brain capacity
averaging 1,450 centimetres, is thick-walled and low-vaulted
—indeed the skull is flattened to a bunlike form, with a sharp
angle at the back of the occiput and attachments for powerful
neck muscles. The brow ridges, so typical of the Palaeoanthropic stock, as of the apes, are very large indeed, forming
a bar of bone projecting strongly over large eye sockets. The
nose is broad, the heavy jaws protruding, while once again we
notice the lack of a projecting chin. The teeth are large, and
the molars sometimes show a peculiarity known as taurodon-
tism, in which the pulp cavities are extraordinarily big and
the roots fused together. The long bones of legs and arms are
clumsy, with thick, bent shafts and enlarged joints; the ankle
bones show the weight to have been carried on the outer
edge rather than the ball of the foot, while the foot itself is

short and very broad. Thus the Neanderthal species that was dominant in Europe and western Asia and adjacent regions of north Africa during the first half of the last glacial age was a short, heavy figure, and as brutish of face as clumsy of figure, in some ways hardly less simian than the *Pithecanthropi* of two hundred thousand years before. Yet the large brain was there, and these men were not only skilled tool-makers but even appear to have had the beginnings of a conscious emotional life (p. 290). It was not until their sudden total surrender before the advance of the then rapidly progressing races of *Homo sapiens* some forty to fifty thousand years ago that their cultural achievements and capacity could be shown to be evidently less than those of our ancestors.

Several human fossils of Neanderthaloid types have been found in Africa, two of them representing a peculiar and highly specialized stock which, like the true Neanderthalers of Europe and Asia, became extinct before the end of the Pleistocene period. The earlier of the two is Saldanha man, whose skull was found in 1953 at a site sixty miles north from Cape Town; the bones of various extinct animals associated with it (an elephant, short-legged giraffe and giant pig) suggest that this individual was living at the end of the last African interpluvial. The later specimen, but a much older discovery, is Rhodesian man found in 1921 during quarrying of lead and zinc ores at Broken Hill, Northern Rhodesia. Its age is uncertain, but the associated fauna is recent. Rhodesian man is distinguished by an extraordinary development of the facial bones and in particular of the brow ridges. The last feature is present also in Saldanha man, whose facial bones are missing. Looked at from the front the skulls show prodigiously massive rings of bone round the eye sockets. Yet in other respects these men seem to have been very close indeed to *Homo sapiens;* their crania are akin to the modern Australoid form, and *Homo rhodesiensis* had straight limbs and upright carriage.[2] A third skull found on the eastern shores of Lake Eyasi in Tanganyika was probably a near contemporary of Rhodesian man, but appears to be more nearly related to the original *Pithecanthropi* than to either Neanderthal or Rhodesian man. With his primitive traits, this individual has proved difficult to classify, but when the much-needed revision is made, he may, like Rhodesian man, be included within the genus *Homo.* These three fossils are enough to suggest that various breeds of men with Palaeoanthropic characteristics survived in Africa, continuing to flourish in remote culs-de-sac just as *Australopithecus* had done before them and the great apes still do today. In the south one group evolved the strangely exaggerated features of the Rhodesian and Saldanha men, a race which may have lived on for a time after *Homo sapiens* had swept the Neanderthalers from Europe and Asia. Possibly the last, most beetling browed, of them all were still hunting in southern Africa when the Solutreans were carving the great reliefs of Cap Blanc some twenty thousand years ago. It seems that in another remote region a Palaeoanthropic species held its own equally long; this was in Java, where the *Pithecanthropi* may have evolved undisturbed throughout the Pleistocene. In the early 1930's excavation recovered as many as eleven skulls from late Pleistocene deposits at Ngandong on the Solo river. Though considerably larger than those of the Djetis and Trinil skulls, the brains of these men had been on the small side with a range from 1,150 to 1,300 centimetres; once again the brow ridges were heavy (though not equal to those of the Africans) but the *foramen magnum* was set as in modern man and, to judge from a single tibia, the limbs were also like those of *Homo sapiens* with none of the clumsy characteristics of the Neanderthalers. Although they had much in common with the Rhodesian and Saldanha men, it seems most likely that these late Java men were the direct descendants of the local *Pithecanthropi*.

Having followed the history of Palaeoanthropic man to the straggling ends that lead to its extinction, it is worth while to give some last thoughts to its significance. We have seen how its late Neanderthaloid representatives had many sharp differences between them, and how it seems probable that such examples as *Homo neanderthalensis* and *Homo rhodesiensis* may well have been the comparable products of long-separated lines of evolution. Looking back much farther we can see a series of similar events. First the Pongidae themselves splitting off from the primate stem, the Australopithecines sending off their *robustus* branch; then the hominids developing their Palaeoanthropic wing, and finally the Palaeoanthropic wing itself regressing in the simian direction in the evolution of the Neanderthal race. Is it not possible that there may be some factor in the natural environment, presumably some chemical factor of nutrition leading towards the development of the common characteristics that we refer to, very roughly, as simian? It should be recalled that while some of these characteristics, such as the prominent mouth and receding chin, were truly 'primitive' in the chronological sense, others, and particularly the frontal torus, are not primitive in that sense but highly evolved specializations common to all the lines under consideration. It is still impossible to prove this theory, but it would suggest an explanation for a trend which appears to have taken place not once but repeatedly throughout the long history of the primates.

We are ready now to return to what must be the main theme of this chapter, as it is the basis of all that follows: the emergence and spread of our own species.[3] It is a history which will take less time than that of the human failures, for as it happens fewer fossils of pre-*sapiens* than early *Homo sapiens* have been recognized. Mention has already been made of the lower jaw from Kanam, Kenya, found in deposits which would date it to the first pluvial and make it a contemporary of Oldoway man. This mandible comes very close indeed to the modern form except that it is rather more massive and has larger pre-molar teeth. After its discovery, it was suggested that the fossil was not in fact contemporary with the apparently associated animal remains dating from the earliest Pleistocene. This remains the opinion of the majority. But if its great antiquity be accepted, then the Kanam jaw undoubtedly implies that the ancestors of *Homo sapiens* had already begun to diverge from the Palaeoanthropic stock by the end of the Pliocene.

For the Middle Pleistocene period there are two other finds of fossil men which could be on the direct line of our own ancestry. But one of them, from Kanjera in Kenya, a site neighbouring on Kanam, has also been called in question. Fragments of four skulls were discovered at this site; they were thicker, and rather lower in the vault than is usual in modern man, but with their high foreheads and lack of brow ridges they certainly qualify as belonging to our species. As, like the Kanam jaw, the correct stratification of the Kanjera[4] skulls is disputed, for an unquestionably authentic Middle Pleistocene man approaching *Homo sapiens* we rely on Swanscombe man, named from a skull (probably a woman's) found in a Thames-side gravel pit in Kent. Two fragments of the cranium were found in 1935–36 and another in 1955; the frontal and face bones are missing. In common with the Kanjera skulls, this one is thicker than is normal today, but the whole modelling of the head is indistinguishable from that of a modern man, while at some 1,300 centimetres the brain capacity is near the present average. Although brows and face are missing, the anatomy of the rest of the head makes it certain that although the features and brow ridge may have been on the heavy side, they did not approach the development found in extreme types of Palaeoanthropic men. The Swanscombe fossil enables us to claim with confidence that men at least close to our own species were living in the Thames valley by the end of the second (Mindel-Riss) interglacial, some two hundred and fifty thousand years ago.[5]

The third find of Middle Pleistocene fossils of Homo sapiens was made in a cave shelter at Fontéchevade, in the Charente Department of France, where a woman's cranium and a small part of the frontal bone of a man's skull were lying among hearth ashes in an undisturbed cave deposit. Except for the thickness of the bone, which seems to be characteristic of these early members of our species, these skulls had high, rounded foreheads and were in every way identical with those of modern man. The Fontéchevade remains had become incorporated in the cave earth in the last (Riss-Würm) interglacial and are therefore approximately one hundred thousand years later than those of Swanscombe man. Above the horizon in which they were found, and divided from it by an unbroken stalagmitic deposit, was an occupation later containing tools of a type almost invariably attributable to Neanderthal man. Whether or no the man and woman had been actual inhabitants of the cave (p. 132), this stratification proves that Homo sapiens was in the area before it was dominated by the Neanderthalers.[6]

With Fontéchevade, we have reached the latest known fossil of Homo sapiens type before the period of Upper Palaeolithic culture and late Pleistocene Age when, with surprising speed, our forebears contrived to inherit the earth and we find ourselves dealing not with different species, but merely with the differences of race with which we are familiar today. We leave a world where biological distinctions inevitably claim much of our interest for one where man's various cultural achievements become all important. Unfortunately this moment of transition is in many ways unusually obscure. While we are confident in our knowledge that men of our own kind were in Europe during the second interglacial and can hardly doubt that they were also in Africa at this time,[7] the main centres from which our kind spread during the last glaciation, and the times and places where the main racial types emerged, remain very imperfectly understood.

This, however, is essentially a cultural problem; all that it remains to do here is to describe the several types of men known to have been inhabiting the Old World during its last glaciation and to see how far they can be recognized as the forerunners of modern racial types. It is logical to begin in Africa, the probable cradle of the species. Apart from such freakish survivors as Rhodesian man, the Late Pleistocene Africans show a division into two contrasting types, an Australoid (resembling the Australian aborigines) and a Bushmanoid, ancestors of the Bushmen who were once more wide-spread in Africa.[8] We know them now as a helpless pygmy race allowed to live only on sufferance, but when first they peopled the continent they were a vigorous race of normal stature. Actually one of the earliest skulls, from Florisbad in the Orange Free State, seems to represent a crossing of the two races, but with Boskop man, represented by a skull cap found in the Transvaal, we have the characteristic Bushmanoid head, wide, with a full smooth forehead, giving a large brain. Both these South Africans were living during the last pluvial phase: Carbon-14 analysis has given the Florisbad fossil a date of 'more than forty-one thousand years old'. Another individual who must have been very much like Boskop man is recalled for us by a skull from Singal, a site two hundred miles south of Khartoum on the shores of the Blue Nile; he, too, was a big-brained proto-Bushman, but his brow ridges are sufficiently developed to suggest a touch of Australoid in his ancestry. The latest of the Bushman ancestors is the man from Fishhoek, again in South Africa, who seems to have lived no more than fifteen to twenty thousand years ago, when the final pluvial was approaching its end. A contemporary of this proto-Bushman in the Australoid branch had been recognized in the skull from Cape Flats near Cape Town. This skull has sufficiently prominent brow ridges to suggest that the earlier 'Neanderthaloids', Saldanha and Rhodesian man, may have been a highly specialized offshoot from the African Australoid type.[9]

From about ten thousand years ago, when the last pluvial was over and the Sahara beginning to return to desert for the last time, in South Africa the Australoids and proto-Bushmen were giving way to the typical small Bushman.

At the same time the first men of Negro race had appeared north of the Equator, the oldest skull believed to be of proto-Negro type coming from Asselar, over two hundred miles north of Timbuktu. Of Late or post-Pleistocene Age, it cannot be exactly dated.[10] In this skull the upper central incisors had been deliberately struck out in early life, a practice still widespread among Africans today. Where they originated is still unknown; we shall see that the arrival of a Negroid race in Europe has been suspected but is not generally agreed. Undoubtedly, however, men closely related to some of the races that took possession of Europe after the extinction of Neanderthal man were present in north Africa during and after the last pluvial. The difficulty of absolute dating on either side makes it unwise to use the African skeletal material to prove the invasion of Europe from Africa or of Africa from

Europe during this period. The connection may in any case have been partly indirect, via east Africa and south-west Asia (p. 145). The oldest skeleton from the cave of Afalou bou Rummel in Algeria is very similar to that of the early Upper Palaeolithic Combe Capelle man from France (below); so too are the narrow-headed, non-prognathous skulls from Gamble's Cave, Elementeita, in Kenya. These Elementeita people were of Mesolithic culture (p. 148) and prove the presence of non-Negro races in east Africa at this late date; supporting evidence is provided by two contemporary, Combe Capelle type, skulls from Oldoway and the Naivasha shelter.

On the other hand the skeletons from the upper levels of the Afalou cave, as well as others from Mectha el Arbi and Beni Segoual, approximate quite closely to a very different European race, the powerful, heavy-featured Cromagnons who, far back in their ancestry, may have had some genetical inheritance from the Palaeoanthropic breeds. The latest discoveries suggest the people of the Capsian culture were not of this type but instead were Mediterraneans. The Natufian Mesolithic people of the east Mediterranean were slender and short, with long heads and delicate features; they seem to represent the original Mediterranean Semito-Hamitic stock before the division into linguistic groups.

In Europe itself remains are much more numerous and their cultural contexts more coherently understood (p. 139). The earliest recognizable type is that of the Combe Capelle skeleton, already referred to for its similarity to the earliest remains from the Afalou cave. This individual was certainly one of the bearers of the first Upper Palaeolithic culture established in western Europe and hence one of the dispossessors of the Neanderthal population. The skull is long and narrow with a small forehead and fairly low vault; it may represent a type ancestral to the modern Mediterranean race—a comparison supported by the presence of Combe Capelle-like skulls in Africa.

The racial type next in point of time is the Cromagnon, the best-known and most distinctive of the late Pleistocene races of Europe. They were a tall, very muscular people with long heads possessing rather loftier vaults than the Combe Capelle type, giving a very high average brain capacity. In spite of the dolichocephalic skull, the face was short with (as we have said) marked brow ridges and a high-bridged nose. This Cromagnon type was powerful of body, and effective culturally as well as physically. It is certainly still represented in the European population today. Probably descended from the Combe Capelle people and very much like them were the

mammoth-hunting Predmostians; on the other hand two skeletons of much the same date found away to the south in the
Riviera cave of Grimaldi have been claimed to show a
Negroid strain. A skull with prognathous face and a broad
nose was also found at Markina Gora in the Voronezh region.
Whereas it is possible that the prominent jaws of the Grimaldi
skulls may be due more to restoration than nature, there can
be no doubt of the Negroid combination of features in the
skull from Markina Gora.

One other of the Late Pleistocene, Upper Palaeolithic races
of Europe demands to be singled out, a type which was one of
those responsible for creating the last and most brilliant Upper
Palaeolithic culture of south-western France. This was Chancelade man, whose skull is universally admitted to have
Eskimoid affinities in its vertical sides, pointed keel, and somewhat broad cheek bones. Although the old view that this
race withdrew northwards in the wake of the ice after the
last glaciation to form the ancestors of the modern Eskimo
has now been much blown upon, it may have an element of
truth in it. There seems no reason to deny that Chancelade
man may have been involved in both the genetical and cultural inheritance of the Eskimo peoples.[11] However this may
be, there is now a convergence of evidence from physical
anthropology, linguistics and ethnology, that the Eskimo
were of Old World origin and that the culture was largely
Asiatic. Their spread into North America is connected with
the appearance of the Palaeo-northern cultures there. One
of the most telling indications of this movement is the occasional occurrence among American Eskimo of Blood Group
B, which is frequent in Asia but absent from the American
Indian population.

It will have been noticed that all these races of *Homo sapiens* who made the population of Europe in the Late Pleistocene even more sharply differentiated than it is today, tended
towards the dolichocephalic, or long, narrow, head form. A
rather broader skull has, however, been found occasionally,
notably at Solutré near Mâcon, and this brachycephalic element appears to have been reinforced in post-Pleistocene
times. At the Mesolithic site of Ofnet in Bavaria there was
found a ritual burial of a nest or cluster of skulls many of
which showed extreme broad-headedness. Thus it seems
that while the forebears of the Mediterranean, Nordic and
other intermediate European types were already in Europe
during the last glaciation, the Alpine race, typical inhabitants
of the great mountain backbone of the Old World, may
have spread into Europe at a rather late date. On the other

hand it is not impossible that the race may have evolved locally from the indigenous population.

In eastern Asia the known remains of Late Pleistocene men are extraordinarily scanty. In the Upper Cave of Choukoutien three skulls were found that probably date from the very end of the period or even from early post-Pleistocene times. They have a general resemblance to the Cromagnon type, but are considered to have recognizable Mongolian features. Roughly contemporary are the only known human remains of the period from southern China; a fossilized skull cap and fragmentary upper jaw from the Kwanshantse valley fifty miles south-east of Cheng-tu. These had belonged to a young girl living in Late Pleistocene times and of much the same racial type as the inhabitants of Choukoutien.

Although there is no doubt (pp. 71 and 148) that human beings began to people the American continent at this time,[12] probably during the last phases of the Würm glaciation, no skeletal remains certainly as early as this have as yet been identified. Of the two least doubtful finds, the girl from Pelican Rapids, Minnesota, and the man from Tepexpan, Valley of Mexico, which would both be about ten thousand years old if they are contemporary with their geological horizon and not intrusive, are both of Mongoloid type. Later remains, and the surviving American Indians, leave no doubt that the pioneers who entered the continent from Siberia to Alaska were predominantly of Mongoloid stock, probably several different groups of Mongol people following one another across the land-bridge. There appears, however, to have been a primitive Australoid strain among them.

Enough is known to enable us to see Late Pleistocene and post-Pleistocene times, say from 40,000 to 8000 B C, as the main formative age for the races of man. This was the period when *Homo sapiens* (after some great concentration of energy, of numbers and perhaps of social organization which may have taken place in north and central Africa or southwest Asia and was certainly constantly renewed in secondary centres) spread throughout the Old World and at last streamed on into the Americas. This was the period, too, when areas of differentiation divided geographically and by other barriers of which we know nothing, incubated the dominant racial types that share the world today. Sun and frost, forest and plain, humidity and dryness, height and latitude, diet and water content, a variable inheritance from the remoter past and the chance movements of peoples, all united during these millennia to give our single species the differences of height and proportion, of facial structure and skin colour, of shade and texture of hair, which make the rich variety of mankind. No other species save our own domesticated dog has so remarkable a range of form while yet remaining one species.

The whole skeletons and scraps of skull that modern man has found and is finding in ever-increasing numbers have given us some glimpses of this great formative process, but there is still a sorry gap between the interpretation of these scattered fossils and account of the races of man as they were in early historic times, and as they remain today save for the prodigious spread of the European races.

To make a full and coherent history linking these fossil records with the racial pattern in historical times is still beyond us. Although our knowledge of human types, so far as their skeletal varieties are concerned, is naturally much greater for later prehistoric periods than for the Palaeolithic and Mesolithic Ages, nevertheless our picture of the establishment of races and their subsequent expansion or decline is still exceedingly patchy.

As will emerge in the course of this history, before the sudden spread of the white races after the fifteenth century there were six major racial groups with more or less well-defined geographical ranges. These were the Negroid, Caucasoid, Mongoloid, Bushmen, Australoid and Polynesian (Pacific) (Map II).

The forest zones on either side of the Equator in Africa were the main range of the Negroid peoples with their very dark skins, often everted lips, and tightly twisted (ulotrichous) hair. Even in this area they varied very much in stature, from the pygmies of the tropical rain forests to the Nilotic tribes, some of which are among the tallest of all mankind. Other black-skinned people with comparable characteristics lived along a scattered trail eastward from central Africa; from south-east India across the Indian Ocean to the Philippines, New Guinea, Melanesia, tropical north-east Australia and Tasmania. It has already been remarked that proto-Negroid skeletons have been claimed for Europe in Late Pleistocene times; the earliest from north Africa dates from about the end of the last glaciation (p. 103). The centre of their racial differentiation is uncertain, but the western Sudan seems the most probable region. Certainly they were already expanding southward at the expense of the Bushman races before the fifteenth century A D, an expansion which continued in the following centuries with the march of the warlike Bantu tribes into east and south Africa. Although material evidence is lacking, the Negroid peoples of southern

Asia and the islands are generally considered to be of great antiquity, especially the forest pygmies of India, the Andaman Islands, the Malay Peninsula, some parts of the Philippines, Melanesia, Australia and Tasmania. Whether all these peoples are related to one another and to the Negritoes of Africa is unknown; it seems probable. On the other hand it is possible to see in them men who were shaped by the rain forests in which they had to find a living.

The Caucasoid or white race of early historic times inhabited a solid territory to the north of the African Negroids, comprising the central land mass of the Old World in north and north-east Africa, Europe, and western Asia as far as India and Ceylon. As might be expected from what is known of their Palaeolithic forebears, they have always varied widely, particularly in the colouring of skin, hair and eyes and in size and bodily form. Dane and Watusi African, Semite and Brahman cover a great range of features. Nevertheless the Caucasoids are generally distinguishable by narrow, often strongly bridged noses, soft and often wavy or curly (cymotrichous) hair, heavy growth of beard and skins which among the majority of Caucasoids are fairer than those of any other race. The extreme unpigmented Nordic type with yellowish or reddish hair, blue or grey eyes and pinkish white skin that burns on exposure to strong sun was limited to Europe and dominant only in the cool and temperate zones in the north and west of the continent. It has been shown to what considerable extent the heavy-featured and muscular Cromagnon type of Caucasoid predominated in Europe, north Africa and Asia during much of the Upper Palaeolithic and Mesolithic Ages; this inheritance is still important among modern Europeans. On the other hand the smaller lighter-built and more delicately featured forerunners of the Mediterranean race seem to have asserted themselves later in the Upper Palaeolithic period. We shall find them spreading from southwest Asia into north Africa rather after the arrival of the Cromagnons there (p. 147). This same light-boned Mediterranean type will be found carrying the practice of farming along the Danube as far as Belgium, and along the Mediterranean shores to Spain, France and Britain.

East of the Caucasoids stretched the vast ranges of the Mongolian peoples, covering all northern and eastern Asia, extending down the Malay Peninsula to Borneo, Sumatra and other East Indian islands (with an extreme western outlier in eastern Madagascar), and including the large offshore islands of Formosa and Japan. Peoples of Mongoloid type were also to be found, if rather sparsely, over the whole of

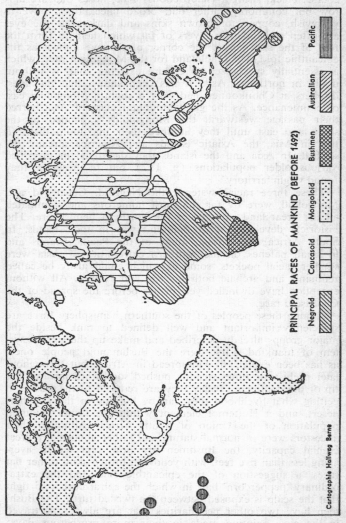

PRINCIPAL RACES OF MANKIND (BEFORE 1492)

Pacific

Australian

Bushmen

Mongoloid

Caucasoid

Negroid

Cartographic Hallwag Berne

MAP II

the American continent. These peoples are characterized by coarse, black, straight (leiotrichous) hair, noses that are narrow but commonly rather flat, broad cheekbones, olive to yellowish, coppery or brown skins and dark eyes; the eyes are often embedded in layers of fat which help to form the fold of the skin across the corner of the eye known as the epicanthic fold. The cradleland for the Mongolian race, which is essentially specialized to endure extreme cold, is without doubt in north-east Asia. It has been shown that the latest dwellers at Choukoutien had only a slightly Mongolian cast of countenance. As the great mountain mass of Asia barred their passage westward, the Mongoloids expanded to the south and east until they attained their maximum distribution in Asia, the Asiatic islands and America already described. In Asia and the islands they destroyed or absorbed various older populations (p. 112) but in America they found virgin territory.

These three racial systems, the Negroid, Caucasoid and Mongoloid, were by far the most numerous and dominated all the great land surfaces of the northern hemisphere. The historical development of mankind was in their hands. In South Africa, Australasia, many of the Pacific islands and in small patches on the southern extremities of Asia were smaller racial pockets, some of which could justly be called remnants and archaic both in race and culture. All without exception have dwindled yet further before the spread of the Caucasoid race.

Among these peoples of the southern hemisphere three are sufficiently important and well defined to rank beside the major groups already described and make up the sixfold system of mankind. First were the Bushmanoid people once, as has been explained, widespread in Africa, but throughout later prehistoric times steadily pushed southward towards the tip of the continent. Today they are reduced to the Bushmen getting what livelihood they can by hunting in the Kalahari desert, and a Hottentot element within the Cape Coloured population of the Union of South Africa. Although their ancestors were of normal stature and rather abnormally great cranial capacity, the Bushmen are now very small, averaging less than five feet, with yellowish brown skin, rather flat faces, a suggestion of the epicanthic fold and the extraordinary 'peppercorn' hair in which the spiral curl is so tight that the scalp is exposed between the twisted tufts. The Bushmen have two other peculiarities that are always portrayed in the cave painting made in their more prosperous days: protruding fatty buttocks and a penis which projects forward without erection. Whether or not one judges them to be attractive, these three bodily characteristics are unique.

The second of the smaller racial groups is the Australoid, a group difficult to define and which may include many archaic peoples surviving from Pleistocene times who are not in fact closely related. In Australia itself there is a considerable contrast between the desert-dweller who sparsely inhabited the greater part of the country and those aborigines, now reduced to near the point of extinction, who lived in the Murray River basin and Gippsland. The hunters of the desert are brown-skinned, tall and slender with wavy hair and beards but little body hair; in the formation of their skulls they seem to show a very archaic inheritance with a larger genetical element from Palaeoanthropic stock than any other living people. This element seems to have been even more marked in the past, to judge from certain skull finds—especially those of Talgai and Cohuna. They have narrow, low-vaulted crania, with bony ridges above the eyes; the teeth are large and often prominently set, the nose broad. They have with reason been likened to Solo man (p. 100). The aborigines of the more fertile and temperate south-east had many archaic features in common with their neighbour, but their bodies were both more massive and very much hairier while their legs and arms were relatively short; in colouring they evidently carried genes for fairness, for their skins when untanned were pale brown, their eyes sometimes green or blue and their hair occasionally red. It has been suggested that these were the first men to settle in Australia, and that they have affinities with a primitive racial strain still surviving, though deeply submerged, in Europe. If they were the first comers, then they were followed later by the desert people and finally by the possible Negrito element in the tropical north-east and Tasmania (p. 108). At present, however, there is no evidence for this sequence and some authorities still believe that the Tasmanians, instead of being partly a Negrito group drifting in later from New Caledonia, were in fact a survival from the oldest population in Australia.

The Gippsland Australians are often likened to the aborigines of Japan, the Ainu, who have long been dispossessed of most of their territories and pushed into the cold northern island of Hokkaido. The Ainu are short and thickset with white to pale brown skin colouring; they have wavy or curly hair which grows heavily on both the face and body; the brow ridges are strongly developed (though much less massive than they often are among the Australians), but the nose is straight. There seems no doubt at all that these earliest in-

habitants of Japan (who may have reached the area before
its complete isolation) have affinities with ancient stocks still
genetically represented in modern Europeans.

The other considerable group of Australoids is to be found
in south and south-east India, where the Dravidian stock,
probably descendants of the pre-Caucasoid aborigines of the
greater part of India, show many of the recognized characteristics; the type is represented again in the Hadramaut and
traces of it survive submerged throughout the East Indies
and Pacific islands. It will be recalled that there was a widespread Australoid element present in Late Pleistocene Africa;
there seems no doubt that this type, whether or not it is
held to be a once coherent and related racial group, represents a survival of an early spread of humanity throughout
much of the Old World; in Africa it virtually disappeared,
in Asia and the Asiatic islands was almost though not wholly
swamped by the southward and eastward spread of the Mongoloid peoples. Only in Australia, that living museum of zoological survivals, could the Australoids remain master of wide
territories, until at last, but inevitably, the white race arrived
to dispossess them of all that was desirable in this their one
great retreat.

The sixth and last of the racial groups is the Polynesian
and Micronesian. These people with their often easy Oceanic
life are of a very generalized human type, usually dark-
skinned with wavy black hair and dark eyes, narrow and
sometimes well-bridged noses and mouths that are neither
prominent nor thick-lipped. Most are of average height,
though here and there, as in Tonga, there is a strain of
exceptionally tall stature. This physically fine stock probably
originated from a mixture of Mongoloid peoples with the
native Australoid or Ainu-like inhabitants of the East Indies,
Philippines and other islands off the Pacific shores of Asia.[13]
As the move to these remote islands of the Pacific was among
the last carrying our ubiquitous species to the humanly habitable corners of the earth, it falls well within historical times
and so will have its place later in this history.

This ends the account of the emergence, spread and differentiation of man as a zoological breed. It is a history that
begins with rival genera and species, then narrows to the
races of *Homo sapiens,* the single species which is mankind.
Through the tens of millions of years of the Cenozoic era
the human frame, so familiar a possession of each one of us,
has been seen slowly shaping among the primates, until by
Pleistocene times a large-brained, upright biped by beginning
the creation of culture has won human status. Throughout

this vast stretch of time the increase in the size and complexity of the neo-pallium or New Brain makes the central theme; in the fossil skulls which are our principal record for the human epic we see the forehead and vault rising, their capacity swelling. Whether or not he is inclined to indulge in the modern name-calling of highbrow and egghead, no one can question that man is distinguished as the highbrow or egghead of the primates. Here, housed within the curved bone plates of the skull, is the most subtle and complex instrument in the world, which, at the command of the whole man, has created the rich and varied cultures, the superb individual works of art, the inspiring if never final systems of thought, that make the history of mankind.

These achievements, the exalted and the humble, have come from the many races of mankind evolved during the last forty thousand years. All races are one in that they can mate together and produce children who may be healthy, fertile, beautiful and intelligent, yet in their remaining separate and various lies one of the delights of the existence of man on earth. That after thousands of years of interbreeding and response to the various conditions of their native lands they may have developed abilities and weaknesses peculiar to themselves seems likely enough and should certainly not be denied. Without this variety our future would be less abundantly promising just as our past would have been infinitely the poorer. No one can claim that a violin is a better or a worse instrument than a clarinet; what is glorious is the whole symphony orchestra. So it is with mankind.

NOTES TO CHAPTER II

1. Professor G. F. Debetz observes that 'the question of man's cradle land cannot be regarded as completely solved. There is no doubt that Australia, America and in all probability northern Eurasia must be excluded as possible zones. The remainder of the earth's land surface (southern Eurasia and Africa) is too vast to be considered as the cradle of the species since the emergence of man most certainly took place on a more restricted territory. At the present time, however, it is impossible to define the boundaries of this territory more exactly. Many scholars favour Africa as the answer to this problem. It was in Africa that the fossil apes—the Australopithecines—which are the most man-like—were found. It is by no means impossible, however, that the cradle of man was one part or another of southern Eurasia'.

2. Professor G. F. Debetz stresses that to some scholars it has not been proved that the limb bones found at Broken Hill belonged to the same individual, or even species, as the skull.

3. Professor G. F. Debetz recalls that, 'the opinions of specialists

sharply diverge on the question of the origin of *Homo sapiens*. The essence of this divergence is concentrated in the question of the genetical interrelations of *Homo sapiens* and the Neanderthal Man. Some specialists claim that the Neanderthal Man was the ancestor of modern man. Others consider that the Neanderthalers and modern man developed independently of and parallel to each other. The more consistent adherents of this point of view even consider it likely that the genus *Homo* descended directly from Pliocene Australopithecine stock while the Pithecanthropi were a collateral branch which developed the extreme forms of massive brow ridge, heavy jaw and other somewhat simian features. The adherents of this conception thus exclude not only the Neanderthalers but also the Pithecanthropi as man's forebears.

'Adherents of the other point of view accept the general outline of the development of the human species from the Pithecanthropic stock to the Palaeoanthropic and on to the Neoanthropic. This outline is substantiated by the fact that all the well-dated Premousterian and early Mousterian finds known to science unquestionably refer either to Palaeoanthropic stock or to even earlier forms. In Europe these are the Mauer jaw, the lower jaw from Montmorin, various fragments from Weimar, the skull from Steinheim, skeletons from Krapina, the natural endocranial cast from Hanovce, limb bones from Kiik-Koba; in Africa there are the finds from Rabat, Eyassi, Saldanha, the remains of Atlanthropi; in Asia the remains of Pithecanthropi and Sinanthropi.

'But also from this point of view there are grounds for assuming that not all the branches of the Pithecanthropic and Sinanthropic stock and the Neanderthalers produced *Homo sapiens*. Many of the early and very early hominids disappeared from the face of the earth without leaving any direct issue. The presence of such specialized features as pronounced taurodontisme (extraordinarily big molar pulp cavities), the distinctive structure of the nasal cavity and other features in West-European Neanderthalers, render highly improbable the hypothesis that they were the forebears of modern man, the more so if one recalls that the Cro-Magnon type of Western Europe differed sharply in his structure from the West-European Neanderthalers.

'It is possible that at the beginning of the Mousterian period there separated from some Palaeoanthropic breed a branch of hominids whose development led to the emergence of *Homo sapiens* at the end of the Mousterian or the beginning of the Upper Palaeolithic. As to the zone where this process of development was most intensive, this remains a matter of dispute. It is possible that this zone included south-west Asia and its large adjacent regions.'

4. Geological observations by P. G. H. Boswell have led many authorities to contest the dating of the human remains found at Kanam and Kanjera to the Lower Pleistocene (Villafranchian) or Middle Pleistocene. See P. G. H. Boswell, 'Human Remains from Kanam and Kanjera, Kenya Colony', *Nature* (March 9, 1935).

5. Professor G. F. Debetz points out that the Swanscombe skull is not universally recognized as conclusive evidence that *Homo sapiens* lived in the Thames valley in the Gunz-Mindel interglacial: arguing from the relation between the width of the occiput and the height of the vault, the relation of the parietal chord to the parietal arch, the *foramen magnum* index, the distance between the inion point and the inner occipital tubercle, many scholars believe that affinities exist with Neanderthal man. X^2 has been worked out on the basis of these features to determine the real extent of the probability of

the Swanscombe skull belonging to modern European series and this probability seems to be practically zero (X^2-test of Karl Pearson for the statistical comparison of characteristics of more than two groups). See Y. Y. Roginsky, 'Concerning the Antiquity of *Homo sapiens*', *Sovetskaya Etnografia*, No. III (1947); S. Sergi, 'I profanerantropi di Swanscombe e di Fontéchevade', *Rivista di Antropologia*, XL (1953), pp. 65–72; F. C. Howell, 'The Place of Neanderthal Man in Human Evolution', *American Journal of Physical Anthropology*, IX, n.s. (1951), pp. 379–416.

6. Some scholars hold that the very fragmentary nature of the Fontéchevade skull makes it impossible to establish an exact diagnosis; it has been pointed out that certain features of the skull bear a resemblance to the Neanderthal type.

7. Professor G. F. Debetz notes that those scholars who do not accept the early dating of the human remains found at Kanam and Kanjera consider that the hypothesis that *Homo sapiens* lived in Africa already during the second interglacial does not rest on actual facts.

8. Dr Birket-Smith points out that in connection with the Bushmen mention should be made of the Hottentots, who are racially related to the Bushmen, and the Pygmies, where this is probably not the case. See K. Birket-Smith, *Wir Menschen* (Zürich, 1944).

9. Professor G. F. Debetz observes that the view that the African Australoids gradually became highly specialized Palaeoanthropic breeds, i.e. approached the Saldanha and Broken Hill type, is contested by some authorities. It is open to objection on the grounds that the only argument in favour of such an assumption would be the prominent brow ridges on the Late Palaeolithic skull from Cape Flats. But prominent brow ridges are not a rare phenomenon in different parts of the world even now as well as in the Neolithic, the Bronze Age, etc. For this reason there is some doubt whether such data are adequate for substantiating a theory of human genealogy which embraces the whole of the Pleistocene.

10. Professor A. C. Blanc remarks that the age of the Asselar skeleton, assigned to the Late Pleistocene, has recently been queried. This dating was given by Th. Monod, but after revising his opinion on this point he now regards this find as relatively recent (post-Palaeolithic). See Th. Monod, 'Sur l'âge de l'Homme d'Asselar', *Historia Naturalis*, I, 4 (1946), pp. 81–2; A. C. Blanc, 'Sull'età geologica dell'Uomo di Asselar', *Rivista di Antropologia*, XXXV (1947), p. 420.

11. The majority of anthropologists today reject the view that an affinity exists between the Chancelade type and the Eskimo. See H. V. Vallois, 'Nouvelles recherches sur le squelette de chancelade', *L'Anthropologie*, L (1941), pp. 165–202. Nor is there any longer much support for the arguments in favour of a connection between the late Upper Palaeolithic Magdalenian culture in western and central Europe and the Eskimo. All the available ethnographic and archaeological data testify to ties linking the forebears of the Eskimo with the Asiatic and American continents, not with western Europe. See H. G. Bandi, 'Die Frage eines Zusammenhangs zwischen dem Magdalénien und der Eskimokultur', *Jahrbuch der Schweizerischen Gesellschaft für Urgeschichte*, XL (1949–50), pp. 75–92.

12. See p. 161, n. 8.

13. Dr P. Bosch-Gimpera points out that many authors have included the Polynesians in the Europiform group. See E. v. Eickstedt, 'Die Biodynamik der Europiden', *Historia Mundi*, I (Berne, 1952), pp. 115–34.

CHAPTER III

THE HISTORY OF THE PALAEOLITHIC
AND MESOLITHIC CULTURES

THIS chapter will attempt to chronicle the events of Old Stone Age, or Palaeolithic times, that is to say the emergence of cultural groups, their movements, mutual influence upon one another, their expansions and disappearances. Not very much will be said about the modes of life, technology, arts and beliefs of the peoples concerned, for these will be the proper subject of the following sections. It is necessary to pursue these events in space and time because without some knowledge of them cultural history cannot be properly understood. Yet for the prehistoric past there is a peculiar difficulty in so doing because our knowledge of these affairs —of political history in the broadest sense—is entirely dependent on cultural remains. Thus there is a grave danger of confusing the expansion or migration of peoples with the spread of cultural traits, as though, in more recent times, we were to speak of a Gothic-architecture people or the migration from Europe of the railroad race.

In very early times when there were virtually no communications between different cultural centres, the danger of such confusions was much less than it would be today. Nevertheless the more we discover about the Stone Age the more apparent it becomes that at some times and places there was no correlation at all between culture and physical type. As the ability to exchange skills and ideas by language or demonstration is one of the most important abilities of our kind, this state of affairs cannot be surprising, but it has taken time to recognize its reality, and earlier assumptions of a close bond between species or race and culture are still being modified.

Though Lower Palaeolithic is essentially a cultural and not a chronological term,[1] it lasted in most parts of the world from the beginning of the Pleistocene to the end of the third, Riss, glaciation, a period of some half million years. During this vast span of years when man was advancing his skill as a tool-maker, and probably also his range as a social, emotional and thinking creature, in crucially important, but to our eyes painfully small degrees, the humanly occupied regions of the Old World can be divided, if somewhat roughly, into two principal cultural divisions. In Africa, round the eastern end of the Mediterranean up to the Black Sea, in southern and central India and intermittently in Europe men were gradually evolving the culture responsible for the first sharply distinctive standard tool form, the Abbevillian and Acheulian hand-axe (Fig. 4). In south-eastern Asia (Java, China, Burma and north-central India so far as present knowledge goes) *Pithecanthropus* and related stocks built up a different and generally less progressive culture which had no comparable creation to rival the hand-axe. This is known as the chopper-chopping-tool complex and shows a high proportion of tools made of rough flakes. A related cultural province extended through Europe as far as Britain[2] (Map III).

Europe and India were thus the areas of overlap where mingling and mutual influences were most likely to occur. In Europe, however, the picture is complicated by the fact that the bearers of the two cultural traditions were not usually present simultaneously, but alternated in response to the climatic pulse of Pleistocene times. Though there may well be many discoveries to disprove the universality of this rule, there is now very considerable evidence to show that during the Lower Palaeolithic period the hand-axe peoples extended northward through Europe with the warm interglacial conditions, while their rivals, perhaps dominated by the Palaeoanthropic stocks, probably hardier and more enduring, took possession of as much of the continent as was habitable during the glacial ages. It was only much later, during the last glaciation, that our own species had become sufficiently well equipped culturally, particularly through the possession of sewn skin clothes, to be able to master arctic conditions and so break this long alternation.

The map will make clear that these territories where the early history of mankind was played were only a small part, about one-fifth, of the land surfaces of our world. America, Australia and probably northern Asia and eastern Europe had not as yet been penetrated by our most varied and adaptable species but remained through hundreds of thousands of years inhabited only by man's fellow animals, those other creatures of evolution that had no such strange destiny as his in an unimagined future.

The oldest tools fashioned by human hands have been

found in Africa. They are water-worn pebbles of lava, quartz and quartzite roughly chipped into blunt points or chopping edges. They have been recognized as belonging to two cultures, the Kafuan and the Oldowan, of which pride of place as the more ancient was given to the Kafuan. The first of these pebble types, usually flaked on one face only, were found in deposits dating back to the beginning of the Pleistocene period. In later phases of the Kafuan culture the pebbles were worked from both sides, the flake meeting to form the edge or point. It was thought possible that the early Kafuan was ancestral to the Oldowan.

Now, however, the reality of this culture, at any rate in its early phases, is being questioned. Perhaps the very rough flaking was made not by man but by natural agencies such as streams, waterfalls or soil-creep. One of the points against the artificiality of the Kafuan-worked pebbles is that in some places they occur in an enormous profusion which suggests the mass production of nature rather than the laborious handiwork of a few struggling hominids. For the present judgement of the Kafuan culture, as of that of the 'eoliths' (below), will have to await further evidence. Probably it will be merged with the Oldowan.

Happily there is no doubt about the credentials of the Oldowan pebble culture. Although it has not as yet been identified in the earliest Pleistocene horizons, it occurs in a number of sites where it can be assigned to a later phase of the Lower Pleistocene and the early Middle period. Mention has already been made of the Oldowan level in the *Australopithecus* cave at Sterkfontein, and of the all-important '*Zinjanthropus*' horizon in the Oldoway Gorge itself. Other sites are Kanam in Kenya, the Vaal valley in South Africa, and Ain Hanech in Algeria, where the pebble industry was associated with artifically rounded balls that may have been used either for throwing or pounding. In the Oldoway Gorge there is evidence of how this, the oldest of human cultures, gradually progressed, for a series of super-imposed deposits show the pebbles being shaped with increasing elaboration and clarity of purpose. By the latest Oldowan levels they are being chipped (though still roughly) from both sides into ovoid forms that can be recognized as prototypes of the Abbevillian hand-axes which occur in the overlying beds (Fig 4). Thus the Oldoway Gorge is of great significance in showing beyond question that the Abbevillian culture and its immediate inheritor the Acheulian grew out of the ancient pebble cultures of the Oldowans.

Although early pebble tools have been found in so many

see table, p. 58.

parts of the African continent, the region where their makers are thought to have advanced to the full Abbevillian type of culture is in central Africa, perhaps in the open country on the forest fringes. On the other hand, when it is considered how uniformly the Abbevillian-Acheulian tradition developed over the whole far-flung region of its prevalence, it is not impossible that the ancestral pebble-tool cultures may have evolved towards the Abbevillian throughout the African continent.

Outside Africa there is no certain evidence for tool-making communities dating from the opening of the Pleistocene, but

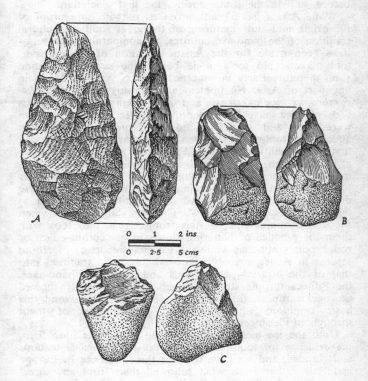

FIG. 4. *Pebble tool to hand-axe: A: Acheulian tool; B: Abbevillian tool; C: Oldowan pebble tools (after Oakley).*

the claims of the European 'eoliths'[3] deserve serious consideration. Perhaps the best known are the English groups from East Anglia. These roughly chipped flints from old land surfaces smothered beneath the Crag deposits of Norfolk and Suffolk may well have been made by hominids who were the European contemporaries of the pebble-tool peoples of Africa. The fact that they were chipped by human hands and not by ice or other natural agents capable of exerting blows or pressures is not universally accepted. Even if none of the known 'eoliths' is an artifact (and this is unlikely), it still remains inherently probable that there were human creatures capable of rough tool-making present in Europe before, and in the south during, the first glaciation.

While Africa has already provided us with sure proof of the origin and slow maturing of the great southern cultural tradition of the hand-axe cultures, no comparable discoveries have been made for the Asiatic tradition of the chopper-tool makers. No tools made before the second glaciation (and therefore Early Pleistocene) have as yet been found in any part of Asia. No implements certainly made by *Pithecanthropus modjokertensis* and other hominids of the Djetis beds of Java have been identified; nevertheless, these men were there, and seem likely to have entered the continent already as tool-makers. When the tools of this stock are first recognized, in the Middle Pleistocene period (for example at Choukoutien), they are still of the most elementary workmanship; it seems likely enough that if their even rougher prototypes were found in ordinary deposits and not in a cave dwelling, their recognition would be quite as uncertain as that of the European 'eoliths'. The probability is that when the first hominids entered Asia from Africa, they took with them the practice of battering stones to get cutting-edges or rough points but that while the various precursors of *Homo sapiens* in Africa steadily improved this basic tradition into that of the bifacial pebble tools and ultimately hand-axes, the Pithecanthropic stock in much of Asia already showed the backwardness, the failure to develop much beyond this basic tradition, which remained characteristic of them throughout Pleistocene times.

Until the ice had melted after the Gunz glaciation then, the evidence for tool-making men outside Africa is tenuous and clouded, and we have to infer their presence in Europe and Asia rather from what followed than from any direct proof. With the first interglacial phase, however, the cultural map of the Old World begins to fill, and by the opening of the Middle Pleistocene with the second Ice Age the distribu-

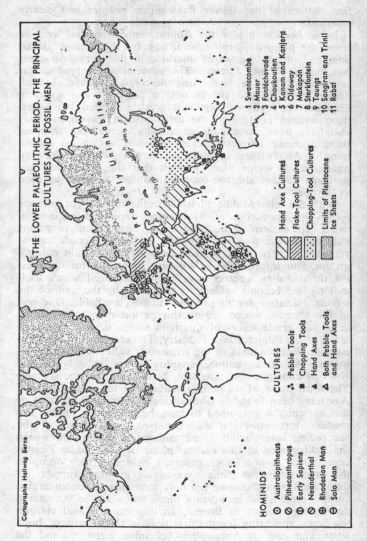

THE LOWER PALAEOLITHIC PERIOD. THE PRINCIPAL
CULTURES AND FOSSIL MEN

1 Swanscombe
2 Mauer
3 Fontéchevade
4 Choukoutien
5 Kanam and Kanjera
6 Oldoway
7 Makapán
8 Sterkfontein
9 Taungs
10 Sangiran and Trinil
11 Rabat

CULTURES

- Pebble Tools
- Chopping Tools
- Hand Axes
- Both Pebble Tools and Hand Axes
- Hand Axe Cultures
- Flake-Tool Cultures
- Chopping-Tool Cultures
- Limits of Pleistocene Ice Sheets

HOMINIDS

- Australopithecus
- Pithecanthropus
- Early Sapiens
- Neanderthal
- Rhodesian Man
- Solo Man

Cartographia Hallwag Berne

MAP III

tion pattern of the Lower Palaeolithic peoples had clearly emerged.

It has been seen how the Abbevillian culture had evolved from the primitive pebble traditions by the second glaciation, and during the warm interlude in this period its creators carried it into Europe. The Abbevillians spread as far as northern France (we, their descendants, have, indeed, named them after a village on the Somme) and southern England. As well as their still crudely shaped hand-axes, these ancient hunters of the early Middle Pleistocene may also have used stone balls as missiles, sometimes chipping them to make perfect spheres. There is as yet no certain trace of Abbevillians in India before the second interglacial phase, yet it seems likely enough that they did reach the southern part of the sub-continent almost or quite as soon as Europe.

With the later Middle Pleistocene the picture (or perhaps rather our knowledge of it) becomes rapidly more complicated. In eastern Asia, where we have been supposing Palaeoanthropic men were making exceedingly crude and as yet unrecognized tools, we can now identify certain cultural groups. Our information is still very slight, but for the present three Asiatic centres have been recognized where toolmaking had become sufficiently advanced by the time of the second glaciation for its products to be classifiable. One was in the Punjab, where during this period men were flaking large and crude flakes of quartzite which have been recognized as the Punjab Flake Industry. The second is in northern Burma, where hunters of the Irrawaddy valley were establishing the Anyathian culture, shaping several roughly defined types of chopper, chopping-tool, hand-axe and large scraper. The third place where human artifacts of the second Glacial Age have been found is Choukoutien, where a single tool of this antiquity is presumed to have been chipped by the immediate forerunners of *Pithecanthropus pekinensis* of the succeeding interglacial. Some authorities would still assign the Peking men to this earliest phase of the Middle Pleistocene, but it is now more generally held that they occupied the caves when the climate was again growing warmer. By the second interglacial we not only have their Choukoutienian culture established in north China, but also the Anyathian developing strongly in Burma, an important related culture, the Soan, appearing for the first time in those parts of India north and east of Abbevillian-Acheulian territory, and the Patjitanian in Java. In Japan a culture identified at Gongenyama appears to be the equivalent of these other cultures.

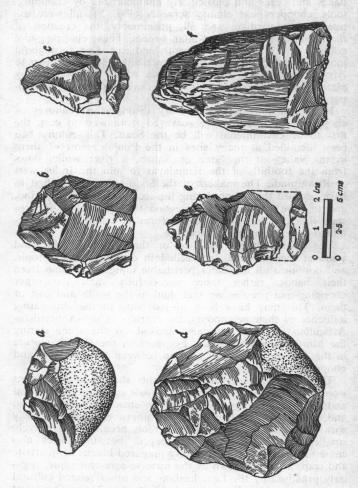

FIG. 5. *Chopper-chopping-tool implements from Asia.*

These were all cultures with implements made on both rough flakes and cores and particularly characterized by chopping-tools, choppers and clumsy scrapers (Fig. 5), all were extremely conservative, and all, presumably, the creation of *Pithecanthropi* and related Soan breeds. These chopping-tool cultures which prevailed in south and east Asia throughout most of the Pleistocene will be described before returning to Africa, Europe and south-west Asia where the events took place which led up to the dramatic developments of the Upper Palaeolithic.

If the far-flung but never very distinguished cultures of chopping-tool tradition are surveyed from west to east, the first to be encountered will be the Soan. This culture had been identified at many sites in the Punjab, most of them in the valley of the Soan or Sohan, a river which flows from the foothills of the Himalayas to join the Indus west of Rawalpindi. The makers of the Soan culture seem first to have peopled the region during the second interglacial period, and to have remained in possession throughout mid-Pleistocene times. Indeed, an evolved form of culture was maintained even during the last Ice Age.

The Soans, during the two or three hundred thousand years at their disposal, succeeded in developing their tools, and doubtless all the other perishable things that came from their hands, rather more successfully than the other chopping-tool peoples we shall find to the south and east of them. This may have been in part due to the stimulating influence of their neighbours, the carriers of the Abbevillian-Acheulian tradition who also arrived on the scene during the Mindel-Riss interglacial. For here in the Punjab we are in the only region of full overlap between the hand-axe and chopping-tool traditions.

The most characteristic implements shaped by the Soans were chopping-tools and choppers made on large round, oval and flat pebbles; they also, however, struck and used flakes, and it is here that their technique improved most markedly with time. Both pebble and flake tools became progressively smaller and more accurately shaped, but the flakes also came to be struck from carefully prepared blocks of quartzite and trap, a mode known as the tortoise-core technique, regularly practised by the Levalloisians and other related cultural groups in western Eurasia and Africa (p. 216). The latest Soans, living during the Riss glaciation and the succeeding warm phase, possessed a culture which had approached very closely indeed to the European Levalloisian, a development which is not found among other chopping-tool cultures and which must surely be due to western influences.

The Anyathians who, as has been shown, were already living in the Irrawaddy valley during Mindel times (the second pluvial of their own region), used mainly fossil wood and siliceous tuff for their tools, the intractable nature of the first leading them to make a high proportion of the hand-adze type of chopping instrument. They maintained this simple tradition with only the slightest improvements in technique right through the Pleistocene Age; it is possible that new influences reached Burma towards the very end of the period, but certainly the manufacture of blade tools, so characteristic of the Late Pleistocene, Upper Palaeolithic, cultures of Europe and Africa was unknown until after the end of Palaeolithic times.

In Java the Patjitanian culture, identified in the valley of the little stream Kali Baksoka and other sites on the south side of the island, has a large number of big rather clumsy tools, the chopper always predominating, made on water-worn pebbles, chunks of stone or massive flakes; it includes, however, a relatively small number of neat flake tools. It has been claimed that the Patjitanian, unlike all the other chopper-tool cultures of south-east and eastern Asia except the Tampanian of Malaya, included tools approaching so closely to hand-axes as to betray influence from the Abbevillian-Acheulian tradition. This seems unlikely, particularly in view of the absence of hand-axes in Burma, a region lying on the natural route from the nearest Abbevillian-Acheulian territories in India. These Javanese implements, which are at least as much choppers as hand-axes, were probably independently evolved to serve comparable purposes. The Patjitanian culture has not been found in direct association with *Pithecanthropus erectus* or with the contemporary fauna of the Trinil beds; at present it is only known to start a little later, in the second half of the second interglacial period, lasting on through the third glacial. There is little reason to doubt, however, that it was made by the immediate descendants of *Pithecanthropus erectus* or that this fossil man himself made a comparable, if perhaps even cruder, equipment of tools. His much later descendants of Late Pleistocene times (p. 100)—who may, as has been said, have been reinforced by invaders of a more evolved physical type—are held to have been the makers of implements found at several sites in the Solo valley; these include flakes and even blades struck from chalcedony and jasper as well as points and picks made from bone and antler. This material has been grouped together as the Ngandong culture, but for the present it has not been proved to be all of one age; nor can it, therefore, all be recognized as the handiwork of *Homo soloensis*.

The Palaeolithic history of Burma and Java has been first recounted because the information from these countries is greatest. There is no doubt that there was a Lower Palaeolithic population in Thailand (Siam) possessing chopper-tools and a cultural tradition similar to that of the Anyathian of Burma, while in Malaya men were making tools strikingly similar to those of the Patjitanians of Java, including even the hand-axe-like chopper. This Malayan Lower Palaeolithic culture has been tentatively named the Tampanian. There are a few traces of Lower Palaeolithic chopper-tool tradition more or less of the Patjitanian type in Sumatra and also in the Celebes. The Celebes, however, are more remarkable for an Upper Palaeolithic population in the Wallanae valley who were making tools on small, thick flakes and occasional blades. This culture is likened to the Ngandong of Java and is found nowhere on the Asiatic mainland, although it is suspected to have been present in the Philippines. Its bearers may have reached the Celebes from Java and the Sunda Shelf route, but the Pleistocene fauna of these islands is entirely unlike that of Java and must almost certainly have come by the alternative route, also open in times of low ocean level, by Formosa and the Philippines. If this is true of the animals, then probably the hunters of the Late Pleistocene also came this way; it is a question which cannot be settled until the presence of peoples with cultural traditions similar to those of Ngandong and the Wallanae valley have been recognized on the mainland.

In southern China very little indeed is known of Palaeolithic man, although the skeleton from the Kwanshantse (p. 106), supposed to be of Late Pleistocene Age, and a few tools suggestive of the chopping-tool type of culture picked up along the gorges of the Yangtze between Ichang and Chunking are enough to show that exploration would discover that this region had its Palaeolithic history. For the present such a history can be attempted only for north China. It centres in the Choukoutien caves, the most important site for the history of Palaeolithic man in the whole of Asia. After the occupation dating from the second glacial represented for us by a single implement, *Pithecanthropus* lived at the main site while fifty metres of cave deposit accumulated. During the whole of the great span of time represented there is practically no change in either the physical appearance or the material culture of the cave-dwellers. The *Pithecanthropi* continued to make their rough and inaccurate chopping-tools and scrapers, some on broken pebbles, some on flakes. Occasionally they utilized, though they can hardly be said to have shaped, implements of bone. These creatures who for so long inhabited the fissured limestone of the Western Hills less than thirty miles from the place where the exquisite city of Peking was to rise, were cannibals, eating human flesh, and more particularly human marrow and brains, for nourishment rather than ritual. They do not appear to have had any of the intimations of immortality which lead to a careful disposal of the dead. The fact that they existed for so long without perceptible evolution of their brains and with only the humblest improvement in the tools they made is held to prove that this part of Asia, so far from having contributed to the main tide of Palaeolithic history, was at this time a sluggish backwater.

In the fissure known as the Upper Cave at Choukoutien all this has changed. The men living there and burying their dead (p. 106) were of our own species, perhaps already showing some mongoloid features. Although the material found is scanty, they were in possession of an Upper Palaeolithic or even Mesolithic culture utilizing polished bone flakes, eyed bone needles and perforated bead head-dresses and necklaces. They also imported sea shells and mother of pearl for ornaments. They evidently used the cave as a seasonal squatting-place at a period which may have been very late glacial or post-glacial—perhaps as late as about 8000 B C.

A centre of vigorous Asiatic Upper Palaeolithic culture lay in the valley of the Huangho between Shensi and Shinsi and farther north on the Ordos plateau. Here in several sites dating from the last Ice Age, clearly earlier than the Upper Cave, hunters had maintained a culture which still showed some conservative inheritance from the chopper-tool tradition of the Choukoutienian and also included flake tools (points and scrapers) made from prepared cores, long blades, backed knives, engravers and many other types which will be found to be characteristic of the rapidly advancing Upper Palaeolithic cultures of Europe and Africa. This Ordos culture, which has sometimes been classified as 'Moustero-Aurignacian', has affinities with the Upper Palaeolithic of Siberia which will be discussed in connection with the first invasions of America.

The history of eastern and south-eastern Asia has been carried down to the end of the Pleistocene period because it was during the whole of that time a peripheral region re-

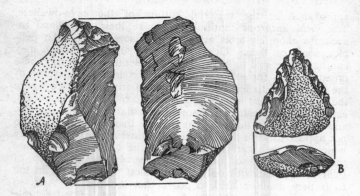

FIG. 6. *Flake-tools from western Europe. A: Clactonian flake-tool (scale 4/9); B: Tayacian flake-tool (scale 2/5). (After Oakley.)*

mote from those parts of the world where man was to take the most significant steps towards higher cultural forms and at last to civilization. Also the chopping-tool tradition was so persistent that it gives a unity to the whole Palaeolithic period in these parts of Asia. This warrants treating it all together, even at the cost of encountering a few intrusive Upper Palaeolithic traits before discovering their origins farther west. It is time now to turn in that direction.

It has already been suggested that when the final phase of the second glaciation rendered northern Europe uninhabitable and most of the rest of the continent bitterly cold, the Abbevillian peoples withdrew southward towards their African cradleland. The peoples who took their place were the makers of a culture known as the Clactonian, which belongs to the group known as the flake cultures to distinguish them from the Asiatic chopper-tool and the African hand-axe traditions (Fig. 6). Their tools were mostly trimmed from boldly struck flakes, many of them evidently designed as skinning-knives and hide scrapers, an equipment better adapted to life in a cold climate than that associated with the hand-axe.[4] Although we know the Clactonians to have been fully established in western Europe near the beginning of the Mindel glaciation, while evidence for the existence of chopper cultures in Asia as early as this is still very scanty, it is probable that the European culture will prove to be an early offshoot from the Asiatic, perhaps sharing a common origin with the early Soan (p. 124). Thus, even if nothing is certainly known about the physical type of the early Clactonians, they may well have belonged to the same general Pithecanthropic stock. Furthermore, while later on contacts between the flake-tool and hand-axe makers in Eurasia undoubtedly led to the mingling and transference of cultural traits, there is good reason to believe that at this stage the two peoples were distinct and that we are free to visualize the departure of the Abbevillians and the arrival of the Clactonians as actual, even if very gradual, migrations.

While the Clactonian hunters were holding their own in the harsh environment of England, France and Germany, the hand-axe peoples enjoyed an unbroken cultural development in Africa greatly improving their techniques and adding to the range of their tool forms (p. 132).

During the second interpluvial the more primitive Abbevillian stage of their culture had passed into the Acheulian with its increasingly finely made and beautifully proportioned implements. Possibly, too, by this time they had spread into India, where the early Madras culture, soon to dominate the whole peninsular area, certainly shows primitive, Abbevillian, forms of hand-axe.

With the melting of the ice for the corresponding long and very warm Mindel-Riss interglacial phase, the hand-axe people advanced once more into Europe, bearers now of the Acheulian culture. The hundred and fifty thousand years of this interglacial saw the heyday of this culture; to judge from the stone tools which alone survive of what may have been a rich if still technically primitive culture, this was the time when it reached its finest development as well as its greatest extent.

A place such as Ol Orgesailie in the Kenya Rift Valley with its lakeside camp sites thickly scattered with hand-axes, cleavers, bolas stones and the bones of wild pig, baboons and zebras, seems to speak of high success in the chase. As to its extent, the Acheulian culture covered much more than half the humanly inhabited world and about a fifth of the total land surfaces of our planet. Acheulian hand-axes, used to follow the steps of this culture like the shreds of a paper chase, have been discovered throughout Africa, southwestern and western Europe as far as the southern half of England, across central and eastern Europe to the Black Sea, in Asia Minor, along the east end of the Mediterranean, in Arabia (though rarely as yet), Iraq, and all over peninsular India extending northward as far as the Punjab (p. 122).

None has yet been found in Iran or Afghanistan, but the Acheulians must be presumed to have reached India by a narrow corridor north of the Persian Gulf and south of the Iranian highlands.

What is perhaps most remarkable about this vast Acheulian territory is the uniformity of its cultural products and the completeness with which new developments, clear-cut (if in our eyes trifling) improvements in manufacture, spread throughout large parts of three continents. If collectors went out from London, Jerusalem, Cape Town and Madras, all four might find hand-axes which could not be distinguished one from the other unless it was by the material from which they had been made. Evolution was, in fact, slow enough for diffusion always to keep up with it. From the Upper Palaeolithic onwards this state of affairs was generally to be reversed, cultural evolution within limited regions far outstripping cultural diffusion; thus it is not until the era of modern communications that we again encounter a comparable uniformity of manufactures over huge areas of human settlement. There remains, however, a need for caution in assuming the absolute contemporaneity of the various phases of the Abbevillian-Acheulian tradition in remote parts of their range. Rapid diffusion in certain directions, persistence in certain areas, may have led to a divergence of tens of thousands of years in the rates of change. Nor is it true that during this period of its expansion the hand-axe culture was everywhere the possession of one species of man.

Even in this time of its flowering during the second interglacial, remains of the actual possessors of the Acheulian culture are rare. In spite of the really vast quantities of hand-axes and other implements of this age which have been found in Africa, suggestive of considerable populations, the bones of their makers are few indeed. The earliest known are represented by the jaws of *Atlanthropus* from Algeria, while the doubtful Kanjera skulls, if their claims are accepted, also belong to this time and culture. In Europe Swanscombe man was certainly shaping hand-axes towards the end of this warm period. While the Kanjera and Swanscombe men have convinced many people that whatever happened during later times when cultural traditions were blending, the Acheulian of the second interglacial was the creation and possession of *Homo sapiens*, the Algerian *Atlanthropus* warns us against such over-simple assumptions. These fossils prove that the Acheulian tradition could be faithfully carried by men who physically had much in common with Heidelberg man, and the general Pithecanthropic stock.

In regions of western Europe where the bearers of the Acheulian and Clactonian cultures must have met during these scores of warm millennia, we have certain evidence of their contact and probable fraternization. A community, for example, living near High Lodge in Suffolk, England, towards the end of the interglacial, made both Clactonian flake tools and hand-axes, and it is impossible to know whether they were Acheulians who had been influenced by Clactonians or vice versa. What is certain is that here we have one of the earliest examples of a process which was to be commonplace in human affairs: the encounter of strange peoples proving a stimulus to change and leading to the creation of a new and fertile synthesis.

It may be that the most important development of late Middle Pleistocene times was the fruit of precisely this synthesis. The Levalloisian culture appears in Europe with the return of the ice for the Riss glaciation. This culture, distinguished by an ingenious and very effective way of making flake tools (p. 217), can be held like all the flake cultures to be particularly well adapted to the preoccupation with cutting meat and preparing hides that most often goes with living in cold or arctic conditions. It has been argued, therefore, that the Levalloisians were the former Acheulians who, sapient as they were, had borrowed ideas from their Clactonian neighbours to equip themselves to face a rapidly worsening climate. This view might be held to find some support from the existence at an earlier date in South Africa of a Levalloisoid method of flaking which was unquestionably devised by the local Acheulians. On the other hand the fact that the true European Levalloisians extended their territory farther to the north and east than the Acheulians had done, suggesting a hardy people capable of living in extreme cold, gives slight support to the opposite view that the Levalloisians were descended mainly from the old flake people, perhaps inspired by their Acheulian contacts. Certainly some Acheulians retreated southward before the advance of the ice, for there is evidence of their arrival in northern Africa.

Such dusty arguments must continue until more is known of this important but comparatively recently recognized culture. Unhappily even less is known of the peoples living to the east of the Levalloisians during and after Riss times who have now come very faintly into prehistory as the Tayacians. This culture, centred in eastern and central Europe and extending from France to Palestine, appears to be a derivative of the Clactonian. It is chiefly important, as will be shown, as having apparently given rise to the culture of Neanderthal man. It would seem an obvious assumption, therefore, that the Tayacian flake culture should have been the product of men of Palaeoanthropic type, possibly of rather extreme representatives of the type. Yet in a cave at Fontéchevade in the Charente Department of France, fragments of several skulls found in hearths belonging to the Tayacian culture were hardly if at all to be distinguished from *Homo sapiens.* As a warning against the exclusive association of particular cultural traditions with particular species, the Fontéchevade men are the counterpart of *Atlanthropus.* On the other hand it is not quite incredible that the skull fragments may represent a feast at which brutish Tayacians devoured several members of our own species—brawn having, for once, had victory over brain.

In spite of the enduring dominance of the native Abbevillian-Acheulian tradition in Africa, a culture comparable to the Clactonian was present in Kenya and the Rhodesias during the third pluvial period. This is the Hope Fountain culture which may have been derived from the Clactonian or Tayacian, in which case it would presumably have been carried into east Africa by immigrants from south-west Asia.

On the threshold of the Upper Pleistocene Age then, eastern Asia was still in the possession of the backward choppertool makers, Africa was mainly inhabited by Acheulians but also had the flake-tool Hope Fountain peoples; south-west Asia was dominated by late Acheulians with Tayacian elements who extended also into Europe, while western Europe was occupied by the Levalloisians. If the end of the Middle Pleistocene period had seen a considerable mingling of peoples and their cultures leading to a complication of the cultural pattern of the Old World, this process was to be vastly increased and accelerated throughout the Upper Pleistocene. As for the physical nature of the human beings responsible for all these hunting cultures, there can be little doubt that while the eastern Asiatics were all of rather low, Palaeoanthropic breeds, in Eurasia and Africa there was a patchy mixture of types already nearer to modern man with a great variety of others showing more or fewer Palaeoanthropic features.

As warmer seasons returned after the Riss glaciation, the Levalloisians seem to have remained in Europe while the Acheulians returned, bringing the ultimate form of their culture which they had been evolving in Africa. While it may be folly to base such arguments on no more than stone implements, the scanty survivals of complex living cultures, it is nevertheless very tempting to see in the smaller, more finicky, aesthetically weaker hand-axes of the Upper Pleistocene a degeneration in the ancient Acheulian tradition extraordinarily similar in spirit to the decline which was to overtake so many cultural traditions during the future history of mankind. Is it legitimate to suppose that this, the very first human culture of some distinction, during the hundreds of thousands of years of its duration went through much the same cycle, the same rise and fall, that has been apparent, with rapidly increasing tempo, in all creative cultures of civilized man?

During the first half of the Riss-Würm interglacial late Acheulians and Levalloisians lived as neighbours in southwest Europe and have left ample evidence of their mutual influence upon one another. The last attenuated phase of the Acheulian culture, known as the Micoquian, shows in its flake tools as well as in the slight and pointed form of the hand-axes an effective borrowing of Levalloisian ideas. Similarly the Levalloisians of this period made hand-axes though employing their own peculiar techniques.

Just as the Riss-Würm interglacial phase saw what might be called a fragmentation of the ancient hand-axe tradition, so also did the corresponding Kanjeran-Kamassian interpluvial of Africa. The very old and distinctive version of the hand-axe tradition characteristic of South Africa (where it is sometimes distinguished as the Stellenbosch culture) seems to have been the parent of two of the principal later African cultures. These are the Sangoan of South and Central Africa and the widespread Fauresmith of British East Africa, the Rhodesias and South Africa. The northern swing of the rain-belts, which at this time was desiccating much of the continent, made the peoples concerned seek out large rivers and lakes or highlands lofty enough to maintain falls of rain and snow. Thus the Sangoans frequented the Zambesi and the Congo, Lake Victoria and the other Great Central Lakes, while the Fauresmith people similarly kept nearer permanent rivers in the south, and lived at high altitudes on Mount Kenya, the Aberdares, Kilimanjaro and other ranges in the eastern part of their territory. In the south the Fauresmith culture was maintained into the last, Gamblian, pluvial period.

In addition to these two offshoots from the native Acheulian, the Levallois culture is generally (though not universally) held to have been brought into Africa from Eurasia, perhaps more immediately from Palestine. Except for an uncertain settlement on the north-west coast, the Levalloisians spread out only in the north-east sector of the continent: in Egypt (as far west as the Kharga oasis), Abyssinia and British East Africa as far south as central Tanganyika.

With the latter half of the last interglacial phase we come to a people who provide something approaching a substantial raft on the uncertain waters of our Palaeolithic history. These are the Neanderthalers and their Mousterian culture (Fig. 7), already established in this time of warm climate even if their heyday was not reached until the Würm glaciation was at its first climax. The very numerous skeletons of this breed that have been unearthed in Europe, Asia and north Africa have always (if they had tools with them at all) been associated with a culture with a strong Mousterian element, even where the Levallois technique and the manufacture of hand-axes (by means other than those used by the Acheulians) show the influence of other traditions. The Mousterian and related flake cultures dating from the end of the last interglacial and the earlier part of the last glacial phase are sometimes described as 'Middle Palaeolithic'.

It has already been suggested that the Mousterian was a development out of the Clactonian or Tayacian which took place in eastern Europe or adjacent regions. Certainly this lies near the centre of its range. The true Mousterian has not been detected in Britain, but it is probable that Neanderthal man did in fact reach so far to the west, for at Creswell Crags in Derbyshire cave-dwellers left tools showing a

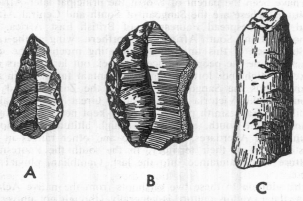

FIG. 7. *Mousterian implements: A: flake point; B: side scraper; C: bone compressor (scale approx. 4/5). (After Singer.)*

Mousterian tradition while at Kent's Cavern, Devonshire, was a Mousterian with Acheuleo–Levalloisian influence very much like the culture associated with actual Neanderthal remains across the Channel in the island of Jersey.

From this western limit Neanderthal man with his culture pure or adulterated has been found through most parts of Europe, in south-west Asia and in north Africa. An extreme north-eastern outpost has been discovered in Uzbekistan, where a cave not far south of Samarkand contained Mousterian implements and the skeleton of a young Neanderthal child who had been buried within a ring of horns of the Siberian mountain goat. Another man of the eastern outposts has been found in Azerbaijan, again with a Mousterian element in the associated culture. A skull of a Neanderthaloid infant has been excavated from the Shanidar cave in northern Iraq.

It has already been shown that the earlier Neanderthalers, those fortunate enough to be born before the advance of the Würm glaciation, were rather less extreme in physical type than those who faced the rigours of this last glaciation. They lived generally in the open, like the Acheulians, whereas their descendants were by choice cave-dwellers. Examples of Neanderthal man from this earlier period have been found over most parts of their total range; one who was alive at the very beginning of the interglacial comes from north Africa (Rabat, Morocco), while two groups of European Neanderthalers fall well within the warm period—those from Germany (Ehringsdorf) and Croatia (Krapina); an individual from Italy was living towards its end. South-west Asia is represented by Palestine, where the Tabun and Skhul men were hunting on Mount Carmel just before the cold began.

Undoubtedly then, the Neanderthal breed had spread far before Würm times, but it was during the glaciation that they appear to have asserted their domination. In western Europe in particular they were evidently numerous and strongly entrenched (Map IV). Some seventy thousand years ago very many cave-dwellings and shelters throughout the region must have been occupied by these uncouth but successful hunters. They were now at their greatest strength as a species and their extreme of bodily development (p. 97).

Between forty and fifty thousand years ago, during the first half of the final glaciation, there was a sudden change in this situation. Sudden at least in the terms of the coarse net cast by our prehistory which still lets millennia slip back into the sea of time. It was a change that must have taken much longer than the time which has passed since the first

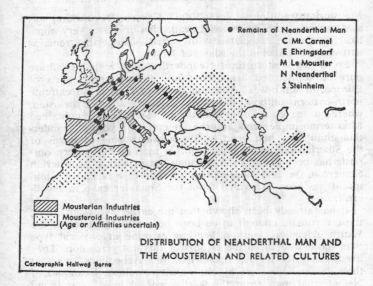

Remains of Neanderthal Man
C Mt. Carmel
E Ehringsdorf
M Le Moustier
N Neanderthal
S Steinheim

Mousterian Industries

Mousteroid Industries
(Age or Affinities uncertain)

**DISTRIBUTION OF NEANDERTHAL MAN AND
THE MOUSTERIAN AND RELATED CULTURES**

Cartographie Hallwag Berne

MAP IV

glimmers of civilization, yet it was swift in terms of what had gone before. Throughout the whole of their range in Africa and Eurasia the Neanderthal species disappeared. The survival of remnants of Palaeoanthropic type in Africa has been recorded (p. 99), and there is every likelihood that comparable human relics will be forthcoming from Asia. In general, however, it can be said that, starting with Europe and west Asia, the entire Old World was emptied of all other groups and *Homo sapiens* left in possession.

By what means the Palaeoanthropic men in all their variety were liquidated can never be known. It is easy, and doubtless partially true, to say that they were defeated by the superior intelligence, better weapons and organization of our own species. Yet sometimes, when thinking of the vast stretches of the earth's crust involved, and the many remote, unwanted corners where they could have survived, one feels that there is more of the *Zeitgeist* in it than this. As with the dinosaurs, so with these men, was there not something more than the environment and their enemies against them? Furthermore, while all proper weight has by now been given to the recent tendency to separate physical type and culture in the Palaeolithic Age and to emphasize the variability of our ancestors, the impossibility of isolating a pure *Homo sapiens* stock far back into the Pleistocene, yet surely this final scene says something for the opposite point of view? In Europe, at least, the picture is fairly clear. An apelike breed in possession of one well-defined cultural tradition was directly confronted and dispossessed by men of modern type and with a totally different material culture. Two breeds, we think two species, met face to face and their faces were strikingly unalike. However much mixed cultural and physical traits had been in the past, in the early Upper Pleistocene there was some centre or centres where men entirely of our own kind had created the beginning of the high hunting cultures of the Upper Palaeolithic, a tradition almost wholly new, remarkably inventive, and, as history was to prove, immensely potent for future growth.

This first crystallization of the blade cultures of the Upper Palaeolithic (p. 241) was one of the crucially important events in human affairs: it is not certainly known where it took place, but recent evidence, as we shall see, points to west Asia. What is perfectly clear is that the whole Upper Palaeolithic movement, if it may be so called, all the important events of a revolutionary age, took place on a limited stage. That stage was Eurasia from France to the south Russian plains and Persia. In Lower and Middle Palaeolithic times eastern Asia had been a backwater remote from centres of creative change; now Africa, too, lapsed into this position. The huge continent which may have seen the origin both of human kind and of *Homo sapiens*[5] and which, in part, was to have so important a place in the first flowering of civilization, made no significant contribution to the stirring achievements of the last glaciation.

Just because it was a revolutionary period marked by the first great acceleration in technological progress as well as the first known expression of man's imaginative power, the historical pattern of the Upper Palaeolithic is much more complicated than anything existing before. Evolution now rapidly overtook diffusion, and it was no longer possible that there should be such far-flung uniformity as that shown by the Acheulian culture. Man became physically more uniform, culturally far more diverse. Throughout the Eurasian theatre the all-conquering *Homo sapiens* split into a number of groups, all in possession of the new blade tradition, but otherwise sharply differentiated, as were those other groups that, towards the end of the period, began to carry late forms of blade culture to the wide territories outside their homelands. Even more than in earlier times, our knowledge of the Upper Palaeolithic is so overwhelmingly much greater for Europe, and particularly for western Europe than for the rest of the primary area, that it is difficult to see the whole prospect in due balance. There is a score of European sites for every one in Asia. Furthermore, western Europe's possession of man's first great artistic creations justifies giving it a peculiar pre-eminence. Nevertheless, in spite of the richness and complexity of the European Upper Palaeolithic, it appears almost certain that the blade tradition did not originate there. The picture given by the great series of classic cultures of the French caves is rather that they were brought in when already more or less fully developed, even though later new groups evolved locally. Europe can show no transitional cultures suggesting the evolution of either the latest Acheulian or the Levalloisio-Mousterian tradition towards the earliest known blade culture, the Châtelperronian.[6] Rather, as has been said, it was brought in by modern man and superseded the Neanderthal's Mousterian with a sharp break.

In south-west Asia, on the other hand, there are signs of an elementary type of blade culture emerging at an earlier date. At Adlun on the coast of the Lebanon a 'pre-Aurignacian' culture of this kind has been found in a geological context which dates it to the last interglacial phase and which can be shown to be *earlier* than the Levalloisio-Mousterian found with the famous Mount Carmel skeletons which showed characteristics both of Neanderthal man and of *Homo sapiens*. This Carmel industry was itself already recognized to contain burins and other blade culture elements not found with the typical Levallois and Mousterian of Europe. It looks very much, then, as though the blade and burin tradition of the Upper Palaeolithic evolved in western Asia, perhaps in the hinterland rather than on the Mediterranean coast, and that it was from there that it spread westward into Europe (as later the Neolithic tradition was to do). The admixture both of racial types and of cultural traditions at Mount Carmel encourages the already likely assumption that this earliest blade and burin development was due to men of *Homo sapiens* stock who came to mingle both their genes and their new ideas for tool-making with that of the Neanderthalers. Their final ascendancy in the same area is demonstrated in a true blade and burin culture known as the Emiran which succeeded the Levallois

Mousterian at Mount Carmel—though not without in its turn incorporating certain Levallois forms.

Thus it seems as though the lands beyond the eastern end of the Mediterranean which were to see the dawn of the Neolithic revolution also played a great part in the earlier and almost equally important cultural innovations of the Upper Palaeolithic. It is here that we should look for the cradleland of the Châtelperronians who dispossessed Neanderthal man in western Europe. It still remains possible, however, that the true Aurignacian which followed the Châtelperronian originated rather farther west, conceivably in eastern Europe. However, it would be rash to assume that any of these ideas about the birth of the Upper Palaeolithic tradition are final. Every year brings new and contrary ideas about these most crucial events in the history of our kind.

In France, where so many scores of rich sites have been excavated, the local sequence of cultures is much more certain, and although further research may well complicate, it is not likely to contradict, what is already known (Fig. 8). Having exposed our present doubts about the origins of the Upper Palaeolithic movement, it will give the most coherent idea of its course if it is described from a viewpoint looking outward from the limestone country of south-west France and northern Spain, where the remains of the gifted hunters concerned are so strongly concentrated. It has been made clear that the earliest of these cultures, the Châtelperronian, which in France is associated with the Combe Capelle race (p. 104), can be detected over most of the Eurasiatic theatre but not in a perfectly consistent form. It was flourishing towards the close of the first phase of the Würm glaciation. The second, Aurignacian culture is almost equally widespread, but shows so coherent an individuality throughout its whole extent that there can be little doubt that here we are dealing with a single migrating race. That race was of the powerful, large-brained Cromagnon type, skilful and artistically gifted; its spread was made easier by the more favourable climate intervening between the first and second maxima of the glaciation. No doubt it was this improvement which encouraged this people to push into Britain, where the Châtelperronian culture failed to penetrate. Although the Aurignacians extended eastward into south-west Asia, they are poorly represented in what is usually recognized as the gateway into Asia—the Balkan countries of eastern Europe. It is possible, therefore, that their migrations did not take them by this expected route but rather along the Pontic

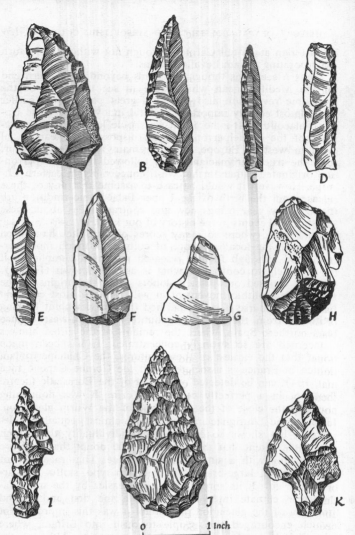

FIG. 8. *Upper Palaeolithic implements from Europe. A: Audi knife blade; B: Châtelperron knife blade; C: pointed Gravette knife blade; D: square-ended Gravette blade; E: awl; F: graver and end scraper; G: Aurignacian beaked graver with notch; H: Aurignacian keeled scraper; I: single-shouldered Solutrean point; J: Solutrean laurel-leaf point; K: Aterian point (after Burkitt).*

steppes and then southward into the Lebanon and Palestine (Map V).

The third culture recognized in France is the Gravettian, sharply distinct from the Aurignacian and probably representing a further development of the Châtelperronian tradition. This continuity suggested by their handiwork is also supported by the physical type of the men concerned, for the Gravettian race, represented best at Predmost in Czechoslovakia (Moravia), is very much like that of Combe Capelle. Whether this development took place in many areas of the original Châtelperronian range, including France itself, is uncertain. It seems more probable that it was initiated in southern Russia. Here an eastern branch of the Gravettian flourished exceedingly among mammoth hunters who pursued their game along the corridor of tree-scattered steppes lying between the northern ice-sheet and the heavily glaciated ranges of the Carpathians and Alps. Some element of their traditions was even carried as far to the east as Siberia, for the mammoth hunters of Mal'ta (near Irkutsk) as well as having blade forms among their tools were like the Gravettians in carving little female statuettes in bone (p. 277). It has already been suggested (p. 127) that the Ordos culture of China also embodied something of the Upper Palaeolithic blade tradition.

It is surprising to find that in spite of the harsh conditions prevailing in the second maximum of the Würm glaciation and even on into the slight recession that followed, makers of the Gravettian culture succeeded in establishing themselves as far into the bleak north-west as Derbyshire in northern England. They remained there until the end of the Ice Age, evolving a local culture known as the Creswellian.

The next event in the cultural history of France seems to have been brief and episodic. The Gravettian was there locally succeeded by the Solutrean culture, distinguished from other Upper Palaeolithic blade cultures by exquisite flint lance or dagger blades showing a highly skilled form of pressure flaking (p. 220). Similar blades are known from Hungary and Bulgaria, and central Europe was once thought to have been the homeland of the Solutreans;[7] recently counter-claims have been put forward for a southerly origin in Spain and even north Africa. In fact it is possible that the Solutrean culture does not everywhere signify any movement of people but rather the adoption by existing populations of the new pressure-flaking technique. Where Solutrean blades appear only sporadically, as in England, it can be supposed that

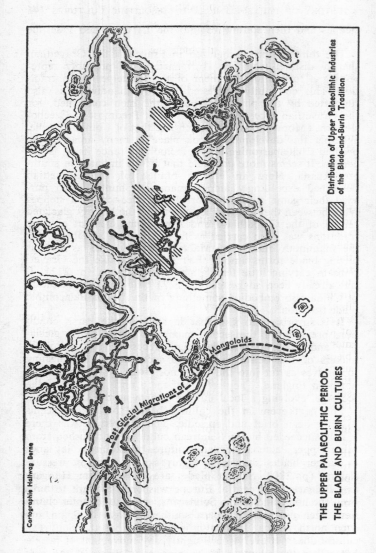

Cartographie Hallwag Berne

Distribution of Upper Palaeolithic Industries
of the Blade-and-Burin Tradition

Post Glacial Migrations of Mongoloids

THE UPPER PALAEOLITHIC PERIOD.
THE BLADE AND BURIN CULTURES

MAP V

these fine products may have travelled from hand to hand as objects of trade.

The savage cold against which the European peoples had to struggle as the Würm glaciation reached a final climax seems to have checked both migration and the spread of ideas, for during this last stage of the Upper Palaeolithic period there was a tendency for cultures to be developed locally and remain in isolation. It has already been mentioned that such a local growth, the Creswellian, managed to survive in the north of England and we find similar offshoots in France and other parts of Europe. They sprang from a mixed ancestry of the older cultural traditions in which the Gravettian was generally dominant. By far the most remarkable among these cultures was the Magdalenian which flourished exceedingly in its homelands in south-west France and northern Spain but also made its influence felt in Belgium, Switzerland, southern Germany and Bohemia.

It was these Magdalenian hunters, finding living easy with the abundant game of the open grassland and tundra of their day, who brought cave-painting, engraving and carving to a superb peak of achievement before its sudden eclipse together with the way of life on which it depended (p. 73). In their art all the Upper Palaeolithic peoples give us the first opportunity in history to enter into communion, however imperfectly, with the mind, imagination and emotions of our forebears. Looking at these studies of the mighty mammoth and rhinoceros, the great oxen and reindeer and bison, the graceful herds of stag and wild horses, each of us can experience according to his imaginative powers something of what it was like to live as a hunter at that time some twelve thousand years ago, when civilization was still hidden from knowledge far in the future, but when self-consciousness and the power to grasp all kinds of mental images was rapidly transforming the human psyche. This art also reminds us, more effectively than any consideration of the similarities which underlie the diversity of the blade cultures, of the unity of all the Upper Palaeolithic peoples, particularly in western Europe. Soon after the arrival of the first blade culture, the artists had been at work and had maintained a tradition, variable certainly, but continuous enough to imply the handing on of ideas and technical methods from one culture to the next.

At this point in the ultimate Palaeolithic it becomes necessary to look once more at Africa, where bearers of blade cultures were at last to make an appearance. Throughout the greater part of the Gamblian pluvial period (correspond-

FIG. 9. *Tool types of the Stillbay culture from Ethiopia. Scale 2/3 (after Leakey).*

ing to the Würm glaciation) the peoples of that continent were content to continue in the Acheulian and Levalloisian traditions, allowing the progressive movement of world history to pass them by to the north. In east Africa the Stillbay culture (Fig. 9) was a moderately vigorous development from the Levalloisian while the Magosian was a still later degeneration from the same root. Both Stillbay and Magosian cultures extended also into the Rhodesias and made themselves felt even in South Africa, but in the south the ancient Acheulian inheritance was still dominant among the possessors of the Fauresmith culture. In central Africa the Sangoans proved themselves equally conservative. In Egypt, as in east Africa, it was again the Levalloisian tradition that lingered alike in the Sebilian of Upper Egypt, in the miserable epi-Levalloisian of Lower Egypt, and the Khargan centred on the Kharga oasis. In north Africa the picture is different and somewhat more vigorous. The Aterian culture, which seems to have originated in the north-western end of the coastal strip and to have spread from thence eastward, suggests a people of some creative energy. It is thought to have grown from the local Mousterian, but its possessors were skilful workers in flint, using, among others, the pressure-flaking technique which has led to a belief that the Aterians may have had some share in the Solutrean culture of Europe (p. 141). They have also been credited with being the inventors of the bow and arrow. Their expansion carried them as far as the Kharga oasis, which they (or their cultural influence) reached at the very end of the Palaeolithic Age; some may have crossed into Spain at an earlier date. It was here in the north that the true blade tradition of the Upper Palaeolithic made its tardy appearance in Africa. The earliest of these is now held to be, not the Capsian as was long thought, but the Dabba culture, known at this relatively early period in Cyrenaica and believed to have been introduced by an influx of people from the east end of the Mediterranean. It is a culture with typical backed blades and burins belonging to the main European and south-west Asiatic tradition and only later developing some local characteristics. The next event appears to have been the beginning of the Oranian culture along the coasts north of the Atlas chain in the regions known as the Maghreb. This culture, which is characterized by a great preponderance of small backed blades, may have been due either to a migration from Spain, or an influence from the Late Palaeolithic cultures there, dating from something like 15,000 to 12,000 B C. By about 10,000 B C, or rather later, it is suggested that

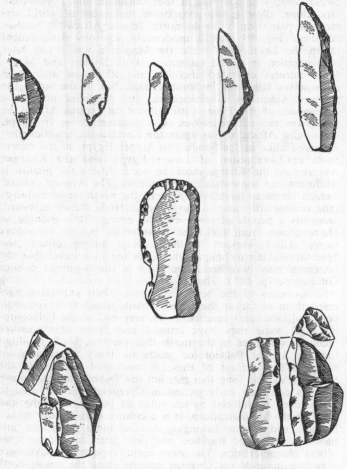

Fig. 10. *Tools of the Upper Kenya Capsian (after Leakey).*

the people of the Dabba culture, living along the southern desert-facing slopes of the Atlas in Algeria and Tunisia, created the Capsian culture. In its earliest form the Capsian included fairly large curved backed blades so much like the Châtelperronian of western Europe that it led to the old belief that this was a very early African blade culture. However, it is now known that from the first it also included small forms approaching the microlithic, and that in its late phase when it was spreading north and east along the coast it had all the true microlithic implements of the European Mesolithic. There seems no doubt that this Upper Capsian was a post-glacial Mesolithic culture. The only Carbon-14 date yet obtained gives about 6800 B C for the end of the earlier or Typical Capsian (Fig. 10).

A very interesting point for the racial history of north Africa (and one which also supports the historical interpretation just given) is that while the Oranian culture is associated at a considerable number of sites with a massively muscled, rather heavy-browed type reminiscent of Cromagnon man, the Capsian seems to have been created by people of smaller, more delicately featured physique comparable to the Natufians and evidently early representatives of the Mediterranean race soon to dominate the region. A survival of the Oranian type may perhaps be recognized in the Guanches of the Canary Islands.

This reconstruction of the spread of Upper Palaeolithic cultures into north Africa and the emergence of Mesolithic cultures there is by no means universally accepted, though it seems to offer the best interpretation of all the known facts. Some would still insist on a much earlier beginning for the Capsian. Some, too, still attribute the lively rock shelter art of east Spain (Fig. 28) to a Capsian invasion of the peninsula. Even if, as seems probable, the east Spanish art was not the work of Capsians, it is thought that much of it was painted at a time when the Capsian was flourishing on the other side of the Mediterranean and may well have had some kind of relationship with the rock art of the Sahara.

This African rock art—nearly all of it incised but with a few rare paintings—is found along the southern side of the Atlas but also southward in the Hoggar mountains and scattered eastward in southern Tripolitania, in the Tibesti massif, Gilf Kebir and even as far as the Nubian Nile. It includes some fine examples of the naturalistic portraiture of wild animals, especially elephants, giraffes, lions and an extinct giant buffalo. These wild animal studies, often life size, are probably the oldest work, just as various groups showing domestic animals and others with obvious connection with historical Egyptian motifs are undoubtedly among the latest. Possibly much of this earlier art was engraved by peoples of Capsian descent who were just beginning to adopt some of the Neolithic cultural traits spreading out from the Nile valley. The Capsians themselves sometimes made very rough engravings, usually only a pattern of lines (in one known instance possibly attempting representation) but it seems unlikely that left to themselves they would have developed this excellent representational talent. On the other hand, Egypt does not seem to be a credible source of inspiration for what was essentially a hunters' art. Perhaps some indirect inheritance or influence from the European Upper Palaeolithic tradition may lie behind these rock carvings of the desert fringes. Among other African cultures that have been mentioned, several, notably the Sebilian and Magosian, developed a microlithic element in their latest phases, while the Kenya Capsian gave rise to the Elementeitan of east Africa, a true Mesolithic culture dating from post-glacial times. In South Africa the Smithfield and Wilton (Fig. 11) cultures were the counterpart to the Elementeitan, but were still in full swing in recent times when the first white settlers arrived. Here, in fact, is one of the first and best-documented examples of the cultural persistence which has allowed peoples living the hunting and food-gathering life of the Stone Age to survive into our modern world. Looking at the flints and other remains of the Wilton peoples who began to pile up their great seaside shell middens at a time when civilization and even farming were unknown throughout the world, suddenly we find them mingling with the copper wire and beads of European traders.

These South African developments are among the outer ripples set up by the changes of the Mesolithic Age; before turning to see what happened nearer the centre, it is necessary to follow another late and peripheral movement of Upper Palaeolithic culture. This is the occupation of America from eastern Asia by peoples who may have had a primitive Caucasian element among them but who undoubtedly in time became predominantly Mongolian (p. 106). It was an event that probably began at about the time when the first blade culture peoples were moving into Africa: there is as yet no certain evidence that our species has been living on the American continent for more than fifteen thousand years.

The route of entry, probably taking advantage of the low sea-level of the last climax of the Wisconsin glaciation, has

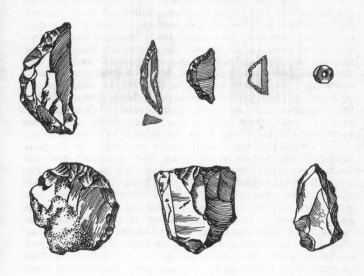

FIG. 11. *Flint implements of the Wilton culture, Northern Rhodesia. Scale 3/4 (after J. G. D. Clark).*

already been discussed. It seems that from Alaska these pioneers followed the Mackenzie river into the northern plains, whence some pushed up the Missouri to cross over into the Snake River valley and so southward on the Pacific side of the mountains, while others used the corridor east of the Rockies (early freed from ice) for their gradual expansion south. The western migrants seem to have swung eastward into the Rio Grande. Equally with all other groups pushing southward and eastward they could have converged upon the bottleneck of Central America before the settlement of the southern subcontinent. The spread of man throughout the New World may have taken up to ten thousand years, for there is some evidence that the extremity of South America was reached about 6000 B C. For us there is something dramatic and moving in the thought of these little groups of hunters setting out to people so vast a realm where no human being had been before them. The feeling persists, even though we know that for them there was no comprehension, only the immediate lure of a coastline, valley or pass, a desire for fresh hunting grounds, and perhaps a trace of that spirit of curious adventure that seems likely soon to lead us on a wild-goose chase to the moon. The newcomers as they spread through northern and Central America appear early to have developed two broadly distinct ways of life, two differing economies, which are inevitably reflected in their material equipment. These two traditions have been distinguished as the Palaeo-eastern and the Palaeo-western.[8] The Rockies roughly divide them, but in the Great Basin area of the south-west United States both are present in equal strength.

The creators of the Palaeo-eastern cultures were big-game hunters whose largest quarry were first mammoth and then bison. Their most characteristic remains are the stone or flint heads from the spears or darts which they probably usually hurled from spear-throwers. Spear-throwers, as we have seen, were used by the Upper Palaeolithic peoples of Europe and they were to have a long history in the Americas, surviving as the *atlatl* into recent times. The lives of the American and of the European hunters of this time, separated by such a vast distance, must have had much in common. Indeed, as we look at photographs of the massive skeletons of mammoth and bison slain by the New World hunters with the spear-heads still lying thrust among them, the imagination seeks to bring them to life by recalling the painting of these beasts, often with spears at their flanks, on the cave walls of France and Spain. Although many of the similarities between these Late Pleistocene hunters of America and Europe were due to a common way of life we shall show that it is not impossible that a real if tenuous historical relationship did in fact exist between them.

The Palaeo-eastern cultures have been distinguished mainly by their projectile points (Fig. 12). As cultures, indeed, they remain flimsy and there is a need for more living sites to be explored before they can be given any solidity and before the real cultural pattern behind them can be established. The earliest at present recognized is the Sandia, named from a cave in New Mexico. Although dating evidence is slight, it may well go back to 12,000 B C or beyond. Next follows the Clovis, in which the distinctive American technique of fluting first appears (p. 248). Points of this type have been found with the remains of mammoth at a number of sites in Arizona, New Mexico and Texas and they are widely distributed elsewhere. They reach north Mexico, Guatemala and Costa Rica. The Folsom culture, with its elegantly fluted points often with a hollow base and little ear-like barbs, was almost certainly derived from the Clovis. Folsom points have often been found embedded in the remains of extinct species of bison (Pl. 1), and the centre of their distribution is the High Plains and the area to the west of them. Both geological evidence and Carbon-14 dating make it reasonably sure that this culture was flourishing by 8000 B C, a time when spreading forest was bringing the big-game-hunting life to an end in Europe and true Mesolithic cultures such as the Maglemosian were developing in response to the change.

While it is impossible here to pursue all the various subdivisions of the Palaeo-eastern hunting peoples of North and Central America (p. 247) something should be said of discoveries made in the Valley of Mexico. Near Tepexpan, about a score of miles north-east from Mexico City, bones of a mammoth (an imperial mammoth, in contrast with the Columban species associated with Clovis points) were found in the silt of a dried lake bed. Between the ribs lay a projectile point. Near by in Santa Isabel Iztapan another elephant was killed with projectile points similar to the Plainview points of the USA. This particular kill was probably made round about 10,000 B C and the spear-head used was of a non-fluted type with a widely scattered distribution extending northwards into Canada. It has been suggested, though at present on quite insufficient evidence, that it may be a weapon type associated with the earliest migrants and diffused by them from the far north down into Middle America. This remains to be proved, but what is certain from the find at Santa Isabel Iztapan is that hunters had carried the Palaeo-eastern cultural tradition as far as the Valley of Mexico before the end of the Pleistocene period.

While the peoples who created and developed the Palaeo-eastern tradition were game-hunters following a life comparable to that of their contemporaries and predecessors in Europe, the economy of the Palaeo-western tradition from the first depended in large part on food-gathering, including the collection of vegetable foods. A major part of the tradition can be distinguished as the Desert culture, a name first used for the Palaeo-western type of cultures of the Great Basin, but now extended to include comparable cultural groups as far south as the Valley of Mexico and as far north as Oregon.

While the centre of gravity of the Palaeo-western tradition is certainly somewhat later than that of the eastern hunters, its beginnings are now realized to be earlier than was once thought. Danger Cave, Utah, for example, was

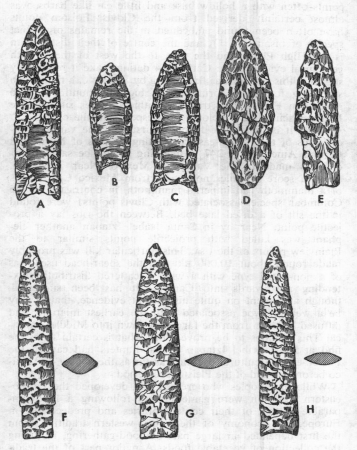

FIG. 12. *Projectile points from North America. A: Clovis point;
B: Folsom point; C: Ohio point (type of eastern United
States); D, E: Sandia points; F: Eden point; G: Scottsbluff point; H: point with oblique flaking. Scale 2/3
(after Wormington).*

probably first occupied by 9000 B C. At this site basketry was already being practised at this time, the oldest known example of it in the world. Thus we begin to see this New World tradition as by no means only a poor and late derivative of the Palaeo-eastern, but one of considerable vigour and originality.

Of its characteristic equipment, it can be said that the projectile point was of less importance than among the hunting easterners. Where it is present it is usually rather smaller, being intended for the killing of smaller game, and forms with side notches or tangs for hafting are common. An early form of tanged point comes from Gypsum Cave, Arizona, while the side-notched type was present at Danger Cave. The troglodytes at the Gypsum Cave had apparently eaten sloth, camel and horse—a warning against any assumption that the Palaeo-western peoples *never* hunted big game. In general in their flint work they made relatively more use of the core than their eastern neighbours; choppers, keeled scrapers and grinding stones were among their most characteristic tools.

Among developed Palaeo-western cultures special mention should be made of the Cochise of the south-west. Although it probably began as early as 7000 B C when mammoth, horse and bison were still being hunted, from the first the extensive use of milling stones shows that the gathering of wild plant foods was an essential part of the economy. The tradition lasted for many thousands of years and is thought at last to have given rise to the Indian cultures known as Mogollon and Hohokam. A counterpart to the Cochise in Central America is the Chalco culture of Mexico.

There is a third cultural grouping within the North American sub-continent deserving mention here: the Palaeo-northern of Alaska and northern Canada. It was first detected on the site of the campus of Alaska University, Fairbanks, and at several Arctic sites, but is now best understood from Iyatayet on Cape Denbigh, Norton Sound, where the industry has been named the Denbigh Flint complex. This complex has some elements, notably a variety of fluted point, probably derived from the Palaeo-eastern tradition to the south, but it is dominated by Mesolithic or persistent Upper Palaeolithic forms reminiscent of the Old World. These include gravers (burins) which have been compared with those found in Mesolithic sites in Siberia and little many-faceted cores from which are struck tiny prismatic blades, or microblades, which also recall techniques found in Siberia and Mongolia. The microblades were made to be fitted into grooved bone points, and both these and the burins are characteristic of prehistoric Eskimo cultures. As we have seen (p. 105) the Eskimo probably originated in the Old World and their cultural traditions were mainly Asian, so that it appears very likely indeed that the Palaeo-northern cultures were introduced into North America by Eskimo immigrants after the original peopling of the New World. This is in harmony with the still tentative dating evidence. Although the Denbigh complex may possibly have been first established as early as 6000 B C it can be considerably later.

The relatively late date of the known Palaeo-northern cultures is one of the difficulties in the way of linking the late glacial hunting cultures of America with those of eastern Asia, whence they must have come. It is not at all impossible that sites along the line of entry in Alaska may now be submerged by the sea. Although a great quantity of new material has been brought to light in Siberia, China and Japan the ages of the various cultures revealed are disputed —estimates differing by as much as ten thousand years. Two contradictory interpretations are current. One that the American projectile point cultures were entirely home-grown—possibly having developed out of the retarded chopping-tool tradition of east Asia. The other, which would appear far more in harmony with the world picture, that the eastward spread of the great Upper Palaeolithic blade and burin cultures into Siberia (Lake Baikal and adjacent regions) took place earlier than is otherwise assumed, and that the settlement of the Americas can be regarded as a yet further thrust from the dynamic expansions of *Homo sapiens* during the final glaciation. Whatever interpretation is accepted at last, it already seems unlikely that close counterparts to the cultures of the earliest American hunters will be found in east Asia. Very much of their achievement belongs to the New World.

The American scene can be allowed to lead into that stage of human history falling between the dying away of the Palaeolithic cultures and the emergence and spread of the Neolithic cultures and rather uneasily distinguished as the Mesolithic phase. For in the sense that they were adaptations to the changing environment of the post-glacial world before the development of agriculture, these later hunting and food-gathering cultures of America can be called Mesolithic. In the sense that they had anything in common with the roughly contemporary cultures that grew out of the Upper Palaeolithic traditions in the Eurasian theatre and in some parts of Africa, they are not Mesolithic. This more limited and more correct use of the title applies to a surprisingly widespread series of cultures in which some of the most characteristic flint and other stone tools were very small (intended for mounting many together in a haft) and often in neat geometric forms (p. 223). This trend towards the use of microlithic flints which was the chief innovation of late glacial and post-glacial times was certainly in part a reaction to the great changes in animal life and vegetation which followed the retreat of the ice, in particular to the spread of forests over the once open hunting lands. The modification of the Gravettian culture in Britain into the Creswellian with its far smaller flints has already been described. Exactly the same dwindling took place in many other Upper Palaeolithic cultures, the Magdalenian, the latest forms of Gravettian and in the Sebilian, Magosian and a number of other African cultures. The usual explanations given are that the new abundance of wood made multiple hafting attractive, the smaller forest animals could be hunted with lighter weapons, and also, perhaps, that large blocks of flint were more difficult to come by. It seems impossible to believe that these causes could operate throughout all the territories in which the dwindling towards microlithic size took place, for some of them were within latitudes where the end of the Ice Age meant desiccation rather than forest growth. However this may be, there is no doubt that this common trend did give a kind of unity to post-glacial cultures or that it was sometimes an independent, indigenous development. There was, however, another influence working in the same direction, spread partly perhaps by actual migrations, more by the borrowing of ideas. The microlithic element in the culture of the Capsians has already been mentioned, and this tradition which involved the manufacture of exact geometric forms (Fig. 22) seems to have influenced in time many of the Mesolithic peoples of Eurasia. Whether the Capsians of Spain and Africa themselves played an important role in originating and diffusing the tradition is not clear, but there are signs that this influence did come from the south into Europe and perhaps south-west Asia.

For the most part, nevertheless, the Mesolithic Age continued the Upper Palaeolithic tendency to develop local cultures, while free movement and group migration among them were probably much less, being discouraged in many regions by forest growth. One very substantial movement, however, there was bound to be: the advance into the habitable parts of northern Europe and Asia which had been covered by ice-sheets.

In France the Magdalenian culture had become the Azilian by pre-Boreal times, and this survived in the more open country of southern and south-western Europe for several millennia. Later, however, other cultures derived from the dying Upper Palaeolithic traditions emerged, important among them the Sauveterrian (formerly known as Lower Tardenoisian) which prevailed over much of France and Britain. Finally Tardenoisian and kindred 'blade and trapeze' cultures became widespread over much of Europe from the Mediterranean to the Low Countries, north-west Germany and south Russia. Although in some sense they represent a late manifestation of Mesolithic culture (they include microlithic forms) it is beginning to be thought that they may have been created by peoples who already possessed some domestic animals—goats and sheep before cattle. If this proves to be so, then we can recognize in them the humble European counterpart to the pre-pottery Neolithic peoples of south-west Asia. Meanwhile the northern territories when first freed from the ice were occupied from Scandinavia to the east Baltic lands by reindeer hunters such as the Hamburgians of north Germany and Denmark who were living still essentially in the tradition of the Upper Palaeolithic and were in part contemporary with the Magdalenians. In pre- and early Boreal times other reindeer hunters developed the Ahrensburg culture of Schleswig-Holstein and the Swiderian which stretched from the Oder to the Volga, through east Prussia, Poland, Lithuania and White and central Russia.[9] In some part of their territory the Swiderians were superseded by the successfully expanding 'blade and trapeze' peoples.

The most interesting and remarkable of the northern cultures were those which developed with the warm weather of full Boreal times (Fig. 13). Peoples who had shared such a Palaeolithic inheritance as the Hamburgian now adapted themselves to a river and seaside life among the forests with determination and vigour; they invented an axe which was effective in felling trees, nets, hooks and all manner of fishing gear; they had good boats and entered into some kind of agreement with the dog for scavenging and hunting. These Maglemosians and their eastern counterpart the Kunda people lived a successful forest life from Denmark to Estonia; they also crossed into eastern Britain, arriving before the rising Boreal seas made it an island about eight thousand years ago. The Maglemosians and Kunda people often decorated objects of bone, antler and amber with chevrons, lozenges and other simple geometric patterns inherited from

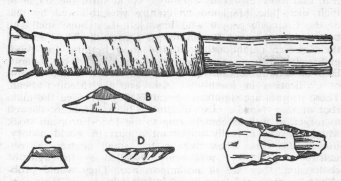

FIG. 13. *Mesolithic implements from Denmark. A: transverse arrow-head, Jutland, Denmark; B: triangle; C: trapeze; D: lunate (microliths); E: transverse arrow-head, Ertebølle, Denmark. Scale 1/1 (after Singer).*

the latest Magdalenian art. They also sometimes engraved highly formalized but quite lively figures of men and animals, and made charming little amber carvings of animals such as bear and elk. Other survivals of naturalistic hunting art are found in the rock carvings of the Norwegian coast stretching up far beyond the Arctic Circle. They were probably the work of hunters who had adapted themselves to sealing and whaling. In the south a group has been distinguished as the Fosna culture, while the northern Komsa culture extends well beyond the Arctic Circle. Both appear to have been introduced from the Baltic by peoples pushing westward round the edge of the ice. The engravings, usually simple outlines on flat slabs of rock, show reindeer and elk, whales and seals. While the Komsa and Fosna cultures date well back into Boreal times, there is no doubt that the tradition of rock engraving lasted for an immensely long time in these last strongholds of the western European hunters;[10] some of the Norwegian engravings probably date from as late as the second millennium B C. Here in these remote northern latitudes was a dim echo of the first great announcement of man's artistic genius made by the Upper Palaeolithic peoples of western Europe.

When seven thousand years ago the moist Atlantic climate caused the northern forests to become yet denser and more difficult to hunt, their inhabitants were forced to concentrate their settlements along salt and fresh-water margins where fish, and more especially shell-fish, could form the staple of their diet. The Maglemosian culture was followed by that of the Ertebølle people who have left their huge shell and bone middens along the shores of Denmark. They and all their eastern neighbours continued their hunting and food-gathering life until they began to be affected by tenuous lines of communication reaching them from the new centres of civilization in south-west Asia and the Mediterranean. These peoples are significant because they provided the main root of that 'Nordic race' which we have not been allowed to forget, as well as contributing to the Indo-European stock which played so really important a part in world history. But at this time when from a few small centres the obscurity of prehistory was being dispelled by the light of civilization, they are of no importance. They would probably have remained 'primitives' indefinitely, as did their contemporaries in South and central Africa and in North America, had they not been within nearer reach of the revolutionary new influences.

Some idea has now been given of the post-glacial world on the periphery of this centre of change and growth. In Europe, Africa, India, eastern Asia and America Palaeolithic hunters have been seen adjusting to the warmer earth they had to live on, sometimes by creating true Mesolithic cultures, sometimes by making rough adjustments in the older tradition. In many places these cultures survived with little change into historic times, in backwaters, such as South Africa with its Smithfield and Wilton cultures, right down to our own world.[11]

It is time now to close in upon the creative centre, the region from which the new way of life was to spread, fast or very slowly, to these peripheral lands. It is probably safe to say that the momentous development from food-taking to food-making was achieved, perhaps with no very sharp point of focus, in an area between four waters: the eastern ends of the Mediterranean, the Black Sea, the Caspian and the Persian Gulf—that is to say, among or on the edge of the uplands surrounding the great Tigris-Euphrates valley where, much later, urban civilization was to be built on the foundations now being prepared.

Although scattered traces of Mesolithic culture have been found over most of this territory, in Palestine, the Lebanon, Syria, Iraq and Iran, they have not as yet begun to tell a coherent story. Among them the Natufian of Palestine is often singled out as of peculiar historical significance; here is a culture whose creators appear to have one foot in the old Mesolithic hunting world, one in the new life of the farmer. These people, who were very fond of ornamenting themselves with necklaces, pendants, shell-bead head-dresses, lived chiefly by hunting and made Mesolithic types of tool. Sometimes the bone and antler hafts had carved animal forms strongly reminiscent of the ancient hunting art. Yet the hafts they carved were for sickles—unmistakable sickles with the gloss of cutting siliceous stems still on them. While it has been supposed that they may have been used for cutting wild grasses, it has also been pointed out that wild crops, falling readily from the ear, are always gathered by beating, and that these glossy sickles must therefore have been used for the reaping of fully cultivated cereals (see p. 366).

In their way of life, still dependent on hunting but reinforced by the harvesting of grain, the Natufians admirably represent the age of transition. So these people, some of whom were buried at the foot of Mount Carmel elaborately decked with fine head-dresses and necklaces, make a fitting subject with which to close a history of the million years during which all mankind knew only the hunting life of the wilderness.

NOTES TO CHAPTER III

1. Professor G. F. Debetz observes that with regard to the classification of the Palaeolithic into Lower, Middle and Upper Palaeolithic, K. J. Narr [*Abriss der Vorgeschichte* (Munich, 1957), pp. 5–6] points out that there are two different ways of classification existing side by side: 'into purely *chronological* stages (valid for the entire area as stratigraphic-chronological units) and *cultural* phases (starting and ending at different times in various areas, and completely lacking in some regions). Some units that were originally seen chronologically eventually turned out to be definable only from the standpoint of cultural phases. . . . This resulted in a good deal of confusion and contradiction: . . . "Middle Palaeolithic" can only be used as a chronological-stratigraphic term, "Mesolithic" as a chronological-stratigraphic one in its early stage, but as a cultural one in its late stage; "Lower" and "Upper Palaeolithic" are ambiguous in both senses. It now seems to have become necessary to effect a clarification, i.e. to distinguish between purely chronological units on one hand and purely cultural ones on the other. This means that one has to use a dual (double-track) terminology. Thus terms that are ambiguous in both senses have to be formulated more specifically: if terms such as "Mesolithic" and "Middle Palaeolithic" are accepted, "Lower" and "Upper Palaeolithic" can only be conceived in a purely chronological-stratigraphic sense . . . . If on the other hand, one keeps to the cultural meaning of the terms, then logically at least the expression "Middle Palaeolithic" would have to be dropped and included in "Lower Palaeolithic".'

K. J. Narr therefore suggests distinguishing between a 'chronological classification' (Lower Palaeolithic, Middle Palaeolithic, Upper Palaeolithic, Mesolithic and Kaenolithic) and a 'cultural classification' (Protolithic, Miolithic, Protoneolithic, Neolithic).

2. Professor G. F. Debetz points out that there is hardly any reason to assume that the 'chopper-chopping-tool complex' spread to Europe from Asia. If there did in fact exist in Europe cultures which can be compared to the 'chopper-chopping-tool complex', it is more likely that these were independent parallel developments. For the time being it can only be establishd that rough flakes and chopping-tools also occur in zones where hand-axes predominate, for instance in Europe; on the other hand, hand-axes are met with, though infrequently, in the province of the 'chopper-chopping-tool complex', for example in Java.

3. The term 'eoliths' (= stones from the dawn of mankind) was introduced by L. Bourgeois in 1863 to denote primitive stone implements ascribed to man of the Tertiary Age. But once the view prevailed that the finds in question were not human artifacts, this term was applied to purely natural products which happened to resemble implements (pseudo-artifacts). Nowadays it appears that in this way some objects have wrongly been termed eoliths in this second sense. On the other hand misunderstandings arise when primitive human artifacts from the Lower Pleistocene are now once more designated eoliths, since at present this term is generally restricted —erroneously—to natural products and pseudo-artifacts.

4. The hand-axe must have been used first and foremost for chopping trees and working wood, or for digging up roots, and must therefore have been connected with cultures in zones of forest vegetation or with warm climatic conditions. In colder climates, as in the tundra, or in the steppe, it may have given way partially or completely to the flaking tools that accompanied it. It is a debatable point whether we can deduce from this the existence of two cultural circles in the earlier Pleistocene (hand-axe and flaking cultures), or whether the flaking cultures are a sign of the impoverishment of the hand-axe cultures conditioned by environmental factors. There is also a number of prehistorians who think that the 'Clactonian' techniques were practised by makers of early hand-axes, e.g. in north Africa, where the Acheul I industries have often been termed 'Clacto-Abbevillian', and 'Levalloisian' by the makers of more evolved Acheulian hand-axes. Again, in some territories, e.g. the Vaal R., South Africa, hand-axes were habitually made from flakes. It is not a matter of distinct cultural traditions so much as alternative techniques. Incidentally, it ought not to be overlooked that H. Warren, the 'inventor of the "Clactonian culture",' has recently expressed his view that the so-called 'cores' of the eponymous site were in reality chopping-tools and that many of the flakes were by-products of the manufacture of such choppers. See K. J. Narr, 'Zur Frage altpalaeolithischer Kulturkreise', *Anthropos* 48 (1953), pp. 773–94.

5. See p. 115, n. 7.

6. It is sometimes maintained that the Abri Audi stage, sandwiched between the Mousterian and Châtelperronian cultures, suggests a transition from the Mousterian to the Châtelperronian in western Europe; at the same time it is pointed out that the Châtelperronian culture in its pure form has so far only been established in France. H. Breuil, on the other hand, argues that there is nothing to show that the Mousterian gradually evolved into the Châtelperronian

along independent lines. He is much more inclined to believe that the Abri Audi stage, which according to him emerged more or less locally, suggests a degenerate Mousterian, already influenced by blade cultures [see H. Breuil, *Les Subdivisions du Paléolithic Supérieur et leur signification* (2nd ed., Lagny, 1937), p. 14]. In this connection it should also be pointed out that there are no indications present in western Europe for the development of the Neanderthal type to *Homo sapiens*. Furthermore, it must be borne in mind that in Asia Minor there exists the Emiran culture, which is akin to Châtelperronian. According to Narr, therefore, the position at present is 'that within the early Upper Palaeolithic complexes of miolithic type the connections extending over vast areas are more prominent than the treads leading back to some such time as the European Protolithic. . . . In order to explain the wealth of miolithic culture in Europe as a European regional continuation of the Protolithic, it would be necessary to presuppose a sharp radical change—which cannot, of course, be ruled out *a priori*, but would be a far more complicated hypothesis than the theory that they originated from other areas.' See *Abriss der Vorgeschichte* (Munich, 1957), p. 13.

7. Dr J. Neustupný emphasizes that in this connection mention must also be made of the Szeletian (named after Szeleta cave in northern Hungary), which may have originated from Lower Palaeolithic forms in central and eastern Europe. Related to the Mousterian, Aurignacian and Gravettian, this is a culture characterized by a large number of leaf-shaped points. See L. Vértes, 'Problematika szeletienu', *Slovenská archeologiá SAV*, IV, 2 (1956), pp. 318–40.

8. Of late there has been some discussion in an endeavour to provide a different interpretation of the split into the Palaeo-eastern and Palaeo-western traditions. The starting-point in this discussion is the fact that, on the basis of the C^{14} dating at Tule Spring (Nevada), we must reckon with the possibility that man penetrated into North America as early as the last interglacial period (before the Wisconsin glacial stage). With this very early immigration late Lower Palaeolithic flake cultures, which were probably widely distributed in north-eastern Asia, are thought to have reached America (offshoots of them may be seen in the Cochise culture in the southeastern USA and northern Mexico). These primitive flake cultures spread fairly rapidly to the extreme south, as is shown by a C^{14} dating to about 6700 B C from the Palli-Aike cave in the region of the Strait of Magellan. In part these flake cultures are believed to have survived for a very long time in various areas of North and South America, their characteristic features being the stone-flaking technique and a primitive mode of existence as food-gatherers.

Some doubt is now cast upon the assumption made hitherto that the appearance of advanced hunter cultures with their characteristic pointed weapons in the course of the Wisconsin glacial stage must be attributed to fresh immigrations. But it is also thought that these cultures in the south of North America may have developed along independent lines. There are various circumstances that support this view. It has not, for instance, been possible to establish really convincing parallels to similar cultures in north-eastern Asia, although there would have to be some there if a fresh immigration had taken place. Moreover, the sites of such hunter cultures in North America seem to be more recent the farther north one goes, a point that tells against the theory of immigration from north to south. Finally, there is already evidence in hand to show that the expansion into Central and South America took place at an early stage. For example, there is the Toldian in the south of the Argentine, labelled by O. Menghin as Late Pleistocene; this may have exerted an influence upon the primitive inhabitants of the Palli-Aike cave in Tierra del Fuego. See A. Varagnac, ed., *L'Homme avant l'écriture* (Paris, 1959), pp. 165–87; O. Menghin, 'Fundamentos cronológicos de la Prehistoria de Patagonia', *Runa V* (Buenos Aires, 1952), pp. 33–43; O. Menghin, 'El Altoparanense', *Ampurias*, XVII/XVIII (Barcelona, 1955–56), pp. 171–200; P. Bosch-Gimpera, 'Asia y América en el palaeolítico inferior. Supervivencias', in *Miscelanea Paul Rivet Octogenario Dicata* (Mexico 1958), I, pp. 49–76; R. S. MacNeish, 'Preliminary Archaeological Investigation in Sierra de Tamaulipas, Mexico', Philosophical Society *Transactions*, N.S. 48, Part 6 (Philadelphia, 1958).

9. On dating and cultural position of the Ahrensburgian and Swiderian culture, see Ch. VI, p. 262, n. 13.

10. The origin of the Komsa and Fosna cultures (jointly also termed Finnmarkian) is still none too clear, but it is probably beyond the bounds of possibility that they originated in the west. The Komsa culture seems to have been introduced from the east along the Arctic shore. Even if the Fosna culture is not derived from it directly, but from offshoots of the Late Upper Palaeolithic Ahrensburgian culture of northern Germany, there is still no reason to assume that it originated in the west. The Ahrensburgian culture, as well as the related and somewhat older Hamburg culture, originated in the east. See Ch. VII, p. 296, n. 2.

11. It may be relevant in this connection to add a few remarks with regard to the value of ethnographical and archaeological analogies. Recognition that an analogy has limits to its usefulness, and may be only partial, is essential; there is a tendency to forget that it *is* only an analogy, and to incorporate it as directly relevant evidence. Sometimes contemporary non-literate peoples are, in effect, treated as if they represented Stone Age man; and material relating to them is used to demonstrate how Stone Age man must have lived. Some archaeologists make use of this sort of analogy, in the absence of any comparable data from their own field; but this is always a procedure to be employed with care. Despite the fact that archaeological evidence tells one little about social structure, or social systems, the criteria used by the author of this part in assessing 'stages of development' (p. 364; also 'stage of social evolution', p. 363) are technological, e.g. stone tools. This in itself contributes to a unilinear view of human social development, to the virtual neglect of other factors which are just as important. It must be emphasized that, according to R. M. Berndt, for example, the identification of Australian aborigines with Stone Age man is a spurious one, since it seizes on a few points of material culture, without paying equal attention to other cultural and social features; and it pushes into the background the similarities between the aborigines and other contemporary living peoples—including ourselves. The same kind of labelling, in what could perhaps be called conceptual shorthand, appears in such statements as that relating to the destruction or absorption by the Mongoloids of 'various older populations' (p. 110). There is a time confusion here, since what is evidently referred to in this and similar examples is the relative length of time one population, as contrasted with another, had been associated with a certain locality: it is a time plus locality

reference, *not* one of 'earlier origin'. As regards the use of analogies, we are confronted by the need for reliable data, as contrasted with the interpretation and evaluation of these data—a problem always particularly relevant where reporting of unfamiliar situations is concerned. Early references are to be treated with extreme caution; and because contemporary published material is often so scattered and so scanty, it may be essential that more than a few sources should be consulted in any reference to them. It is equally essential that personal views should not be taken as statements of more general relevance.

CHAPTER IV

MIND

THE expansion of consciousness is a main theme of history. Nothing has greater significance than the development and exercise of the combined mental powers of intellect and imagination, the two springs of human greatness. This must be the estimate of the humanist; if it were added that it is through these gifts that God has made us aware of divinity, then there are few people in the world who would challenge it.

In man's animal past as one of the primates, the sharpening of sight at the expense of the more lowly sense of smell that went with living in trees contributed to a heightening of mental faculties; only birds, carnivores and primates are equipped with a specially sensitive spot on the retina which provides for great acuteness of eyesight. When to this sharpness of sight the stereoscopic vision was added, while the habit of grasping branches and seizing insects and fruits produced a flexible hand, the way was open for further advance. An ape or monkey fingering at the same time as it scrutinizes some unfamiliar object offers a good symbol for the dawn of both conscious apprehension and skill. Much has sometimes been made of the great importance for human evolution of the hand with its opposable thumb; it was important, certainly, but only as the servant of a waxing brain. The hands of the higher monkeys would be perfectly capable of the finest skills had they a mind to set them to work; monkeys could be watchmakers had they ever conceived the notion of time.

A further stimulus to mental growth was given our ancestors when they left the trees and a mainly vegetarian diet and began to adapt themselves to living in relatively open country and eating meat.[1] It may be that the actual chemical constituents of meat were of benefit to their brains; undoubtedly its nutritive value, so much greater than that of herbs and fruit, relieved them of the necessity of perpetual

eating. More important, the need for a creature with a
relatively flat muzzle and lacking sharp claws or canine
teeth to kill, skin and break up animal food must have led
first to the use and then to the manufacture of tools. Once
manufacture had begun, our forebears had stepped to an
altogether higher plane of concentrated visual attention and
manipulative skill. It may be that the controlled use of the
hand helped to develop another essential human faculty, that
of speech.[2] It has been found that movements of the hand
provoke a sympathetic movement of the mouth, and it may
be that a habit of communicating by gesture helped to in-
duce the controlled emission of sounds.

Here again, however, there is need to be chary in any
recognition of cause and effect. Just as monkeys and some
other primates have hands capable of executing skilful tasks
were their brains equal to it, so, too, their lips, palate and
vocal chords are probably capable of speech. It is the brain
power that is lacking. It is easy to say that the need for
acute vision, the ability to manipulate, the necessity of cutting
up meat, the purposeful concentration required to make tools
all led to the multiplication of brain cells in hominid and
human skulls, while each multiplication of cells led in turn
to a further advance in functions. To this we can add the
further idea favoured by many biologists that 'man is a
foetalized ape', that is to say that the direction of human
evolution was towards resembling the young and not the
mature primate, and that this postponing of physical ma-
turity gave opportunity for a longer period of learning and
experiment and further increase in brain size. All this interplay of cause and effect can be made to seem very convincing after the event. Yet we should remember that for
thousands of years the Egyptians seemed to have very good
reason for thinking that the rising of Sirius caused the Nile
to flood. It may be that the ultimate cause of the waxing
of the human brain, of the expanding of consciousness within it, remains as remote from our knowledge as the mountain sources of the Nile were to the Egyptians.

If causes are best treated with caution, there is no doubt
that the strengthening of mental power came with the vast
expansion of the cerebral cortex of New Brain in man. The
two hollow hemispheres of the human cerebrum are so large
that they have become deeply folded and convoluted to
house them within the plates of the skull. The great size of
the frontal and temporal lobes is particularly characteristic
of man, and they include among their millions of nerve cells
many groups not enslaved to exact functions but with the

storing of memories and their association. Memory, association, leading to image-making powers, these are the capacities necessary for full self-consciousness, for the awareness of past and future, intelligent anticipation and the building of traditions to bind the long life of the race. There is a sequence in the functioning of memory that can be seen passing from the biological into the cultural realm. First the cerebral storing of innumerable items of experience, then their concentration into images that begins the breakdown of the wholeness of experience and hence to the control of life's matrix; next the formation of fixed symbols and more especially the sound symbols of language that make it possible to sharpen the identity of things by the giving of names and to transfer memories and images from one living human being to another. Finally the invention of writing that extends memory outside the living group to all generations of all mankind. By these means what started with the momentary experiences of single individuals may be built into a great and long-lived cultural tradition.

The self-consciousness that intensified with the elaboration of the cerebral cortex, making man more and more aware of his actions and of his separation from nature, was to take two main and opposing directions. One was towards controlling the environment. This led immediately to tool-making and then on to the whole accelerating course of our technical and scientific advance. Here analysis, the breaking down of the whole into manageable parts, has been the means, and the ends are wholly practical and material. The other direction is towards reuniting the part with the whole, man with the universe from which his consciousness seemed to divide him. This way led to ritual, art, religious faith, mysticism and some aspects of philosophy. Metaphor, simile, symbolical enactments and other unifying forms have been the means, and the ends, essentially, are not practical or material.

The very evident weakness of archaeology as a proper basis for history is its helpless dependence on material remains and the resulting tendency to over-emphasize the first of these two great ways of human endeavour. Thus, for example, it is not until the sudden appearance of art and ritual burial towards the end of the Palaeolithic Age that we have anything beyond the faintest hint of man's inner, unifying existence although undoubtedly this must have been increasing and refining even while in his extraverted and practical life man went from battering pebbles to shaping a hand-axe. We can assume at the intellectual level a growing ability to categorize and to draw conclusions from the past for the benefit of the future. At the imaginative level there must have been mounting power to picture things (and particularly objects of desire such as game animals) when they were not before the eyes, comparable to the ability to visualize the completed tool within the unshaped block of stone. The beautiful shape of the hand-axe itself can, indeed, be used as a proof of the early emergence of an aesthetic sense. It has even been suggested that the finest of these tools, those which seem so much more exquisitely worked than practical necessity demanded, may have become cult objects like the ceremonial axes of the Caledonian islanders or the very unwarlike silver maces often brought out on state occasions in western Europe.

Whether or not these implements came to possess some special imaginative significance or *mana*, their satisfying proportions show that already a quarter of a million years ago the imaginative mind had its own sense of rightness in pure form which, whatever its source, still holds good for us today.

Consideration of the source of these aesthetic judgements leads to the question of inherent mental patterns of all kinds. It may well be that man's feeling that certain proportions are right or beautiful has always been derived from his participation in the natural world, animate and inanimate, organic and mathematical, from which he emerged. But beyond that there is a widely held and also strongly contested view that human beings are born with certain innate mental forms which have come into being through the experience of the evolving species. They are inherited just as the similarly evolved bodily parts are inherited, but as they are mental they tend to be expressed in cultural forms, most obviously in religious myths, which although they differ in outward form with the tone of the culture concerned, often appear to have an underlying unity that is worldwide and timeless.[3] These archetypes might correspond on a higher, more complex plane to the undoubtedly innate sense of aesthetic rightness and such universal tendencies as the grotesque in art, animal forms, dragons and other recurrent artistic manifestations.

Although many people cannot accept this idea of the inheritance of mental forms, it is surely far more likely than that we are born with a mental *carte blanche*. At the level of instinct we accept the idea readily enough, even though the instinctual bequest from the past may be highly complicated. Weaver birds, for example, after six generations of having been reared among other birds and deprived of their own proper nesting material, can still in the seventh generation weave their ingenious nests when given the opportunity. At some time in the remote past this species gradually perfected a most unusual form of dwelling construction, and the pattern for it has become fixed in the brain and central nervous system so that it can be repeated at any time by reference to this 'instinctive' pattern book. Surely, then, it cannot be impossible for man to inherit patterns at a more imaginative level from the repetitive experience of twenty thousand generations? Or, having inherited them, that he should find expression for them in myths and other cultural forms?

At least the possibility is strong enough for it to be unscientific to ignore it, particularly when considering the diffusion of cultural traits. When two peoples at some distance from one another possess some peculiar implement, design, myth, in common it may well have been transferred by trade, migration or a spreading influence. These contacts should always be looked for, but if they cannot be detected, then there remains the alternative that the trait represents two independent expressions of a common mental pattern.

Whether or not human beings inherit mental furniture of this kind, there is no doubt that we bring with us from the past very much more than our bodily parts. Forty thousand years after the death of the last Neanderthaler, *Homo sapiens* still carries with him a most powerful inheritance of passions and emotional tendencies acquired through the ages. Even inquisitiveness, the desire to explore, is an emotion proved to exist already in animals. Some modern men have liked to think of themselves as wholly rational and their fellows as potentially so, yet others have concluded that our species is never capable of carrying out a rationally formed intention. The whole course of human history in which so many great peoples have hurled themselves to self-destruction, seems in many ways to support this second point of view. Some rationalists might be happier to have it otherwise, but if we lost our emotional inheritance with its energetic power to galvanize the imagination, the whole creative life of our kind would soon be withered, parched as a mummy.

The mental history of this vast formative time of humanity resulted in the emergence of language, of art and religion and of technical skills and primitive science. The other achievements will be discussed in subsequent chapters, but spoken language, a purely mental manifestation which has left us no material embodiment, deserves a place in this more general account of the development of mind.

The new mode of inheritance that came with the spoken word has as much claim to be the distinguishing mark of humanity as the ability to make tools. Without it all cultural progress had to be empirical, all instruction of the new generation entirely by practical example. It has, indeed, been said that 'speech is the correlative of the tool', and that 'man seems to have started to use some form of language at the same time that he learnt to fabricate tools'.

Yet there is no absolute justification for this association; no more than that the intelligent use of hand and eye in manufacture was one part of the general sharpening of faculties which made speech possible. It cannot be too much insisted upon that language and its voiced expression were an invention; they are not innate in the human species as are the songs of birds or the calls of animals. If a child were brought up in silence, it would not produce any articulate speech; there is even some evidence to suggest that if a child is not in a position to learn to talk at the normal time, in the second and third year after the period of free babbling, it is immensely difficult for it to learn at all. The complementary aspect of these facts is, of course, that any baby reared in a foreign land will learn the language of its adopted country perfectly. An Eskimo baby would readily learn to speak Parisian French, a Parisian one an Eskimo dialect.

The genesis of spoken language remains obscure. We do not know why or how the great invention began. Apes have a considerable range of emotional cries, and are given to dancing and rhythmical drumming to express mood. The white-faced gibbon is said to sing by moonlight and at dawn. Apes can also, though laboriously, be taught to enunciate a word or two. Yet they have never themselves taken the first step towards articulate speech. To the question why man did so we can only revert to the old shuffling of cause and effect and say that it was due to his growing brain power, to the associative capacity of his huge cerebrum. To the question how, though nothing can be proved, it is possible at least to attempt a factual answer.

The most coherent account of the origin of spoken language which has been devised claims that the first symbolic sounds were uttered as the accompaniment of gestures, particularly of gestures of the hand. The supporters of this theory point to the sympathy existing between hand and mouth which shows itself in such things as the movements of a child's tongue during writing, or gesturing as an ac-

companiment to talking. Apes also often synchronize movements of the hands and lips. Certainly, too, primitive peoples
such as some of the Australian and North American Indian
tribes still maintain a fairly exact sign language which may
be a development from an early mode of communication.
The Arunta, for example, have such a language with over
four hundred and fifty signs made by the hands and arms.
A means of communication by a kind of general pantomime is employed by the uneducated born deaf and seems
to be universally understood; it might be said to be the
one form of symbolic communication which really is natural to our kind.

The history of the emergence of language and speech,
then, put forward by those who believe that the symbolic
sound was at first secondary to symbolic gesture, implies
this sequence. First a stage of general pantomime with a
subsidiary accompaniment of mouth babble. The babble
might sometimes give rise to established 'holophrases' or
conglomerations of syllables meaningless in themselves but
together expressive of a particular state or happening. Secondly a stage in which pantomime and babble began to
give way to more precise gestures associated with correspondingly more precise sound symbols or words. In this
stage the beginning of directed thought can be assumed.
The third stage sees the complete supercession of pantomime
and babble by systematized signs and words. While in the
more progressive societies gesture symbols and holophrases
were abandoned, in others they have been retained until
this day. Sign languages have already been discussed; an
often quoted example of a surviving holophrase comes from
Fuegans, among whom *mamihlapinatapai* is said to signify,
'the state or event of two persons each looking at the other
and hoping he will do something that both desire but are
unwilling to undertake'.

Once the third phase was reached, the isolation of individual items or objects of experience had been achieved
and analytical thought made possible. From that time language was likely to flower rapidly, with syntax, vocabulary,
and such special categories as numeration keeping step with
general cultural development towards increasing abundance
and complexity. Some support for the derivation of speech
from gesture is provided by the anatomy of our brains.
There is no precise speech centre; instead it is controlled
from a large cortical area extending from just in front of
the visual area, across the auditory to the edge of the motor
region. This area is always found in the left hemisphere in

right-handed individuals and in the right among the left-handed.

The result of isolation by naming is of special importance. The uneducated born deaf (who offer a fair analogy in certain respects to mankind before language) are unable to break down the world confronting them; they experience life as a continuous procession of total events, and their attempt to communicate leads to a miming of these unanalysed events. Individuals in this position can remember but cannot reason logically and are therefore most unlikely to be inventive. The story has often been told of how Helen Keller, blind, deaf and dumb, was suddenly reached in her dark silence and made to realize that 'everything had a name'. From this fateful moment when her governess held her hand below a tap and repeated once again the sign for water, her mind began to apprehend the world about her and she was soon in full symbolic communication with her fellows. Mankind made this same step towards isolation and control through naming, but infinitely more slowly than Helen Keller for there was no governess in his primeval world, and every sound symbol had to be shaped, remembered, transmitted by individuals who could not at first know what they were doing.

Even if the theory of the origin of speech from gestures is not accepted, the sequence of development from free babbling through holophrases to increasingly exact word sounds must be somewhere near the truth. Whether it was a process which, like most inventions, took place in one region and then spread to other societies, or whether it occurred in many centres independently is unknown. Certainly the great number of distinct language groups show that the later stages of development took place among many isolated societies. The legend of the Tower of Babel presents the opposite of the truth. Today there are no living languages as simple and undeveloped as those of the earlier Palaeolithic hunters are likely to have been. Nevertheless some, such as the numerous aboriginal tongues of Australia, are believed to include genuinely primitive traits, and the existence of languages in varying stages of development has helped to suggest the historical development of word sounds.

Young children of all linguistic groups are found to master the different consonantal and vowel sounds in a closely comparable order. This progression begins after the end of the babbling age when all possible sounds are used haphazardly. All over the world at the succeeding stage infants learn first to distinguish and sound the vowel *a* and the consonant *m,* and then the consonants *m* and *p.* Hence the widespread occurrence of words resembling *papa* and *mama* for the first object to be distinguished in the dawning mind —the parents. The vowels *a, i* and either *e* or *u* are established before the others, and certain primitive tongues use only these three vowels. Again certain sounds such as the sibilants *s* and *sh* and the fricatives *f* and *th* are among the last to be mastered by children and are absent in many of the languages of Oceania, Africa and America. A more general rule is that consonants formed in the throat do not come under the child's control until after those formed by lips, tongue or teeth, a sequence reflected in the universal presence of front (mouth) consonants in all languages while in the more primitive back consonants are lacking.[4]

Confirmation of this ordered emergence of symbolic sounds is provided by aphasiacs suffering from progressive lesions of the brain. These unfortunates lose control of sounds in precisely the reverse order to that in which children gain it; if they are healed the order of relearning repeats the childish one. Thus it seems to be proved beyond reasonable doubt that the sound sequence repeated by young children, aphasiacs and the languages of the world broadly represents the order in which word sounds were established during and after the third of the theoretical stages already proposed for man's first invention of language. Just as the foetus recapitulates some of the steps of our bodily evolution so each baby generation repeats the steps by which its remote ancestors gradually won the power of speech on a hitherto wordless planet.

At what time in our history did men take these first steps? Many different answers are given to this question, and it seems unlikely that we shall ever know which is correct. Probably from the beginning of tool-making early in Pleistocene times Palaeolithic man communicated by sounds more explicit than those of the apes; perhaps by holophrases expressing total states or events. It has been pointed out that individuals in this condition, like the uneducated born deaf, are unable to use such undifferentiated blocks of experience for conceptual thought and are therefore unlikely to make inventions except by happy chance. In the Lower Palaeolithic period the hand-axe, although it was gradually improved, remained in use as the dominant tool form for over a quarter of a million years. It has been argued, and cogently, that this almost unimaginable slowness of change demonstrates a lack of inventiveness that could only survive among societies without fully articulate speech.

The Middle Palaeolithic cultures achieved some more rapid
changes if no very important advance; with the Upper Palaeolithic there was a rapid acceleration, marked by a purposeful elaboration of specialized tools and weapons (p. 217) and
the birth of a visual art in command of almost all the
techniques practised today (p. 272). Even the most dispassionate estimate of the Upper Palaeolithic phase cannot
fail to reveal it as the time when man first seemed to take
a grip of himself and his surroundings and lay the necessary foundations on which, with such astonishing speed,
civilization was to be built. It is most likely that a most
important factor within this new awareness, this new sense
of purpose, was that the latest Palaeolithic hunters had at
last succeeded in bringing speech to a point where the precise naming of things and the elementary discussion of ideas
had become possible.

An alternative interpretation allows a rather higher capacity for speech to Lower Palaeolithic man but delays the
moment of revolutionary progress until the Neolithic Age
when a settled life, more stratified society and greater numbers of possessions provided an obvious incentive, while at
the same time suggesting sharpened mental powers. This
point of view has its adherents, but on balance the evidence
would seem to support the opinion that it was during the
last glaciation that men first learnt to talk coherently together, to discuss simple problems, make plans, and pass
on their accumulating lore to their children.

This is not to deny that the great social changes of Neolithic times had a powerful effect upon language. Vocabularies must have been quickly enlarged, most of all by the
words devised by potters, weavers and specialists of all kinds.
Words for counting up to high numbers would also have
to be invented; it has been found that hunting peoples
seldom have words for numbers above a very few; numeration was needed only when more sedentary peoples began
to produce a surplus of goods.

Nothing has been said of the speech of hominids other
than *Homo sapiens*. While probably the earliest *Pithecanthropi* made even less progress in language than their more
highbrow contemporaries, as even apes are anatomically
capable of uttering words, there is no reason to doubt that
so skilled a tool-maker as Neanderthal man was possessed
of at least a rudimentary language. On the other hand his
conspicuous lack of inventiveness suggests that it was not
far advanced; failure to develop a fully articulate language

may have been one of the cultural handicaps leading to his final submergence.

It is interesting to consider how far language reflects the nature of the culture to which it belongs. Tongues are notoriously easily imposed and assimilated, being transferred by conquest, cultural dominance and migration. Nevertheless, many are still spoken by the racial or cultural groups in whose mouths they were formed, and it is always permissible to seek in them the distinctive cultural flavour of their creators. The Latin, Chinese and Arabic linguistic groups have strongly contrasting grammatical systems: do they express the spirit of their peoples? Many have claimed that they do, but such judgements must always be subjective. It is certainly reasonable to say that while the Indo-European languages were originally of great grammatical complexity, the leading European tongues have all been severely simplified as a result of their long use in the service of abstract thought.[5]

When it comes to vocabularies, a close connection with culture is obvious and inevitable. The Arunta tongue of Australia, in many ways poor and primitive, is wonderfully rich in kinship and ceremonial terms—a reflection of the tribe's preoccupation with family relationship and totemic ritual. Turning to the opposite extreme of development, the English pride themselves on being well equipped to speak of home, the French of love.

A recent discovery of brain science may prove to be of at least indirect linguistic significance. Differences in the electrical rhythms of the brain cells have been found to divide individuals into two principal types: those who tend to think in visual images, and those whose thought is largely verbal. Evidently, then, these two modes indicate some profound mental distinction. May it be that peoples who, like the Japanese, have an exquisite sense of the visual arts and crafts while seeming somewhat uninterested in logical thought and means for its expression, include a high proportion of individuals who think in images, while European and other western peoples who have a passion for abstract thought and have shaped their language to its needs, contain a correspondingly high proportion of verbal thinkers?[6]

One further aspect of speech and language deserves a few words. Man has always been a gregarious species, and this must have been of the utmost importance in the earlier stage of language formation. If, as is assumed (p. 190), the hunting group usually acted under a leader, words of command to control behaviour must have been among the first to be established. But if group life helped to develop speech, at a later stage the possession of a common tongue undoubtedly helped to consolidate and isolate the social group, however large or small. Ever since languages proliferated, the other man's incomprehensibility has made him a foreigner.[7]

NOTES TO CHAPTER IV

1. Professor A. C. Blanc points out that many authors have challenged the view that our ancestors left the trees and only then began to adapt themselves to living in relatively open country; instead, they consider that life in trees of apes is a form of specialization which the human species never went through.

2. Professor G. F. Debetz suggests that the use of the hand in the process of labour activity and of the practical transformation of objects of nature for the purpose of satisfying the material requirements of man conditioned the formation and development of his spiritual faculties: thinking, attention, memory; it complicated and improved such psychic functions as sensation and perception. And our ancestors' requirements for communication, ensuing from joint activities, conditioned inevitably the beginning and development of speech.

3. Professor G. F. Debetz doubts that 'mental forms' constituting the contents of our consciousness are inherited. While adhering to established facts of science, one should, according to him, admit that only physiological mechanisms of thinking and consciousness as a whole are inherited, but not concrete notions or ideas.

4. On this approach W. C. Sturtevant makes the following comment:
    'The order of differentiation given here is *not* universal. Iroquoian languages, for example, lack *m* and *p*, hence Iroquois children do not "distinguish" between *a* and *m* or *m* and *p*. The statements as to *s, sh, f, th,* and the vowels are open to similar objections with regard to other languages. It must also be said that the vowel system of languages differs. Some Caucasian languages have only *one* vowel; others have a dozen or more. A language with three vowels—or one or twenty—or a language lacking *s, sh, f,* or *th,* is in *no* sense "more primitive" than any other. French lacks *th*; English and most west European languages lack *ł*, a voiceless *l* which is present in Welsh and many other areas of the world (it is especially common in North American Indian languages). But this does not make French more primitive than English, or English more primitive than Welsh or Navaho.
    'The "universal presence of front (mouth) consonants" is at least debatable. Such statements are impossible to prove—the next previously undescribed language to be analysed may prove them to be wrong, and it is impossible to search all the literature at present available. "Back" consonants are present or absent without regard to the "primitiveness" of the speakers or the language. English and French lack the German and Scottish *ch*, a back consonant which also has a spotty distribution elsewhere. Arabic has back stop consonants lacking in western Europe. Such facts have nothing to do with the development of language. The statements of the author about young children and aphasiacs may or may not be relevant;

and most linguists would deny that any such distinction can be made with regard to "primitive" and "advanced" modern languages.'

5. Dr W. C. Sturtevant points out in this connection that grammatical change has occurred in western Europe as it has everywhere else. Whether or not it has been simplified here is debatable; many who think so say also that the change took place in the direction of Chinese, which they believe to have a 'simpler' grammar. This has certainly nothing to do with any supposed advantage possessed by Indo-European speakers over Chinese or Arabic speakers in capacity for abstract thought. Consider the situation as it was in about AD 1300 or 1400—would not an objective observer have then considered Arabic and Chinese cultures more 'advanced' and capable of abstract thought than any Indo-European cultures, except perhaps that of India? The structures of the respective languages were then essentially the same as they are today.

6. Dr W. C. Sturtevant feels that the contrast drawn between the Japanese on one hand and Europeans and other western peoples on the other as regards their capacity for logical thought is not necessarily valid. The fact that, for example, Zen Buddhist thought is not comprehensible to most western Europeans because it is so different from European philosophy is surely not an argument in favour of the view that the Japanese do not think logically.

7. Professor G. F. Debetz considers that the relationship of man and his environment, and the forms of social labour which develop in the course of this relationship, are fundamental in determining the progress of early man in such basic aspects as the manufacture of tools and weapons, the construction of dwellings, the development of speech, artistic creation, and even the rise of religion. It was through work that the consciousness of man was moulded, that speech and art came into being: the mutual relations between man and nature, related to the character and level of the development of labour, could have exercised a decisive influence also on the rise of religion and on its elementary forms.

CHAPTER V

SOCIETY

THE gradual, continuous emergence of the human body and the human mind from their animal ancestry has already been traced. It remains to watch artificially created, traditionally inherited forms of society growing from origins as little artificial and as little traditional as the animal family, pack or herd: body, mind and society, the trinity from which culture has grown.

Without society man's mental powers could never have matured—their transmission remains dependent upon it. This is obvious enough. What is perhaps more often overlooked is the individual's helpless dependence upon social tradition; without education into that tradition even the most innately gifted would remain seemingly idiotic. The born deaf are incapable of conceptual thought until reached—rescued—by their fellows; children who have grown up in the wilds or in solitary confinement appear to be hardly human and, as has been said, may never gain full mastery of language. Mozart, had he been born deaf, might have been living a moron's life at five years old instead of performing before the courts of Europe.

The forms of social life in which human intelligence and full consciousness were first incubated must have been of the simplest, having more in common with the family than with our extended social structures. The stages by which they emerged from those of the natural animal community are inevitably far more difficult to trace than the stages of man's bodily evolution. Archaeological evidence is so slight that we have to depend almost entirely on comparisons; on the one hand with animal species most nearly related to the hominids and on the other with the seemingly most primitive surviving societies of hunters and food-gatherers. Both these sources of evidence are plainly unreliable, particularly analogies drawn from modern 'primitives' who may have changed considerably in social structure even if their cultures still seem to belong to the Stone Age. Nevertheless, it is reasonable to suppose that these surviving hunting societies are examples of an extension of the slowness of change characteristic of prehistoric times and that they are therefore likely to preserve social tendencies once universal among mankind.

For the beginnings of human society, the habits of the great apes should offer the most useful comparisons. Surprisingly, our knowledge of the social life of these fellow primates in their wild state is incomplete and disputed. The African apes, the gorilla and chimpanzee, seem normally to live throughout the year in kindred groups numbering from a dozen to a score. Chimpanzees, however, may occasionally form much larger companies. The group seems to be to some extent dominated by one or more powerful adult males; yet at the same time the females with their young of various ages form a company of their own within the group, spending much of their time apart from the males.

Undoubtedly the long period of helplessness and immaturity so distinctive of young primates and human children was as vital to the development of society as it was to the development of the brain (p. 165). For many months the young ape clings to its mother, and cannot fend for itself until after it is three years old; it remains sexually immature until its tenth year.

When our forebears left the forests and began game-hunting in more open country the size of the group is likely to have enlarged and its social co-operation to have intensified. While in an arboreal life each individual could readily pick up food for itself, game-hunting is enormously more effective if undertaken as a corporate effort. Baboons, the other primates that have taken to the ground and to flesh-eating, live in large communities and have been observed to hunt together, sometimes even forming a ring and closing in on their quarry.

As for the sexual and domestic aspects of the social life of the earliest men, opinion differs sharply. It has often been claimed (and the claim is still repeated) that the great apes normally mate for life and monogamously. This piece of wishful thinking has been quite certainly disproved. Gorillas, chimpanzees and orang-utans are undoubtedly polygamous, the successful males having possession of all or several of the females in their band. On the other hand the fact that the apes resemble man in having no limited rutting season and are willing and able for sexual relations throughout most of the year, must encourage the closely knit kindred group even as it militates against brief seasonal mating and the seasonal and wholly promiscuous life of the herd. When man emerged from among the primates it was to make monogamy a possible, though by no means a necessary, ideal.

The practice of exogamy, or marriage outside the individual's clan or other immediate social group, is almost as universally prevalent among primitive peoples as is the horror of incest among all mankind. What is regarded as incest, it must be remembered, depends entirely on the type of social structure. There are highly moral societies where the marriage of a brother and sister is permissible while the marriage of distant cousins belonging to the same clan is a horrifying sin. How did the various exogamous systems and the sense of incestuous sin grow from a group life assumed to be comparable to that of the apes?

One explanation has had many followers from Darwin to Freud. This is based on an interpretation of the natural primate family group as being dominated by the most powerful adult males who have possession of the females and keep the young males from them. The deprived sons then leave their group to capture or attract females of another group either to join them or to found a new group free from the tyranny of the old fathers. With mankind this habit of seeking a mate outside the group becomes a custom and then a social and moral law whose non-observance leads to sin and guilt.

An alternative explanation depends on the contrary view that the primate family was essentially matriarchal, based on a lasting and indissoluble association of mothers and daughters. The sons would then slip away from the jealous and possessive mothers, sometimes merely making surreptitious visits to the young females of other groups, sometimes taking up residence with them under the awe-inspiring eye of the mother-in-law. While both these interpretations are over-simplified and exaggerated, studies of primate life, particularly among Japanese monkeys, have shown that both could contain elements of truth. Most of all, however, these studies have warned us against generalizations by showing that there is a wide range of social patterns, not only between species, but even within species according to local circumstance.

It appears that dominance among the males depends on seniority. When younger males become mature enough to seek independence from the male elders, they frequently form sub-groups, going about with their own females and tending to avoid the old leaders. (It has not yet been estab-

lished whether mature males who remain in their groups are
barred from intercourse with their mothers.) On the other
hand in one instance a young male monkey who had always
enjoyed high status as the offspring of a dominant mother
remained at the centre of his group and was able to take
over the leadership directly. Yet another closely observed
group of Japanese monkeys had no male leaders, the status
of the offspring depending on that of the mothers. This
group was joined by two males coming from outside.

How important the defence of territory is among the
primates is uncertain. Some authorities go so far as to
claim that it plays a greater part in maintaining group
solidarity than do sexual relationships. With redtail monkeys
small kindred units are able to move freely within a territory
held in common—an arrangement similar to that shown in
the hunting groups and tribes of Australia (p. 183).

While it seems to be confirmed that in its power aspect
the structure of most primate society depends on the dominant male elders, the closer and more continuous coherence
of the females and their young is of profound significance.
It might well be that when among the early hominids possessions and a home base began to gain in importance, this
mother-dominated sector of society would have increased
its influence. Today it is unfashionable to talk about former
more matriarchial orders of society. Nevertheless, there is
evidence from many parts of the world that the role of
women has weakened since earlier times in several sections
of social structure.[1]

So against the exacting climatic background of Late
Pliocene and Pleistocene times we have to picture animal
behaviour evolving into social conduct; kindred groups becoming the exogamous clan within the tribe; instincts and
habits of sexual intercourse and mating being more and more
artificially directed and circumscribed until any infringement
of the code gave rise to a social interplay of condemnation
and guilt. All these steps from natural animal life with its
predominantly biologically inherited patterns to traditionally
acquired and consciously enforced social organization must
have been taken so gradually over the hundreds of thousands
of years available that there was no kind of break between
them. At no point in time, even though the point were allowed to cover several millennia, would it have been possible to say, 'This is no longer the animal family or horde
but society; this is no longer mating but marriage; this is
no longer male and female but husband and wife'.

Archaeological evidence for the emergence of human

society before the Upper Palaeolithic Age is necessarily exiguous. The relative abundance within limited areas of the
remains of *Australopithecus* suggests that these little ape-
men lived in bands of some size; the more dubious evidence that they were successful hunters of baboon and other
agile game would speak for cunning co-operation in the
chase and perhaps specialization of the males as hunters.
The caves at Choukoutien with their relics of men, women
and children (as we can now call them in respect of their
status as hominids) suggest family life of a kind, strengthened
by the occupation of a chosen dwelling and sharply de-
marcated from the surrounding tide of animal life by the
possession of the hearth fire. The ability of these men to
kill deer must now more surely than with the Australopithecines be taken as proof of the organized hunting party,
while the gathering of hackberries may very well have been
a task undertaken by the women.

A special social problem is posed by the very strong
evidence at Choukoutien for cannibalism: several of the
skulls were broken in a way that suggested the individual
had met a violent death and the skull been opened for the
removal of the brain. Cannibalism is of very many kinds,
sometimes ritual, sometimes frankly indulged in to satisfy a
taste for human flesh sometimes induced by necessity. Some
primitive peoples have been recorded to eat their dead as
the most respectful form of disposal, some again to kill their
old people of necessity and eat them for respect and wisdom.
The skulls at Peking, however, rather suggest that this was
not domestic cannibalism of any kind, but a killing of individuals belonging to other groups. If this is so, then already
by the second interglacial age men were recognizing members of their own species as enemies outside society and fit
to be eaten.

It would be of immense interest to know whether the
social organization of the more progressive races on the
Neanthropic wing of advance differed from that of the
Pithecanthropi. The Acheulian occupation of the Tabun
cave on Mount Carmel with its hearths and litter of food
bones is not in this respect to be distinguished from
Choukoutien. The famous Acheulian site of Orgesailie in
Kenya was an open-air encampment beside a lake in the
Great Rift valley. There were no surviving traces of either
substantial shelters or of hearths. It is only perhaps worth
reflecting at this point that while the haphazard tools of
Peking man (p. 239) look as though they might usually
have been made at the moment they were wanted, Acheulian

hand-axes, and the chipped stone balls found at Orgesailie and thought to have been joined by thongs for use as bolas (p. 118), must have been made deliberately and in advance of need. At Crayford in Kent a flint-working floor was found where Levalloisian knappers had flaked great numbers of tools at some time during the last interglacial phase. It was a regular workshop. Thus although there is not likely as yet to have been much specialization of occupation, every man making his own tools, there must have been a very real specialization in the use of time, with hours or days set aside for the labour of manufacture.

Before passing on to the Upper Palaeolithic and Mesolithic population whose social structure can best be considered in relation to that of modern hunting peoples, something should be said of the Neanderthal breed, living in the forward-looking era of the Upper Pleistocene yet physically so retrograde. The intensely cold climate in which they lived during the latter part of their dominance drove them wherever possible to be cave-dwellers. Such harsh conditions may perhaps have reduced the normal size of the social group and knit it closer together. There are a few hints that among these creatures the family bond was more strongly developed than it had ever been before. Ceremonial burial, the interment of food and weapons with the dead, which is found first among the Neanderthalers, suggests a heightening of family and social feeling. Notions of the dead living on, the wish to provide for them, mean that they have an emotional survival in the minds of the living. That is where the after-life takes place. It is true that provision made for the dead may be to appease dangerous ghosts, but the fact that a young child could be buried with as much care and ceremony as any adult should mean that an emotional bond was paramount.

The Neanderthalers were brave hunters, going out successfully after mammoth and rhinoceros and therefore presumably working together. They, like *Pithecanthropus,* appear to have been cannibals with a strong partiality for brains.

There is very good reason to guess that among the advantages enabling the Aurignacian and other Upper Palaeolithic people to oust the Neanderthalers was a superior social organization. We know they had better tools and weapons and have supposed them to possess a more effective language: it is most likely that they would also have formed much larger social units, with a considerable tribe that could be rallied under some form of central leadership. Most of the peoples who have maintained a hunting economy into modern times have a more or less complicated system of clans within the larger body of the tribe. In Australia, where a Stone Age way of life survived intact into the eighteenth century, there were some three to five hundred tribes in all, each with its own dialect or distinct language. The normal living unit was of twenty or thirty individuals (among the Tasmanians smaller still), but they would meet together for jamborees at times of year when food was plentiful and the whole tribe would confirm its unity through feasting and dancing. Even the tribes themselves had a few bonds that might draw them into a loose confederation. A rather similar state of affairs existed in North America, with an even more bewildering number of tribal languages, proving a long period of isolated evolution even among neighbours and confederates.

It is impossible from archaeological evidence to detect the existence of tribal units. Most of the cultures described in Chapter III are evidently too big to represent any kind of coherent social organization; the Aurignacian and Maglemosian, for example, would have been united only by a general cultural inheritance such as would have been common over vast territories in Australia. Conceivably we may in time be able to detect tribal division within these larger cultural patterns; it has already been tentatively suggested that Mesolithic Britain can be split into five tribal areas. Again it is possible that a very clearly defined invasion of new traditions into a limited area such as that of the Solutreans into western Europe may represent a movement with as much social solidarity as that of the peoples of the folk migrations during the European Dark Ages.

As for total numbers, they would still have been very small. Although such inventions as the spear-thrower and bow and arrows would certainly have appreciably increased the food-winning capacity of the most advanced of the Upper Palaeolithic peoples, no hunting economy wholly dependent on the natural food supply can support more than a very thin population. The inhabitants of the whole island continent of Australia at the time of its discovery by western man probably numbered between a quarter and a third of a million. In Alaska when it was purchased by the United States the population was about twenty thousand to over half a million square miles; in the North-West Territories there were no more than six thousand five hundred natives to over a million and a quarter square miles—the variations between the two being from one in twenty-five square miles to one in two hundred square miles. This is a wide range, but even in Alaska human beings were certainly very thin on the ground. One is reminded of an eighteenth-century traveller in a very different part of North America who reported, 'there are very few Californians, and in proportion to the extent of the country, almost as few as if there were none at all. . . . A person may travel in different parts four and more days without seeing a single human being.'

The conditions in Alaska and the North-West Territories have enough in common with late glacial Eurasia for comparison to be useful, and on this basis it has been estimated that in Upper Palaeolithic times the winter population of the peninsula later to become the British Isles was about two hundred and fifty. Certainly under glacial conditions Britain was very much on the fringe of the habitable world, and there is no doubt that in more favourable areas such as south-west France and northern Spain the big game was enough to support many more hunters; the same may have been true in the pluvial conditions of the most favourable parts of Africa. Nevertheless it is safe to say that the number of men, women and children living on this globe twenty thousand years ago was very much less than are now packed into the little space of London or New York. One species was about to begin the expansion that was to alter the face of the continents, but as yet a world traveller would have found men 'as few as if there were none at all'.

While then we can be fairly sure that the Upper Palaeolithic hunters lived in groups of from half a dozen to thirty and that these groups may have formed larger tribes of up to a thousand individuals, it would be interesting to know whether they had also developed certain other forms of social organization that are widespread among surviving hunting peoples and often of very great importance in the shape and colour of their lives. Many of them throughout the Old and New Worlds have a system of clans which may or may not coincide with the group living together; it has become customary among anthropologists to distinguish between the clan in which descent is matrilineal, probably the older custom, and the gens in which children belong to their father's group. Within the clans and gens there may be further subdivisions with social, educational and religious duties to the community: curing societies, rainmakers and the like. Almost invariably the clans and gens are exogamous and to contract a marriage within them would be regarded as incestuous; sometimes the choice of husband or wife is quite narrowly limited to boys and girls of a particular kinship within the appropriate clan.

Two further social ingredients are commonly though not universally related to the exogamous clan system. Very often the clan is totemic, and very often admission[2] is related to initiation rites involving fear and physical pain or mutilation that seem to symbolize the idea of death and rebirth into the full life of the tribe. Both these conceptions are powerful and highly elaborated among the native Australians.

Totemism has been defined by Fraser as 'an intimate relation which is supposed to exist between a group of kindred people on the one side and a species of natural or artificial objects on the other side, which objects are called the totems of the human group'. The 'objects' are most often living creatures, as for examples in the Australian kangaroo and witchety grub totems. Although there may be a strong religious undercurrent, the totemic relationship is essentially a social one, the men feeling kinship and affection for their totem, both being descended from common ancestors, usually ambivalent figures, with animal and human aspects. Frequently it is tabu for the human members of the totem to eat their animal kin for food, although they may have to partake of it ritually in a communion meal. A notion is often found, particularly in Australia, that the totemic animal spirit enters into the woman and begets the child so that the relationship is renewed with every generation. It is at once apparent how this idea of totemic conception and of all the members of the clan being one flesh almost presupposes exogamy and a matrilineal basis for clan membership, particularly when it is remembered that, even allowing for anthropological enquirers being deliberately misled or baffled by habits of thought which allow two explanations to be equally true, it appears to be a fact that Australian and a few other primitive peoples did not understand biological paternity or accept a necessary connection between sexual intercourse and conception.[3] If when all society was young this ignorance was more nearly universal, descent through the female line was, of course, inevitable. In Australia itself a majority of the tribes has developed partially patriarchal institutions, the women going to live in their husbands' families and being much reduced in status.[4] This is not true of all the tribes, and, moreover, there is much to show that formerly matrilineal descent and matrilocal marriage were general and the status of women very much higher. This state of affairs still prevails among very many societies in North America and Africa and among the Dravidians of India; relics of it persist in Melanesia, Micronesia and Indonesia. Nor is it limited to uncivilized peoples, for it is evident in the background of Egyptian and Homeric society, while among the Cretans the position of women seems to have remained exceptionally high.

The very widespread prevalence of various combinations of clan structure, exogamy, totemism and matrilineal descent encourages a belief in their extreme antiquity. Is there any evidence for their existence among the hunting peoples of the Upper Palaeolithic Age? Most of what little there is must come from Europe, for the works of art that put us suddenly in touch with the minds and feelings of these fellow-men provide many of the hints on which we have to build. A carving on a bone plate from Raymonden shows a dismembered bison with two lines of men, evidently ritual participants, drawn up on either side. The impression here of a ritual meal of the kind associated with animal totemism is very strong. In addition to the famous 'Sorcerer' from the Trois Frères cave (Fig. 33) there are several other pictures of men wearing pelts and horns or antlers, or alternatively of beings intended to be half animal, half human. Some of these may merely represent hunters disguised to enable them to approach their game, but modern analogies make a ritual identification seem by far the more likely meaning. As for the Sorcerer himself, he must either represent an animal-human ancestor of the totemic type or a man fully identified with an animal, his totem or otherwise, in fertility rites for the increase of the species.[5]

In the remarkable scene of the fallen man and wounded bison at Lascaux (p. 276) the man appears to be bird-headed while planted beside him is a wand with a bird on its top; it is possible that this picture has totemic significance, showing the human member and his totemic emblem.[6] Both Aurignacians and Magdalenians shaped and carved bone and antler plaques in ways extraordinarily similar to the Australian churingas or totemic spirit lodgings, even employing the circular and spiral motifs which with the Australians symbolize the spirit-tracks or pathways. Meander patterns painted or incised in caves have also been likened to the painted 'maps' of spirit journeys which form so important a part of Australian rituals and are very prevalent, too, among the ideas of North American Indians. One or two of the Magdalenian plaques are notched or pierced for attachments and may therefore have been used as the special kind of churinga known as the bullroarer which the Australians used to simulate spirit voices at initiation ceremonies. Again, it has been hazarded that the stencils and imprints of hands, some of them (at Gargas in the French Pyrenees) shown with fingers missing, might be connected with initiation ceremonies and mutilations. This is much more certainly likely to be true of the skulls with front teeth knocked out which date from the Upper Palaeolithic in north Africa (p. 104) and from the Natufian Mesolithic in Palestine.

As for the vast and magnificent array of the animal cave-paintings themselves, can they be said to have totemic significance? This will be discussed more fully in connection with their magico-religious meaning; here it is only worth pointing out that in the western territories of Australia members of a clan would make representations of their totem animal on cave walls and retouch it at appropriate times to secure the fertility of the species. Palaeolithic paintings do show such retouches, and it is just conceivable that the different game-animals depicted, bison, reindeer, cattle and the rest, might have been the property of totem clans. Yet there is no doubt that in this ancient art, so much freer and so incomparably finer than the Australian pictures, the religious and aesthetic emotions were paramount.

As for the prevalence of the matrilineal family, is it permissible to see evidence for it in the 'Venuses' and other carvings of women so popular among the Upper Palaeolithic peoples from Aurignacian to Magdalenian times? It would be very rash to be confident of a social significance in these cult objects, nevertheless such a recognition of fertility and the female principle (p. 278) might be allowed to indicate an habitual recognition of the power of motherhood unlikely in a wholly patriarchal society.

Taken together this evidence is surely enough to prove the existence among the hunters of Palaeolithic and Meso-lithic times of ideas and rites comparable to the totemism of modern hunting peoples. On the other hand it cannot be said to prove the exogamous clan system; the religious and magical implications are there, but the social side of totemic organization cannot be demonstrated. The Australians them-selves are said to have believed that their animal cults and ideas of brotherhood preceded their clan system. Neverthe-less, if the very early emergence of the matrilineal family and the custom, and later law, of exogamy which has been put forward (pp. 179–80) is correct, the original and per-sistent association of the social and cultic aspects of totemism must be accepted. Taking into account the striking economic and technical similarities between the Australian cultures and those of the Palaeolithic, the fact that they appear to have been carried early into Australia and to have continued there free from later contamination, and finally the near similarities between them and other primitive survivals throughout the world, combine to make a very strong case for believing that the entire totemic life of these surviving Stone Age cultures perpetuates something of what was evolved by Palaeolithic man between ten and fifty thousand years ago.

The only other indications of social structure and the size of living units are provided by dwelling places. Caves tell us nothing more than has already been suggested (p. 180), but there are a few house sites dating from Palaeolithic and Mesolithic times that are slightly more revealing (p. 199). Among the tribes of southern Russia who had shaped their lives to mammoth-hunting and had to live in regions both caveless and bitterly cold, houses of substantial size were built (Fig. 14). Some of about 5 metres square (or rather roughly oval) would have held a family group of up to a dozen, while the cluster of long, narrow houses on the banks of the Desna at Timonovka could have sheltered a community of as many as sixty men, women and children. If the reconstruction is correct, the pit-dwelling or earth-house at Kostienki by the Don with a length of 15 metres is easily the largest building known to date from before the beginning of farming economies. Unless it was a men's club house, it must presumably have been occupied in sections by a number of families, a domestic arrangement found in the long houses of the north-west coast Indians of America.

For the Mesolithic period the fairly numerous hut sites often suggest small family units. A study made of such sites on the English Pennines, admittedly an impoverished area, has shown that there the Sauveterrian hunters and food-gatherers moved about either in little family parties or in small groups that could camp in about four huts, each only large enough to hold from three to five people.

A discussion of houses leads naturally to what is one of the most essential social characteristics of the purely hunting life—whether of late glacial or any other times: its restlessness. Food supplies will not allow the hunter to settle down except in unusually favourable conditions such as those offered by the abundance of salmon once to be caught along the north-west coast of America. Even if game is plentiful, it may shift its range with the seasons, obliging the human hunters to do likewise. In Upper Palaeolithic times in Europe caves were normally used only as winter dwellings, the groups probably returning autumn after autumn to the same familiar shelter. During the warmer weather they remained on the move, living in temporary shelters quickly built and

readily abandoned. Among the more advanced Upper Palaeolithic peoples of Eurasia summer quarters were probably
neatly built round huts of the kind sometimes roughly sketched
on cave walls that have been likened to the hogans of the
nomadic Navaho Indians of the American south-west; in
some regions no doubt men made do with simple wind-
breaks like those put up by the Tasmanians and that most
wretchedly equipped people, the Fuegans.

The last Palaeolithic hunters in western and north-western
Europe depended very largely on reindeer hunting and must
have trekked far in the wake of herds that, like those now
tended by the Lapps, might travel hundreds of miles for
their summer pasture. It so happens that we know the more
southerly reindeer hunters, the Magdalenians, from their
winter cave-dwellings, while their northern counterparts, the
Hamburgians, we know from their summer camps along the
edges of lakes and ponds in the glacial valleys of Schleswig-
Holstein where there was abundant grazing in the warm
months from June to September. Nearly all the habitations
of the Maglemosians of the succeeding Mesolithic period to
have been discovered are of similar waterside summer camps
where they resorted for fishing, fowling and hunting; very
little is known of their winter homes. Those latest Mesolithic peoples who, like the Ertebølle folk of Denmark, took
to a strand-looping life largely dependent on shell-fish and
other sea food seem to have settled down and lived permanently in one place thus presaging the sedentary habits
that were to come with farming.

For the shifting life led by hunters where food is not
easily come by, the Australians provide a useful analogy,
moving as they do from caves to rough huts and wind-
breaks in the open. A vivid picture of a life controlled by
seasonal rhythms, with change of territory and habit and
type of house, is still to be seen among the Eskimo. In
particular the Eskimo of the Barren Grounds have the same
close dependence on the caribou as had the Magdalenians and
Hamburgians on the European reindeer.

The life of the hunter is restless, dangerous and most uncomfortable, but blessedly free from the monotonous tedium
that was to come with farming and reach a climax with
the well-regulated factory and office. It is probably, in fact,
the life preferred by most men to all other (in contrast here
with women); they were conditioned to it for a million years
and in the modern world still return to it as a rare privilege.

Social evolution has generally been in the direction of a
simplification of such structures as the exogamous clan and

its intricate rites, customs and prohibitions, side by side with
an immense increase in the economic and functional complexity of society. Every economic advance has seen an increase in specialization of function, a heightening of special
skills, until today most of us would be without food, clothes
or shelter if suddenly left to fend for ourselves.

Among the Palaeolithic hunters there can have been very
little specialization indeed; every man and every woman possessed all the knowledge and all the skills proper to their
sex. A division between the sexes there certainly was; women
probably never hunted any large game, but contributed to
the food supply by collecting wild plants, roots and fruits,
and any other edible crop that could be gathered with a
baby in arms or on the back and toddlers alongside. There
is no reason to doubt that from the earliest times the stay-
at-home women were the cooks, and, where the climate demanded it, the preparers of pelts and leather for clothes.
When the needle was invented towards the end of the
Upper Palaeolithic period, the tailoring of garments probably became as special a feminine skill as it is among the
Eskimo. To judge from Australian analogy, the stone-working was done by the men only.

All the men would have taken part in hunting and tool-
making, although it seems very likely that as equipment
became more elaborate, involving the use of bone and antler
as well as stone and wood, some individuals may have been
recognized as particularly neat-fingered and ingenious and
have been enabled to do rather more manufacture and less
hunting. Specialization cannot go much farther than this in
a hunting economy, for without an assured surplus of food,
the full-time artisan cannot be supported. Probably, however,
the group was always ready to contribute to the support
of a few specially gifted individuals such as shamans and
medicine men, sometimes exceptionally intelligent or quick-
witted, sometimes with what we should call a low threshold
to the unconscious, and therefore able to attain the trances
and possessions believed to put them in touch with the spirit
world. In Europe, too, it may well be that artists were allowed to be part-time specialists, for the very great technical
skill developed must have demanded laborious cultivation.
It is interesting to notice that in many instances where the
painting of a game animal has been marked with spears or
darts for hunting magic (p. 284), this has been done by a
clumsy hand, suggesting that the magical rites were carried
out by a medicine man other than the artist. Among the
South African Bushmen, whose cave-paintings have some-

thing in common with the Palaeolithic tradition, the artists formed a clan of their own.

As for leadership within the hunting group, clan and tribe, prestige is likely to have derived from age with its knowledge of tribal tradition, from strength or prowess in the hunt, and from special gifts of the kind already described. Perhaps grandmothers commanded as much power and respect as grandfathers, if the arguments in favour of a matrilineal and matrilocal system of marriage and descent are correct. Nor is it impossible that women were among the leaders in ritual life; certainly the scenes from the Mesolithic rock paintings of eastern Spain (Fig. 28) show women taking an important part in dances and other rites. Character and good sense must have counted among the gifts of leadership then as ever since. For example, among the Andaman islanders the 'Big Man' who is honoured even above the tribal elders is chosen not only for success in hunting and fighting, but also for kindness, generosity and a sound temper.

An absence of private ownership minimized the need for government and the enforcement of law. To judge from Australian and other analogies, the tribe would have had some vague possession of its whole territory, while smaller areas within it would have been vested in the family or clan. This ownership by family or clan was probably not absolute, all members of the tribe having a right to hunt over the entire tribal lands—at least for certain animals or at particular seasons. All game killed would belong equally to the group and be scrupulously shared, perhaps with the best portions going by right to elders and medicine men. Individuals would have owned only their tools and weapons and personal ornaments; even ritual gear is likely to have been a communal possession.

As for crime and punishment, the intimate participation of the spirits makes the whole conception very different from the legal codes of secular societies. Crimes of wounding or murder committed against an individual are likely to have been avenged on the principle of the *lex talionis* by his or her fellow clansmen; civil and secular offences against the tribe such as certain infringements against the marriage laws and treasonable consorting with the enemy would be immediately punishable by common consent.

A pictorial record of an ancient punishment is preserved in the 'execution' scene among the paintings in the rock shelter of the Cueva Remigia in eastern Spain. Probably by far the commonest offences were those committed against the spirits. Such sins as witchcraft, failures in ritual observance, and above all the breaking of tabus were more dangerous to the tribe than secular crimes. Among modern primitives they may sometimes be punished by social ostracism, or by outlawry, in itself almost a form of death sentence. More often, however, the breaking of a tabu is expected to bring its own punishment—and does so. The terrible dread of the anger of unseen spirits felt by the offender, enhanced by the wrath and fear of his fellows, is more effective as a deterrent, more dire as a punishment, than anything that can be imposed by secular authority. It seems to be a far more potent sanction than was the fear of hell in mediaeval Christendom, for suffering was expected to be immediate and not conveniently postponed to a future world.

It need hardly be said that the social morality evolved by long custom for the protection and well-being of members of a tribe or other group did not apply to 'foreigners'. As among modern societies, to inflict discomfiture and death upon members of other social groups was not crime but admirable bravery or cunning. Mention has already been made of the evidence for the destruction of enemies among the Pithecanthropic and Neanderthal men. There are one or two instances of flint points found lodged in human skeletons of Upper Palaeolithic Age. The Mesolithic painting of the five warriors in La Mola Remigia shelter setting off apparently in feather head-dresses, and brandishing bows and bundles of arrows, looks very much more like a raiding than a hunting party. Then there is the famous discovery in the cave of Ofnet in Bavaria of two nests of skulls, one with twenty-seven heads, the other with six. These might conceivably be the relics of ancestor worship, but as each skull had neck vertebrae attached, many of them with marks of cutting, and as, moreover, a very high proportion were of women and children, ruthless head-hunting is the more convincing explanation. Among the Nagas of Assam a woman's or child's head was as good as a man's and very much more easily come by. It seems reasonable to assume that as mankind became more numerous in late glacial times, so raiding and petty warfare increased and intensified.

If the use of analogies from surviving hunting peoples must be accepted with caution when the organization and conduct of the larger social units are being considered, it evidently becomes even more hazardous when dealing with the smallest unit: the biological family. Here archaeology can offer no corroborative evidence of any kind, while on the other hand the bewildering variety of forms and customs found

among primitives suggests that they may be of relatively
recent origin; if the economic and technical development of
a people is retarded, a great deal of energy may be expected
to go into the elaboration of social forms as well as into
its ritual life. Perhaps, then, it is legitimate to guess that
among the early hunters the rules and etiquette governing
marriage and married life had not yet evolved the burdensome
and sometimes repellent complexity found among their descendants.

While modern analogy is obviously worthless for these
marital intricacies, it may be helpful in the case of certain
more generalized and widespread observances. On the question of polygamy, it suggests that while this may often have
been permissible, and even greatly to be desired, the economic realities of the hunting life are likely to have enforced
monogamy, except perhaps in favoured circumstances and
for specially privileged leaders. As for polyandry, it seems
only to prevail where the conditions of life are very harsh.
Whatever the theoretical forms of marriage, comparisons
suggest that adultery was probably prohibited but often
tolerated, and divorce readily allowed by mutual consent.
Indeed, the possibility remains that at least during the earlier
part of the Palaeolithic Age the idea of lifelong mating had
not been formalized, and there were no established marriage
procedures.

We are almost certainly on safe ground in using one other
general analogy: the bond between mother, father and children would have been very much looser and less exclusive
than is usual in the monogamous societies of the modern
world. Romantic love is, of course, the creation of high
civilization where art and literature play a great part in
heightening, even while refining, sexual passions and emotions; but on a much humbler level, it is true to say that
primitive people rarely expect marriage to mean close and
continuous companionship between the parents, or between
father and young children. Sometimes marital customs seem
specially designed to keep husband and wife distant and
even hostile. But even where monogamous marriage is the
rule and affection recognized, nothing like the closed biological family of western civilization would be considered toler-
able. Boys and girls, men and women, would resort much
with their age and sex groups, playing, working and celebrat-
ing with them as a matter of course. And where the hunting
group remained small, meals would normally have been communal. In particular there would be no close association between a father and his children before the age of puberty.

Of all the artificial creations of human society, the idea of the perpetually loving and responsible father of young children is probably the farthest from natural instinct.

The last word in any account of early forms of society must be to insist on the subservience of the individual to his tribe. To judge from the unanimous evidences of surviving tribal societies, the tribe was seen as a timeless procession of the dead, the living and the unborn, attended by all the unseen powers of the spirit world. To this procession of life, which could only be maintained by the proper adherence to its traditions, the individual was wholly subject. Or perhaps it would be more correct to say he was lost in it through total participation. Men and women may have been considerable personalities, without having fully isolated themselves from the consciousness of the tribe. Indeed, the ideal of the free-standing human being was hardly formulated before the Greeks, hardly fulfilled before the Renaissance; for these people it was remote from all experience. They thought, felt, and acted as members of a group, and in this they were daily confirmed by dancing, initiation and all the other rites that held them in bodily and psychic unison.

NOTES TO CHAPTER V

1. Dr R. M. Berndt and Professor K. Birket-Smith consider that in general little attention is attached today to the problem of the priority of matriarchy or patriarchy. The issue of matrilocal and matriarchal versus patrilocal and patriarchal was the subject of a good deal of unprofitable discussion. Modern British social anthropological work has shown that this crude dichotomy is quite inadequate for any thorough study of descent, inheritance and social status. Professor G. F. Debetz considers that the ape-like ancestor of man entered the stage of labour already as a 'social' animal with strong gregarious instincts. The ever-growing significance of hunting big game, the constantly increasing complexity of making stone tools, the use of fire for heating and preparing food, the use of natural shelters and caves against unfavourable environmental conditions and for storing tools—all this naturally conditioned the development of social ties; consolidated socially, the elementary zoological associations of people that had formed earlier, complicated and differentiated the forms of relations between members of the human herd.

2. Dr K. Birket-Smith points out that initiation does not mean admission to the clan but admission to adult status, which may imply admission to the totem cult where one exists.

3. Professor R. M. Berndt observes that many aborigines draw a distinction between 'physical' and 'spiritual' conception, with the strongest emphasis on the 'spiritual' aspect; they are not alone in this, since in many human societies the 'spirit' or 'soul' is not thought to come into being merely at the moment of conception—

i.e. when the bodily substance first begins to take form. This is not to say that they had a detailed and accurate knowledge of the connection between sexual intercourse and conception; but with a number of them, where careful enquiry has been made in their own language, it is clear that some well-established linkage was acknowledged (e.g. the semen forming the child's bones, the mother's blood the child's blood and flesh).

4. Professor R. M. Berndt feels that the topic of the status of women, in any society, seems to lend itself to exaggerated and emotionally unbalanced comment, in which 'one side' is emphasized at the expense of the other, and the problem is rarely seen in perspective. Aboriginal women were, traditionally, subordinated to men in certain respects; but the converse also held good. Anyone acquainted with this topic should know what sort of evidence to look for in discussing it, and to separate 'fact' from misinterpretation of fact.

5. It is worth noting that many experts hold the view that the 'Sorcerer' of the cave of Trois Frères belongs to the same realm of ideas as the 'lord of the animals'; if this is so, it would not be a man in disguise but a supernatural being exercising power over game, upon whom depends the hunter's success in the chase. See H. Breuil, *Four Hundred Centuries of Cave Art* (Montignac, 1952).

6. The well-known 'bison scene' in the 'puits' of the cave at Lascaux is interpreted in several different ways. It has been given a totemistic explanation and interpreted as an initiation scene [see H. Danthine, 'Essai d'interpretation de la "Scène du Puits" de la Grotte de Lascaux', Sédimentation et Quaternaire (1949), pp. 213–20].

   Mention should also be made of the view advanced by H. Kirchner [see 'Ein archaeologischer Beitrag zur Urgeschichte des Schamanismus', *Anthropos*, 47 (1952), pp. 244–86] that it is connected with a Shamanist ritual. According to this theory the anthropomorphic figure would be a human being (shaman) collapsing in a state of complete ecstasy.

CHAPTER VI

MATERIAL CULTURE OF THE PALAEOLITHIC-MESOLITHIC AGE

DWELLINGS

AMONG the creations of cultural evolution that have made man the most adaptable of species, able to flourish from the Equator to the polar circles, houses and other forms of shelter are, together with clothing, evidently the most important. Birds and some animals are builders and tunnellers, but each species is limited to its own instinctively inherited pattern, whereas man has adapted his dwellings to all kinds of surroundings, all temperatures, all raw materials and also to his own very various demands dependent on taste, habit and economic and social organization. Thus, even while still at a humble stage of development, men will build with tropical leaves, with skins and felt, with twigs, boughs and timbers, with whale and mammoth bones and stone, earth and turf, with ice and snow. Men will build in jungles, on mountain slopes and steppes, by river and sea-shore, on swamps and over water. They will design their houses for a little family or for large kindred and clan groups, as club rooms or for many families to live side by side under one roof; for peace or for war. They will set them singly or in small clusters—but very seldom, so long as they remain hunters, in clusters large or permanent enough to be true villages.

In this context of the Stone Age it is hardly necessary to say that as well as building houses, man has long been glad to accept the very solid shelter offered by natural caves and overhanging rocks or cliffs. It would, however, be unwise to assume that caves and rock shelters were the earliest form of human habitation, for if man first emerged in Africa he was not often in need of solid walls and roof and is likely to have lived very much in the open. It is true that the Pleistocene Australopithecines may have occupied the rock fissures where their bones were found, but we have no evidence that their, and our, Pliocene forebears did likewise, while the remains of one of the oldest known cultures, the Oldowan, have normally been found in conditions suggesting their creators lived in the open. Indeed no such evidence for cave-dwelling has been recognized in Africa before Late Acheulian times. There is no sign of Africans having used fire before this same period, and it may be that men could not live permanently in caves until they had fire to protect them from marauding carnivores.

Again, it is true that the Choukoutien caves are the earliest known human habitations, but then the chance of occupation litter surviving in caves and so making it possible to recognize them as dwellings is immensely greater than it is for exposed sites. Except when extreme cold drove them into caves, men must from the first have roved freely over the open countryside, perhaps in the earliest times making only wind-breaks or light roofs against rain and sun, but later, as will be shown, quite substantial houses.

Caves have a continuous history of occupation throughout later Palaeolithic and Mesolithic times. Indeed, men have taken advantage of this form of free shelter until the present day. In Britain it has been said that there were never so many cave-dwellers as in the Roman period; during its excavation, it proved that one of the Arab workmen had himself been born in the Tabun cave of Mount Carmel where a female Neanderthal skeleton was unearthed.

The Choukoutien caves were inhabited by *Pithecanthropus* during the second glaciation; caves in the Makapan Valley in the Transvaal, in the Cape Province, at Mount Carmel in Palestine and Palmyra in Syria and in Jersey in the Channel islands, gave shelter to late Acheulian man during the last interglacial. After this, sites are too numerous to specify. The Neanderthalers were so much cave men that Mousterian sites in the open are exceptional.[1] Although Europe, and especially south-west Europe, probably has the greatest concentration of caves occupied intermittently throughout later Palaeolithic times, there are long-tenanted caves in many parts of Africa, including the famous Bambata and Elementeita caves in Kenya and a number along the Mediterranean littoral. Many more than are at present known are likely to be recognized in Asia as research develops. In the New World most of the pre-agricultural sites are in the open, but the earliest known culture is named after a cave-dwelling, that of Sandia in New Mexico. Several caves occupied rather later than these, but still in pre-agricultural times, have been recognized in Oregon and Utah.

The name of troglodyte may suggest a being living far from

the daylight, but this is not in fact true of the prehistoric cave-dwellers. They maintained the centre of their home life just inside the cave-mouth where shelter was combined with daylight and a ready escape for the smoke of the great fires that were so essential a part of cave existence. The depths were normally visited only for executing works of art and for the magic rites connected with them (p. 267). In selecting a cave-dwelling for bitterly cold winters, Palaeolithic man showed a natural preference for those facing south or westward, and this choice made the terrace so often present outside the entrance a good working place on fine days. There tool-making was often done, and, very probably, skins stretched out and cleansed and clothes sewn. Occasionally, too, the dead were buried outside in the terrace bank. It must be remembered that the type of habitation usually known as the rock shelter was at least as popular as the true cave. This was a living place established under overhanging cliffs or large rocks where, although there were no natural walls, the overhang made a good roof. Neither caves nor shelters have as yet yielded evidence of artificial walls or fences, yet it seems exceedingly unlikely that these admirable efficient hunters had not devised at the very least screens of skins to add to the warmth and security of the natural vault.

Nowhere in the world is there so much to encourage an imaginative reconstruction of Palaeolithic life as the Dordogne region of south-west France. In the great limestone valleys of the Dordogne system, and particularly of the Vézère near Les Eyzies, where the rivers have eroded steep, and often overhanging, cliffs, there are scores of desirable caves and rock shelters (Pl. 2). Such dwellings with tools, weapons and all the litter of occupation on their floors, with paintings and sculpture on their walls or in the depths behind them, and with the bones of the hunters themselves buried there, are so numerous that they are sometimes within sight and even hailing distance of one another. Making allowance for the fact that not all were inhabited at the same time, there must often have been a stir of life between them. It is easy, and surely permissible, to picture the formation of hunting parties, visiting by courtship parties, and large gatherings round fires where meat from the communal hunt was being roasted. Sometimes medicine men, artists and other leaders, perhaps horned, masked and clad in pelts, must have made solemn entries to carry out their hunting and fertility rites at the images deep in the rock. At certain times, perhaps at mid-winter to turn back the sun, perhaps in the early spring for the fertility of the game animals, there may have been ceremonies drawing hunters from afar for their celebration. During the hard, bright winter nights there must have been fires making wavering patches of light at point after point along the limestone cliffs.

Cave-dwellers invariably allowed their lost or discarded possessions, their food bones and other rubbish, to accumulate beneath them, often to a depth of several metres and sometimes until the cave became choked up and quite uninhabitable. With the encampments in open country which, as we have seen, our ancestors certainly used over as long a period as caves, there are no such favourable conditions for preservation. The chances of their surviving in recognizable form over many thousands of years are slender indeed. The Acheulians had a preference for encampments beside rivers and estuaries and lakes. A large proportion of the flint implements found in river gravels and other natural deposits are likely to have been derived from exposed living sites of this kind, having been carried away by streams, floods or soil movement. Occasionally, however, a sufficient concentration of occupation material has remained in one spot to mark it with some certainty as the site of an encampment of some kind even if no traces of any structure remain. The best defined Lower Palaeolithic site of this kind is Ol Orgesailie in the Kenya Rift valley, where the rise and fall of the level of the lake by which it was situated have preserved much of the domestic rubbish under layers of silt. Here Acheulian hunters had left behind them on the floors of flimsy huts, wind-breaks or whatever form of shelter they may have used, astonishingly great quantities of their hand-axes and cleavers, and the chipped stone balls thought to have been used to make bolas. They had thrown down their food bones where they ate (as was of course the universal practice), and these prove them to have lived mainly off wild pig, zebra and baboon. None of the bones showed the mark of burning, nor was there any trace of hearths at Orgesailie; it seems possible, therefore, that in a warm climate men did not as yet invariably make use of fire. Another well-defined lakeside Acheulian settlement was at Torralba in Spain. Here, however, the hunters had command of fire.

No post-holes or other marks of buildings were preserved at this site, although the extreme concentration of flints and bones suggests that they existed. The earliest actual remains of man-made buildings date from Upper Palaeolithic times and come from Czechoslovakia, southern Russia and Siberia. All of them appear to have belonged to mammoth hunters of Gravettian culture, whose highly specialized way of life obliged them to live in caveless country even during the winter season. One group of three huts lying within a few hundred metres of one another is at Vestonice on the lower slopes of the Pavlov hills in Czechoslovakia, a site long famous for its mammoth bones, and for Palaeolithic carvings and models (p. 273). All three were set near small springs and on a specially prepared floor hollowed from the slope of the hill; not very much more can be reported of the third of these houses as it has only been partly excavated, but the remaining two, standing 80 metres apart, are of very great interest. One of them was roughly oval in plan, measuring about 15 by 9 metres and floored with limestone grit. Five hearths in shallow depressions ringed with flat stones lay along the centre line, while small pits that may have been for storage had been dug just inside the house wall. No certain remains of post-holes or roofing material were found, and it is possible that this building never possessed a substantial roof, but was protected by a series of wind-breaks or lightly built shelters. Quantities of stone and bone tools and some personal ornaments were scattered round the hearths, while near the central one flint-working had been carried on so intensively that over a thousand flakes had accumulated within a space no more than a metre square. This long house with its several hearths is judged to have been the communal dwelling of a family hunting-group or clan.

A large kitchen midden was discovered along the banks of the rivulet flowing near the hut. This may formerly have been a marsh where the bones of mammoth, reindeer, horse, fox and wolf had been thrown and allowed to sink into the slime. Also near the hut was the grave of a forty-year-old woman who had been buried in a manner fitting for the wife of a mammoth hunter. She had been laid in a shallow grave, strewn with red ochre supplied with tools and then covered with the great bony plates of mammoth shoulderblades.

The other hut was smaller, nearly circular and with the floor partly sunk into the hillside in such a way that a low roof would probably have followed the line of the slope. The roof had been supported on uprights about 12 centimetres in diameter and perhaps slightly inclined inwards towards the centre; they were secured in their rather shallow sockets by collars of large stones, and further supported by internal struts. The roof itself appears to have been made of branches, grass and earth, and perhaps covered with hide and weighted with mammoth bones. A certain amount of ash, bones, and other refuse had been thrown on top. The whole hut was enclosed in a circular wall of limestone and clay 6 metres across. This must be the most ancient true wall built by human hands known to survive on earth. More remarkable still is the hearth in the middle of the hut which is surrounded by the overhanging edges of a vaulted structure of the same material as the wall, and evidently the base of a beehive-shaped oven or kiln. Its floor was covered with a thick sooty layer, and the inside of the kiln walls was burnt to a reddish colour. The layer of soot contained more than two thousand clay pellets, some of them showing finger marks, and mingled with them some fragments of the clay modeller's art—the heads of two bears and a fox, some unfinished statuettes, and legs broken from animal figures. In short, it seems that this was a kiln, the oldest ever to have been discovered, and that it was used to harden clay figures of the kind for which Vestonice is already well known.[2] Furthermore, the excavators believe that this was no ordinary dwelling house, but perhaps the quarters of a Palaeolithic medicine man, the sacred den where he shaped and hardened the images of beasts and of women to be used in his hunting and fertility rites.

The charcoal from Vestonice suggests a cold type of coniferous forest, and the animal remains, too, are of a kind to be associated with extreme cold, perhaps with tundra conditions. Probably the dwellings there were inhabited near the beginning of the last phase of the Würm glaciation.

Another comparable, but slightly earlier, mammoth-hunters' encampment in Czechoslovakia is at Ostrava-Petrovice on the left bank of the Oder (Fig. 14). Here there had been three oval huts from 6 to 8 metres long and each with a pair of hearths set on the middle line. In one of the huts, lying under a mammoth molar, was a miniature torso of a woman carved in haematite, and more realistic than most of the Gravettian Venuses. Domestically the remarkable thing about this settlement was the use of coal for the fires. The Ostrava coal measures come to the surface quite close to it, and the hunters had learnt enough about the properties of the material to prefer it for fuel to the scanty supply of pine logs.

The medicine man's hut at Vestonice is unique, but the other Czech dwellings are sufficiently like some of those in the Black Earth country of south Russia to show that these mammoth-hunters of Gravettian culture followed closely similar ways of life throughout wide territories. These loess-land dwellings usually stand on the banks of a great river, and

on the present somewhat insufficient evidence appear to fall
into two main types, one sunk well into the ground and
remarkably like the winter earth-houses still used in circum-
polar regions (for example, by the Kanchadals of north-east
Siberia), while others were tent-like and comparable with
the summer tents of the Canadian Eskimo.

The best specimens of the earth-house type are the group
of six elongated rectangular dwellings, measuring about 3
by 12 metres, uncovered at Timonovka on the Desna river
near Briansk. Here the floors might be sunk as much as
3 metres into the ground and the huts were entered by a

FIG. 14. *Upper Palaeolithic houses at Ostrava-Petrovice, Silesia.*
(*Reconstruction*)

ramp, sometimes at one end, sometimes in the middle of the
long side. The vertical walls seem to have been lined by a
timber revetment, and the roofs to have been made of logs
laid across the trench and piled with the excavated soil and
kitchen refuse. One or more hearths were sited near the
entrance, but in one instance the problem of getting rid of
the smoke was apparently met by constructing a hood or
chimney of clay-covered bark. Fires, however, were also lit

in the open; both hearths and flint-knapping floors were found near the settlement. These subterranean houses, lit by stone lamps, must have been snug refuges in winter and have offered a welcome haven from arctic winds.

The Russian dwelling most nearly comparable with those at Vestonice was found at Kostienki on the River Don. It, too, was some 15 metres long, with a floor slightly hollowed into the ground and with hearths set along the axis. Although the excavators report post-holes to support a roof the evidence is doubtful, and it may be supposed that here as at Vestonice there was not a substantial or continuous roof but perhaps several shelters or tent-like coverings of skin. There may have been other yet longer communal dwellings of this kind at Kostienki. So successful were the mammoth-hunters who lived there, that the site has long been famous for an abundance of mammoth bones and teeth; as early as the eighteenth century they interested Peter the Great enough to make him order an investigation.

There was another long, roughly rectangular house with slightly sunken floor and hearths, and quantities of mammoth remains at Pushkari, on the Desna, but more interesting is a dwelling near the Don, that of Gagarino close to Lipetsk. This was more clearly of tent-like construction. It had been an uneven oval some 5 metres across with the floor sunk to a depth of half a metre, and mammoth tusks and stone slabs lying round the edge of the hollow. These were almost certainly used to weigh down the edges of skins which may have been stretched over a framework of sticks such as those used for their summer tents by the Canadian Eskimo. When camp is shifted, the tents are removed and the weights left lying in a ring. It is a striking fact that the tent-houses of mammoth-hunters found far to the east by the Siberian Lake Baikal (p. 143) were of much the same type, apparently with mammoth phalanges for weights, while away to the west the reindeer-hunting Hamburgians of Schleswig-Holstein favoured the same kind of dwelling, using stone blocks to take the place of bones as weights. The dozen or so habitations of Palaeolithic men recognized between Moravia and Siberia have been described in some detail, for poor though their remains are, and difficult to interpret, they gain distinction as the first known examples of domestic architecture. A dozen huts and houses for the whole of the Old World—this can represent only a small fraction of the total number raised (or sunk) during Upper Palaeolithic times. Nevertheless the human population was still so very sparse that, except in a few unusually favoured regions, these diminutive centres of human life must have been thinly scattered and isolated almost beyond our comprehension. It is worth giving some space to these few pioneer buildings as the harbingers of the countless millions of houses that by the end of this history will have sprung up to embellish and to disfigure the earth.

For the Mesolithic Age again, nearly all the evidence for artificial houses comes from Europe. A larger number of sites is known, but it is true to say that the huts represented generally appear to have been smaller and flimsier than those of the preceding age. The growth of forest and thickets vastly increased the amount of material available for making shelters, but shelters of a kind even less likely to survive (except in bogs) than those built when wood was very scarce. Nor did the warmer climate demand the digging of earth-houses.

Where they could, Mesolithic builders chose sites on sandy or gravelly soils where the vegetation would have been light. But in Europe at least, the post-glacial millennia saw much bog formation round the edge of glacial lakes, and the Mesolithic people fishing, fowling and hunting in this kind of country developed some skill in camping on marshy ground. At Duvensee near Lübeck Maglemosians inhabited a knoll set amid the bog, laying birch-bark floors and making hearths of sand on them where fires could be lit in safety.

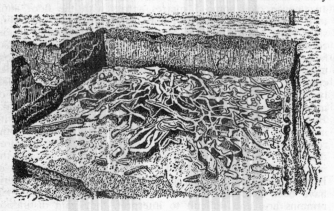

Fig. 15. *Mesolithic dwelling platform, Star Carr, Yorkshire, England (after J. G. D. Clark).*

At Star Carr, Seamer, in Yorkshire, other Maglemosian deer-hunters and fishers, camping among reed swamps on the edge of a lake, had made a dry platform with birch brushwood, including some quite substantial trunks (Fig. 15). At neither of these sites, despite the preservation of wood, was there any sign of huts, and it can only be guessed that tents were pitched on them. On the other hand on the bog of Aamosen on the Danish island of N. Zealand squarish huts floored with birch and pine bark were detected. Walls and roof appear to have been made with slender uprights set into the subsoil round the floor and pulled together at the centre. This same kind of light construction was also detected at Bokum in Hanover, though here the plan of the hut was an irregular oval. Probably it was used at many other sites where nothing has survived beyond slightly sunken floors, hearths and occupation rubbish. Wattle and daub may have made the covering of one hut in Belgium, but all the evidence suggests that true frame construction was not used in Europe, nor so far as is known anywhere else, until the Neolithic period.

Sometimes Mesolithic huts are found in small groups, as for example on the English Pennines (p. 188) and at Farnham in Surrey; small seasonal settlements of this kind were probably usual, but when we come to one of the size of that at the edge of the Federsee moor in Württemberg with as many as thirty-eight huts (again constructed of branches and with sunken floors) it is necessary to be cautious; this was evidently a popular camping site, revisited year after year. It may well be that not all the huts were occupied at one time. It is unfortunate that almost nothing is known of the dwellings inhabited by the Ertebølle folk (p. 158) whose steady food supply enabled them to avoid seasonal migration.[3] Although their huge kitchen middens survive to bear witness to their vast consumption of sea foods, and particularly of shell-fish, of the houses they must have inhabited through the centuries no trace remains.

FIRE, COOKING AND FOOD

The domestic arts practised in these caves, shelters, huts and houses were not highly developed, although here as in other spheres there was certainly a conspicuous increase in skills in later Palaeolithic times. Those which called for special tools will be described presently, but here in direct relation to the dwelling places something should be said about fire, food and cooking.

It has already been insisted that the control of fire was one of the first and most important of human achievements, though warmth, protection, and even the hardening of wooden implements probably all preceded cooking among its uses. It may well be that the *Pithecanthropi* of Peking, the earliest users of fire at present known, may not have made fire but only maintained it when it had been naturally ignited. Among modern primitives all possess fire-making appliances except the Andaman islanders, who have either lost or never possessed the art. Many, however, do their best to save the labour of kindling by keeping their fires going—sometimes even on a clay hearth laid on the bottom of a canoe.

When we reach the Acheulians, it seems much more likely that great fires such as those that burned in the Tabun cave on Mount Carmel or in the Cave of the Hearths in the Makapan valley were artificially kindled. In the present stage of knowledge Asia is in the van of fire-making with the Choukoutien hearths dating from the second glaciation; Europe follows with evidence of fires for the second interglacial at such mid-Acheulian sites as Torralba, while Africa lags behind with no sign of fires (and no true cave-dwellings) before Late Acheulian sites of the last interglacial period.

There are two principal ways of making fire, though each has many variants. One consists in making sparks by percussion, the other in friction between two wooden surfaces, creating a fine wood dust that finally kindles enough to light the tinder. The only solid evidence of fire-making in Palaeolithic or Mesolithic times is for the first method, some cave-dwellers having made a strike-a-light from flint and a lump of iron pyrites. The friction methods include the fire-plough in which a piece of hard wood is rubbed to and fro in a furrow in softer wood, the rather similar fire-saw in which a sharp-edged stick such as bamboo is sawed across a slit, and the fire-drill where a hard pointed stick is rotated in a socket. The drill may be twirled between the palms but is made much more effective if rotated by means of a thong, cord or bow-string looped round it. It seems certain that one or more of these techniques would have been perfected before the end of the Mesolithic period. Here is an invention likely to have been made independently in different regions, always with variations determined by the nature of the woods available.

As for fuels, wood was of course usual (two kinds of pine, spruce, willow and birch were identified at Vestonice) but in treeless tundra bones were sometimes resorted to, as they were by the mammoth-hunters at Kostienki. The use of coal at Petrovice, the first known in human history, has already been described. The stone lamps burning fat used in the earth-houses and by cave artists (Fig. 25) may well have served to give warmth as well as light, as they do among the Eskimo.

Fire was certainly used for roasting meat already in Lower Palaeolithic times, but probably, like their modern successors, the ancient hunters always ate some of their meat raw. It is often suggested that boiled food was unknown before the invention of pottery, but it would have been quite possible for Upper Palaeolithic women to have learnt how to boil in leather vessels by the means, often employed in later pre-historic times, of dropping in hot stones. Since the discovery of the Vestonice kiln, it has even become rash to assume that the cooking oven was never used at this time, although it must have been most exceptional as no signs of it have been detected in any cave-dwelling.

As for food, the subject is too vast to be treated in any detail. The quest for food was early man's main preoccupation and its variety enormous. Between the Equator and the ice-caps, between the extremes of Pleistocene climate, the range of foods offered by the animal and vegetable kingdom is beyond description, while man himself was as nearly omnivorous as any animal can be. It may be supposed that fruit, roots and perhaps insects were eaten in much greater quantities when and where the climate was warm, while flesh must have been consumed on a huge scale by the European hunters of the last Ice Age. In the 'Zinjanthropus' horizon in Oldoway Gorge were the bones of many creatures which had apparently been consumed by this hominid or by his hypothetical destroyer (p. 90). They included those of lizards, frogs, birds, rats and mice. Of the giant species of pigs, sheep, cattle and giraffe prevalent at the time only the young seem to have been eaten. The *Pithecanthropi* ate a large proportion of venison, and so also did the Acheulians on Mount Carmel, while such specialized reindeer-hunters as the Magdalenians must have had a surfeit of it. Indeed, the wide range of the many species of deer, antelope and gazelle must have made venison one of the most important foods of pre-agricultural times. The Acheulian hunters in Kenya have been shown to have eaten pork as well as zebra and baboon; on Mount Carmel in addition to a basic diet of venison (mostly deer and gazelle), hippopotamus and even tortoise varied the meals. Communities of Middle Palaeolithic culture living in the Huangho valley in China enjoyed large quantities of ostrich eggs.

The excellence and variety of food enjoyed by the successive Upper Palaeolithic hunters of Europe was, indeed, most remarkable. They had an abundance of wild cattle and horses, pigs, bison, ibex, red deer, in the rather warmer phases, reindeer and mammoth predominating during the arctic periods when tundra returned. But in addition to flesh they also ate fish and fowl; arctic grouse and ptarmigan, salmon, pike, trout, bream and other fresh-water fish. In America the diet of the early hunters was comparable, allowing for the differences in the game available. Mammoth and bison were important food animals, as were the camel and the wild horse. The huge ground sloth was hunted in some regions, and so too, before its extinction, was the mastodon. Hearths uncovered in Texas, where fires were probably burning about ten thousand years ago, in addition to the remains of most of these large game animals, yielded also those of coyote, prairie dog and rabbit; there were also mussel shells and hackberry seeds. Among the peoples belonging to what has been called the Palaeo-western tradition (p. 151) the diet would have included a considerably higher proportion of small creatures as well as of wild plants of many kinds.

With the forest growth of post-glacial times Mesolithic man, so far as Europe is concerned, experienced a noticeable change of diet. Not only were the reindeer and mammoth entirely replaced by red deer, long-horned cattle (*Bos primigenius*) and other forest species, but the amount of sea-fish, shell-fish and birds consumed must have mounted sharply, especially in the summer months. The diffusion of the bow, followed by specially designed fowling arrows (Fig. 13), increased the number of birds available for food. The fortunate survival of one picture among the east Spanish rock paintings, showing a woman who has descended a cliff to reach a wild bees' nest,[4] proves to us that honey was eaten where conditions were warm enough for it to be obtainable.

Although the proportion of meat and hence of protein in the diet of the ancient hunters would normally have been much higher than among agriculturalists, vegetable foods must always have been eaten to maintain health. Though vitamins were not discovered before the twentieth century, the need for them was empirically recognized from the earliest times. As roots, fruits and leaves normally decay without trace, our knowledge of what was eaten in this way is very slight. Mention has already been made of the hackberries gathered by the *Pithecanthropi* at Choukoutien; hazel nuts were eaten by Palaeolithic man in Europe, and in quantity by his Mesolithic successors; walnuts, wild pears and the seeds of water lilies have been found in Mesolithic middens in different parts of Europe. It can be taken for granted that these odds and ends which are all that are now known to us represent a very considerable consumption of vegetable foods gathered by the women and children to supplement the meat brought home by the men. It has been suggested that the reindeer-hunters may have eaten the half-digested mush from the stomachs of the deer—a rich source of vitamins still appreciated by the Lapps and Siberians.

Towards the close of the hunting ages the consumption of grasses and other seed plants either wild or semi-cultivated probably increased in some regions, as it certainly did, for example, among the Natufians of Palestine. This people harvested enough grain to justify making mortars for grinding it. They may be supposed to have eaten the meal both in some porridge-like form and as unleavened bread. With this cereal element in the diet becoming so considerable, we are on the threshold of an agricultural life.

DOMESTICATION OF THE DOG

There is a tendency, not altogether mistaken, to regard the Mesolithic period as a tardy epilogue to the Palaeolithic, an interim period when in most regions mankind was, as it were, waiting for the coming of farming to change the whole basis of life. Yet progress was made during Mesolithic times even in regions remote from the cradlelands of farming, and in one development in particular it was quite clearly looking forward to the Neolithic Age and not backwards towards the Palaeolithic. The domestication of the dog by Mesolithic man was not of great importance in itself but of very great interest as a preliminary advance towards what was to come.

How man came to gain control over this first of the wild animals to be drawn into his social orbit is as much disputed as is the species originally involved. Hunting peoples are inclined to make pets of wild animals; some of the Australian tribes tie them up in their camps, and wallabies, opossums and, more significantly, dingoes may become quite at home among them. This friendliness between one form of life and others, particularly as manifested in the overspill of maternal affection in woman, may have contributed to the domestication of the dog. But probably the most effective advances were made not from man's side but from the dog's. If wild dogs of a species small enough not to be dangerous began to frequent camps to pick up offal and discarded bones, they would have been more than tolerated for their services as scavengers; then special scraps would have been thrown to them, they would have been petted, and gradually turned into fully domesticated watchdogs and companions. According to this view these homely functions came before the dog was trained to take part in hunting, while his skill in herding could, of course, only have been fostered with the advent of farming. It still remains possible, however, that from the very beginning of their association dogs joined men in the chase, following the more intelligent species in the hope of pickings at the kill. This interpretation of events would gain some support if it were proved that the original wild species to be tamed was the smaller breed of southern wolf, the candidate which on the whole seems to be the most promising.

True domestic dogs have been identified on Mesolithic sites in several places; among the Tardenoisians in Brittany and the Maglemosians in Denmark. A dog owned by the Palestinian Natufians seems to have had a jackal-like ancestry.[5] The earliest European breed seems to have been fairly small and of a generalized form most comparable to a chow. It has been named *Canis familiaris palustris* because it was first identified in Swiss lake-dwellings of the Neolithic Age. It shows the reduction in size and in length of muzzle that was to follow domestication in the case also of the food animals. On the other hand the earliest dog remains from the Belt Cave (p. 307) were those of a very large animal.

THE DEVELOPMENT OF TOOLS AND WEAPONS

The shaping of tools has been generally adopted as the criterion of human status because among the fossil remains that provide our only other means for recalling the emergence of our kind it is impossible to make a dividing line between man and primate ancestor. The size of the brain relative to that of the body, though useful as a rough indicator, will not do as the final distinction. Tools not only offer a proof of mental concentration with at least some slight skill and forethought, but, when they are of stone, possess the supreme advantage of durability. Therefore both theoretically and for expediency the dictum that manufacture maketh man is a sound one.

A number of other creatures use tools—insects, birds and mammals. Among the primates a baboon will pick up a stone to kill a scorpion and also deliberately dislodge scree and rocks on a hillside to bombard pursuers. Chimpanzees in captivity have been known to join sticks together to make a longer one, even biting the end of the smaller piece to make it fit the socket. This is the nearest approach to tool-*making* to have been observed among other species than our own, but such essays seem only to be made when there is an immediate objective in view, and furthermore have never been known to occur among apes in their natural surroundings. The shaping of even the crudest tool in advance of any particular need demands mental powers nearer to conceptual thought and an imaginative realization of the future.

It has already been suggested that the immediate predecessors of man must have attained to a tool-using stage. The next stage, achieved by the first hominids, was distinguished by the intentional but haphazard manufacture of tools. Man had become a tool-maker, but possessed no mental pattern book to enable him to repeat standard forms designed for definite purposes. This second stage on the path of technical progress is well represented by the Oldowan culture with its pebbles broken into rough edges and points, and again by the culture of the *Pithecanthropi* at Choukoutien. Among their descendants in eastern Asia this haphazard type of manufacture lasted immensely longer than in the more progressive parts of the world (p. 126).

The third stage beyond tool-using and haphazard tool-making was first most clearly achieved by the creators of the Abbevillian-Acheulian tradition: this was characterized by the production of a standard implement of well-defined form but very little specialized in function. The fully evolved hand-axe with its point, its broad, cutting base and straight-edged sides, its weight and clubbableness, could serve all the simple needs of Lower Palaeolithic life—it could pierce, dig, cut, stun,

FIG. 16. *Spear-thrower in use
(after Linton).*

or serve as a missile, all after a fashion with the lack of full efficiency that goes with unspecialized design. Even among the Abbevillians and Acheulians, however, there was evidently some slight specialization of function, for the flake tools used side by side with the hand-axes may be presumed to have had their own uses, perhaps for cutting and scraping where a keen edge was necessary. Furthermore it must be remembered that more effective missiles and narrower points than those provided by the hand-axe were probably obtained in wood.

The Lower Palaeolithic flake cultures, best represented by the Clactonian, included no tool form so regularly standardized as the hand-axe, yet, as will be shown, the method of flaking was consistent and fairly distinctive. It has been suggested, though with insufficiently exact justification (p. 128), that these flake cultures were better adapted to existence in conditions of extreme cold. It is certainly true that none of their tools appears to have been serviceable for digging up roots or grubs, a job for which the pointed hand-axe was probably used in warmer climates. Instead flake tools of the Clactonian type would have served very well for cutting up carcases and scraping skins. It will be recalled that the oldest wooden implement known to us, a sharpened spear-point, was of Clactonian handiwork.

In the flake-tool developments succeeding the Clactonian there seems to have been a continued emphasis on the same function of dealing with carcases and skins. As we shall see, in these Levalloisian and Mousterian cultures progress does not show itself so much in functional specialization as in improved techniques of manufacture. In the final stages of the Acheulian the hand-axe became so small that its usage must have changed considerably. In this period we begin to find the spasmodic appearance of tools made on long flakes already approaching the blades that were to dominate the technology of the Upper Palaeolithic peoples.

In the Upper Palaeolithic Age man began to make the tool fit the task with an altogether new precision. There was also a sudden increase in the tempo of change. Among tools made upon flint blades, the knife was of the utmost importance, while scrapers were made in a wide range of standard forms designed for particular purposes. The invention of the chisel or burin, the gouge and awl made possible the development of working in bone and antler that was another important element in the technical advance of the Upper Palaeolithic cultures. The repertory of bone implements advanced from simple spear-points to barbed spears and true harpoons, fish gorgets and (with the Magdalenians) to the eyed needle. Burins and gouges and awls are of great historical interest in that they are the first implements designed not for direct use but to make other tools; with them technology is gaining depth. They were also the first tools to be used for purposes that were not in our sense practical—for carving and engraving works of art.

Most significant of all the material achievements of Upper Palaeolithic man was the invention first of the spear-thrower (Fig. 16) and then of the bow and arrow, the one using the principle of the lever to increase the efficiency of human muscles, the second the more advanced principle of the concentration of energy. The possession of such long-distance weapons enormously increased the effectiveness of hunters who had to kill swiftly-moving game in country where good cover was scanty or absent.

The Mesolithic peoples of Europe made further useful additions to the equipment of the chase, particularly for the fishing and fowling that formed a considerable part of their economy. In addition to nets and fish-traps, they invented the bone fish-hook as an improvement on the gorget, an effective perforated harpoon, complex fish-spears and arrows with various types of bone and flint heads specially designed for shooting birds (Fig. 17). But the most valuable achievement of the more northern among the Mesolithic peoples was certainly the perfection of the heavy-hafted axe and adze which enabled them to fell trees and develop carpentry, including the shaping of dug-out canoes and paddles.

Apart from these various devices that the Mesolithic hunters contributed to the world, they made a drastic technical change that was of no very lasting importance. This was, of course, their adoption of multiple settings of small and sometimes minute flints both for cutting edges, points and barbs.[6] The finest of the geometric microliths called for most delicate craftsmanship. The practice of setting microliths in projectile heads was maintained by the earliest American Eskimo. Towards the very end of the period, in regions adjoining the cradleland of agriculture, microlithic implements looking forward to the coming age begin to appear— such as the reaping knives used by the Natufians.[7] The northern forest peoples, too, learnt how to make polished and perforated tools of stone.[8]

This brief history of man's development of his tools from the first tentative breaking of pebbles to the skilled manufacture of a wide range of specialized equipment at the end of the hunting age must be followed by some

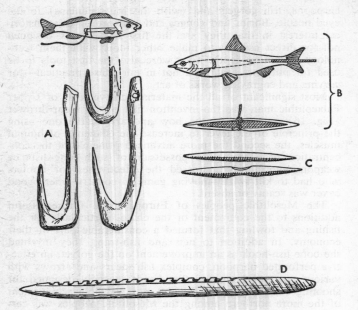

FIG. 17. *Mesolithic fishing gear and modern comparisons. A:
bone fish-hooks of the Maglemosian culture, showing
possible method of securing bait (scale 2/3); B:
modern Finnish gorgets; C: gorgets from lake-side
village, Switzerland (scale 1/1); D: Maglemosian
leister prong from the bed of the North Sea (after
Singer).*

account of the technical methods involved and by a description
of the leading tool types characterizing all the many cultures
of Palaeolithic and Mesolithic times.

THE WORKING OF FLINT AND OTHER STONES

Flint, a nearly pure silica, together with the volcanic glass
known as obsidian, undoubtedly offered the best natural
material for tool-making at all generally obtainable by prehistoric man. Harder than steel, they are fine-grained and
remarkably homogeneous and can therefore be most accurately worked by various methods of fraction. Chert, more

widespread throughout the world than true flint and very commonly used for implements, is also composed of silica, but very much coarser-grained and more faulty. The ancient tool-makers used these stones wherever they were available, but were sometimes reduced to such intractible materials as schist, granite, quartzite, or fossilized wood. Once the manufacture of stone implements by grinding and polishing became a common practice among the Neolithic peoples the tough, igneous rocks came into their own, although flint and obsidian remained the only good substances for delicate work.

If a faultless piece of flint is struck vertically with another stone the fracture can be perfectly conchoidal, the lines of fission radiating outwards from the point of contact to form a cone like a limpet-shell. If the blow is struck obliquely (as in tool-making it invariably is) then only half or less of the cone will penetrate the flint, forming the little swelling usually known as the 'bulb of percussion' at the base of the detached flake and leaving a corresponding hollow on the main body of the flint. After thousands of generations had employed more or less random striking, man learnt that he should direct his blow at a point near the edge of the block at an angle of about 120 degrees to the direction he wanted the fracture to take. Two main methods of procedure could be followed: either the detached flake could be worked up into the implement or the implement could be formed from the main block, flakes being detached to shape and trim it. It has been seen that this distinction between flake and core tools is a very significant one for the classification of Palaeolithic cultures.

At first the blows were struck with another rounded stone; the earliest pebble tools were made with random blows of this kind, while the hammer-stone technique had been more fully mastered by the Abbevillian hand-axe makers. It might sometimes be supplemented by a second method by which instead of the flint to be worked being struck with a hammerstone, it was itself hit against a much larger immovable anvilstone. This anvil technique was particularly effective for detaching very large flakes.

The great disadvantage of both methods was that the shrewdness of the blow of stone on stone produced large bulbs of percussion on the flake and correspondingly deep 'negative bulbs' on the core. The deep depressions thus formed along the edge of a core tool made it impossible to keep the line at all true; in all Abbevillian hand-axes the edges are more or less jagged and irregular. The discovery that made possible the smooth workmanship of the best Acheulian

examples was that the bulbs of percussion were greatly
reduced if instead of a hammer-stone a cylindrical bar of a
softer material was used. Experiments have shown that the
limb bones of horses and other sizeable animals are ideally
handy for the purpose, but as few such hammer-bones have
been found even on sites where the cylinder hammer had
undoubtedly been employed, it is assumed that branches of
tough wood with the bark removed were more often used.
Not only does the yielding surface spread the blow through
a wider line of contact, so flattening the bulb, but it can
be directed exactly on the edge of the tool instead of at a
little off it. The blows are made quickly and lightly from
the wrist, and further control is obtained by pressing the
fingers against the point where the flake is to be detached.
Thus it must be recognized that to achieve the smooth flaking,
straight edges and true form of the finest Acheulian hand-
axes men had already accumulated considerable knowledge
as well as skill in the niceties of stone-working. It was, of
course, knowledge empirically acquired, and the process of
learning took some quarter of a million years.

The next technical innovation affected the flake cultures.
The Clactonians and Tayacians had obtained their flakes by
the use of hammer-stone or anvil; the Clactonians with their
preference for large, coarse flakes must commonly have employed the anvil method. The flakes were detached freely
from the core, and if further shaping was required it was
done subsequently as secondary trimming or 'retouch'. Work
of this kind could be done very quickly and the resulting
tools were neither elegant nor closely standardized. The new
device characterizing the Levallois culture was so to prepare
the block of flint that a perfect and completed flake tool
could be struck off with one carefully directed blow (Fig. 18).
One side of the block was flaked all over to form a low,
convex surface usually oval in outline; at one end cross
flaking made a flat platform roughly at right angles to the
worked face. By striking this platform correctly the greater
part of the convex surface could be removed as a symmetrical, oval flake tool, the upper side fully worked, the underside
formed by the flake surface, and the butt showing portions
of the transverse flake scars of the striking platform. This is
the true Levallois flake, and the block bearing the large scar
of the flake is known as a tortoise-core. It is likely that for
the crucial blow to detach the laboriously prepared flake, the
Levalloisians used a bone or wooden punch which was applied
to the platform and then struck with hammer-stone or wood-
en cudgel.

This efficient Levallois technique was perfected in Europe during second interglacial times, but at what is thought to have been a considerably earlier date the early Acheulians of South Africa had developed a comparable method for making hand-axes. They detached a flake large and thick enough to be turned into a hand-axe by a little further working on the underside; the flake was, in fact, being used to simulate a core. These two far separated occurrences of the tortoise-core method may perhaps represent an early instance of that surprisingly rare phenomenon: independent invention. A comparable form of flake hand-axe is found in south and central India.

No very significant technical invention in stone-work was made during the last interglacial phase—although it may well be that somewhere pioneers were beginning to experiment in the blade-flaking methods that were to be fully developed in the Upper Palaeolithic cultures. The thick, heavy flakes of the Mousterian culture which suggest its descent from the Clactonian and seem well suited to the hands of the squat, thickset Neanderthal men were trimmed in a manner sufficiently distinctive to be worth mentioning. The edges of their characteristic points and cutters were chipped with blows directed so much into the implement that instead of the flakelets peeling smoothly off they drove into the flint and broke off short leaving a tiny vertical face or step at the tip of each scar. This is known as step flaking.

Many of the new departures in stone tool-making that form so important an element in the great forward movement of the Upper Palaeolithic Age were dependent upon the discovery of a new way of striking flakes. As the whole

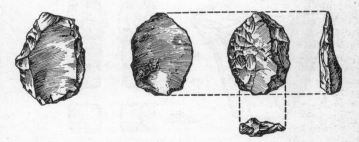

FIG. 18. *Manufacture of the Levallois flake.* Left: *tortoise-core.* Right: *the detached flake, scale 1/3 (after Singer).*

group of Eurasiatic cultures get their general name from
these blade flakes their manufacture demands full description.
The distinguishing features of the blade from which so many
specialized tools were made are the narrowness and the parallel sides, suggesting the steel of a modern table knife; a
common measurement for a blade would be four inches long
by barely an inch across. It should be remembered, however,
that exactly the same kind of flaking continued into the
Mesolithic repertory, though now on a miniature scale.

To make good blades (Fig. 19) it was often necessary to
take a nodule of flint and break it cleanly across, a fracture
that can best be secured by striking a projecting knob in a
precise and cunning manner. To judge from modern analogy,
the half-nodule was then rested on the knapper's thigh with
the fractured surface uppermost. Blows were then delivered
round the edge while at the same time the flint was rolled
in such a way that the flakes almost peeled off. A number of
these blows delivered all round the block would soon remove
the rough outer cortex and leave a fluted or multiangular
centre, conical or cylindrical, and of the purest unweathered
flint. The process of peeling off could now continue with
perfect blades as the result. The blows could either be struck
at the junction of two of the flake facets to produce blades
with a single central keel sloping down to the sharp parallel
edges, or they could be struck at the centre of a facet to
detach the whole of it together with half of those adjoining
on either side, so making a blade with a flat centre and
bevelled edges. These slender, keen-edged blades were now

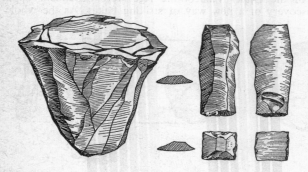

Fig. 19. *Manufacture of flint blades (modern), Brandon, Suffolk. Left: flint core with blades replaced. Right:
blade ready for division into gun flints (after Oakley).*

ready as the blanks from which many typical Upper Palaeolithic tools could be made.

A new technique capable of the finest of all flint work
came to the fore in Upper Palaeolithic times and is seen
at its best in the Solutrean; this is pressure flaking, used for
secondary trimming on blades and other flakes. In its simplest
form it was used both to form a steep strong working edge
for a scraper or to blunt one edge of a blade to make the
back of a knife on which the finger could be pressed without
hurt. The need was, in fact, to remove a number of minute
flakes evenly along the original sharp flake edge. This can be

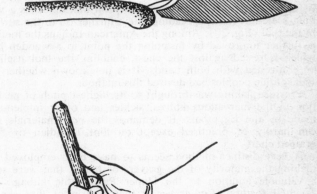

FIG. 20. *Pressure flaking. A: the flaking tool pressed from
below (after Singer); B: as practised in N.W.
Australia (after D. S. Davidson).*

done with a small hammer-stone, but not without danger of both breaking the flake (particularly if it is a slender blade) and battering the fingers. These dangers are avoided by the pressure method in which a flint fabricator is pressed upwards against the underside of the edge to be trimmed or blunted with sufficient strength to detach a little flake; this can be done at great speed so that the whole edge is retouched in a few minutes. The fabricator itself is very little specialized in form; any rough flake with a blunt squarish edge or nose will do; specimens are found in most Upper Palaeolithic sites.

The far more delicate form of pressure flaking first exemplified on Solutrean spear-heads (Fig. 8, J) could not be done with a flint fabricator but required a pointed tool of bone, hard wood, ivory, or a long incisor tooth. This point is placed against the edge to be worked in much the same way as before, but is given a rather sudden push that detaches a very thin, scale-like flake, spreading much farther on to the surface of the tool (Fig. 20). Among the American Indians the method is further improved by fastening the point to a wooden haft which is rested against the chest, enabling the tool itself to be controlled with both hands. It is not known whether the Palaeolithic peoples had devised this method.

Pressure flaking was brought to its highest pitch of perfection in the marvellous knives, sickles and other implements made by the Egyptians. It demands the best materials and can hardly be practised except on flint, obsidian or fine-grained chert.

A very distinct method seems to have been employed for making the majority of the gravers or burins that were such a valuable addition to the Upper Palaeolithic kitbag. The essential feature of a graver is that a strip of flint should have been struck off down the edge of a blade or other flake at right angles to its main surfaces; the narrow facet thus obtained may dissect with the ordinary flat end of the blade with an end blunted by retouching or with another graver facet identical with itself (the *bec de flûte* type). The result is a chisel edge, with a breadth equal to the thickness of the blade; a curved gouge-like variant can be produced by making several graver facets on one side dissect with a single one on the other. There is an enormous variety of both gravers and gouges, but it seems that most were made by the same technique. The end of the blade to be converted into a graver was trimmed into a blunt point and this rested on a fixed anvil-stone. If the blade was held at the right angle, a sharp tap on its side detached the graver strip as the result of indirect impact through the anvil. If the blade was turned round and a tap delivered on the opposite edge a second graver facet could be made to dissect with the first to produce a *bec de flûte*. Experiment has shown that this ingenious use of the ricochet blow is much quicker and more effective than striking directly downwards from the blade end.

In many ways the methods used to make microliths were

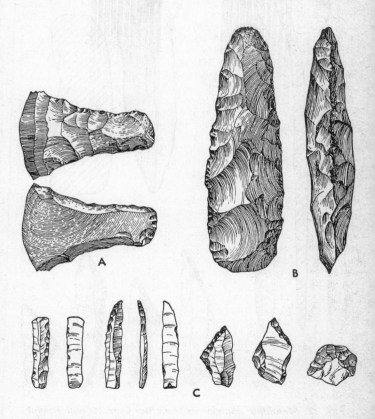

FIG. 21. *Mesolithic implements. A: tranchet axe; B: adze or core axe from Denmark, scale 1/2 (after Klindt-Jensen); C: microliths from Jalahalli, Mysore, scale 1/1 (after Seshadri).*

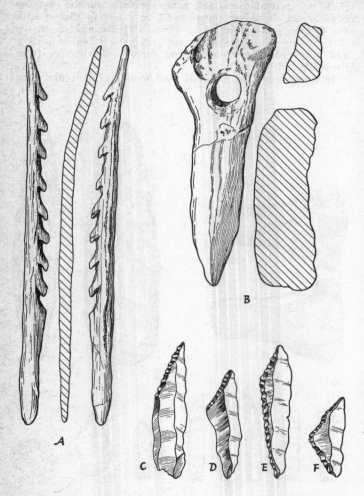

FIG. 22. *Mesolithic implements from Star Carr. A: antler point (scale 1/2); B: mattock head, elk antler (scale 3/8); C–F: microliths (scale 1/1 (after J. G. D. Clark).*

similar, but one or two developments deserve mention. It appears that for trimming or blunting the backs of these small or even diminutive blades into lunates, triangles and their other forms, a fabricator was devised that would detach a number of the minute retouch flakes simultaneously, so trimming a whole edge in one movement. Again, these same forms came to be made by chipping two notches deep into one side of a little blade (or on opposite sides for a trapeze) and then snapping off the ends beyond the notches between the fingers, and retrimming the resulting breaks. For a very long time the snapped-off ends were known as micro-burins and accepted as tools instead of the waste products that they really are.[9]

The north European Mesolithic peoples devised a new trick of flaking to give a sharp yet strong edge to their wood-cutting axes and adzes. These *tranchet* edges were formed by the intersection of two large flake scars, the flakes having been detached by blows struck crosswise at right angles to the main axis of the tool. Another very significant innovation among these peoples was to peck axes, mace-heads and picks from hard rocks, sharpening the edges by grinding, and making a hafting hole by boring from both sides. These tools, made in small numbers by the Maglemosians and Ertebølle people, clearly look forward to Neolithic techniques (Figs. 21 and 22).

WORKING IN BONE, ANTLER AND IVORY

It is a little surprising that these materials do not seem to have been used for tool-making before Upper Palaeolithic times, but presumably they were found too intractable until man was ready to go forward to specialized tools, among them the graver. Like stone, bone was utilized before it was manufactured. The Peking men and after them the Neanderthalers used solid pieces as chopping-blocks, and broken long bones for sleeking skins and other odd jobs; we have already seen how long bones may also sometimes have been used for flaking hand-axes.

When bone-working began at the hands of Upper Palaeolithic man, it was at first mainly by rubbing it down on sandstone or some other rough surface. In this way awls, lance-heads and other points could be made—a form of tool still often found in use in quite recent times. This method was also used for the so-called Lyngby axe, the first effective tree-felling implement in the north. But soon the use of

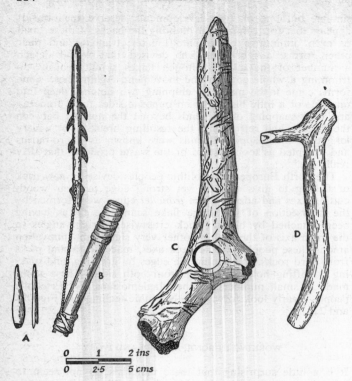

FIG. 23. *A: Aurignacian split-base bone point; B: Magdalenian harpoon; C: Magdalenian bâton de commandement (after Oakley); D: Lyngby antler axe. Scale 1/2 (after Singer).*

gravers made skilled cutting and carving feasible; it is no-where better shown than in the exquisite barbed harpoon-heads and ornamented spear-throwers of the Magdalenians. Boring of holes, presumably with flint awls or drills, was soon mastered, as is shown in *bâtons de commandement*, perforated harpoon-heads, and, at its most precise, in the Magdalenian needles. At first this drilling must have been done by hand, but by Mesolithic times at latest we can be reasonably sure that the bow-drill had been invented.

The hollow centre of bones must always be an obstacle to

the manufacture of large accurately shaped tools; among the later Upper Palaeolithic and Mesolithic peoples an ingenious way of obtaining strips of solid bone and antler was much in use. A graver was used to cut parallel furrows at the required distance apart, and when they had gone deep enough a blow at the top would detach the strip between them. This method was used for harpoon and leister heads, and probably also to obtain narrow spalls to be rubbed down into needles.

The working of bone, antler and ivory both for implements and works of art was brought to greater perfection by the Magdalenians than by any other primitive people. Their skill and artistry have been approached only by the Eskimo.

WORKING IN WOOD

There is no reason to doubt that wood was utilized and worked as early as stone, but it seldom survives to remind us of the fact. The oldest known wooden artifact in the world is the pointed end of a yew-wood spear found with Clactonian tools in the water-logged Elephant Bed at Clacton-on-Sea in England. The end had been sharpened with flint flakes. Second to it comes a complete spear, also of yew-wood, found inside the skeleton of an elephant at Lehringen in Germany. This weapon, evidently most effectively used, had been made by Levalloisians, and they hardened the point by fire. The hollow scrapers, or spoke-shaves, that occur in one form or another throughout most of Paleolithic times, were almost certainly used for shaping wood, and, to judge from Australian analogies, so too were other forms of scraper that have sometimes been too readily assumed to have been exclusively used for preparing skins.

We do not know when stone tools first began to be supplied with wooden hafts, though it was probably not before the time of the Middle Palaeolithic cultures. Such usage, however, became very common among the Upper Palaeolithic and Mesolithic peoples who must have mounted tanged dart-heads, spear-heads, drills and other tools in wood, as well as the great range of microliths that were set in wood to make barbs, points and continuous cutting-edges (Fig. 24). Bone harpoon-heads and leister prongs were also attached to wooden shafts. With the invention of the bow and arrow (p. 145) stone-tipped and all-wooden arrows must have been added to the repertory. Large bows, evidently of wood, are shown in eastern Spanish cave paintings of Late Palaeolithic and Mesolithic Age. The Maglemosian bows preserved in a peat bog at Holmegaard in Denmark were well designed and skilfully executed; cut from a single piece of elm, the longest was about 145 centimetres. The arrow-shafts associated with them had grooved ends, presumably to take flint heads.

In Europe, whence so large a proportion of the evidence must still be derived, true carpentry blossomed with the spread of forest in the Mesolithic Age. The northern peoples felled trees on a considerable scale, used their axes and adzes to hollow dug-out canoes (with the help of fire), carved canoe paddles and boomerang-like throwing-sticks—in addition to the bows, arrows and many other shafts and hafts already mentioned.

TRAPS AND NETS

From the beginning of his history man was able to kill animals swifter and stronger than himself. The cunning that made this possible revealed itself most clearly in the setting of traps. As we have seen the use of implements can begin quite empirically by the snatching up of handy sticks and stones, but to make and set a trap demands a very considerable degree of imaginative foresight. It is impossible to know when it began. No doubt driving herds over cliffs or into pits, morasses and other natural danger-spots must have preceded deliberate constructions. The branch-covered pit with a stake at the bottom may early have been devised for killing elephants and other heavy animals. Modern Congo pygmies to this day dig holes in which they conceal themselves below piles of dung (to disguise their scent) and leap up to disembowel a passing elephant.

The first possible evidence for the construction of traps is that of the Magdalenian paintings in the Font-de-Gaume cave in the Dordogne. Certain sketchy drawings once known as 'tectiforms' have been interpreted as fall-traps, mainly because in one of them a mammoth appears to be floundering. But as the Palaeolithic artists often made quite haphazard superpositions, this interpretation is by no means certain, and it remains equally probable that the tectiforms represent summer huts. The most ancient traps to have survived are fish-traps dating from Atlantic times in Denmark—probably the handiwork of the Ertebølle people. These are of a type still in use in Europe today, making one of the most interesting known examples of the persistence of a simple but efficient invention. They are known also from tomb-paintings of the Egyptian Old Kingdom. The type is a basketry cone or

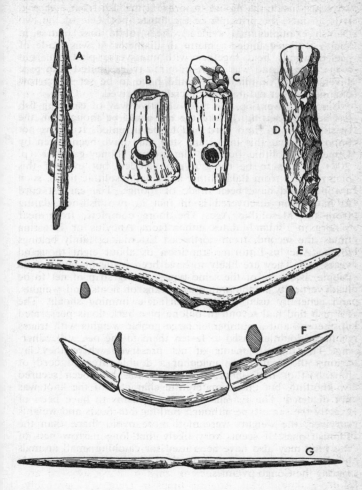

FIG. 24. *Mesolithic implements from north-west Europe. A:*
bone arrow-point with flints, Skåne, Sweden; B and C:
Maglemosian perforated antler sleeves; D: a 'Thames
pick', Farnham, Surrey (all scale 1/3); E and F: wood-
en throwing-sticks, Jutland (scale 1/4); G: bow stave,
Holmegaard, Denmark (length 145 cm.) (after Singer).

tube, closed at the bottom and with internal funnels, one always just inside the mouth, to prevent the fish from escaping. It is, in fact, the principle of the lobster-pot. One of the two Danish examples had evidently been quite four metres in length and just under a metre in diameter; it was made of peeled wands held together with transverse plaits of split twigs. The second was made of birch twigs plaited with pine slivers. Traps of this kind would have to be set in narrow channels, either natural or artificially contrived.

Since its invention, the most effective way of catching fish has been by netting. Before the net could be thought of, the twisting of fibre into cord had to be invented. It seems not impossible that this important step may have been taken by Upper Palaeolithic hunters; the woman honey-gatherer (p. 208) appears to be using a rope ladder, but even if this picture dates from Palaeolithic and not Mesolithic times, such a rope could have been made of thongs. The earliest cord to have been discovered is in fact in two fish-nets dating from the Mesolithic Age. The more complete, from near Viborg in Finland, dates either from Ancylus or Littorina times; the second, from north-east Estonia, certainly belongs to the Ancylus-Littorina transition of about eight thousand years ago. They are likely to have been made by late Kunda people. Both are of the seine type—a long strip of net to be held vertically in the water by means of floats and weights, and generally used to catch surface-swimming shoals. The Finnish find had seventeen oblong pine-bark floats perforated at one end and a number of large pebble weights with traces of fibre, doubtless used to fasten them to the net, still adhering. The tiny fragments of net preserved where they lay against the floats were made of a double-threaded cord of lime bast or nettle-fibre; the reticulation had been secured by knotting, but unfortunately the character of the knot was not detected. The Estonian specimen seems to have been of exactly the same type although nothing but floats and weights survived; the weights were of a more ovoid shape than the Finnish ones. It seems very likely that long narrow nets of this kind may also have been used for catching small animals by drives in undergrowth, a method still in use—for example among the Congo pygmies.

BOATS AND OTHER TRANSPORT

No actual remains or pictures of Palaeolithic boats have been found, nor is there any evidence implying sea passages by Palaeolithic peoples. Nevertheless, it seems almost certain that they must have used logs or rough rafts on lakes and rivers from time to time, particularly after they became interested in fishing.

The use of the seine fishing-net implies the use of a boat, even if one end is attached to bank or shore, and it so happens that the oldest known boats also date from Mesolithic times in northern Europe. One, from Drenthe in the Netherlands, has been dated by Carbon-14 to about 6300 B C. It is a dug-out canoe made from a pine trunk with solid, roughly-squared bow and stern. Fire had been used in the hollowing process. The second, also a dug-out canoe, comes from the silt of the River Tay in Perth, Scotland. It had been shaped, also with the help of fire, from the trunk of a Scots fir, and measured rather under a metre across the gunwales; neither bow nor stern was well enough preserved for its form to be distinguishable. This canoe had been made in the second half of the Ancylus Lake period, and can probably be credited to the Maglemosians. Maglemosian steering paddles with oblong or roughly rectangular blades have been found in both Denmark and England.

LAMPS

For the greater part of his history, man is unlikely to have had any artificial light beyond the fugitive flicker of fires and torches. In some regions where suitable wood was available he may have collected resin and used lumps of it for torches. The oldest known lamps were used by the Upper Pa-

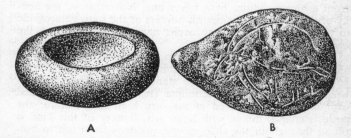

A   B

FIG. 25. *Upper Palaeolithic stone lamps. A: La Madeleine (scale 1/2; after Peyrony); B: La Mouthe, length* c. *12.8 cm. (under-surface).*

laeolithic hunters of western Europe, probably mainly for light-
ing the artists when they were at work in the depths of the
caves. They were shallow saucers, sometimes with a broad
tongue projecting from the rim to form a handle (Fig. 25). The
finest known example of this kind of lamp comes from the cave
of La Mouthe in the Dordogne; it is very carefully finished, of
good proportions and with a pleasing engraving of an ibex on
the base. Eskimo who have comparable, though larger, lamps
use blubber from seal or walrus for fuel and a wick of moss.
Possibly the Stone Age Europeans may have done the same,
for seal remains, though uncommon, have been found in their
cave litter at most periods, while live seals are several times
represented in their art. Usually, however, they must have
made do with ordinary fats.

Curiously formed oval containers with rounded bases are
one of the two pottery forms commonly found in the middens
of the Ertebølle people, and it is thought they were used as
blubber lamps. Seal bones, though not abundant, occur at
very many Ertebølle sites.

It is quite probable that, like the Eskimo, the Palaeolithic
and Mesolithic hunters occasionally used these lamps as a
source of heat and for small jobs of cooking.

POTTERY AND OTHER CONTAINERS

Pottery was almost certainly an invention of the Neolithic
Age that went with the more settled life of husbandry. Its
occurrence at Mesolithic sites in northern Europe and east
Africa is therefore thought to be merely a product of the
overlap of periods and the borrowing of a useful invention
from a higher culture by a lower one. Nevertheless, the ability of the Moravian mammoth-hunters of the Late Palaeolithic
to harden figurines in clay ovens must be recalled, and the
evidence cautiously judged.

In the Ertebølle kitchen middens, besides the oval containers
already described as possible blubber lamps, remains of large
jars with pointed bases are the standard form. They have all
been made by the coil technique (p. 403), often burnished
with a pebble, and fired at no very high temperature; the
paste is coarse, mixed with large grit. Pottery of this kind is
found throughout the shell-mound middens from top to bottom and must therefore date back at least to between 4000
and 5000 B C.

It may be guessed that the hunting peoples of the Palaeolithic Age used leather vessels and sewn-up skins for containing

liquids, but we have no proof of it. The Spanish honey-gatherer must be mentioned again, for she appears to be carrying a handled leather bag to receive the comb. The attractive art of working the silvery-white bark of the birch was probably widespread among the northern peoples during the Mesolithic period when this tree was abundant. Rolls of birch bark up to thirty inches long were found at the lake-side encampment of Maglemosians at Star Carr in Yorkshire, and pieces have also been found at a Maglemose site in Denmark. No vessels have as yet been discovered, but even if the bark was most commonly used for boxes, quivers and the like, containers made of it could presumably have been caulked to make them watertight.

CLOTHES AND ORNAMENTS

Clothing is both practical and anti-practical, a means of keeping alive and an acutely uncomfortable, painful or even dangerous means of displaying wealth or spiritual and social status. It is possible to argue that when our ancestors first took to dressing themselves it was for the unpractical reasons. Supporters of this point of view quote the Fuegans, who seem cheerfully to survive in a cruelly cold climate with no more than a skin slung over the shoulder; the need of clothes to keep warm, they say, is due entirely to habit, and man first covered his body from a desire for display. It would be wrong to scorn this point of view, for we are far too inclined to expect primitive man to be like ourselves in always putting what we regard as practical needs before more imaginative or purely psychological ones. Nevertheless, it does appear certain that clothing served an essential physical need in the Stone Age, and must rank after tool-making and the control of fire as one of the products of human ingenuity enabling our kind to adapt to a world-wide range of environments.

As the earlier hand-axe users seem generally to have avoided very cold climates by migration (p. 117), they may not have had much need for protection; the conditions offered by the second and third interglacials were probably relatively easy everywhere. The early flake tools look as though the preparation of skins was among their uses, and by the time we come to the Neanderthalers it is usually assumed by higher authorities than the popular illustrators that they wore pelts further to protect them from the glacial cold that unquestionably drove them to cave-dwelling.

With the Upper Palaeolithic Age both art and the remains

FIG. 26.
*Upper Palaeolithic
fur clothing. Fig-
urine in ivory.
Mal'ta, Siberia—
slightly enlarged
(after Singer).*

of material culture lift us on to certain ground. Some of the fine awls and points that were made throughout the period seem best suited for piercing leather in order to stitch it while the fine bone needles of the Magdalenians could have been used for sewing as perfectly neat as that practised by the Eskimo and some North American Indians on their well-tailored and beautiful leather clothes. A Gravettian statuette from Mal'ta, Siberia, shows a man wearing a hood and closely fitting body garment and trousers of skins with the fur outside (Fig. 26); these seem to have been made all in one piece like the 'siren suit' of the English in the Second World War. Most of the female statuettes of the period, being cult objects, are naked, but one seems to depict a small apron worn at the back between the buttocks. One of the very few naturalistic portraits of human beings, the carved, engraved and painted head and shoulders of a bearded Magdalenian hunter from Angles-sur-l'Anglin in the Vienne department of France shows him wearing a fur robe, well up at the back of his neck and open at the front to show a high-necked garment worn underneath. Crossing the Pyrenees to the late Palaeolithic and Mesolithic paintings of eastern Spain, we find the men nearly always portrayed naked, whether they are hunting or fighting—a fact suggesting that men normally only clothed themselves when the climate was cold. Some of the women in these paintings, on the other hand, are wearing long skirts, apparently with peaks at the front and back, although their upper parts seem to be naked except for broad armlets.

To judge from the imprints of broad-toed naked feet found in some of the French caves, foot-coverings were not usually worn. It seems unlikely, however, that these hunters did not tie leather or pelts on to their feet when they had to go on to ice or snow.

It remains to consider the special costumes donned as disguises or ceremonial attire. A number of paintings and engravings in the French caves show men wearing animal masks and pelts, and the only difficulty is to distinguish between those which certainly represent men taking part in the animal-evoking masked dances and other rites so nearly universal among modern primitives, and the few that may perhaps portray hunters dressed up in the skins of the animals they are stalking—a practice commonly found among the Bushmen of South Africa and shown in their art. It seems just possible that the bison-headed man at the famous cave of Les Trois Frères, Ariège, is such a disguised hunter, but on the whole he seems more likely to be taking part in a ritual, and this must be the explanation of most of these pictures. There are little jumping chamois-horned figures from Teyjat, a seeming mammoth-dancer and other masked forms from Combarelles, and a naked man and woman with animal masks engraved on a piece of bone at the cave of La Madeleine, as well as others less easy to identify. As for the famous painting known as the 'Sorcerer' from the same cave of Les Trois Frères, it may represent a shaman or medicine man, but there is something about this most strange antlered figure that suggests rather that an animal deity or ancestral spirit is being portrayed.

The Stone Age hunters must also sometimes have decked themselves on other occasions than religious ones—and particularly for battle. The line of five warriors from the Gasulla Gorge in eastern Spain are wearing head-dresses, some of them apparently feathered.

Among the most interesting discoveries at the Maglemosian lake-site of Star Carr, Yorkshire, were several frontal bones of deer which had evidently been used for head-dresses. The antlers had been cut off, the bone itself shaped into a rough frontlet and perforated, evidently for the reception of feathers or some other embellishment.

These frontlets are the only known surviving relics of the masks, head-dresses and other gear so vividly recalled for us by Stone Age art. With personal ornaments, often made of durable materials, much more has been preserved. Decorating the face and body, changing its colour, perforating the flesh for the reception of ornaments, reshaping the skull, to do these things was one of the earliest desires of man, and one that has only grown more subtle with civilization. The motives seem to be strangely mixed. Ornaments can come to be the mark of an age group, a clan, a tribe or of leadership within the tribe, and so satisify the wish for some mark of exclusiveness and at the same time of membership always so strongly developed in children. They may also satisfy the craving for the rare and precious possession. Again, there seems to be deeply rooted in human psychology a notion *qu'il faut souffrir pour être beau*—or *belle*. Finally, perhaps there is something rather better than all these urges, a certain divine discontent that has made man dissatisfied not only with his surroundings but with his own person. He has wished to change and beautify his face and body; sometimes it may be in a kind of poetic emulation of the birds and flowers that he so often plunders for the purpose.

FIG. 27. *Upper Palaeolithic pendants from La Madeleine*. Left: *canine tooth*. Right: *engraved bone (after Capitan and Peyrony)*.

If, as it appears, the *Pithecanthropi* brought back bright quartz crystals to their caves at Choukoutien because they were pleasing to the eye, it seems likely that they may already have been inclined to deck themselves with feathers, or anything of striking colour or form. But with ornaments as with so many other creations of culture, it is not until the Upper

Palaeolithic Age that we begin to find tangible evidence of their existence. In Europe skeletons have often been found with ivory and bone pendants (Fig. 27), and with necklaces, bracelets, legbands and headgear made of shells and bone beads. Beads have usually been made from dentalium, spondylus, cyclonassa, cowrie and other shells, from small vertebrae and occasionally from fossils, all carefully drilled for threading. Shells have often been carried hundreds of miles from their home seas. Particularly fine necklaces and shell head-dresses decked some of the Grimaldi skeletons. In the triple burial in the Barma Grande cave, for example, the skeleton of a man still displayed a necklace in which teeth made spacers dividing regular rows of beads of nassa shells and fish vertebrae. This necklace, by chance held intact by a clay deposit, suggests that scattered beads in other burials may once have been threaded with equal excellence of design. Teeth with an hour-glass perforation through the root were popular, particularly the curiously lobed canine teeth of stags. Among forty canines of bear and lion apparently worn as a necklace and belt by a Magdalenian buried at the Abri Duruthy at Sordes, nearly half were finely engraved, with seal and fish among the animals portrayed.

The same love of personal finery spread with Upper Palaeolithic traits to eastern Asia. At Mal'ta and other Siberian sites there were well-made beads and pendants of ivory and bone; in the Late Upper Palaeolithic or Early Mesolithic occupation of the Upper Cave at Choukoutien bodies have been buried wearing cylindrically shaped bone pendants, beads of perforated fish vertebrae and sea-shells, and with pieces of mother-of-pearl. The shells and mother-of-pearl had been brought from the coast one hundred and twenty miles away. Pieces of red haematite found in these Chinese graves make another link with the west, for ochre and other red oxides often occur in Upper Palaeolithic burials in Europe, and although it is believed that the dead were laid with it for magical reasons (p. 290), there seems good reason to suppose it was also used as a body paint by the living. An instance of a pendant which was certainly worn as an amulet comes from Petersfels; the form, though highly schematized, is derived from the female statuettes, and was presumably a fertility charm. Probably the perforated cut-out animal heads, usually of horses, that form an attractive element of Magdalenian home art were also worn as amulets.

The traditional ornaments of the Upper Palaeolithic remained popular among the Mesolithic peoples. The Maglemosians wore amber beads and pendants, sometimes enriched with geometrical patterns, as well as a great range of perforated teeth—those of bear, aurochs, wild cat, otter, wild boar and deer have been recorded. In the microlithic culture represented at Langhnaj, Bombay State, dentalium shells accompanied burials. By far the finest Mesolithic ornaments, however, come from the Natufian cemetery at the Wadi el Mughara in Palestine. Several of the skeletons there had coronets and caps of dentalium shells, and one necklace in which these shells seem to have been used as spacers between bone beads carefully cut and polished into twin lobes, probably phallic in intention.

APPENDIX TO CHAPTER VI

LEADING TYPES OF TOOLS AND WEAPONS CHARACTERISTIC OF THE PALAEOLITHIC AND MESOLITHIC CULTURES OF THE WORLD

1. LOWER AND MIDDLE PALAEOLITHIC CULTURES

The Kafuan and Oldowan Cultures

The implements of these African cultures, the oldest known in the world, are made entirely on water-worn pebbles of lava, quartz and quartzite. The Kafuan, if indeed it is a true culture, is represented mainly by flattish oval pebbles with two or three flakes removed to make crude chopping, cutting and scraping tools. Sometimes the rough primary breaks show further flaking, always on one side of the pebble; in the latest form of the culture hollow scrapers and wedge-shaped points can be distinguished. In the Oldowan culture the pebbles were usually more fully rounded. The same chopping, cutting and scraping tools are at first characteristic, but in the latest form they were chipped much more extensively and on both sides to produce roughly oval bifacial tools, the bases still consisting of the unworked surface of pebble. These bifacial pebble tools are clearly ancestral to the true Abbevillian hand-axe.

The Abbevillian-Acheulian Cultures

These core-tool cultures (which include the Stellenbosch of South Africa) are typified by the hand-axe, although flakes were sometimes utilized and occasionally shaped into rough side-scrapers. The commonest type of hand-axe is a tongue-shaped implement with one end quite narrowly pointed. (They are often described as pear-shaped, but the pear in question would be a flattened one.) In the earlier Abbevillian specimens the broad end is often unworked, consisting simply of the natural surface of pebble or flint nodule. In all Abbevillian hand-axes the edges tend to be zigzag as a result of the deep flake scars left by the hammer-stone blows; with the Acheulian the cylinder-bar technique gave straight edges, often with one side sharper than the other. The advanced Acheulian repertory includes more rounded, ovate forms. In South Africa, where suitable small nodules were not readily available, hand-axes were often made on thick flakes worked on both sides; as thinner, more elegant forms developed with the Acheulian culture, flakes were often used also in Europe. Many of the hand-axes associated with Swanscombe man were shaped from such stout flakes. Although the hand-axe in all its phases shows astonishing uniformity throughout its range in Africa, Europe and Asia, certain local variants can be distinguished. In Africa and India a variety known as the cleaver has a large flake surface at one end producing a flat, axe-like edge. In western European ovate hand-axes the sides often show a sinuous line like a very open S which appears to have been intentional. No variety of hand-axe, so far as is known, was ever hafted.[10] The latest phase of the Acheulian is distinguished as the Micoquian, the typical form of tool being a small and very pointed hand-axe usually made from a flake.

The Clactonian and Tayacian Cultures

The Clactonian was predominantly a simple flake culture in which the flakes were struck off, probably on a fixed anvil-stone, in such a way as to make a very prominent bulb of percussion. The base of the flake (striking platform) was plain, without the flake scars left in preparing the platform for the Levallois flake, and at a characteristically open angle (about 120 degrees) to the main flake surface. The edges of these coarse, irregular flakes were often retouched all round the edges to make scrapers and knives. Hollow scrapers or spoke-shaves were an established form, and must sometimes have been used to trim the shafts of pointed wooden spears. Cores, often with the crust of the nodule left on one side, were further trimmed to make a kind of heavy chopper. The Tayacian, another flake culture, is related to the Clactonian and somewhat later. Newly recognized, its tool types are at present ill-defined; the flakes are usually smaller than the Clactonian but equally rough.

The Punjab Flake Culture

This simple flake culture is the oldest known from the Indian sub-continent. It consists entirely of large flakes with plain striking platform at a high angle to the flake surface, thus generally recalling the Clactonian technique. A steep narrow retouch seems sometimes to have been applied to the edges, but usually there was no secondary working.

The Soan, Anyathian, Tampanian, Patjitanian, Choukoutienian and Related Cultures

All these cultures belong to the chopper and chopping-tool group of south and east Asia. Of the three most characteristic implements: (a) the chopper is like a large coarse scraper, but more commonly made on a core instead of a flake; it is flaked only along one side of the upper surface to produce a rounded or straight cutting-edge; (b) the chopping-tool is made on a core or tabular chunk of stone and has a single cutting-edge made by flaking from both surfaces; the intersecting scars of coarse flakes produce a sinuous or zig-zag edge; (c) the hand-adze is a core tool usually of tabular form with the cutting-edge at one end and in the opposite plane from the long axis in the characteristic adze fashion; this edge is trimmed on the upper surface only.

The Early Soan culture of Pakistan and East Punjab is the most westerly of the Asiatic chopper-chopping-tool cultures, following the Punjab Flake Industry. It includes both flake and pebble tools, the flakes generally with plain striking platform at a high angle to a flake surface with a large bulb of percussion in the Clactonian manner. The choppers are made on pebbles flaked over the upper surface and along one side; the chopping-tools, also on pebbles, may show the characteristic zigzag edge. The Soan at this early stage belonged entirely to the Asiatic tradition. The Late Soan which dates from the third glaciation, probably extending into the following interglacial, in its first phase is a refinement of the early culture with the choppers and scraping implements smaller and more neatly made. Already there is some progress towards the prepared striking platform, tortoise-core technique. A few parallel-sided flakes, or flake-blades, are also included. In the second phase Late Soan B, the tortoise-core method has become characteristic and the culture is in many ways close to the Late Levalloisian of western Europe, although choppers made on pebbles still persist.

The Burmese Anyathian culture tends to divide into two according to whether tools have been made on silicified tuff or the intractable fossil wood. Where tuff has been available, choppers predominate, followed by chopping-tools and then adzes. Flakes also are present, usually irregular and with plain, high-angled striking platforms comparable to the Clactonian; rarely these flakes have been retouched to make scrapers. In the fossil wood implements the difficulty of flaking except across the grain has produced a very high proportion of tabular tools worked at the narrow end; nearly 80 per cent of tools are adzes, most of them with a single cutting-edge, a few double-ended and in both forms with a retouch that gives the edge a slightly scalloped outline. The repertory is completed by choppers and chopping-tools in much smaller numbers.

The little-known Tampanian culture of Malaya has the usual assemblage of flakes, chopping-tools and choppers, the latter characteristically with rounded or oval cutting-edge, including some that are very steep-ended. As in the Patjitanian, a crude hand-axe-like tool occurs.

In the Patjitanian culture of Java large, coarse flakes often with the outer crust remaining on the butt are common, usually without secondary working; such core tools as exist are usually made on pebbles or small boulders. The chopper is the predominant form, but chopping-tools also occur and adzes made on very massive flakes. Implements that have been described as proto-hand-axes are an unusual feature of this culture, but as these oval and sometimes pointed forms are flaked on one surface only and merge imperceptibly into ordinary chopping-tools, they are likely to be a local derivation with no influence from the Abbevillian-Acheulian tradition.

At Choukoutien itself the great majority of the broken pieces of quartz, sandstone, chert and other stone artificially broken were not recognizable as implements; flakes seem more commonly to have been utilized than cores, and a few were retouched to make crude points and scrapers. Pebbles and oval boulders had been made into both choppers and chopping-tools, but these were infrequent. In the upper levels a more careful selection of material had been made, and the resulting greater use of chert led to somewhat better-looking tools, but with no real advance in design.

The Levalloisian Culture

It is impossible altogether to isolate a Levalloisian culture, so closely does it appear to be related to the Acheulian tradition and so often is it found mingled with other cultures, particularly the Micoquian and Mousterian. The Levallois technique has already been described, and some description given of the resulting tortoise-core and Levallois flake. The typical cutting-tool or side-scraper made by this method is oval or sub-rectangular and often a considerable size; sometimes, however, triangular flakes were struck, ranging from a broader to a very narrow pointed form. As has been said, secondary retouching was usually unnecessary on these carefully prepared flakes, but some points seem to have been further thinned at the base as though for hafting. In the later Levalloisian of the last interglacial period, a small, bifacial, heart-shaped hand-axe was often included in the repertory.

The Mousterian Culture

In so far as the term Middle Palaeolithic has validity it can be applied to this culture, together with the versions of it showing Late Acheulian and Levalloisian influence. The pure Mousterian flake culture shows its Clactonian ancestry in the use of rather thick flakes with plain striking platforms; an assembly of tools usually shows a somewhat monotonous repetition of two standard types, a D-shaped side-scraper and a triangular point or knife—in both the retouching is careful and usually in the stepped flaking technique. A third implement typical of this culture is the small discoidal core, presumably used as a rough scraper or chopper. In the latest phase there is a tendency for the points and side-scrapers to be smaller.

The Sangoan Culture

This culture developed from the Acheulian tradition as a special adaptation to wet tropical forest conditions of central Africa. It is typified by four types of implement: a gouge or chisel worked on both faces, an elongated pick or adze, an axe with a *tranchet* edge and a long lance-head.

The Fauresmith Culture

This culture developed the old Stellenbosch (Acheulian) tradition into small slender hand-axes and cleavers, but a very

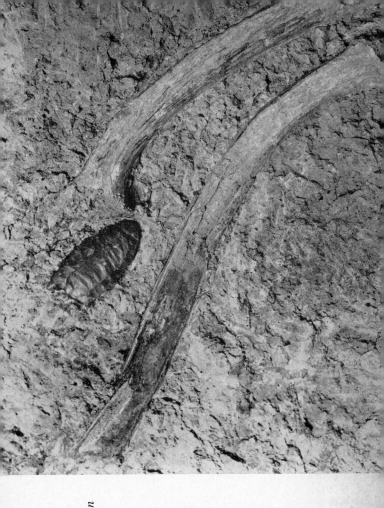

1
Folsom point and associated fossil bison ribs embedded in matrix,
Type Station, Folsom, New Mexico

[D.M.]

2 *Valley of the Vézère near Les Eyzies, Dordogne, France*

3
Palaeolithic
Cave
Painting I:
crouching
bison from
Altamira,
Province of
Santander,
Spain

[l'Homme

[l'Homme

4 *Palaeolithic Cave Painting II: cow and horses from Lascaux, Dordogne, France*

(a)   [l'Homme, *photo Max Bégouen*

5 *Palaeolithic sculptures*

    (a) *Clay bison from Tuc d'Audoubert, France*
    (b) *Wild horse and boar from the frieze at Le Roc, France*

(b)   [l'Homme, *photo Henri Martin*

(a) [Willcox

6

African Rock Painting

(a) *South African Bushmen. Steatopygic figures*

(b) *The Sahara Masked Hunter*

[l'Homme, *photo R. Perret* (b)

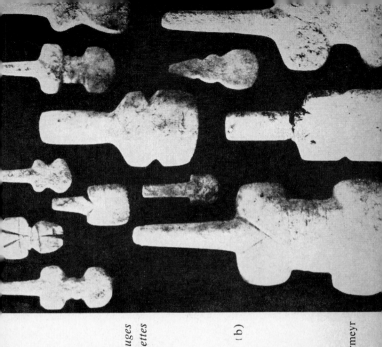

7

Comparison of Palaeolithic and Neolithic 'Venuses.'

(a) *Vénus de Lespuges*
(b) *Cycladic statuettes*

(b)

(a)

[Schachermeyr

[l'Homme,
photo
J. Oster

(a)

[*photo Josephine Powell*, T.H.

8 *Selection of Asiatic Painted Pottery*
   (a) *from Sialk, Persia*
   (b) *from Yang-shao culture, China*

(b)

[O.M.

(a) [Kenyon

9 *Neolithic Jericho*

   (a) *Clay-modelled head*
   (b) *The Great Tower*

(b) [Kenyon

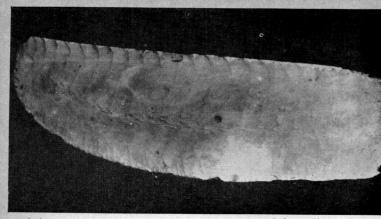

(a)   [*photo Chuzeville*

10   (a) *Ripple-flaked flint knife blade from Gebel-el-Arak,*
          Egypt. Gerzean culture. Paris, Louvre.
      (b) *Sialk: carved sickle handle with human figure*

(b)   [*Ghirshman*

(a)

11   *Megalithic Architecture I*

    (a) *Malta: Tarkien temples, main altar of the middle temple*

    (b) *Malta: Mnaijdra temples, the interior*

(b)

12
*Megalithic
Architecture II
Ireland, New
Grange: stone
lying before the
entrance*

[P.W.I.]

high proportion of all tools was now made on flakes and may have been intended for hafting. In some regions carefully shaped round stone balls probably were used for bolas.

2. THE UPPER PALAEOLITHIC BLADE CULTURES

The Châtelperronian Culture

The earliest of the known blade cultures included among its tools the simple end-scrapers, spoke-shaves, and several forms of graver that occur throughout all these Upper Palaeolithic cultures, but is distinguished by a particular form of knife blade. The Châtelperronian knife is made from a blade with one edge straight and razor-like, the other gently curved over towards the point and blunted by steep retouching. The most primitive version of it (sometimes particularized as the *Audi* point) is broader and made from an ordinary longish flake rather than a true blade.

The Aurignacian Culture

This culture (formerly known as the Middle Aurignacian, when the Châtelperronian was Lower, and the Gravettian Upper, Aurignacian) includes some of the most skilful and distinctive flint-work of Upper Palaeolithic times; it is also marked by the first introduction of true bone-working. The flint-working is particularly marked by steep trimming with narrow, parallel-sided flake scars that gives a finely fluted effect. This is found on end-scrapers, small roundish scrapers looking like little cores, on keeled scrapers and a complicated form of beaked graver or gouge (*burin busqué*). The bone implements included little pins or awls and, most characteristically, the split-based bone point, evidently a light spear-head, that had the one end ground and polished to a point, the other split (but not *cut*) to receive a wedge-ended shaft. They also include *bâtons de commandement*, or portions of antler with one or more holes driven through them. The name signifies a belief that they were used as ceremonial sceptres, but although this may conceivably have been true of some of the richly carved examples later made by the Magdalenians, there is no need to doubt that the Aurignacian specimens were wholly functional, probably used either for straightening shafts, or softening leather thongs.[11]

The Gravettian Culture

This culture shows its derivation from the Châtelperronian in the knife blade that is its most distinctive tool. The Gravettian form is inclined to be rather smaller, and the blunted back is straight, parallel with the cutting-edge, instead of curving forward to the point. Probably two or more of these blades were set in a grooved wooden handle to produce a continuous blade—thus presaging the multiple settings so characteristic of the Mesolithic Age. Points, probably dart-heads, with a kind of tang and a shoulder on one or both sides, make another new type appearing at the end of Gravettian times. Bone was less skilfully used than in the Aurignacian culture. Among the eastern Gravettian mammoth-hunters, however, ivory was made into wedges for splitting wood and bone.

The Solutrean Culture

The Solutrean culture of southern France and northern and eastern Spain is sharply distinguished by an extraordinary mastery of pressure flaking, displayed at its most exquisite in the willow-leaf and laurel-leaf lance points. These weapons range in length from about two inches to as much as a foot in exceptional specimens. Often they are pressure flaked all over both surfaces. The later Solutrean is characterized by the addition of a tanged point with a shoulder or low barb on one side only; unlike the Late Gravettian shouldered points these are pressure flaked and very exactly shaped. In this last phase of the south-west European Solutrean some local specializations developed. A large concave-based point is typical of the north-west Spanish coast (where the single-shouldered type is unknown), while in south-east Spain a true winged and barbed point occurs which is in every way comparable to true arrow-heads of later times.

The Hamburg Culture

This northern counterpart[12] of the Magdalenian was, like it, specially equipped for reindeer hunting. The flint repertory is of pure blade type with end-scrapers and several varieties of graver; a blade ending in a narrow point or awl is particularly common. The most distinctive flint implement, however, is a tanged point with a single shoulder. As a piece of equipment, presumably a dart-head, this can be compared with the shouldered points of the Gravettians, but the form is different. Reindeer antler was freely used for tools, though not perhaps with quite all the skill of the Magdalenians; the repertory included a single-sided barbed harpoon-head, recalling the Magdalenian but differing from it.

The Creswellian Culture

This can be regarded as the English counterpart to the Hamburgian and related cultures of Holland and north-west Germany, although the development probably took place locally. The blade tools, and particularly backed knives, became smaller until they approached true microliths and included geometric forms such as the trapeze.

The Magdalenian Culture

The Magdalenian reindeer-hunters' culture, with its large Gravettian inheritance, includes many kinds of the end-scrapers, gravers and other blade tools characteristic of the Upper Palaeolithic tradition, but is specially distinguished by a wide range of implements beautifully made from bone, ivory and reindeer antler. These show a rapid evolution towards greater efficiency and more perfect execution until towards the latest phase of all when deterioration set in, a mark of the general decay of the Upper Palaeolithic way of life. This progressiveness is best exemplified in the history of bone lance- and harpoon-heads. From the earlier phases of the culture there are only simple lance-heads with polished points and bases either bevelled to fit into a shaft, or cleft to receive one (the difference between the *split* base of the Aurignacian and the *cut* fork of the Magdalenian is invariable). In the middle of the culture's history true harpoons with detachable heads appear; at first they are notched along both sides to increase their grip in the wound. Later very finely cut barbs like curved teeth are carved along one side of the head, and then later still it evidently proved more effective to have rather larger barbs set alternately on either side of the head. At first the double-sided barbs were as well carved as the single, but at last, when degradation was setting in, they became angular, coarse and unsightly. Harpoons have to possess some means of fastening the line which is to remain attached to the head when it leaves the shaft; in the French Magdalenian harpoons this is provided by a raised collar just above the pointed base, while in Spanish specimens there is usually a perforated lug.

Other notable additions to the long list of bone and antler

implements are spear-throwers, often magnificently carved with game-animals, *bâtons de commandement* far more numerous and ornate than the Aurignacian prototypes, antler hammers, fish gorgets (the straight forerunner of the fish-hook) and eyed needles that appear to have been ground down in sandstone grooves. In very many ways, most strikingly in the harpoons and spear-throwers, this hunting and fishing equipment of the last of the great European Palaeolithic cultures resembles that in use among the Eskimo until recent years.

The Emiran, Athlitian and Keberan Cultures

These cultures represent, or partially represent, the eastern extension of the Eurasiatic blade culture tradition. The Emiran is a transitional culture comparable in this respect with the Châtelperronian, with a strong survival of Levalloisian forms and technique. It includes a rather squat-backed blade, and, as a diagnostic type, the Emira point, a small triangular blade trimmed at the base as though for hafting. There succeeded a period of true Aurignacian dominance (p. 139) before the Athlitian which, while showing a fairly direct descent from it, nevertheless possesses a distinct individuality in implements made largely on tabular flint. A simplified form of the keeled scraper and beaked graver preponderates.

The Keberan shows a sharp break with the previous cultures, and should certainly be regarded as being as much transitional between the Upper Palaeolithic and Mesolithic traditions as is the Capsian. It maintains the standard line of gravers and scrapers, but also includes true microliths, including a few geometric forms. The characteristic tool is a small blunted-back blade sharply pointed at both ends.

3. THE UPPER PALAEOLITHIC CULTURES OF THE INDIAN SUB-CONTINENT

Knowledge of this period in the Indian sub-continent is still too slight to allow any clear demarcation of cultures. But it is beginning to be clear that a distinct Upper Palaeolithic tradition can be recognized which embodies something at least of the blade-and-burin techniques. In the north the appearance of flake blades in the Late Soan is not sufficiently definite or accurately dated to be worth consideration as yet, but in central India in the valley of the Pravara (a tributary of the Godavari) an industry overlying the latest Acheulian horizons has very real Upper Palaeolithic characteristics. The implements, made of agate, chert, chalcedony and jasper, include scrapers, blades, a few burins and cores. Blades about an inch long with blunted back merge imperceptibly into a wide range of end and side-scrapers. This 'Upper Pravara' has been likened to the Kenya Capsian and may represent the beginnings of a similar Indian development.

A further suggestion of a true Upper Palaeolithic tradition comes from Khandivli about a score of miles north of Bombay. Here in beds of clay and gravel again lying above a horizon containing Acheulian hand-axes was a developing blade industry. At the uppermost level it included quite evolved burins of the angle, polyhedric and parrot-beak type.

4. THE UPPER PALAEOLITHIC CULTURES OF SOUTH-EASTERN AND EASTERN ASIA

An extraordinary slowness in development characterizing this vast region meant the survival right through the end of Palaeolithic times of the ancient chopper-chopping-tool tradition. As far as is at present known the intrusion of new forms, evidently deriving from the Eurasiatic blade-tool source, can be detected only in north China and Siberia.

The Ordos Culture

This north Chinese Upper Palaeolithic culture still manifests a strong survival from the Choukoutienian, including choppers made on pebbles. There is also a Moustero-Levalloisian element represented by points and side-scrapers. But the blade tradition shows itself in very simple forms of graver and backed blade; indeed, the presence of blades up to 15 centimetres in length shows that this Upper Palaeolithic technique was fully mastered.

The Baikal Culture

The flint implements included in this Siberian culture show almost the same blending of old and new forms as does the Ordos. Here, however, the addition of an array of bone tools, as well as the famous statuettes from Mal'ta, makes the Eurasiatic, and presumably mainly Gravettian, intrusion more clearly evident. Bone tools of western type include awls and eyed needles. At one site large laurel-leaf points flaked on both sides were associated with barbed bone points; the date, however, appears to have been late, and there is no doubt that these Palaeolithic types last well into post-glacial times.

5. THE UPPER PALAEOLITHIC AND LATER STONE AGE CULTURES OF AFRICA

The Middle Stone Age Cultures of South Africa

These confusingly named cultures which followed the Fauresmith during late glacial times no longer include hand-axes or cleavers but flake implements of Levallois manufacture and shaped into slender lance-points flaked on one or both sides. The latest of these cultures show a microlithic element.

The Stillbay Culture

This is one of the African cultures in which the Levallois tradition lingers. Most tools are made on Levallois flakes; they include the usual points and side-scrapers, but are mainly distinguished by points flaked on both sides and suggesting diminutive hand-axes. In the latest Stillbay of Kenya these points had become leaf-shaped and very fine, apparently worked by pressure flaking.

The Tumbian Culture

This culture of central Africa is now often included as a late plase of the Sangoan. It shows a survival of Acheulian forms with a pick-like tool derived from the hand-axe.

The Sebilian Culture

This Egyptian culture is derived from the Levalloisian and in its early form consists of implements made on very small Levallois flakes and with steeply retouched edges; a squat form is particularly characteristic. Later, although the Levallois technique continues, tools become smaller, first with backed blades of lunate form and finally with true micro-liths resembling the Natufian types. This latest Sebilian can be accepted as a Mesolithic culture.

The Aterian Culture

This north African and, perhaps, Spanish flake culture is thought to be descended from the Mousterian. Its most typical manufacture is a small tanged and barbed point, usually with a plain flake surface on the underside and flaking over the upper. It has exactly the appearance of an arrow-head and has brought the Aterians the credit of having invented man's first long-distance weapon—the bow and arrow. The Aterians also made small leaf-shaped lance-heads recalling Solutrean workmanship.

The Capsian Culture

This is the only true blade culture in Africa other than its coastal counterpart the Mouillian. Starting as a Late Upper Palaeolithic culture with the usual repertory of blades, scrapers and gravers, in its Mesolithic phases it developed microliths including such so-called geometric forms as the triangle, lunate and trapeze, all of them made on bladelets and blunted where required with steep retouch. All were intended for hafting as arrow-points, knives or barbs.

6. THE PRE-AGRICULTURAL CULTURES OF AMERICA

The cultures which developed in North and Central America from the time of the first settlement fall into two main groups, roughly divided by the Rocky Mountains. These are the Palaeo-eastern and the Palaeo-western. A possible subdivision of the second of these is the Desert culture of the Great Basin, and this term is now being extended to include a much wider range of loosely related cultures extending from the Valley of Mexico to Oregon and from the Pacific coast to the eastern foothills of the Rockies.

These two groups, which overlap extensively, particularly in the south-west of the United States, are the outcome of different modes of life. The Palaeo-eastern, characterized by lanceolate, pressure-worked projectile points, was based on big-game hunting; the Palaeo-western, in which projectile points were generally less important and core tools, choppers, keeled scrapers and grinding-stones were typical, depended economically on food-gathering, and especially on the collection of vegetable foods.

A third tradition, the Palaeo-northern, spread over Alaska and Canada at a rather later date.

The Sandia Culture

The projectile heads typifying this probably earliest of known American cultures are flaked on both sides and have a broad tang with a single shoulder. What appears to be the older form is somewhat rounded: leaf-shaped save for the shaping of the tang and shoulder; a better-worked and perhaps slightly later form is much narrower and more nearly parallel-sided, sometimes with a concave base. These flint points have been found in association with bone points very similar to themselves in shape, and with beaked scrapers and a variety of utilized flakes.

The Clovis, Folsom and Other Fluted-Point Cultures

These cultures are all distinguished by varieties of a projectile head with a single long flake removed on either face to make central concave flutings or channels. These two flakes were removed *after* the point had been fully flaked over both faces. This technique is not known from any other part of the world.

The Clovis point appears to be the most primitive form typologically, and was probably also the oldest in time. These heads are larger than the better-known Folsoms, and the fluting does not extend far up them; they have the same hollow base, but there is no fine retouch along the edges. Clovis points have often been found lying embedded among the remains of mammoth. They have also been found in association with tapering, cylindrical bone shafts with one end bevelled, possibly foreshafts used with spear-throwers, or (more probably) themselves projectile points comparable to the earlier bone lance-points of the Old World Upper Palaeolithic.

The most numerous, widespread and best-known of the fluted points are the Folsom, a name which was long applied to all fluted types. The typical form is leaf-shaped but with a deeply hollowed base giving barbs, which, however, do not project outwards but continue the line of the sides. The greatest width tends to be about two-thirds of the way towards the tip, with a slight taper towards the base. The edges show fine retouching, and the workmanship of the pressure flaking is excellent. These points fall roughly into a longer and a more stumpy version probably designed for different species of game. Also typical of the Folsom culture are two types of knife, one fluted like the point but with a blunt base, the other made from the spall removed for the fluting. Folsom points have also been found associated with many types of scraper, including nosed and keeled, with spoke-shaves, drills or awls, sharp points probably used for engraving bone (not gravers in the Old World sense), cores shaped into rough choppers, and hammer-stones. They also occur with bone awls, punches and points, and with perforated slivers of bone that may be either needles or pendant beads.

Another group is distinguished, mainly on geographical grounds, as the Eastern Fluted points; they have a general resemblance to the Clovis points, but a special Ohio variety has a constriction above the base giving the tangs a projecting ear-like appearance.

Eden, Scottsbluff, Plainview and Other Parallel-Flaked Points

This group of point types, thought to be a little later than the fluted forms, were formerly loosely known as Yuma points but are now subdivided. All of them show fine pressure flaking making long parallel-sided flake scars. The Eden point is long, slender and almost parallel-sided although with a slight taper towards the point; there is a broad central tongue at the base with shoulders too slight to be called barbs; the flaking goes horizontally across the point up to a pronounced median ridge. The Scottsbluff (widely distributed in North America) is very similar except that the blade is wider, the median ridge less, the shoulders more pronounced. The Eden and Scottsbluff points were undoubtedly sometimes used by the same people and it has been recommended that the two should be combined as the Cody Complex. The Plainview point has no shoulders but is parallel-sided often with a slightly hollowed base; the outline is relatively rather more squat than the previous varieties. They have been found associated with various scrapers and blades which were probably used as knives. Other forms identified, but with no kind of cultural connotation, are the Brown's Valley point, a broad thin leaf-shaped variety with flat or slightly hollow base; the parallel ripple flaking runs obliquely instead of horizontally across the blade. Points with this oblique flaking (usually running downwards from left to right) can be seen as forming a sub-group within the parallel-flaked point family, but they have not as yet been assigned any general name. The San Jon point is like a thicker flat-based Plainview point. Some of these ripple-flaked types must have persisted into late post-glacial times.

7. THE MESOLITHIC CULTURES OF EUROPE AND WESTERN ASIA

The Azilian Culture

Some gravers and scrapers on blades survived from the Magdalenian ancestry of this culture, but generally it consists of great numbers of microliths, including geometric forms made by the notched or micro-burin technique. Small round thumb-scrapers are also frequent. The most typical ingredient of the culture (other than the painted pebbles, p. 272) is a harpoon-head usually made in red-deer antler. It is a very poorly made affair when compared with the Magdalenian forerunner, flattish in section with barbs roughly nicked out on one or both sides. The attachment was sometimes by a projection at the base, more typically by means of a hole cut through the shaft. It has been suggested that in the latest form the harpoon was made thinner and the perforation higher (about half-way up the shaft) in order that the head should 'toggle' or twist round sideways in the wound, so securing it more firmly than any barbs could do.

The Sauveterrian Culture

This culture, formerly known as the Lower Tardenoisian, represents the last gasp of the dying Upper Palaeolithic way of life in post-glacial Europe. At a number of French sites it is found stratified between the Azilian and the true Tardenoisian, but it was not itself derived from the Azilian. Rather it was a parallel development from Upper Palaeolithic traditions. While scrapers and a few gravers maintained these traditions, microlithic tools dominated and the micro-burin method of manufacture was employed (p. 223). While tiny blades were used by the Sauveterrians, the little pointed flake was the most typical blank from which these deft craftsmen worked up their finished microliths. Among these, while elongated triangles, sometimes minute in size, and narrow steeply battered points, were made, penknife, crescent and lanceolate shapes were usually turned out in the greatest numbers. While best known from France and Britain, the Sauveterrian also extended farther north and east. In some regions it lingered on to the end of Mesolithic times.

The Tardenoisian Culture

The French Tardenoisian, which seems to be centred on the region of the Île de France, can be taken as representative of a number of related cultures flourishing in Atlantic times from the Iberian peninsula and the south of France to the Low Countries, Germany, Poland and south Russia, and given unity under the title of the blade and trapeze cultures. They include microliths, particularly broad-based points, and the micro-burin technique was used as in the Sauveterrian. Most characteristic, however, were various trapeze forms, some presumably used as arrow-heads, made across the breadth of broad flint blades (Fig. 13). Characteristic of the Tardenoisian in particular was a trapeze in which one of the angles was a right angle. It is not known whether the blade and trapeze cultures grew up locally in Europe, perhaps as a result of Neolithic influences on Mesolithic traditions, or whether they represent migratory movements. If the latter, there may have been two main streams, one westward from south Russia, one northward from the Mediterranean. It is possible that their creators, though still largely following the Mesolithic hunting and food-gathering way of life, had already become herders.

The Ahrensburg, Remouchamps, Swiderian and Other Tanged-Point Cultures of the North European Plain[13]

These cultures deriving from the Hamburgian and other final Palaeolithic sources in northern Europe all possess a closely similar range of implements only to be distinguished by minute difference of manufacture, particularly in the shaping of the tangs of the characteristic points. Gravers and round end-scrapers continue from the Palaeolithic; other implements are microlithic but do not show the perfect geometric forms typical of the Tardenoisian and were not made by the micro-burin technique. The tanged points generally have one oblique side blunted by steep retouch and the tangs formed by retouching from the flake surface; sometimes, however, the retouching is on the upper surface also. The Ahrensburg is distinguished by little points with hollow base,[14] and the Remouchamps by the inclusion of triangles. Bone and antler implements appear to be limited to simple points. The Komsa and Fosna cultures represent the spread of the tanged-point tradition down the coast of Norway (p. 157). The flint tools repeat the types already described, but as these cultures survived late, they include the wood-cutting core axe borrowed from the Maglemosians.[15]

The Lyngby Culture

This culture of northern Germany and Poland, Denmark and south Sweden is known only from heavy reindeer antler axes, adzes and hafts. In each the base of the antler is used, the massive brow tine being cut obliquely parallel with the handle for the axe, obliquely at right angles to the handle for the adze, and straight across for the haft. The edges of the cutting-tools have been ground on stone, while for the haft the tine is hollowed out—but what was hafted is unknown. It is believed that the Lyngby people also used rather large, coarse versions of the tanged point of the preceding period (Ahrensburg, etc.). The Lyngby axe is the oldest true handled axe in northern Europe.

The Maglemose[16] and Kunda Cultures

These cultures stretching across northern Europe from Britain to the east Baltic countries show an equipment specially designed for tree-felling and carpentry on the one hand and fishing and fowling as well as hunting on the other. Working in bone and antler was highly developed, coming second only to the Magdalenian in skill and variety. Several types of graver and rounded scrapers still persist from the Upper Palaeolithic repertory, but their numbers are not very great as microliths predominate. The most highly evolved and minute forms of the Late Tardenoisian are normally absent, and little blades blunted obliquely or down the whole of one side are the commonest types. The micro-burin technique was employed but perhaps not very extensively. Local variations are noticeable within the Maglemosian microlithic equipment, most conspicuously in the more evolved and precise forms, including many triangles, found in Zealand. The composite hafting of blunted microliths in wood is proved by the occurrence of two close together in the breast-bone of an aurochs at Vig, Zealand. The micro-blades found in slotted bone handles show no retouch, perhaps because the bone could resist a sharp edge as wood could not.

The important innovation among the flint implements in both these cultures is the heavy axes, adzes and picks made on cores. All of these are sharpened (and were resharpened) by means of the intersecting *tranchet* flakes (p. 223). Some of the more rod-like forms may have served as chisels. There begin to appear in the Maglemose culture a few examples of the *grand tranchet* or flake axe characteristic of the succeeding Ertebølle culture.

The introduction of implements pecked out of hard, igneous rocks and ground down for points and cutting-edges is an important innovation in the Maglemose culture; whether it began without outside influence cannot be quite certain, but it seems likely that this kind of stone-work developed out of grinding and polishing bone and antler—as in the Lyngby axes. They include oval pebble-axes with ground edges, and pebble hammer-stones with pecked finger-grips, round mace-heads perforated by drilling from both sides (probably with a stick and grit), and, by far the most elaborate form, a kind of perforated pick, sometimes with projections on either side of the shaft hole. These advanced forms may have outlasted the Maglemose period.

Wooden tools and weapons include fire-hardened points probably used as pikes; throwing-sticks made at the junction of branch and trunk; 'sleeves' for the reception of axes and adzes; paddle-rudders of willow (the earliest examples known in the world); arrow-shafts and the fine elm bows with thickened handgrip and flattened staves known only from the Holmegaard bog in Denmark. Fire seems often to have been used to help out flint tools in Maglemose carpentry.

The range of tools made in bone and antler is very great, and most typical and important among them is a series of bone points, some barbed, some set with flints. The range is too great for description. In the majority of carved specimens the barbs occur on one side only. The flints set in grooves, on the other hand, are invariably double-sided, the bone tapering to a sharp point above them; the flints are sometimes set to project slightly like rather small barbs, but are sometimes almost parallel with the shaft and continuous as though their prime purpose was to cut. Of the various barbed bone points, a few with large barbs and a perforation were probably true harpoons, but most of them were fish-spears, or leisters, and fowling weapons. For both these purposes one, two or more points (up to as many as eight) would have been mounted together on a wooden haft. Both in the Maglemose and Kunda areas such points have been found in pike skeletons, and it is likely that spearing these great fish was one of their principal uses. A rare type of Maglemosian arrow with conical head, to judge from recent north Russian analogy, was probably used to shoot fur-bearing animals with minimum damage to the pelts.

Other bone tools were axes and adzes with and without haft holes, sleeves for hafting flint axes, awls for leather-work, a kind of broad needle probably used for netting, and fish-hooks—seemingly a Maglemosian invention, in which the curved base appears generally to have been opened by boring and not cutting. A type of pointed tool made of elk bone which occurs in the Kunda culture in the east Baltic region has been confidently identified as an ice-pick.

When it is remembered that the Maglemosians and Kunda people also had devised good fish-nets and fish-traps, and the Kunda people also the sledge, it becomes apparent that although they failed to go beyond hunting and food-gathering,

the extreme skill and thoroughness with which they exploited
their difficult environment was worthy of the successors of
the gifted Upper Palaeolithic societies.

The Ertebølle Culture

The equipment of this Danish and north German culture
reveals it as a more or less direct descendant of the Maglemose, but with considerable changes of emphasis. The existence of pottery in the kitchen middens (p. 230) seems to
indicate an outside influence not visible in the tools and
weapons.

The Ertebølle people made core axes and adzes, but their
number dropped sharply in relation to the *grand tranchet*
axe which was made on a stout flake. Similarly, although
there may be said to be a microlithic element in the
Ertebølle culture, it is almost exclusively represented by trapezes, including many long narrow varieties, all of which were
hafted as arrows with a cutting-edge instead of a point. In
Egypt this form was used exclusively for fowling, and this
may well have been true also among this northern people.
It is a curious fact that in its inclusion of a large number
of different types of graver and of convex, straight and
concave scrapers on the ends of blades (sometimes up to
six inches long) the Ertebølle culture is nearer to the Upper
Palaeolithic tradition than is the intervening Maglemose.
Pecked and ground stone maces continue to be made with
hour-glass perforations, but new types of stone implements
are the round-butted axe, sometimes with a gouge-like edge
(Walzenbeil), and a type (the Limhamm axe) which, as one
face is much fuller than the other, must presumably have
been hafted as an adze. Among bone tools points are very
rare, while a little comb has been invented. Perforated antler
axes for a wooden haft are very common, whereas adzes
are few. A new type of antler axe uses a tine for the
perforation, thus securing a kind of socket or collar for
the haft.

The Asturian and Larnian Cultures

The Asturian culture, belonging to poor strand-loopers
on the north coasts of Spain and Portugal, includes in its
piled shell middens rough pebble-axes and quartzite scrapers
but is typified by the Asturian pick, a large pebble-tool
trimmed to a point at one end and doubtless used to detach
the limpets that formed a main item of diet.[17]

The Larnian of the north-east coasts of Ireland has sometimes been linked with the Asturian but with little reason. This Irish culture shows an element of the northern forest culture (presumably Maglemosian) impinging on an earlier Mesolithic tradition. It is represented by coarse core axes and by the Larne pick, a thick curved tool with a deep keel along the upper surface.

The Natufian Culture

This culture, centred on Palestine and extending also into Egypt, Syria and Lebanon, has been several times quoted for the transitional position between a hunting and agricultural economy revealed in its material equipment. The Natufian is a true microlithic culture; microlithic forms comprise many backed blades with square or slightly oblique ends, triangles, a few trapezes, and most characteristic of all, crescents (or lunates) that were probably used for tipping reed arrows. Larger implements include tanged arrow-heads, several types of graver, scrapers on the ends of blades and picks that may have served for turning the soil. The famous sickles are straight with handles sometimes ornamented with animal carvings, the blade formed by backed microliths set in a groove in the bone. Many blades show the siliceous gloss along the edge said to come only with cutting straw. Cylindrical pestles are pecked from hard rocks, the handles slightly ornamented; cup-like stone mortars have been greatly deepened by wear, presumably grain-grinding, and in one instance the bottom has been worn right through.

8. MESOLITHIC CULTURES OF CENTRAL AND EASTERN ASIA

There is no doubt that peoples with true Mesolithic cultures had penetrated far into south-western and central Asia in post-glacial times, but discovery is still in so early a stage that cultures cannot be properly defined. Sites in eastern Iraq (Zarzi and Pelgawra) seem to show a very late, perhaps Gravettian, type of Upper Palaeolithic culture verging towards the Mesolithic with microliths and the micro-burin technique, while Karim-Shahir, a fully Mesolithic site, shows less precise and well-made forms among its microliths. This site has been compared with two caves (Hotu and Belt) in the foothills of the Elburz mountains in north central Iran. At the Belt cave, however, as well as backed blades and other rather ill-defined types comparable with Karim-Shahir, there are crescents and rough geometrical microliths

—triangles and trapezes. Moving northward from Iran into western Turkmenia there is scattered evidence for Mesolithic settlement. The most certain comes from the cave of the Dam-Dam-Cheshme, where there was a Mesolithic horizon with large crescents recalling those from the Belt cave, as well as small pointed blades with steep retouch, miniature disk scrapers and conical microlithic cores used as scrapers. There are no true geometric forms here, and the link with Iran seems at present to be a weak one. Farther east in Uzbekistan there are many surface sites of uncertain age, but the cave of Katta-Kurgan has a pre-pottery level that seems more certainly to be Mesolithic. There is little doubt that, as would be expected, Mesolithic culture survived in this central Asian region well after the Neolithic phase had begun in Iran and other regions to the south-west.

In India, Mesolithic cultures are equally ill-defined, and judgement is further confused by the fact that the manufacture of microlithic flint tools undoubtedly continued not merely into the Neolithic Age but well on into historical times. At Khandivli just north of Bombay, one of the very few sites to have yielded an Upper Palaeolithic culture, this blade-and-burin culture seems to have developed into an overlying Mesolithic with microlithic blades, points, crescents, awls and fluted cores. The same range is represented at two nearby sites at Marve and Manori Point. Microlithic cultures recognized in the Gujrat region of Bombay State have not been dated, but at Langhnaj a microlithic industry including lunates seems to be definitely 'pre-pottery' and probably a true Mesolithic industry. Dentalium shells and a series of crouched dolichocephalic skeletons appeared to be contemporary with the microliths. Together these sites suggest that more research would establish a clear-cut Mesolithic culture in western India. In the east there is evidence for a similar post-glacial reduction of a blade culture to a microlithic one in the Krishna and Godavari valleys. Here the microliths include backed blades, crescents, triangles and fluted cores. Farther south in the Tinnevelly district of Madras microliths were found in fossil sand-dunes, but their age is uncertain, and this is true also of many sites in central India. Mention should be made of a non-microlithic culture identified at Sukkur and Rohri in Sind, which includes many flakes, tools described as 'hand-axes' and long blades and fluted cores. This culture may date in time from the Late Mesolithic and has been thought to be the source of the ribbon-flake blades of the Indus civilization.

In the far east of Asia, it seems that both in the Yenisei-Baikal regions of Siberia and in the Ordos region of northern China the curious blend of Upper Palaeolithic blade tradition with the far older chopper-chopping-tool inheritance continued through the post-glacial millennia, possibly even into Atlantic times. No microlithic cultures have been identified there. Great numbers of surface sites have been found throughout Inner and Outer Mongolia showing a mixture of Neolithic with microlithic forms of tool. The great bulk of material is undoubtedly of the later age, but it is probably right to recognize a Mesolithic sub-stratum perhaps dating back to the sixth millennium B C. The one stratified site in which a pure Mesolithic stratum was present was at Shabarakh-usu, Outer Mongolia, while there is a comparable culture without the usual admixture of axes, arrow-heads and other Neolithic forms at Ikhengung, Inner Mongolia. The microliths are very neatly made on narrow blades struck from little fluted cores. Awls, perforators of all kinds and small end-scrapers are frequent types and geometric varieties are lacking.

A microlithic industry that may be classified as Mesolithic has been found among the sand-dunes of the Lo river, in the province of Shensi. The microliths include points, triangles, round scrapers and fluted cores.

9. THE MESOLITHIC CULTURES OF AFRICA

It has already been stated that the latest phases of both the Capsian and Sebilian date from post-glacial Mesolithic times. The Upper Sebilian of Egypt has much in common with the Palestinian early Natufian, even while keeping small forms of the Levallois flake and tortoise-core as a mark of its descent from this culture. Gradually Mesolithic cultures supplanted the belated descendants of the Acheulian and Levallois tradition throughout east, central and South Africa. In South Africa these so-called Late Stone Age cultures began about six or seven thousand years ago and lasted until recent times.

The Magosian Culture

In east, South and central Africa variations of this culture are the first to include true microliths, even while keeping many forms from the earlier Middle Stone Age cultures. In

Kenya the latest Magosian sites have pottery, sufficient proof of its late survival.

The Wilton Culture

This is a true microlithic culture of the African Late Stone Age; probably it began about 4000 B C and thus overlapped in time with the end of the European Mesolithic Age. As has been explained, it was still in being when Europeans reached South Africa. It is ubiquitous from Kenya to the Cape, and is remarkably uniform, showing less regional variation than the Magosian. In the Wilton culture the old prepared core technique, still lingering in the Magosian, was discarded at last and the typical microliths were made in the true tradition of miniature blades and fluted cores. They include crescents and other geometric forms and numbers of small double-ended and thumb-nail scrapers. What has been distinguished as the Wilton of east Africa still includes a small, degenerate form of Stillbay point. Pottery may have incised decoration with chevrons and other geometric designs.

The Elementeitan Culture

This is a microlithic culture, descended from the Kenya Capsian, prevalent in east Africa in very late Mesolithic times. Microliths include crescents and other backed bladelets and other characteristic tools are double-edged blades with the bulb trimmed away and probably hafted as knives; end-scrapers, a few gravers and bone awls. The pottery has incised decoration and both round and flat bases occur.

The Smithfield Culture

This is a non-microlithic culture roughly contemporary with the Wilton and lasting equally late. Its characteristic tool is the end-scraper.

The Late Stone Age Cultures of Central Africa

The Magosian gave way to three Late Stone Age cultures in central Africa: the microlithic Wilton in more open parkland and scrub, the Smithfield in the dry valley of the Middle Limpopo, and the Nachikufan of forest country. This forest culture seems to have begun by 4000 B C and lasted until two or three centuries ago. Microliths include the transverse edge arrow-head. Later a tree-felling and wood-working equipment of ground and polished axes and adzes was adopted.

10. POST-PLEISTOCENE CULTURES IN AMERICA

There is perhaps insufficient justification for a division between late glacial and post-glacial (terms which of course include the corresponding pluvials) cultures in America, as they show no such sharp distinction as that which separates the Upper Palaeolithic and Mesolithic cultures of the Old World. Although chronology is still very unsteady, there is every reason to suppose that many of the projectile point cultures already described continued well into post-glacial times. Others seem to have developed at this time; one, the Gypsum point, represented in the famous Gypsum Cave, Nevada, with its well-preserved remains of giant sloth and camel, is a long, slender diamond form. This occupation probably dates from about 8000 B C and is possibly related to the Pinto point culture, distinguished by peculiar fish-shaped points with two pairs of tangs. At about this same time, corresponding with the beginning of the Maglemose culture in Europe, hunters were first occupying the Ventana Cave, Arizona, using points very much like the Folsom but unfluted, together with choppers, gravers and scrapers. They hunted horse, ground-sloth, tapir, jaguar and wolf.

While the various hunting groups pursued such game as this with their distinctive types of projectile points, three cultures call for special distinction.

The Cape Denbigh Culture

This important site on the north Bering Sea coast represents a culture coming closer than any other to the Old World Mesolithic tradition, and in particular to the Mesolithic of Siberia. The equipment contains an element seeming to look back to the Upper Palaeolithic, with gravers, keeled scrapers, end-of-blade scrapers and blade knives; it also includes true microliths with micro-blades struck from little fluted cores and probably set in grooved bone or antler points. Many of these little tools are exquisitely worked with oblique ripple flaking. The Denbigh has many features in common with early Eskimo cultures, and it seems reasonably certain that this and related Mesolithic cultures widespread in Arctic regions from Alaska to Greenland provided the basis for the cultural tradition of the Eskimo.

The Cochise Culture

This culture, known from the south-west of the United States and northern Mexico, is contemporary with the later point cultures, probably starting a little before 8000 B C, but is essentially based on a food-gathering economy dependent on wild seeds, nuts and roots. Some hunting was certainly always carried on, possibly with wooden lances as no stone points are found among the implements—but the great number of thin, flat milling-stones and small *manos* are enough to show that vegetable foods were of dominating importance. Other implements found in the earlier Cochise culture (the tradition lasted until our era) are scrapers, knives and axes made by percussion and not pressure flaking.

The Chalco Culture

This culture from the Valley of Mexico seems to be related to the more northerly Cochise although later in date. The implements are made of basalt and include choppers, scrapers, gravers and a few points. Milling-stones again suggest some dependence on vegetable foods.

An earlier tradition with pressure flaking preceded the Chalco in the Valley of Mexico, but it is at present too little known to be given definition as a culture.

NOTES TO CHAPTER VI

1. Professor A. C. Blanc points out that there are nevertheless exceptions to this rule, as, for example, in Italy, where the dune country along the Tyrrhenian and Ionian seaboards was much frequented by Mousterian hunters; for this reason many sites in the open air are to be found in this area. Also the well-known Mousterian sites at Saccopastore, Torre in Pietra and Monte Amiata are open-air stations. See A. C. Blanc, *Torre in Pietra, Saccopastore, Monte Circeo*.

   On the position of the Mousterian culture in the Pleistocene sequence of the Rome area: G. H. R. v. Koenigswald, ed., *Hundert Jahre Neanderthaler* (Cologne, Graz, 1958), pp. 167–74; A. C. Blanc and E. Tongiorgi, 'Studio dei giacimenti quaternari del Monte Amiata', Società Toscana di Scionzo Naturalo, *Atti*, XLVI (1936).

2. Professor J. G. D. Clark suggests that there is an alternative explanation in that the clay models may well have been in the nature of 'doodles'—shaped in idle moments from lumps of soft clay and dropped or thrown into the fire. In other words it could be that the firing of these models was merely incidental and not by design. The fireside would after all be the most likely place where such activities would be carried on.

3. P. Simonsen ['Nye fund fra Himmerlands Ertebølle Kultur', *Aarbøger for Nordisk Oldkyndighed og Historio* (1951), pp. 199–

226], has described houses cut into the slope above the midden at Ertebølle itself and also at a site on the coastal slope at Vegge on a narrow inlet of the Limefjord, N. Jutland.

4. Professor L. Pericot García comments that the well-known scene of the honey-gatherers in the Cueva de la Araña near Bicorp (Valencia prov.) can also be interpreted differently: firstly, the figures appear to represent not women but two men (the basket carried in front of the lower figure should not be confused with breasts); secondly, the two honey-gatherers seem to be climbing up, not down, to the nest of the wild bees. See E. Hernández-Pacheco, *Las pinturas prehistóricas de las cuevas de la Araña (Valencia)*, (Madrid, 1924), pp. 88–93.

5. Professor F. S. Bodenheimer asserts that the *Canis matris optimae* of the Natufians has been erroneously identified as a pariah-dog, and is certainly not of 'jackal-like ancestry'. See p. 82, note 1.

6. Professor J. G. D. Clark points out that multiple settings of small, sometimes minute flints were hardly a Mesolithic invention: microliths (and indeed the notch technique resulting in 'micro-burins') were already a feature of Upper Palaeolithic cultures in the western Mediterranean.

7. Professor J. G. D. Clark affirms that the Natufians (and the Fayumis) did not use sickles, but reaping knives. The idea of cutting slots in handles (whether of bone or wood) was certainly known to the Mesolithic Maglemosians of north Europe, who employed it especially for a type of weapon-head (so-called bird-arrows).

8. In the eldest American Eskimo cultures this Mesolithic tradition of setting flint blades in the edges of projectiles is retained. See H. B. Collins, 'Eskimo Archaeology and its Bearing on the Problem of Man's Antiquity in America', *American Philosophical Society, Proceedings*, 86, No. 2 (1943), pp. 220–35; 'Origin and Antiquity of the Eskimo', Smithsonian Institution, *Annual Report for 1950*, pp. 423–67; 'Radiocarbon Dating in the Arctic', *American Antiquity*, XVIII, 3 (1953), pp. 197–203.

9. Professor L. Pericot García remarks that although the majority of scholars nowadays hold the view that the micro-burin is a waste product formed when microliths with geometric forms are manufactured from blades, there are still some authors who reckon with the possibility of micro-burins with the function of tools. In support of this opinion they point to: the appearance of micro-burins without triangles and trapezes in Upper Palaeolithic and Neolithic industries; the occurrence of 'macro-micro-burins' showing that it is not exclusively a question of a microlithic technique; and the production of micro-burins from the bulbous part or from very narrow blades, rendering impossible a simultaneous development of microliths in which geometric forms are evident, etc. See C. Barrière, *Les Civilisations Tardenoisiennes en Europe occidentale* (Bordeaux, 1956), pp. 73–82.

10. Professor J. G. D. Clark points out that some prehistorians at least have been impressed by certain Australian haftings and the recovery of early wooden objects from South Africa suggests that evidence may yet be forthcoming.

11. A further interpretation of the '*bâtons de commandement*', which is of importance for the structure of the European Upper Palaeolithic, has been given by H. Kirchner ['Ein archaeologischer Beitrag zur Urgeschichte des Schamanismus', *Anthropos*, 47 (1952), pp.

244–86]: he regards the branches of antlers with one or more perforations as drumsticks and correlates them with Shamanistic ceremonies. See also K. J. Narr, 'Bärenzeremonien und Schamanismus in der älteren Steinzeit Europas', *Saeculum*, X, 3 (1959), pp. 233–72.

12. Professor J. G. D. Clark comments that the Hamburg culture is only from a chronological point of view a counterpart of an early stage of the Late Magdalenian. It belongs to a quite distinct cultural tradition with sources in east central Europe and possibly even in south Russia. See K. J. Narr, 'Formongruppen und Kulturkreise im europäischen Palaeolithikum', 34. *Bericht der Römisch-Germanischen Kommission* (1951–53), pp. 1–40.

13. Professor J. G. D. Clark points out that since the dividing-line between the Upper Palaeolithic and the Mesolithic in temperate Europe has, in the light of climatic-geological and cultural data, generally been set at 8000 B C (Younger Dryas/Preboreal dividing-line), the Ahrensburgian, Remouchamps and Swiderian cultures are nowadays ascribed by most authors to the Upper Palaeolithic, and not, as was previously the case, in part to the Mesolithic. For seen chronologically they do not yet belong to the Preboreal, and do not display any of the cultural features characteristic of the Mesolithic. See A. Rust, 'Ueber die Kulturentwicklung des endglazialen Jungpalaeolithikums in Nordwesteuropa', *Festschrift G. Schwantes* (Neumünster, 1951), pp. 48–58; J. G. D. Clark, 'The Earliest Settlement of the West Baltic Area in the Light of Recent Research', Prehistoric Society, *Proceedings*, XVI (1950), pp. 87–100.

14. According to A. Rust (*Die alt- und mittelsteinzeitlichen Funde von Stellmoor*, Neumünster, Holstein, 1943), the Ahrensburgian culture is characterized in particular by tanged points. In contrast to the somewhat older and kindred Hamburg culture there is a complete absence of 'zinken' and shouldered points.

15. Professor J. G. D. Clark recalls that these 'cultures' have been treated more recently by E. Froundt ['Komsa-Fosna-Sandarna', *Acta Archaeologica*, XIX (1948), pp. 1–68]. They represent a coastal spread from the western Baltic area to northern Norway and were flourishing at the time of the Ertebølle culture. However, Froundt probably minimizes the antiquity of the first spread. An intriguing possibility is that the Fosna-Komsa culture represents an early coastal adaptation, traces of which are submerged in the western Baltic region. This in turn supports the idea that the western Baltic coastal culture stemmed from the Ahrensburgian—the source of the 'tanged points' which in turn developed into the rhombic arrows of the Carstesminde culture.

16. In this connection mention must be made of the Proto-Maglemosian, represented by such sites as Klesterlund and Star Carr. It dates from the Preboreal. See J. G. D. Clark, *Excavations at Star Carr* (Cambridge, 1954).

17. It has been suggested by Professor L. Pericot García that the Asturian in the north-west of the Iberian peninsula is much older than had previously been assumed. See F. Jordá Cordá, *Prehistoria de la región cantabrica* (Oviedo, 1957). It should also be mentioned that simultaneously there seems to have existed a similar culture in north-eastern Spain. See M. Pallarès y L. Pericot, 'Ils jaciments asturians del Montgri', Institut d'Estudis Catalans, *Anuari*, VII (Barcelona, 1921–26), p. 27.

CHAPTER VII

ART AND RELIGION

THE flowering of the visual arts among the Palaeolithic hunting peoples of Europe has a high claim to be recognized as the most improbable event in human history. After a million years during which development, in so far as we can observe it, was so slow that hundreds of generations might live and die without making the smallest change in their culture, men began to create works of art which can rival anything that has been achieved in the last ten thousand years. This earliest painting and sculpture illuminates the truth that essentially there is no progress in art. The ideas, the range of experience it expresses, become more subtle and varied, its associations richer, but in so far as art is the direct expression of intense imaginative experience, it does not progress. The genius of different peoples, different cultures, flowers and fades; no just judge can say that the latest shows any advance on the earliest. But that true imaginative expression (as distinct from decoration) should have appeared so soon, that truly is astonishing. So astonishing that we have to try to forgive those savants who for very many years refused to recognize the authenticity of the Altamira paintings, allowing their discoverer to die under suspicion of having faked them.

It is impossible for us to know what efforts towards this kind of expression had preceded the cave art of Europe.[1] It looks as though the *Pithecanthropi* brought back quartz crystals to their caves at Choukoutien for the sake of their sparkle, and it may well be that early men commonly took flowers, feathers, bright stones and other things whose colours and shapes for some reason please the eye, and wore them in their hair or hung round their necks. This kind of natural adornment is widespread among modern primitive peoples and may well represent a very ancient impulse. It has already been argued that the form of the best Acheulian hand-axes is fine enough, sufficiently removed from purely practical needs, to demonstrate the existence of an aesthetic sense in their makers. This is true and would have further significance if they were in fact sometimes used for symbol or ceremony. Yet although the creation of these perfect forms comes much closer to true art than the mere collection of pretty natural objects, it cannot be said to have attained it. Something nearer to it may perhaps have emerged in forms that were not visual and leave nothing to remind us of them. It is quite possible that already before the Upper Palaeolithic Age men were beginning to dance and perhaps to chant or sing. (We cannot allow our species to be outdistanced by the white-faced gibbon.) For this age itself there is evidence for ceremonial dancing, and as it has been argued that the men of this time were equipped with a fully expressive language, there can be very little doubt that side by side with the visual arts there developed verbal art, largely poetic, probably including epic tales, ancestral pedigrees and the kind of poetic litany now often found accompanying totemistic and other rituals among primitive peoples. But of all this, apart from a few scenes in the eastern Spanish rock paintings and the direct, strangely moving, testimony of the marks of dancing feet on the clay of cave floors, nothing survives.

Palaeolithic paintings and engraving on the walls of caves and cave shelters is almost entirely limited to western and south-western Europe and to possible examples in a number of regions throughout Africa: round the Sahara, in east Africa, Southern Rhodesia and South Africa. Unfortunately, evidence for the age of much African rock art is dubious or lacking; but it seems that although some examples date from late glacial times, much is later, and no African painting is as old as the earliest recognized in Europe. The distribution of the carved figurines, most of them 'Venuses', is different, extending eastwards as far as Siberia with the Gravettian type of culture of which they generally form part. They do not occur in Africa. Of these little carvings, some, such as the Venuses of Lespuges, Willendorf and Brassempouy, are works of art; others are hardly more than cult objects or fetishes.

It is impossible not to regard the French and Spanish regions as offering Palaeolithic art *par excellence*. Here three principal centres can be distinguished. One is in south-west France, mainly in the departments of the Dordogne, Corrèze and Vienne, with a strong concentration in the ravine of the Vézère. The second is farther south, on the northern slopes of the Pyrenees, most sites falling within the Ariège and

Haute Garonne departments west of Tarascon. The third, north Spanish, centre is in the Cantabrian Mountains westwards from Bilbao, most of the caves lying to the north, between the watershed and the Biscay coast. In addition to these three regions that between them include almost all the finest cave art, there are caves with paintings or engravings in the provinces of Guadalajara and Madrid, at Parpallo on the east coast south of Valencia and in the extreme south round Malaga. While these scattered Spanish sites belong basically to the Franco-Cantabrian tradition, Parpallo and the southern group have certain affinities with a loosely defined Mediterranean province of Palaeolithic art, which comprises caves in the lower Rhône valley, on the Ligurian coast of Italy, central Italy, Apulia, and western Sicily with the adjoining islet of Levanzo. The art of this province has a high proportion of geometric and other non-representational forms. One fine engraving comes from Holland, and a remote northern outlier is a single poor specimen of engraving on bone from Creswell Crags, Derbyshire, in the north of England.

Along the eastern coast of Spain paintings occur, usually on more or less exposed rock surfaces, which belong to a quite distinct artistic tradition. Although a few authorities still hold to the view that they were executed in Palaeolithic times, the balance of opinion is now heavily in favour of attributing them to the Mesolithic phase in Spain. One telling piece of evidence in favour of this dating is the fact that the Palaeolithic art of Parpallo is quite uninfluenced by the style of the east Spanish paintings, although the cave lies in their midst (Fig. 28).

The art of the Franco-Cantabrian regions just defined is divided between painting, incising and relief carving on cave walls or detached blocks of stone, and *objets d'art,* many of them carved weapons, found among other remains of occupation, usually at the cave-mouth. For convenience, these two divisions are usually distinguished as cave and home art.

Home art is necessarily almost limited to the plastic forms and engraving, but some examples of small paintings on stone have chanced to survive where many more must have perished. A very large number of stones painted with both animal and geometric motifs were found in the cave-dwelling of Parpallo, Spain, most of them in the Solutrean level.

Some of the finest work, most of it Magdalenian, is found on implements, particularly on spear-throwers (Fig. 29). It consists of carving in high relief with the body of the animal most ingeniously adapted to the implement; animals treated

FIG. 28. *East Spanish rock-shelter paintings. A: ritual scene, Cogul, near Lerida (after Burkitt); B: hunting scene, Cueva de los Caballos, near Albocácer, Castellón (after J. G. D. Clark).*

in this way include mammoth, reindeer, ibex and a few examples of birds. The perforated antler objects known as *bâtons de commandement* (Fig. 23) were also often embellished—the flat surface offering an excellent field for engraving. Cylindrical bone rods deeply carved with gold scrolls and spirals seem more certainly to be a true ceremonial bâton or sceptre. Ornaments form another group within the range of home art, some of the most outstanding being little perforated cut-out profiles of animals' heads that were probably worn as amulet pendants. The decorated lamps and paint containers and the fish palette form another small group. Many works of home art, however, are found not on implements and other possessions, but on broken-off pieces of bone, ivory, antler and stone. As well as a tremendous range of engravings, these pieces include some fine carvings in the round, such as the horse from Lourdes and the really superb horse's head from Mas d'Azil (Fig. 29). The Venus figurines are usually found in the ordinary litter of occupation, and therefore make an additional category within the home art.

Turning now to cave art, there are a few sites such as Cap Blanc, Angles-sur-l'Anglin and Pair-non-Pair where the art is found on the walls of an inhabited cave or rock shelter. But this is exceptional. A very large proportion of cave art is found in the inner recesses of the long, narrow and often water-coursed caverns characteristic of the limestone country of south-west France and north-west Spain. Many famous works of art are in situations which must always have been immensely difficult to reach, involving the negotiation of dangerous chasms, waterfalls and the narrowest fissures. When it is remembered that the artists had first to explore these perilous, eerie galleries, the haunt of the cave lion and huge cave bear, and then to set out to execute their works with no more light than was given by torches and fat or blubber-lamps, and probably no more sure means of rekindling it than a piece of flint and a lump of iron pyrites, it is obvious how determined they were to reproduce their animal images far into the depths of the earth. They deliberately and strenuously sought cave walls far removed from the familiar outdoor world and the domestic life of the cave entry.

Many of the most famous caves are exceptionally deep and tortuous. At Font de Gaume there is a tunnel almost too narrow for a large man to squeeze through, and a crevice, difficult of access in itself, where an engraved lion and painted rhinoceros are so high up and in so cramped a

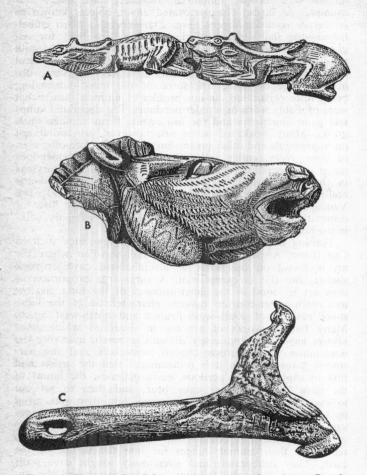

FIG. 29. *Upper Palaeolithic carvings. A: reindeer, ivory, Bruniquel, scale c. 1/2; B: horse head, reindeer antler, Mas d'Azil; C: bird on spear-thrower, reindeer antler, Mas d'Azil (restoration).*

space that the artist must have worked balancing on a companion's shoulders. La Pasiega demands the negotiation of a chimney with an underground river hurling itself below, followed by further long and dangerous winding, creeping and scaling before the great painted hall can be reached. Montespan must be approached by underground river, and it takes three hours to struggle through to the chamber where the bear effigy with the fallen skull and spear holes stood; Tuc d'Audoubert must also be reached by water, after which nowadays visitors must climb by means of pegs and ladders and crawl through a low tunnel to gain the place where the famous clay models of bull and cow bison lean against the rock wall surrounded by the prints of dancing feet. Further proof of the desire to make these images far into the ground is provided by caves such as Niaux, where the artists have ignored a long cave passageway where the walls were well suited to painting or engraving, and started work only at a depth of eight hundred yards from the entry.

MESOLITHIC AND 'ARCTIC' ART

The true, imaginative art of the Upper Palaeolithic cultures can be said to have died with them. It may be that the tendency towards conventionalization and the use of abstract or geometric designs apparent in the latest Magdalenian art shows that the great naturalistic tradition was already dying, but certainly it was killed at last by the spread of forests and the ending of the old way of life. The people who created the Maglemose and Kunda forest cultures may have been in large part the descendants of the Palaeolithic hunters, but they had lost their artistic genius. So far as is known, all they normally attempted was the decoration of tools and weapons with very undistinguished geometric patterns. Antler hafts and axes, bone net prickers and other everyday objects were ornamented with zigzag, chevron, triangle, hatched band, lozenge, checker and net patterns, or simple lines of dots. These might be incised, pricked or drilled—probably with the help of a bow-drill. Occasionally antlers were polished and ornamented in the same style as the implements; as they seem to have had no practical use they may have served magical purposes.

Many of these motifs popular among the northern Mesolithic peoples are the same as those developed among the Magdalenians at the very end of Upper Palaeolithic times and are likely to be directly derived from them. The net

and checker patterns which were new developments may
well have been suggested by the roughly contemporary invention of fish-nets (Fig. 30).

In addition to the purely geometric patterns, both Maglemose and Kunda peoples exceptionally used motifs derived
from human or animal forms. Sometimes these occur on perforated plaques and were probably worn as amulets. An
animal, possibly a pig, roughly carved in the round from a
piece of amber and itself decorated with geometric patterns
comes from Resen Mose in Jutland, but even this degree of
naturalism is rare. There are one or two instances, the
best known from Ystad, Sweden, where fine engravings,
seemingly mere doodles, depict fish and deer in a life-like
manner recalling the Palaeolithic tradition.

Of much greater artistic merit is the Arctic art represented
by rock engravings and occasional rock paintings in Scandinavia—most of it found near the sea or by rivers and
lakes. So, too, are the knives and axes carved with animal
heads that are found in regions adjoining the Arctic but
generally lying rather to the east of it in Sweden, Finland,
and Russian Carelia.

It has been thought that the Arctic rock engravings of
elk, bear, horse and fish, more particularly the naturalistic
style prevailing along the northern coast of Norway, are
derived from Upper Palaeolithic art. However, as the nearest
affinities are with the earliest style, which is certainly some
tens of thousands of years more ancient, it seems that the
likeness is due to the common inspiration of the hunting
life and not to any cultural relationship.[2]

The Arctic art may have begun in the Maglemose period,
but it certainly flourished during the Ertebølle and probably
lasted well on into the centuries when Neolithic cultures
were being established in the more southerly regions of Scandinavia. If, as is probable, the rock engravings were related
to the animal-headed axes and knives, then this late survival
is almost certain, for these tools have metal counterparts in
Russia and seem to have been copied from them. Thus it
seems that while farming was spreading throughout the rest
of Europe, in these northern latitudes the survival of the
hunting life led to the occasional recrudescence of more or
less naturalistic animal art, though the artists never achieved
either the skill or the high imaginative expression of their
Palaeolithic predecessors.

In southern Europe, with the exception of the east Spanish
rock art, much of which, as we have seen, dates from Mesolithic times,[3] representational art disappeared even more com-

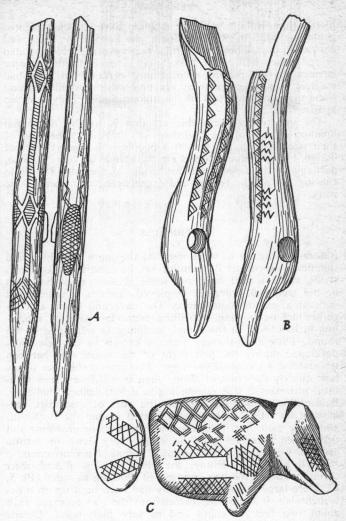

FIG. 30. *Mesolithic art: engraving and sculpture. A: from Langeland island, 11/16"; B: from Ostrolçka, Poland, 9/32"; C: from Resen Mose, Jutland, 7/8" (after J. G. D. Clark).*

pletely than in the north. The Azilians have left their painted pebbles—found in northern Spain, the French Pyrenees, and eastern France. These are natural water-worn pebbles painted in red ochre with dots, bars, wavy lines and other simple devices. As the pebbles seem almost certainly to have had magical uses, these patterns are probably all symbolic, and some may be derivatives of the human figure. They have no artistic value.

The only other Mesolithic art that is worthy of special mention is that of the Natufians of Palestine. The best of their necklaces (p. 236) show a people with a good sense of design, but their masterpieces are the animal carvings in bone, particularly the fawn from the handle of a sickle. This little carving has all the feeling and expressiveness of Palaeolithic work.

TECHNIQUES

Before passing on to what must be the more absorbing and significant aspects of Palaeolithic art, its cultural background, styles, content, and meaning, some account must be given of the technical processes employed. This is a subject not without a general significance. The cave and home arts together include drawing, stencilling, engraving, painting, modelling in relief and in the round, sculpture in relief and in the round. Thus almost every process known to us today was developed during the first flight of the visual arts between ten and thirty thousand years ago. This remarkable fact shows how quickly the brain of *Homo sapiens* will invent new technical processes if it is responding to a well-defined challenge. Palaeolithic art was undoubtedly the work of specialists, perhaps of an artists' clan such as existed among the Bushmen, and these men must have become conscious of problems and determined to solve them. So at the very dawn of artistic creation we find this extraordinary technical inventiveness.

Starting with modelling, the bison of Tuc d'Audoubert certainly affords the best example of working in relief (Pl. 5, a). Here large masses of wet clay had been built up on a detached slab of rock and formed into the two animals, each about two feet in length and in very high relief. Details such as the eyes and mane had been added with a pointed tool, while ears and horns were neatly pinched up between finger and thumb. In their deep cavern these models kept their moisture through the millennia and when discovered by modern man showed only slight cracking. Among the few surviving examples of modelling in the round, probably a popular form but one with a poor chance of survival, are the statuettes and animal figures from Vestonice. The female figurines are made of a mixture of clay and pulverized mammoth bone; it has been shown how some of these Vestonice models had been hardened in an oven (p. 201).

The finest works of relief sculpture are those cut from the living rock of the cave walls or on detached slabs that might be either leant against the walls or laid face downwards on the floor. This kind of work, such as the frieze of life-size horses at Cap Blanc and the slabs carved with ibex, bison, reindeer and other species at Le Roc (Pl. 5, b), seems generally to have been finished with quite fine gravers, but must presumably have been roughed out with coarser tools. Gravers and gouges in all the wide range in which they were designed must have been the principal tools used for carving bone, antler and ivory for the reliefs (such as the exquisite work found on spear-throwers) and small sculptures in the round that form so delightful a part of the home art. The Magdalenians probably used their saw-edged blades for this work, and concave scrapers may have had their special uses for carving in the round. The technical mastery displayed in the best of this home art suggests that the handling of the hard materials that alone endure may have been preceded by carving in wood. When very hard substances were to be sculptured (such as the limestone of the famous Venus of Willendorf) the general form may have been roughed out by pecking before the final shaping was undertaken with gravers. In all this carving, and particularly in tough materials, the fact that gravers could easily be given a new edge must have been of very great advantage.

Gravers were probably also used for the incised type of engraving characteristic of the best Palaeolithic work. There have been a few instances of worn gravers found lying on ledges close by an engraved cave wall. On the other hand in both north and South Africa incised outlines appear to have been executed by peoples who did not make this type of engraving tool. Occasionally, and particularly in the Arctic art of Scandinavia, rock engraving was done not by clean incision, but by pecking—that is by a succession of small blows delivered with a pointed punch. A third method, also used in the Arctic rock art, consisted of engraved or pecked outlines being worked into highly polished grooves, probably with a wooden tool and sand as an abrasive.

Engraving was quite often combined with painting in Palaeolithic cave art; it occurs at many sites including Les

Trois Frères, Font-de-Gaume, Altamira and Lascaux. In these cases the graver was commonly used to draw the outline, the colouring being added later; sometimes, however, it was also used to suggest fur. It is an interesting chance that the work of art which has the best claim to being recognized as the earliest portrait of a human being, the bust of a bearded man from Angles-sur-l'Anglin, combines engraving (both for outline and to represent fur on the cloak), painting and partial low relief.

It was not in the plastic arts or engraving that the hunter artists showed their greatest virtuosity and elaboration of technique. It was in painting—and here of course the preparation as well as the use of colours is involved. The usual pigments were ochres, or oxides of iron, ranging in colour from chocolate to light red, orange and yellow. The reds can be called varieties of haematite, the oranges and yellows of limonite; they occur naturally, usually mixed with clay and other earthy impurities, and little heaps of them, evidently carefully collected, have been found in cave-dwellings. Other common pigments were oxides of manganese that gave a brown and a blue-black, while burnt bone or soot was used to obtain carbon blacks. These pigments were ground to a fine powder, sometimes at least with specially made pestle and mortar. A very neatly finished conical pestle of mammoth ivory was found at Vestonice, while a stone mortar comes from the Dordogne region. The powders were stored colour by colour in holders that include stoppered bone-shafts, shells, hollow stones and even human skulls. Before application they seem sometimes to have been mixed with a water base, sometimes with fat. A bone palette from the Dordogne, beautifully carved in the form of a fish, may well have served for this mixing of colours.

All the pigments used, with the exception of the carbons which can be fugitive and inclined to oxidize, are absolutely permanent. Sometimes, as at Lascaux, a thin glassy skin of calcite has sweated from the limestone, covering the paintings and making them fast and impermeable—a natural glaze more effective than any devised by man. As well as these liquid colours, the artists seem occasionally to have prepared sticks of mineral pigments and used them like crayons.

The application of the liquid paints to cave walls with any accuracy must have been difficult, for although limestone sometimes offers a whitish and fairly smooth surface, it must always be more irregular than paper, wood or canvas. One very simple method was to apply them with the fingertips, usually as a single broad outline, but rarely doubled or

trebled by the use of more than one finger. This finger painting is often practised by modern primitives, and a sophisti-
cated form of it has been perfected by the Chinese. Narrower
outlines were drawn with a solid point, probably a piece of
sharpened wood or a quill, before being filled in with colour;
at Altamira very dark outlines and touched-in details were
executed by this method. Sometimes the sticks or crayons
already described served for the first outlining—it appears
they were used, for example, on the unfinished rhinoceros
in the pit at Lascaux.

For other, more fluent types of outline there are signs that
brushes were used. Some modern peoples make brushes by
chewing the ends of fibrous plants, and this simple procedure
may have been followed by their Palaeolithic forerunners. On
the other hand it is hard to believe that such skilled and
inventive artists would not have used the fur they so often
handled to make themselves finer instruments. Brushes may
also have been used for washes and broad shading effects,
but this kind of true painting seems to have been more
usually done with the fingers, or with pads of moss or fur;
sometimes instead of being spread smoothly the pad was used
very effectively in a kind of stump work technique. Again,
a smaller pad or the end of a stick might be employed for
pointillist painting.

Certain pictures, for example the lovely 'Chinese horses'
at Lascaux, show such smoothly graduated tinting and shading that it has been supposed they must have been executed
with some form of spray. It might be by means of blowing
dry powder through a tube on to a prepared fatty surface,
or again by squirting liquid colour through the lips. Experiments have proved that mouth spraying is feasible; whatever may be true of the finer kind of work, it seems almost
certain that this method was used for the negative hand-
impressions that are among the earliest forms of cave-
painting. The open hand is applied to the cave wall and the
paint squirted round it to make an image that is in fact a
form of stencil.

Finally it must be recorded, although this is a matter of
artistic method rather than of technique, that the Palaeolithic
artists appear sometimes to have made rough sketches on
slivers of bone (and probably, though lost to us, on the clay
of the cave floor) to serve as studies for their finished murals.

This account of the various media and methods so brilliantly mastered by the first known artists is enough to prove
the high degree of professionalism they added to their innate
gifts. We can hold in our hands their gravers, gouges and

saws, their pestles and mortars, their crayons, palettes and paint-holders, the little lamps that gave them light, and picture them as careful craftsmen as well as inspired artists. Though rather simpler, their equipment was not, after all, very different from what men have used ever since.

SUBJECTS AND STYLES

The limitations of Palaeolithic art are chiefly apparent in choice of subjects. In the Franco-Cantabrian tradition painting is almost entirely restricted to animals, although in sculpture and to a lesser extent in engraving, men and women are more often portrayed. The animals are most commonly shown singly, and when they are in groups, as in the line of stags' heads at Lascaux, they are not composed into a scene nor related to one another pictorially. With the stylized groups of mammoth and reindeer engraved by the late Magdalenians when their art was already waning there is pictorial composition of a sort, but it is already almost schematic (Fig. 32, A). Generally the beasts are standing, walking or running, but the amount of movement put into them varies greatly. For example at Lascaux most of them, though full of an intense life, nevertheless have a kind of poetic stillness and calm about them, whereas at Altamira they are caught up in a tremendous dynamic energy. Rare and unusual attitudes have been chosen, giving a greater sense of event. Examples are the leaping cow and falling horse at Lascaux and the famous crouched bison at Altamira (Pl. 3); from these and other examples it seems that these odd attitudes have usually been suggested to the artist either by some natural peculiarity on the cave wall (the falling horse and crouched bison) or by an impulse to avoid an earlier painting (the leaping cow; Pl. 4). This latter impulse is unusual, bespeaking the true artist rather than the servant of magic and religion; more often successive studies were imposed one on the other or allowed to overlap with little care for appearances.

There are also rare exceptions to the rule that there are no scenes in the Franco-Cantabrian art.[4] One is the charming picture of a pair of reindeer at Font-de-Gaume, in which the female is kneeling with lowered head, while the male is bending forward towards her; it is simple enough, but there is a relationship between them and one conveying a sense of tenderness. But the one scene which might claim to be the first narrative picture in the world is in the pit at Lascaux where a man (very schematically drawn) appears to be lying dead, while before him a bison stands in a curious rigid attitude as though about to fall, its intestines hanging from its belly and a broken spear at its side. Different interpretations have been made of this scene, some of which try to include the rhinoceros standing at a short distance from man and bison; we can never know what the story was, nor whether it was an actual happening, or drawn from some camp-fire epic, but there is no doubt that this unique picture was composed to illustrate some event. It told a story, and this was something altogether new.[5]

The dead man at Lascaux is drawn in the stick style popular with small children, and nearly all paintings and many engravings of human beings (which are not numerous) are either schematic or childishly crude; frequently, as we have seen, they appear masked or with animal attributes. Practically never is the artist trying to express the essential character of the human body in the way that he would express that of bison and reindeer, ibex or mammoth. The

FIG. 31. *Upper Palaeolithic 'Venuses'.* Left: *Vestonice, Moravia.* Centre: *Laussel, Dordogne.* Right: *Willendorf, Lower Austria (after Singer).*

nearest approach to an exception is the head and shoulders study of a bearded man from Angles-sur-l'Anglin, but even this is tentative when set beside the superb animal studies. There are also the engravings, full of grace and movement, in Addavra Cave on Monte Pelegrino, Sicily.

Turning to the carvings of women, and the occasional male figures found with them, we are in an altogether different realm of emotional expression (Fig. 31). The Venuses and other figurines with their much wider distribution and evident magico-religious significance within the Gravettian culture might be dissociated from the rest of Palaeolithic art if there were not several works serving to link them. Most significant of these are the women holding bison horns and the hunter from Laussel, carved in low relief on slabs lying on their face in a Gravettian cave-dwelling in the Dordogne, and the three great female figures carved on the cave wall at Angles-sur-l'Anglin. This second site is of particular importance for relating the female figures with other Franco-Cantabrian art, for here they had been carved side by side with animal sculptures of bison, ibex and horse, and furthermore were the work of Magdalenian artists. At both places the female figures closely resemble the Venuses, being shown naked, grossly fat or pregnant, and with little attention paid to so unimportant a feature as the head. At Laussel the faces are blank, at Angles-sur-l'Anglin the head is not represented at all.

It seems then, that although in some instances the same artist might carve an animal and a female figure large or small, the inspiration underlying their creation was quite different. In portraying animals the artist was inspired to express the essential appearance and nature of each species, achieving a form of brilliantly heightened realism; in the female figures he did not want to show the female of his kind in this same spirit of heightened realism, but rather the idea of woman as the source of all fecundity. He portrayed not woman but fertility.

The subject-matter of the predominantly Mesolithic rock-shelter art of the eastern Spanish littoral differs sharply from the Franco-Cantabrian. In that scenes and events are common, it might be said to be intellectually more advanced, but in both execution and imaginative feeling it is inferior. Not only did the east Spanish artists like to compose scenes, but they had no inhibitions against including human beings. Their paintings often show men hunting deer with bow and arrow, and there is the lively group of five warriors wearing head-dresses, also armed with bows and arrows. More famous still is the ritual scene at the cave of Cogul where a party of women clad in long skirts is loosely grouped round a much smaller figure of a man or youth (Fig. 28, A). The east Spanish paintings are usually small in comparison with the Franco-Cantabrian; there is plenty of movement in them, particularly in the hunters, but both men and beasts are rendered in a curiously attenuated and brittle convention, without either the feeling or the high realism of the greater tradition (Fig. 28, B).

African cave-painting (Pl. 6) has much in common with that of eastern Spain, though some of the animal studies are rather superior. In Libya, Southern Rhodesia and South Africa there are single animals and hunting scenes very much like the Spanish, showing the same brittleness and attenuation, the same high-stepping sense of movement. It is to be expected from what has already been said of the persistence of Stone Age traditions in South Africa, that scenes that may in truth date from late glacial times merge almost imperceptibly into pictures of Bushmen fighting Kaffirs and of Boers arriving with their wagons.

Hitherto we have been content to call all the Franco-Cantabrian art 'Upper Palaeolithic'. How far is it possible to attribute it to the successive cultures that we have seen to follow one another in this part of Europe? Not very accurately. Although the home art is always found in its proper cultural context, it is only exceptionally that it is possible to connect the cave art with the tools and other datable possessions of its creators. At the cave of Pair-non-Pair in the Dordogne a succession of levels containing the usual domestic rubbish of Gravettian and Aurignacian occupiers had accumulated against a wall covered with engravings, completely masking them. The levels suggested the engravings had been made by the first of the Upper Palaeolithic inhabitants, or at latest by the Aurignacians. Again at La Mouthe in the same region as the cave where the decorated lamp was recovered, occupation litter left by Magdalenians had blocked the entrance to galleries containing a few works of art. At Cap Blanc the frieze of horses was buried by Magdalenian deposits. From the study of sites such as these, of others where one style of painting or engraving has been executed on top of one or more earlier ones, by comparisons with the home art, it has been possible to build up an approximate sequence of styles and to relate them with more or less confidence to successive cultures. From this it appears that every west European culture from the Aurignacian to the final flowering of the Magdalenian included cave and home art. The germ of Upper Palaeolithic art evidently may have lain in the original Châtelperronian culture,[6] and from this developed among the peoples believed to be directly descended from the Châtelperronians—the Gravettians and Magdalenians. On the other hand the Aurignacian, which, like the Solutrean, represents an intrusive culture although one seemingly less alien, is the first in which there is certain evidence for works of creative art. The Solutrean has been credited with possessing art forms, particularly sculpture such as that at Le Roc. Undoubtedly the Solutrean inhabitants of the cave of Parpallo on the south-east coast of Spain practised both painting and engraving, mainly on small slabs found incorporated in the rubbish of the cave floor. The historical picture seems to be, then, that once cave art had taken its place as part of the traditions of the hunting peoples of western Europe, it was adopted by all comers. Perhaps artists' clans became strong enough to secure the continuity of their tradition. That a tradition could continue with only slight changes of essential style over a period of between twenty and thirty thousand years, which is what our present chronology suggests, seems today almost incredible. Yet when we think of the immense slowness of cultural development in the preceding hundreds of thousands of years, it is apparent that in these beginnings of human history the passage of time must be measured by their own standards. There is the continuity of rock painting in South Africa to convince us that primitive artists can continue to paint in much the same way while millennia go by.

For the developments and changes of style that did mark the course of Palaeolithic art, knowledge is still very incomplete. One high authority has tried to recognize two complete cycles of development, the first taking place during the earlier part of the Upper Palaeolithic period and dominated by the Aurignacians, the second belonging to Magdalenian times. However, these cycles were difficult to define and distinguish, as was proved when the marvellous painted cave of Lascaux was discovered in 1940, and its styles could not be satisfactorily assigned to one cycle rather than the other. For the present a simpler scheme must be preferred. An early phase, which began with the Aurignacian culture, can be distinguished by simple outline paintings and engravings, the animals usually shown in dead profile with only two legs indicated; they tend to be lacking in movement, and the eye is often not shown. That the artists were pioneers, still groping towards the solution of elementary problems, appears most of all in the drawing of the horns and antlers, which are always shown as though they were seen almost full face even though the body of the beast is in profile. In spite of these weaknesses, even in this opening phase of their art the Palaeolithic painters and engravers already manifest their gift for expressing the essential character and feeling of each species. Most of the representations of hands, positive (made by impressing a paint-covered hand) and negative (made by the 'stencilling' process) seem to date from this opening stage;

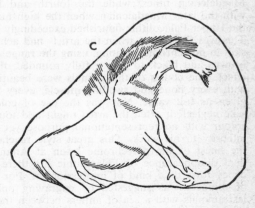

FIG. 32. *Upper Palaeolithic engravings from the Dordogne. A: two mammoths, Font-de-Gaume, on cave wall (after Burkitt); B: head of reindeer, La Madeleine, on bone (after Capitan and Peyrony); C: horse, Abri Labatut, on stone (after Graziozi).*

so do meandering lines traced with a stick or finger-tips
on clay, and known to science as 'macaroni'. It is followed
by a second phase, evidently roughly corresponding in time
with the Aurignacian and Gravettian cultures, in which much
greater mastery has been attained; animals are now shown
with four legs and with antlers and horns, all in perspective.
The artists are already displaying considerable skill in breaking the outlines and varying the breadth of stroke in such
a way as to suggest roundness and solidity. The eye is shown,
generally as an oval, and other interior details are indicated.
Those authorities who believe the Lascaux paintings to be
mainly pre-Magdalenian must include also in this second
phase monochrome paintings in which the whole body is
filled in with a flat wash, and even paintings in two colours
in which the modelling of the animal is suggested with remarkable success.

To the third phase belong the 'stump' and pointillist styles,
as well as a continuation of flat washes, and of partial washes
used to suggest modelling. In Cantabria during this period
a school of engravers, using very fine lines, learned to indicate the third dimension by an extensive use of shading. The
combination of engraving with painting was also much favoured. This phase was certainly developed during earlier
Magdalenian times, while the fourth and last corresponds
with the later Magdalenian when the high hunting culture of
the Upper Palaeolithic flourished exceedingly before its death.
This was the period when the artists had achieved wonderful
skill in polychrome painting, using the range of yellows, reds,
browns and black to give a fully rounded, three-dimensional
effect. The bodies of the animals were beautifully modulated
with every bone and swelling muscle, every fold and hollow
given its full value. Nor was the use of colour for its own
sake neglected; often the artist might add touches of glowing
colour with no representational purpose yet adding life and
intensity to his work. This great style reached its climax in
the finest of the polychrome bison at Altamira. Before the
final disappearance of Palaeolithic art there was some tendency towards a kind of impressionism. For instance a herd
of reindeer was suggested by engraving only the first and
last animals with a sea of antlers between them, while mammoths were rendered without legs, the feet alone being
sketched in. There was an increase in the use of geometrical
patterns, some of them derived from representational forms.
They included zigzags, triangles, hatched ribbon and lozenge
patterns among rectilinear patterns, semicircles, rings and
spirals among curvilinear.

THE MOTIVES AND INSPIRATION OF THE ART

It has been said that Palaeolithic art can claim to be the most improbable event in history, and fundamentally it is as impossible to explain why it occurred as any of the other sudden upsurges of creative genius in the arts that, happily for us, have marked the course of our human existence. The tides of the human psyche ebbing and flowing in society remain largely mysterious. Yet at a rather more superficial level there are explanations and interpretations to be made. On the one hand there are the permissive factors. While material prosperity can never be the cause of artistic genius, a society cannot support its artists without an economic margin. Thus there is no doubt that the abundance of game to be hunted in south-west Europe in Late Pleistocene times made a necessary foundation for the development of Palaeolithic art. Although the artists were probably themselves hunters, it seems very likely, particularly as skill and professionalism grew, that in exchange for their artistic services to the community they only had to hunt part-time and were supplied with food while at work in the caves. On the other hand there are the uses of art—meaning its uses to society and not the satisfaction it gives to its creators. A healthy artistic tradition is seldom without some more or less practical function, and in primitive societies where there is no recognized division between intellectual, practical and religious activities, art must always be an integral part of everyday life.

There is long-standing dispute between those who have wished to see cave-painting and its related forms as an activity undertaken for its own sake, for self-expression and the creation of beauty, and those who see it as a purely practical activity undertaken to secure good hunting. This conflict is entirely in the minds of the disputants. Even in the twentieth century, when life is lived so much in watertight compartments, no one ever thinks of asking whether the painters of easel pictures work for self-expression or because they intend to sell their canvases. To try to separate art and magic and religion in the unified life of early man shows the folly of the over-analytical mind.

There is no doubt at all that cave art had its magico-religious function. In particular it served that form of it known as sympathetic magic, which depends upon a belief that similarity or relationship is identity, and that anything

down to an image or related part of a thing will affect the
thing itself. It is an idea which has constantly recurred
even in civilized life. Potatoes when first introduced into
Europe were thought to cause leprosy because the appearance of some of the tubers suggested the disease. It is well
known that in modern Europe and America people still make
images of their enemies and stick them with pins to secure
their death, and this practice makes an exact analogy to one
aspect of the Palaeolithic hunters' magic. A considerable
number of paintings have spears or darts drawn or scratched
on the animals' flanks. There are many instances at Lascaux.
At Niaux there is a famous example in which three little
pits, naturally formed, have been enclosed by the outline
of a bison, and each furnished with a dart to give the
semblance of wounds. Clearer still was the evidence at
Montespan, where the body of a bear, roughly modelled in
clay, was found with a bear's skull lying in front of it suggesting that this dummy had once been draped in a pelt with
the real head attached at the neck. The clay of the body
was pierced with spear thrusts.

If one form of sympathetic magic was used to ensure
successful kills, another was to cause an increase of
life. Some of the painted beasts are undoubtedly intended to
be gravid, while the careful representation of bull and cow
bison at the Tuc d'Audoubert, and the signs of rites having
been celebrated in the cave, is very suggestive of fertility
magic. That this conception went far beyond sympathetic
magic to form the basis of a fertility religion with a great
history before it in Eurasia is shown unequivocally by the
Venuses and other crystallizations of the Mother Goddess
concept (p. 278). The scene at the east Spanish cave of
Cogul with the group of women surrounding a man may
perhaps represent celebrants in such a fertility cult of which
there will be more to say presently (Fig. 28).

A third type of evidence for the close association of cave
art with magico-religious activities is that provided by the
various drawings of men with animal disguises and possibly
of beings that are part man, part beast, part divinity like
the great 'Sorcerer' of Les Trois Frères himself (Fig. 33).
Indeed this cave as a whole proclaims its ritual use as obviously as any chapel. Passages deep in the rock lead into a small
chamber with walls thickly netted with engravings of many
kinds of animals, including the strange group of a man with
bison head and other animal attributes dancing behind two
weird hybrid beasts, apparently in a state of sexual excitement. From this chamber a tunnel with further engravings

FIG. 33. *The 'Sorcerer', cave of Les Trois Frères, Ariège (after a drawing in the collection of the Musée de l'Homme, Paris).*

curves upwards to give access to a window opening into a chamber some twelve feet above the floor, a place where an officiating medicine man could appear with dramatic effect and dominate participants gathered below him. It is extraordinarily stirring, then, to find that the antlered, phallic, hypnotically staring figure of the 'Sorcerer' has been painted and engraved on the rock face just beside this opening.

This magical element in cave art must have had less force in the home art. It is quite likely that when deer, mammoth and ibex were carved on spear-throwers, it was believed that these images might help to make them effective against the animals represented. On the other hand no one can doubt that the carving was done partly for the pleasure of doing

and regarding it, for it is pre-eminently decorative. Still more
is this true of such little carved objects as the fish palette
from the Grotte de Rey and the bone silhouettes of animals
and even the superb horse head from Mas d'Azil and the
horse from Espelugues, Lourdes. What conceivable purpose
other than decoration can the artist at La Mouthe have had
when he engraved an ibex on his lamp?[7]

There is no doubt that cave art, and to a lesser extent
the home art as well, served the animal cult, part magical
and part truly religious, that underlay the lives of these hunting peoples. The status of the individual and the life of the
tribe were wholly dependent on the multiplication of the
game herds and success in hunting them, and art responded
to the urgency of these two great needs. Utilitarian in themselves, they cannot be separated from a religious impulse
towards a form of communion with animals and nature, a
participation mystique.

And in this religious aspect we rediscover Palaeolithic art
as genuine imaginative expression, its creators as true artists.
Just as mediaeval painters could work entirely in the service
of the Christian Church, just as modern painters work to
sell their canvases to furnish houses and galleries, so too
(and indeed much more consistently) could the painters of
the last glaciation work in the service of hunting and fertility
magic and still remain artists. From that time to this there
have been great numbers of primitive peoples living throughout the world, yet none has had a representational art to
approach theirs. Peoples who, like some of the Australians,
make strikingly effective pictures in connection with hunting
magic lack their realism and technical skill. More often no
attempt at realistic representation is made, and symbolic
designs or enactments supply the identification needed for
sympathetic magic. A visual identity between the image and
the object has never been considered necessary. Yet in the
whole range of Palaeolithic material only one example is
known with anything of the inartistic and grisly character
often found among the properties of the primitive magic
worker—that is the dummy bear with the real head that had
been set up in the sanctum at Montespan.

All the rest may have been intended for magical usages,
but was at the same time a true art, and an art in what
we have come to call the humane tradition. In fact it comes
closer to Chinese drawing and painting than to any other,
and the Chinese were inspired by a mystical conception of
the relationship between man and nature. The art itself makes
it abundantly clear that the Stone Age artists knew an intense

self-identification with the animals they portrayed. Perhaps with a strengthening self-consciousness due in part to the development of fully expressive language, a factor which would also have heightened their image-making powers, these people felt a need to re-affirm their participation in nature. A modern poet has said that 'the poetic image shows the artist seeking to express unity with all that is and has been', and this was true of the first artists as of the latest. Various attempts have been made to suggest that the cave-painters used dead beasts as their models, or that the sight of shadows suggested the idea of painting shapes on the cave wall. Such ideas are entirely misleading. Anyone with any understanding of the creative process must know that the artists working in these fastnesses so remote from the outer world carried with them intense and emotionally charged images of the animals on which their lives were centred. The creative act, as in all true art, had already taken place in the imagination; the pigments, the gravers, served only to give it material expression. With all utilitarian magical functions apart, this element of communion with their animal subjects made the activity of these artists at one with the religious life of their societies.

MAGIC AND RELIGION IN THE PALAEOLITHIC AGE

Many aspects of the religious life of Palaeolithic times have already been touched on in considering mental development, social organization, hunting and domestic customs and artistic expression. This is inevitable, correctly emphasizing the unity of primitive life, the fact that magic and religion served practical ends and that practical life was always suffused with magical and religious meaning. It remains only to give rather closer attention to those matters that we are inclined to isolate as religious—ideas about the soul, spirits, divinities and conceptions of a supernatural realm of existence.

As man's consciousness drew him apart from the great concourse of unselfconscious nature from which he was emerging, he was bound to turn to look at nature, and having contemplated it to seek to explain what he saw, to affect it for his own ends, and finally to regard it with awe and reverence and a desire for reunion. In these three urges, one intellectual, one practical, one mystical, lay respectively the germs of myth, magic and religion. But in contemplating the universe about him man saw it through the instrument of

his mind, which was anything but a clear mirror of nature.
It projected emotions, dream and memory images, and above
all intuitions of its own unconscious depths, on to the outside
world.[8]

Thus human consciousness has always found much of itself
in the universe. At its simplest, when hardly emerged from
its thoughtless past, it saw all nature as full of a similar
consciousness, endowing things, physical phenomena and animals equally with life, feelings and purposes. Winds, storms,
stones, trees, animals—all, like man himself, were imbued
with spirit. This state of mental relationship with the world
has sometimes been known as animism; the further state (and
they cannot, of course, be sharply distinguished) when the
spirits began to take shape as individualized divinities has
similarly been called the daimonic view of the universe. With
further strengthening of conscious powers divinities tended to
take larger, more abstract forms. It seems that while the
individual mind was still closely bound up with family, society
and nature, and when, moreover, women and maternity
were probably still dominant in family and social structure,
there was a tendency for the idea of the divine life and
fertility to be expressed in the form of a Great Goddess.[9]
As intellect gained in power, greatly increasing man's isolation, and as laws and prohibitions built up the conscience
(call it the super-ego, if this language is preferred), then the
masculine god waxed and assumed the throne in the human
mind.

Holding the spirit-filled conception of the universe, and
subject to all the good and evil chances of human life on
earth, early man was certain to form the notion of luck and
to try to make the spirits favour him by means of magical
compulsions of the kind already described in considering
Palaeolithic art. Probably, too (though we have no material
evidence for it), man indulged the dark side of his nature by
using black magic to force the spirits to do harm to his
enemies, public and private. Not only was man's dawning
consciousness made aware of the outrageous vagaries of 'luck'
but also of death—something more than the worst dart of
ill luck. Death with its emotional shock and power to stir
the unconscious has always been one of the great forces
behind the religious impulse and magical activities. The idea
that a man's spirit should continue to live, perhaps be reborn
into another body, which was to have so long and vast a
history before it, appears to have been one of the first to
emerge among our Palaeolithic ancestors.

Although the spirit ancestors might have to be managed

by magical devices, death was certainly more bound up with
the religious impulse than with magic. It is clear that Palaeolithic man already felt the true religious impulse towards
reverence and desire for reunion with the divine. It poured
itself very largely into cults of the animals on which all
human life depended, but it also went so far as to attain the
idea of the Great Goddess. An interesting sidelight on the
growth of animal cults of a more or less totemic kind is
provided by the experience of two German refugees who
decided to live alone in the African veldt as hunters. They
discovered that after a year or so of this hunting existence,
they not only dreamed nightly of animals, but also of themselves turning into animals. Primitive man does not disas-
sociate the dreaming from the waking world, and it is easy
to see how dream experiences could enhance the natural,
emotional and reverential attitude towards the animal life-
givers and help to shape totemic beliefs.

Meanwhile a more or less rational curiosity, a wish to
explain the world of which he was growing more and more
objectively conscious, led man to weave all that he saw
of nature, society and culture into myths in which spirits
and divinities of every magnitude naturally played a dominant part. So stories were made and repeated, but always in
evolving forms, to explain the creation of the world, language,
crafts and above all the life and death of man.

The first indication we have of our remote predecessors
being troubled with metaphysical intuitions (however little
brought into consciousness) is in the careful disposal of the
dead by Neanderthal man. Probably the earliest examples of
such burial are those at the Wadi el Mughara in Palestine
(p. 138). Here the bodies of the Neanderthaloid inhabitants
had been laid in trenches cut in the cave floor and joints
of food and flint weapons put beside them. Mention has already been made of the burial of a Neanderthal child at
Tshik-Tash in central Asia that seems to have been made in
a shallow slab-lined grave, surrounded by horns of the mountain goat, their points stuck into the ground. More remarkable
still were the interments at the rock-shelter of La Ferrassie
in the Dordogne. Here two adults had been buried against
the back wall of the cave, one in a natural recess, one in
what seems to have been an artificially deepened cavity,
and their bodies protected by a covering of stones; near
them a child's skeleton had been placed in a small trench,
the skull being laid on one side, the limb bones towards the
other. The trench was roofed by a slab of stone with circular
depressions, or cup-marks, hollowed out on the under-side.

In a ditch near the child's grave were animal bones and cinders, suggestive of cooked offerings or the remains of a funeral feast. The well-known burial of an oldish Neanderthal man at La Chapelle-aux-Saints in the Corrèze had been made with equal ceremony. The body had been placed in a carefully dug trench in a little sepulchral cave, and round it were ranged a number of the finest Mousterian points and scrapers. A pit, with animal bones and a bison horn, comparable to the ditch at La Ferrassie, had been dug at the entrance. Usually the Neanderthalers were buried in the attitude of sleep, gently flexed and lying on one side; several were accompanied by red ochre, generally supposed to represent the life-giving properties of blood.

These interments, some of them elaborate enough to deserve their description as ceremonial burials, certainly indicate some form of a belief in a continued existence after death. Food, implements and red ochre are all proof of it. It suggests that already these people had an idea of physical continuity, with the dead ancestors still in being among their living descendants.

Other evidence for ritual practices among the Neanderthalers is slight. The discovery at Monte Circeo in Italy of a Neanderthal skull, its base broken out to remove the brain and set in a hole within an oval of small stones, may mean that the cannibalism of this people, though it seems often to have been merely gastronomic, sometimes assumed a ritual form.

Though sometimes more elaborately furnished, the burials of the Upper Palaeolithic and Mesolithic peoples did not greatly differ from those of the Neanderthalers. There was, however, a greater variety in the positions in which the bodies were placed: occasionally they repeated the sleeping posture of their predecessors, sometimes were extended at full length on their backs, sometimes on their sides with the knees up to the chin (presumably generally having been bound in this posture), a style to become very usual in Europe and north Africa in the succeeding Neolithic Age and widely prevalent among the modern primitive peoples of Africa, Australia and America. With the supposed negroid skeletons in the cave known as the Grotte des Enfants at Grimaldi, the body of an old woman had been laid beside a youth's, both in a crouched position; in the neighbouring cave of Barma Grande a man, youth and woman had all been laid extended in a single grave. The practice of interment after the flesh had decayed, another custom frequent among primitives and usually linked with the idea of a final setting free

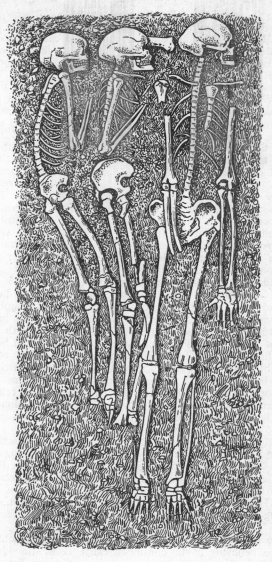

FIG. 34. *Upper Palaeolithic triple burial, Barma Grande, Mentone (after Verneau).*

of the spirit to join its fellows, seems not to have been observed before Mesolithic times. The habit of burying the dead in the cave-dwelling, and, so far as we can tell, continuing to live in it, suggests they were not feared—and indeed could safely be furnished with unbroken weapons (Fig. 34).

Frequently the body, and particularly the head, was protected by stone slabs forming a rudimentary tomb, and accompanied by grave furniture and food. We know that men, women and children were often buried wearing pendants and necklaces, hairpins and other ornamental objects, and this suggests that they were laid in their graves fully clothed. Some of the skeletons in the south of France (notably at the Grimaldi caves of Cavillon, Barma Grande and the Grotte des Enfants) were unusually richly decked with ornaments and were overlaid with shells looking as though they had been attached to skirts and head-dresses. This tradition is exactly continued in the rich accoutrements of the Natufian burials on Mount Carmel (p. 159). In east Asia the same ideas were introduced by the Upper Palaeolithic immigrants; at Mal'ta a three-year-old child had been interred under the foundations of a hut wearing a necklace, pendant and chaplet and accompanied by miniature tools.

It has already been said that ochre had frequently been either sprinkled over the corpse or painted on it (as among the Bushmen); a similar symbol for the life force may have been intended in the tusks and horns sometimes laid with the dead. The youth in the Pavilland cave, south Wales, had been steeped in ochre and furnished with the entire head of a mammoth; a mammoth tusk accompanied a burial at Brunn in Moravia. If symbolism was in fact intended in this funerary use of horns, it should be related to the three carved reliefs of women holding bison horns from Laussel; in religious cults of later times the creative force of the beast was considered to be expelled through the horn point.

It would be wrong to leave the question of burial practices and their religious implications without again mentioning the nests of skulls of Mesolithic age at Ofnet in Bavaria. It is possible to regard these skulls as belonging to revered persons and even as evidence for some cult of the dead or of ancestors. The evidence has already been given, however, for preferring to interpret these skulls as the relics of head-hunting.

If their funerary rites reveal the Palaeolithic and Mesolithic hunters as believing in the continued existence of individuals after death and a strong sense of group solidarity between these dead and the living, the animal art and other evidence suggest that this belief was probably related to animal cults akin to modern totemism. All the indications of totemic ideas among these ancient hunting peoples have already been stated in connection with their possible social implications (p. 185). Though it is still slight, there is more to suggest something akin to the religious aspect of totemism existing among the Upper Palaeolithic hunting peoples than there is, or can ever be, for the social. It is unlikely that either ritual or belief had become so formal or so elaborate as in later times, but there seems every reason to suppose that the dawning religious impulse of the human psyche went out towards animals and animal life with a sense of wonder and a desire for communion with them. The emotional content of the animal paintings themselves, the evidence from the art that men dressed themselves in animal guise and were capable of imagining a being like the Trois Frères 'Sorcerer', all strongly support such an interpretation. The scene of human figures ranged round a dismembered bison from Raymonden may well represent a ritual meal of the kind partaken of by some totemic clans; the comparable one from La Madeleine of a procession with bowed heads approaching a gigantic bison figure might be a rendering of some form of the propitiation ceremony, of seeking forgiveness from the animals to be killed, so often performed by hunting peoples in Australia, Africa and America (Fig. 35).

Other more particular analogies can be found, though identity can never be proved. Central Australian tribes keep their sacred *churingas*, pieces of wood or stone carved or painted with symbolic designs, in appointed caves. They are 'spirit houses' signifying the conjunction of the divine, animal and human aspect of the totem. They are also the houses where spirits await reincarnation in the human mother's womb as part of the perpetual renewal of the totem, and in this sense are shown to initiates undergoing the rites that give them rebirth into full membership of the clan. Objects strikingly like the *churingas* were in the possession of the Magdalenians, while the stones engraved with symbols from La Ferrassie might have played a similar part among the Aurignacians. Even more suggestive are the painted pebbles of the Azilians. It is also worth commenting that the Australians, on entering the caves to fetch the *churingas*, impress the palms of their hands near the entry to establish their right of passage, a practice that might conceivably be reflected in the hand-impressions and stencils found at Gargas and Castillo.

While the central Australian tribes keep movable sacred symbols in caves, the Karadjeri people of the west make sacred cave-paintings. These followers of the Rainbow Serpent believe that by making or retouching paintings at sacred localities within the caves they can promote the fertility of

FIG. 35. *Upper Palaeolithic rituals. Engravings from the Dordogne. A: Raymonden; B: La Madeleine (after G. R. Levy).*

the totemic species. Their practice of retouching old paintings is of particular interest when it is remembered how many of the Palaeolithic works have been repeatedly redrawn. Like the *churingas*, the Karadjeri paintings are held to unite the individual with the totem and the divine ancestor, and the continued use of old ones serves to maintain continuity with this ancestral past.

One other possible analogy can be detected between the rites and beliefs of modern primitive peoples and those of the Palaeolithic hunters. A conception of spirit ancestors coming to the world through lakes, caves or other openings in the ground and making intricate journeys that have to be re-enacted by their descendants is so widespread that it might claim to be a part of that inherited mental furniture already discussed. Comparable ideas are found, too, in the myths and rituals of civilized peoples. The Australians make the most exact and complex maps of these journeys in the form of ground-paintings, and themselves go in procession from sacred spot to spot, following the divine route; American Indians have comparable rituals. The 'macaroni' of the early cave-paintings and other abstract designs such as the strange curvilinear patterns sometimes carved by the Magdalenians have been likened to these maps of spirit journeys. It has also been suggested, perhaps with more justification, that the long, tortuous routes which had to be followed to reach many of the painted caves were deliberately undertaken as a form of re-enactment.

It seems that totemism has special need of art forms in order to make the image of the undying and divine totemic life—something more real than any of its individual expressions in man and beast. While the Australians imparted a certain power to their stylized and even schematic paintings, the Palaeolithic peoples of Europe had extraordinary artistic gifts and so were able to give their images more than the natural force, vigour and significance of the living animal. It is easy to see how the urge for finer and more perfect imaginative expression in the artists coincided with this wish for religious imagery in the whole community and led at last to the highest achievement. Here was a unity of purpose and inspiration greatly to be envied by our outcast artists of the twentieth century.

The shrine established by the Natufian hunters by the spring at Jericho suggests that already by Mesolithic times men were honouring the 'lifegiving powers' of the waters— or, in other words, the 'spirit of the spring'. Local cults of spirits of such natural features were probably universal in prehistoric times, persisting behind all other religious forms.

There remain the female statuettes or Venuses whose significance must be more purely magical and religious than any other element in Palaeolithic art. It can be said that sex provided the only emotion in the life of early man that could rival that roused by the game animals. That is true, and the emotion so engendered must help to explain the artist's inspiration. The life-size female figures on the cave wall at Angles-sur-l'Anglin with their open vulva may even have been used for sexual rites; carved phalluses are not uncommon in the caves. Yet most of the Venuses are not essentially sexual, but rather expressive of the great basic idea of procreation, fertility, the continuance of life. They are extraordinarily like the Mother or Earth Goddesses of the agricultural peoples of Eurasia in the Neolithic Age and must be directly ancestral to them (Pl. 7). Indeed, it may be that just as this goddess presided over the megalithic and other tombs of the later age, and the crouched bodies within can be seen as awaiting rebirth from her womb, so the bodies buried in the caves awaited renewal through the power symbolized by the Venuses.

The concept of the Mother Goddess may be said to be almost as universal as the religious impulse itself. Whether she is an inherited figure of the human psyche, or one created by the common experience of life itself, we cannot presume to judge, but she seems to have eternal life. Her power waxes and wanes, sometimes she is almost dispossessed by her son or by the divine father, but she lives on in the mind of man whether he calls her Nentinugga, Ishtar, Hathor, Isis, Hera or Mary. Certainly the concept of the goddess has grown more subtle and refined intellectually with the development of consciousness, and yet from the earliest time the intuitions of the artist have been subtle and fine. The Venus of Lespuges, carved perhaps twenty-five thousand years ago, is not only lovely and harmonious of form, massive and yet full of grace, but also perfectly expresses, in her bowed head and the superb resignation of her poise, the feminine principle, with its recognition of the glory of life and the need for its continuance. The Venus of Lespuges may have had no annunciation of a coming god, but she knows that she is to bear man and his spirit through all eternity.

NOTES TO CHAPTER VII

1. For Professor Debetz, the aesthetic reflection of reality and creative art are not primordial. They took shape at a rather high stage of development of human society and consciousness. One of the necessary factors of creative art is the technical aspect, physical labour associated with certain work habits. But these habits have not come into being suddenly, by themselves. A determining factor for the origin of art was that in the process of social labour man, in the course of time, not only became more deeply cognizant of the world around him, practically mastering shape, colour and other properties of objects, but also learned when making tools to produce the forms that he required according to a pattern or plan previously conceived. Labour is older than art and is the basis of its origin.

2. Dr P. Bosch-Gimpera feels that the striking affinities between Aurignacian art and the much more recent 'Arctic' rock engravings and paintings, which were recognized by A. W. Brøgger as early as 1906, are definitely not traceable back to direct links between the Upper Palaeolithic of western Europe and the Mesolithic/Neolithic of Scandinavia. The relationship must, however, be of an indirect character. We have to bear in mind the following: (1) that at least the Middle and Late Aurignacian of the west have close relations

with the east; the same applies also in the case of Aurignacian art; (2) that in the east the Aurignacian (or Gravettian) did not give rise to Magdalenian, as in the west, but instead there was a retardation leading to the Mesolithic; this eastern Upper Palaeolithic, too, yields works of art—especially *art mobilier* (home art), but also individual instances of rock pictures (Melitopol area, Sea of Azov); (3) that in northern Norway 'Arctic' art is primarily the product of the Komsa culture, which is thought to have originated in the east. This raises the possibility that the origins of 'Arctic' art reach back to the Upper Palaeolithic in Russia, and are thus indirectly related to Aurignacian-Gravettian art in western Europe. See J. Maringer and H. G. Bandi, *Art in the Ice Age* (London and Basle, 1953), pp. 161–3.

3. Today the prevalent view is that Spanish Levant art dates from a relatively late period. It is possible, although there is no proof of this, that its origins go back to the Upper Palaeolithic. But in the main it must be 'Mesolithic', even if there may be a certain chronological overlap with Neolithic cultures. See J. Maringer and H. G. Bandi, *Art in the Ice Age* (London and Basle, 1953), pp. 132–42.

4. Professor A. Varagnac points out that in Franco-Cantabrian minor arts, too, there are several examples of composite scenes. Among those that are of considerable interest is an engraving on schist from the cave of Péchialet (Dordogne), in which a bear attacking (?) a man, and behind it another human figure, can be identified. See H. Breuil, 'Œuvres d'art paléolithiques inédites du Périgord et art oriental d'Espagne', *Revue anthropologique* (1927), pp. 101–8.

5. See p. 195, note 6.

6. Most authors consider that the Upper Palaeolithic art of western Europe begins only with the typical Aurignacian (= Middle Aurignacian). See H. Breuil and R. Lantier, *Les Hommes de la Pierre Ancienne* (Paris, 1959), pp. 180–1. But it is still an open question whether the representations of hands (in Gargas, for example) could have been painted already during the Châtelperronian (= Early Aurignacian). See L. Kirchner, *Jungpalaeolithische Handdarstellungen der franko-kantabrischen Felsbilderzone* (Göppingen, 1959).

7. For Professor A. Varagnac it is nevertheless conceivable that this representation of an ibex on the lower side of the lamp, which would not normally be visible, had some magic significance. This view is indirectly corroborated by the fact that even today special powers are ascribed to the 'buck' in folk-lore.

8. Professor W. Koppers remarks that the hypothesis that religious ideas developed from the impersonal to the personal is regarded by some scholars as a purely subjective (evolutionist) view. The fact that elder groups of people, known to ethnological research, are constantly attempting a new interpretation of personality seems to prove the contrary. Impersonal (pantheistic) ideas in general unequivocally represent a younger development.

9. Professor W. Koppers asserts that in the light of present knowledge many historians of religion reject the idea that the belief in a Great Mother Goddess is of relatively great antiquity. They hold this view to be as outmoded as Bachofen's theory that matriarchy preceded patriarchy.

SECTION TWO

THE NEOLITHIC

CLIMATIC PHASE	MILLENNIA B.C.	BRITISH ISLES	IBERIA FRANCE SWISS LAKES	LIGURIA	SOUTH ITALY SICILY WESTERN ISLES	BALTIC REGION AND N. EUROPEAN PLAIN
SUB BOREAL	2					*Development into*
SUB BOREAL / ATLANTIC	3	FIRST HENGES (L.N.) RINYO-CLACTON (Orkneys) MEGALITHS FENGATE MORTLAKE EBBSFLEET WINDMILL HILL — PETERBOROUGH	MEGALITHS S.O.M. WESTERN NEOL. (CHASSEY-LAGOZZA CORTAILLOD)		DIANA SERRA D'ALTO	LATE NEOLITHIC PASSAGE GRAVES (M.N.) DYSSER T.R.B. INTERACTION WITH EUROPEAN NEOLITHIC — FIRST NORTHERN
ATLANTIC	4		MICHELSBURG ALMERIAN (Spain)	LAGOZZA CHIOZZA		RÖSSEN LENGYEL DANUBE I
ATLANTIC	5		IMPRESSED WARE (S and E Spain)	IMPRESSED WARE	MOLFETTA STENTINELLO (Sicily) (S. Italy) IMPRESSED WARE	ERTEBØLLE (mesolithic)
BOREAL	6		*Mesolithic*			
BOREAL	7	SEPARATION (from Continent)		*Cultures*		
BOREAL	8					

OF THE OLD WORLD

BALKANS DANUBE VALLEY SOUTH RUSSIA	AEGEAN AND LEVANT	EGYPT	WESTERN ASIA	INDIA	FAR EAST

Metal Using Cultures

				INDUS CULTURES	YANG-SHAO (North and Central) — NEOLITHIC
PRE-YAMNO TRIPOLYE	LARISSA DIMINI (L.N.)				
CULTURES	KNOSSOS E.N. (Crete)		PROTO-LITERATE URUK (S.M.)	PRE-INDUS VALLEY CULTURES	SOUTH— LUNG SHAN (East Coast)
	VINČA SESKLO (M.N.)				
DANUBE I		BADARIAN	UBAID (N.M. & S.M.)		
KÖRÖS	P R E - S E S K L O	FAYUM B			
STARČEVO	KHIROKITIA (p.p.) (Cyprus)	FAYUM A	HALAF (SY.)		
			SAMARRA		
			NINEVEH (N.M.) SIALK (P.)		
	OTZAKI IMPRESSED WARE	TASIAN	HACILAR HASSUNA (ANAT.) (N.N.) MERSIN		
			(ANAT.)		
			BELT CAVE (N.M.)		
			JARMO (p.p.) N.M.		
			JERICHO (p.p.)		
			NATUFIAN Mesolithic		

N.M. = NORTH MESOPOTAMIA
S.N. = SOUTH MESOPOTAMIA
P. = PERSIA
SY. = SYRIA
ANAT. = ANATOLIA

CHAPTER VIII

THE HISTORY OF THE NEOLITHIC CULTURES

For something like a million years men had been living as hunters. For the last forty thousand of them it is true, they had so developed their powers of mind, imagination and skill that they had emerged into full human stature. Yet still, like all the other creatures that had evolved with them on the face of the earth, they were wholly dependent on what nature provided for shelter, clothing, and above all for food. Such supplies were often precarious, almost never constant, and kept men ever on the move. Possessions were a handicap, even children had often to be limited in number. The most important change that ensued when man began to control his natural environment was that he was enabled to settle down. Great possessions became at least a possibility, substantial and enduring monuments were worth the building. Children could live where their parents had lived, inherit what they had made; their numbers could increase.

One distinguishing mark of the first phase of the new farming economy was the establishment of settled villages. The idea of raising a few crops by deliberate sowing, of keeping young animals taken from wild herds, may have happened at several times and places in human history. It seems almost certain, indeed, that the whole agricultural revolution was achieved independently in the New World[1] (p. 349). Profound changes had to be made to adapt it to the climate of eastern Asia. Nevertheless it does at present appear that the enterprises and discoveries that enabled farming to support the settled village community was achieved only once and within a limited region in the Old World; from there the new knowledge together with seed grain and breeding stock were carried outwards by cultural borrowing and the movement of peoples. It is the purpose of this chapter to try to describe first the emergence of the new economy and then its diffusion. A place must be found also to discuss an independent establishment of agricultural communities in America.

This spreading change of the economic foundation of existence constitutes what has been called the Neolithic revolution. It is at once apparent that it took place only over a great range of time. Beginning some eight or nine thousand years ago in its cradleland, it took between three and four thousand years to reach western Europe on the one hand, China on the other. Indeed, as is well known, Bronze Age cities were already in being before the first farmers sowed their crops and led their flocks and herds in western Europe. Yet the concept of the Neolithic Age remains useful so long as it is understood that it is not a time phase falling between exact dates, but represents the period between the end of the hunting way of life and the beginning of a full metal-using economy, when the practice of farming arose and spread through much of Europe, Asia and north Africa like a slow-moving wave.

The Neolithic economy generally depended upon mixed farming. The oldest settlement sites known to us were already dependent on both domestic animals and cultivated cereals. If before this either stock-breeding or agriculture were ever independently established as the basis of a full farming existence, we have no knowledge of it. As for nomadic pastoralism, although it is true it might easily be overlooked as it leaves scanty traces, it is a very highly specialized mode of life and may not have been perfected until relatively late. Certainly, on the vast Eurasiatic steppes where it was afterwards to flourish it does not seem to have emerged until several millennia after the earliest settlement of mixed farmers. Pastoralism will be discussed in due course, but it cannot for the present be included in any account of the origin and spread of early Neolithic culture.

The practice of farming and life in settled hamlets can be accepted as the first mark of the full Neolithic revolution. Certain particular items of material culture so often accompany it that they deserve mention in any general definition of Neolithic culture. One is the polished axe or adze, made either of igneous rock or flint (p. 421), the other the straight sickle, more or less on the Natufian model. The crafts of potting and weaving were soon to become the most important additions to Neolithic culture, but they were, as will be shown, secondary traits following upon the essential innovations in farming life and equipment.

It has already been said that the cradle of the farming economy with more or less settled villages has proved diffi-

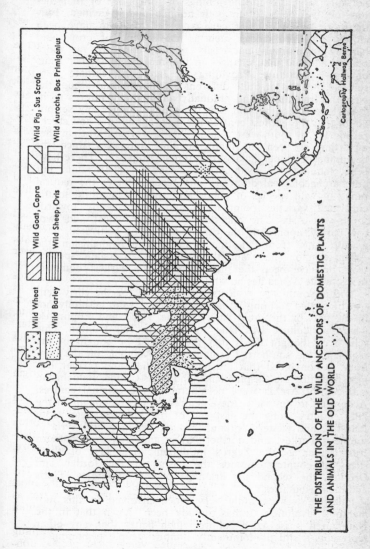

Wild Wheat

Wild Barley

Wild Goat, Capra

Wild Sheep, Ovis

Wild Pig, Sus Scrofa

Wild Aurochs, Bos Primigenius

Cartography Hallweg Berne

THE DISTRIBUTION OF THE WILD ANCESTORS OF DOMESTIC PLANTS
AND ANIMALS IN THE OLD WORLD

MAP VI

cult to place exactly in either time or space. Perhaps it is not surprising, for the beginnings of things are of their nature elusive, being often both humble and ill-defined. Furthermore, this particular genesis is not likely to have been closely localized. Ideas such as the sowing of crops and herding of animals can easily spread; they are far more readily adopted than changes in tool-making and other traits of material culture. Providing the land and climate were suitable, peoples of quite different traditions could accept the Neolithic revolution and gradually adapt their cultures to it.

At least it can be said that there is no longer any serious doubt that the earliest centres for both agriculture and stock-raising lay in south-west Asia, well within that Eurasian theatre that as seen all man's leading initiatives since the beginning of Upper Palaeolithic times (Map VI). There have been claimants for north Africa and even for Abyssinia, but both archaeological discovery and recognition of the natural range of wild species of plants and animals ancestral to the cultivated varieties point more and more clearly towards south-west Asia. The ancestors of emmer wheat and two-row barley, apparently the cereals first to be cultivated, have a wide range from Palestine to Persia and Afghanistan; the Asian mouflon sheep and the urial, also an Asiatic species, seem to have been the precursors of the earliest domestic herds, while Africa has no wild sheep.

Within south-west Asia itself the search for the early centres of settled farming is narrowing. They were certainly not in the flats of the great valley of the Tigris and Euphrates, where agriculture was later to come to full fruition. One school of thought holds that they should be sought in the region of the southern Caspian basin. Another, on the contrary, is convinced that the high Anatolian and farther Iranian plateaux, the Caspian basin and trans-Caspia, Baluchistan and central Arabia were peripheral to the original centres. According to this view, these centres should be sought in the hilly country along the east end of the Mediterranean from Palestine and western Jordan, through Lebanon and Syria to southern Turkey, and northern Syria and Iraq and southern Iran as far as the Zagros mountains. The first of these strips of country contains the basins of the Jordan and Orontes, the second the drainage of the Euphrates, Tigris and their tributaries.

Palestine was certainly very much involved in this momentous revolution. It has already been shown that in the Natufian it possessed a culture which better than any other represents a still predominantly hunting people beginning to harvest grain or seeds. At the famous *tell* of Jericho, an oasis lying nearly one thousand feet below sea-level in the Jordan valley, we can see this culture developing into a full Neolithic one. The first event at this most historic site seems to have been the establishment of a shrine, probably dedicated to the life-giving properties of the spring, by hunters with a Lower Natufian culture. This was followed by the same people settling down in a permanent or regular seasonal settlement, living in flimsy huts of a kind appropriate to a semi-nomadic existence. This settlement, which may be called proto-Neolithic, developed without a cultural break into a full Neolithic community which, with its substantial houses and defences, has been claimed as a true town. Here in the first town of Jericho the stone implements still show a Natufian inheritance. Carbon-14 dating has assigned an age of about 7800 B C to the shrine and indirectly one of at least 7000 B C to the beginning of the full Neolithic phase.

Thus there is no doubt that at Jericho the eighth millennium saw the local evolution from a Mesolithic hunting to a Neolithic farming economy. But this is not likely to have been the only area where this all-important change took place. Another village site that might be expected to contribute to our knowledge concerning the step to a farming economy is Qalat Jarmo on a spur of the Kurdish hills in the Tigris drainage area. Economically it does so, for the earliest of this series of superimposed hamlets look as though they were inhabited by a community very near the beginning of food production. Carbon-14 dating has given somewhat conflicting dates for Jarmo. The readings at first suggested an age on either side of 4750 B C, but more recent tests have pushed it back as early as 6500 B C. Here, however, there is little in the range of flint and obsidian tools to prove descent from the Natufian culture; equally they fail to show any close relationship with the very late Gravettian of the nearby caves of Zarzi and Palegawra. Nor do they derive from the culture known from Karim Shahir and Shanidar which was a parallel development to the Natufian.

There are two other sites evidently of great importance for the tracking down of farming origins. They are the Belt and Hotu caves, lying close together above the southern shores of the Caspian Sea. In the Belt Cave purely Mesolithic occupation was succeeded by a Neolithic one that contains some of the oldest dated remains of domesticated animals, perhaps about the beginning of the sixth millennium B C. Yet here there is no clear continuity between the two: the

Neolithic culture cannot be said to derive from the Mesolithic.

Perhaps the best way to convey a picture of the beginning of the farming life will be to describe the particular sites already mentioned before going on to a more general account of the Early Neolithic Age in south-west Asia. They are undoubtedly among the earliest examples of their types of site known to us, and if we advance from a cave-dwelling occupied by still unsettled stock-breeders, to a permanent village and then on to a stone-walled settlement so substantial that it merits the name of town, we must in fact have followed the economic course of the Neolithic revolution. Also Belt Cave, Jarmo village and Jericho between them span the whole region within which farming is likely to have originated.

These sites represent different aspects of the pre-pottery Neolithic cultures now known to have been widespread in south-west Asia, and which further research may conceivably show to have spread far into Europe as well. The first stock-breeding inhabitants of Belt Cave had no pots; at Jarmo potsherds were only beginning to appear in the latest hamlet; while at Jericho two successive occupations had accumulated four-fifths of the Neolithic *tell* before potting was introduced. This pioneer phase, then, is clearly distinguished from the well-known later Neolithic (or Chalcolithic) cultures of south-west Asia which were emerging by the middle of the sixth millennium B C, and which are distinguished by their fine ceramics. Evidence for the westward spread of pre-pottery Neolithic is still sketchy, although there are a number of possible sites in Thessaly. At Khirokitia in the south of Cyprus a large farming community was established by 5500 B C. Although at first a few clumsy attempts at potting were made, the craft was completely abandoned in favour of excellently-made stone vessels.

The first occupation of the Belt Cave was by Mesolithic seal hunters who probably lived there at the end of glacial times some eleven thousand years ago; there followed a second, still Mesolithic, occupation dating from the seventh millennium, and then a third when the cave-dwellers may or may not have raised grain but certainly possessed domestic sheep and goats. Carbon-14 gave this horizon a date of 5840 B C with an error of some three hundred years either way. During the second half of the same millennium true mixed farmers were living in the cave, people who had sickles to reap grain, made pottery of a rather soft and poor ware and in addition to sheep and goats kept first pigs and then cows. The neighbouring cave of Hotu seems first to have been lived in during this last Neolithic occupation, but it continued to be inhabited after the Belt Cave had been abandoned. The rubbish of the last occupation included fine, hard, painted pottery of a kind not quite identifiable with any known elsewhere.

The people of Jarmo evidently lived more or less permanently in their little village, building multi-roomed rectangular houses of compacted clay or pisé (Fig. 38A), sometimes set on stone foundations and with reed floors. They had such built-in furniture as baking ovens and basins sunk in the floor. Although they did not know how to fire pottery, even the earliest inhabitants cut and ground excellent bowls and other vessels from smooth stones of pleasantly variegated colour; they used stone also for such personal ornaments as beads and bracelets. They possessed that most distinctive Neolithic tool, the ground and polished stone axe, and its variant, the adze. Other agricultural tools were sickles and simple grain rubbers or querns. They imported obsidian for tools and also used chert; and a considerable part of their equipment was microlithic, suggesting a strong inheritance from Mesolithic tradition. The main crops of these villagers were emmer and einkorn wheat, and barley, but their emmer was more primitive than any other cultivated wheat known to us, its spikelets varying so much in size and form as to make it evident that very little selective cultivation lay behind it. As for their stock, almost all the bones belong to the domesticable species of sheep or goat, ox, pig and dog, but it cannot be proved that they were all fully domesticated. For their household divinity the people of Jarmo evidently revered the Mother Goddess, possessing clay statuettes of her seated figure. They also made little clay models of their livestock that may have been used for magical or religious cults.

Some account of the early happenings beside the perennial spring at Jericho has already been given. We have to picture first wandering parties of hunters and food-gatherers visiting their shrine, probably only at certain times of year. Then the growth of a permanent or semi-permanent settlement of clay and wattle huts whose owners, while still making their tools and weapons much as before, were probably now beginning to practise the cultivation of grain crops on a modest scale. Next, about nine thousand years ago these same people took a step forward, and on the remains of a long series of collapsed and rebuilt huts of the first rough settlement raised much more substantial round houses, probably looking like a cluster of large beehive ovens, and defended them with a strong masonry wall and a round tower. This earliest full Neolithic settlement at Jericho has quite properly been called a town.

Not enough has been excavated of this most ancient town for it to be possible to say very much about the lives of the population. Their stone implements still show their descent from the Lower Natufian tradition; they had large stone querns for grinding flour by rubbing. As we have seen they had not learnt the art of potting. The sun-baked bricks from which their houses were built were of a highly distinctive form (p. 386).

Of the second pre-pottery Neolithic occupation at Jericho much more is known. The older population seems to have been completely supplanted by a new one with a distinct though indirectly related culture. This is the Tahunian culture which hitherto has been known only in a far more humble context. As they have been known away from Jericho the Tahunians led a semi-nomadic life, maintaining the Mesolithic tradition of hunting, food-gathering and living in caves, even while they practised shifting agriculture and kept herds of goats. Their culture, too, had been derived from the Lower Natufian, but along different lines from that of their predecessors at Jericho. How the Tahunians acquired the enviable oasis and came to lead there a quite elaborate urban existence is a historical problem as yet unsolved. Certainly their lives must have contrasted with those of their cave-dwelling kinsmen almost as sharply as those of the modern city-dwellers of Palestine with the lives of the Bedouin who pitched their goat-hair tents not far from the city suburbs.

The domestic architecture of this second pre-pottery Neolithic town of Jericho was far more advanced than that of the first. As we shall see (p. 386) the houses were rectangular, of an elaborate courtyard plan and quite excellent in their finish. One house seems to have had a little chapel with a cult stone set on a pedestal in a niche, while a large rectangular building with a stone basin is thought to have been a public temple. The massive defences were maintained with a few alterations. It is estimated that this Jericho of the later seventh millennium B C with its houses packed inside its walls must have had a population of at least three thousand.

Like the villagers of Jarmo, the citizens of Jericho used bowls and dishes cut from stone. These were of the soft local limestone which could be given a pleasantly polished surface. It seems very likely that they also had containers of leather and of wood. For their tools they used mainly flint but occasionally obsidian. The relatively large numbers of sickle blades, typically with finely serrated cutting-edges, together with many querns, are a proof of the importance of agriculture. No hoes were found, and the presence of many perforated stones suggests that weighted digging sticks were used instead. The oasis may have been the centre of irrigated gardens and orchards, but we have as yet no tangible evidence for the cultivation of vegetables and fruits at this early date. Few bones of domestic animals have been discovered, but in the neighbourhood of the temple building there were a number of rough clay models of goats, sheep, cattle and pigs that appear to represent domesticated livestock. A great proportion of the bones found were of deer and other wild species, and these, together with the arrowheads, are enough to prove that in spite of its urban pretensions hunting was still of substantial economic importance at Jericho.

The presumed temple with the little clay figures suggests some kind of animal cult inviting comparison with Jarmo. Two female figurines of the Mother Goddess type were also found in the vicinity. The most remarkable cult objects from the Jericho of this phase, however, are embellished skulls. These are human skulls, usually though not always without the lower jaw, that have had the flesh parts reproduced in clay and cowrie shells set in the sockets in a most striking semblance of eyes. Several skeletons with the skull removed but with the lower jaw still in position have been found in the settlement, suggesting that these were native dead and not the loot of head-hunting or war. This could, indeed, already be inferred by the skilful care taken in modelling the faces and the fact that they were carefully buried under house floors. One can suppose that the people of Jericho wished to keep the ancestral spirits with them. A bone bead carved in the form of a head gives a further hint that some cult of the human head was established among them.

Why was Jericho so exceptionally progressive? Why were three thousand people living there in comfortable houses when all around them their contemporaries were living in rough little hamlets or caves? The explanation seems to be in the fact that Jericho grew up beside a very important oasis. Not only did this perennial water supply encourage good cultivation of both grain crops and, possibly, orchards, but its management necessitated social organization and the feeling of community. Just as the need to co-operate in

hunting animals much stronger and more fleet than themselves must have extended social obligation outside the
bounds of the family in Palaeolithic times, so now the control of irrigation demanded a new sense of co-operation and
respect for law in a settled population.

A word should be said about the later Neolithic occupation of Jericho after its citizens had taken to the use of
pottery. The first pottery was rather soft, tempered with
chaff, of a drab colour sometimes enlivened by the use of a
pink slip. At the same period the inhabitants began to store
their grain in pits lined with unbaked clay, recalling those
at Tell Hassuna. A model of a two-storeyed building, possibly a granary or sanctuary, gives a rough impression of
the contemporary architecture. But what is really remarkable in this settlement (known to archaeologists as Jericho
IX) is the evidence it provides for a local pantheon. A shrine
housed three images, made of unbaked clay with shell eyes,
representing a bearded man, a woman and a child, a most
interesting trinity to find being worshipped six thousand years
ago.

The Belt cave-dwelling, the village of Jarmo and the larger
settlement of Jericho have been singled out because they
represent some of the earliest steps towards the achievement of the Neolithic revolution. Belt has early evidence for
domestic animals; Jarmo is one of the oldest settled villages
as yet unearthed, while Jericho is an astonishing proof, still
hardly assimilated into our understanding of the period, as
to how quickly organized community life could be achieved
on a large scale once the farming economy had been established. It is difficult to follow these studies with any
generalized account of the peoples and cultures of these regions during Early Neolithic times: almost every site seems
to have its own localized culture. This, indeed, must to some
extent represent the truth: every community made its own
adjustments as it took over agriculture and stock-raising and
began to settle into permanent villages (Map VII). A few
sites, however, can be recognized as representing cultures
that had at least a modest range and some influence beyond their own immediate area. One of these is the Tell
Hassuna in Assyria on the west flank of the Tigris that appears undoubtedly to have been founded after the first occupation at Jarmo. The earliest settlement here has much in
common with the earliest at Nineveh and at Matarrah; it
even seems to have had some influence as far west as the
Amouq—the plain of Antioch. The inhabitants of this village, happily situated at the junction of two perennial

streams, from the first made pottery. Almost from the beginning, too, they were capable of producing pleasing painted and incised wares, the painting usually showing simple rectilinear patterns in black. Their pisé houses were both round and rectangular and were equipped with ovens and clay-lined storage pits (the earliest form of storage was in large roughly fired jars sunk into the ground). These stores, primitive saddle querns and broad-bladed chipped stone hoe-blades show the Hassunians to have been considerable agriculturalists, while the bones of cattle and sheep or goats seem to be those of domesticated flocks and herds. At the same time the villagers hunted such wild game as gazelles and onagers with slings and darts. Here again as in nearly all Neolithic peasant settlements from south-west Asia to Britain, a Mother Goddess appears to have been venerated and was made visible in the form of clay figurines. In short, the Hassuna culture shows a way of life only a little advanced from that of Jarmo, the innovations being pottery, hoes and better means of storing grain; it may well be that the wheat itself had been improved by selection beyond the haphazard crops sown at Jarmo.

In the later settlements towards the top of the Hassuna *tell,* where the houses had several rooms fitted with pivoted wooden doors, the inmates were using, as well as their own painted and incised earthenware, pottery which was slipped and painted with extremely effective designs. These include both patterns seemingly derived from basketry, and amusing stylized animal figures. This attractive crockery is known as Samarra ware and it is rather more widespread than the Hassunian. It has been found at Nineveh, Matarrah and at Chagar Bazar, while the site after which it is named is a cemetery situated just above the Tigris mud-flats some way to the south of Hassuna, where some fine specimens of it had been placed with contracted burials. Altogether it was used from Sakje Geuze west of the Euphrates to beyond the Tigris in Assyria, but it seems usually to have been acquired by local peoples as a pleasing possession, and it is hard to define a true Samarra culture.

As for the absolute dates during which farming was being adopted and developed here, round the upper Tigris and Euphrates, the early Hassunian settlements must have been established about the middle of the sixth millennium, while the popularity of Samarra ware was a little later.

What is quite certain is that the Samarra period overlapped with that of a culture known as the Halafian, and the Halafian is a full Neolithic culture. Tell Halaf itself is well

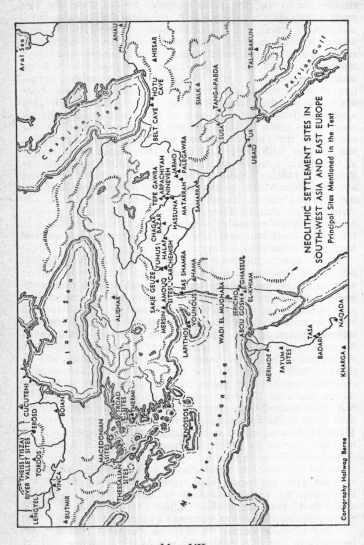

Aral Sea

ANAU

HISSAR

TAL-I-BAKUN

Persian Gulf

Caspian Sea

HOTU CAVE
BELT CAVE

SIALK
TANG-I-PABDA

TEPE GAWRA
CHAGAR BAZAR
"UNUS"
ARPACHIYAH
NINEVEH

SUSA

UR

UBAID

SAKJE GEUZE
MERSIN
AMOUQ SITES
"CARCHEMISH"

HALAF
PALEGAWRA
JARMO

PATEGAWRA

MATARRAH

SAMARRA

Black Sea

ALISHAR

HASSUNA

RAS SHAMRA

HAMA

LAPITHOS
YOUNOS

KNOSSOS

TROAD SITES

HERMI

MACEDONIAN SITES

THESSALIAN SITES

VINCA

BOIAN

TOROS

EROSD

CUCUTENI

THEISS (TISZA) RIVER VALLEY SITES

LENGYEL

BUTMIR

WADI EL MUGHARA

ABOU GOSH
JERICHO
GHASSUL
EL-KHIAM

MERIMDE

FAYUM SITES

TASA

BADARI

NAQADA

KHARGA

Mediterranean Sea

NEOLITHIC SETTLEMENT SITES IN SOUTH-WEST ASIA AND EAST EUROPE

Principal Sites Mentioned in the Text

Cartography Hallwag Berne

MAP VII

to the west of the sites hitherto discussed, lying near the head waters of the Khabur. The culture, mainly, it must be admitted, distinguished by its pottery, made its influence felt from the Iranian foothills east of the Tigris right across the parkland of the upper Tigris and Euphrates and their tributaries to the Mediterranean coast of southern Turkey and Syria.

Many of the great *tells* of this region, in addition to Hassuna and Halaf itself, have their Halafian horizon; Nineveh, Carchemish, Arpachiyah among them. Although hunting with the sling continued as before, mixed farming was now fully established, with cultivated varieties of emmer and barley, two distinct breeds of cattle, sheep, goats and pigs. There does not seem to have been much change in domestic architecture from that of the later Hassunian type of house, but curious circular buildings with low domed roofs were a new introduction almost certainly intended for ritual use. At Arpachiyah, where the Halafian settlement was rich and long-lasting, cobbled streets survive to give us some idea of the town-like atmosphere that must already have existed among close-packed houses.

The Halafians were skilled workers in stone, able to use obsidian for vases and beads; they were also evidently practised in that second craft that goes with potting as one of the great Neolithic inventions—spinning and weaving. They even possessed small beads of copper, but these seem to have been obtained from native copper and do not imply a knowledge of metallurgy. Chert and obsidian remained the material for tools, and the forms do not show any very significant change from the Hassunian—polished stone axes and adzes, obsidian knives and sickles, coarse chert hoes.

The Halafians were pre-eminent as potters, using kilns in which they could raise a temperature of 1,200° F. Their wares were hand-made but extremely thin, usually a creamy buff with a slipped surface. Shapes were elegant and of the highest aesthetic merit, while painting was used to give (in the finest pieces) a rich polychrome effect in red, black and white on buff beneath a lustrous surface. Many of the patterns were geometric, and might converge on a central rosette or Maltese cross, but in Halafian as in Samarran ware, deer, horses, and bulls' heads, all highly stylized, were also deftly shaped into the design. This fully developed Neolithic culture is generally thought to have originated in Assyria, where a steady cultural development can be observed, particularly in the pottery.

Pushing on now to the easternmost limit of the possible

cradlelands of farming, we have to consider Iran. In the Zagros foothills sites such as Tang-i-Pabda and Bakun probably represent early, pre-Ubaid settlement (p. 317), but too little is as yet known of them for it to be possible to judge their significance. Inland, on the Iranian plateau near Kasan, an important settlement grew up beside an oasis at Sialk. The earliest village here appears to have been contemporary with the Hassunian and Samarran, while the second shows signs of Halafian influences. At the very beginning of the settlement, the villagers may have lived in reed huts, but they soon moved into pisé houses. They practised mixed farming with cattle and two breeds of sheep. Their grain crops have not as yet been identified, but they were certainly of great importance in their economy. The fields were prepared with hoes and the harvest reaped with sickles made of rib-bones set with flint teeth. The handles of these sickles were sometimes carved with naturalistic figures, making them surprisingly similar to their faraway Natufian counterparts. One of these carved sickles affords a glimpse of the peasants who wielded them: a stocky little figure wearing a kilt fastened at the back and what looks like a band tied round his forehead to catch his sweat.

Here, as in nearly all the other villages of the time, hunting was still a necessary part of life, the men going out with slings and clay pellets in pursuit of gazelle and other game. Sialk was truly Neolithic in culture, yet a few pins and little awls of copper were in use there; like the beads of it at Tell Halaf, they were probably hammered from native metal. Cosmetics, ground by means of miniature clay pestles and mortars, appear to have been in use among the living, while the dead, buried in crouched positions under and between the houses, were customarily either painted or sprinkled with red ochre.

In the later village, where Halafian influence has been detected, mud bricks were used for building, pig and horse bones appear (though their owners may not have been domestic breeds), hoes were improved, rather more native copper produced and trade extended to bring in turquoise, carnelian, and beads from the Persian Gulf.

In Turkmenia a number of communities forming a single cultural group developed towns round the oases in the foothills of the Kopet-dag. These people lived in pisé houses and made painted pottery, usually dark brown geometric and tree-branch designs on a whitish or red background. At one town, Kara-tepe, the excavators believed they had identified a shrine where both the floor and two square altars had been painted black. Here again the economy depended upon the cultivation of wheat and barley and the raising of sheep or goats. These towns appear to date from the third and fourth millennia B C with the earliest settlements on at least two sites (Jeitun and Namazga) going back as far as 4000 B C.

Returning once more westward after having pursued farming origins to the eastern extremity of our region, a crossing of the narrow mountain belt dividing the Euphrates from the Mediterranean drainage brings us to the relatively well-watered lands of the Orontes basin and the Syrian coastal plain, the Amouq and eastern Cilicia. Here again are Early Neolithic villages which had had a long history before the arrival of Halafian influence from the east brought painted pottery and the use of the sling. This influence made itself felt as far as the Mediterranean coast at Ugarit (Ras Shamra), and on to the *tells* of Judaidah and Kurdu on the Amouq plain, where, however, the Halafian pottery was at first merely imported. There are signs in the repertory of stone implements used by the earliest villagers, and particularly in their microlithic forms, of descent from local Mesolithic cultures of the Natufian type. But still no direct links have been proved.

The early villages of this whole region have a considerable degree of unity. From Byblos, Hama (in the Orontes valley) throughout the Amouq to the important site of Mersin in Cilicia the earliest settlements have a culture distinguished by a dark-faced, burnished pottery often with incised geometrical designs. Polished axes, toothed or other flint and obsidian sickle-blades, projectile-points and stone vessels were generally in use among them from the first. Usually, too, the houses seem to have been of pisé, roughly rectangular in plan and, at Byblos and Ugarit, with limed and burnished floors reminiscent of Jericho. Not very much is directly known of their cultivated plants or livestock.

No pre-pottery Neolithic settlements have as yet been recognized in all this region; if in time they are, their relationship with Mesolithic tradition should prove significant.

While the Halafian culture and its influences were spreading widely from their probable homeland in Assyria, a new culture was coming into being in the lower reaches of the Tigris-Euphrates valley, particularly at the head of the Persian gulf where the heavy silt brought down by the rivers had built up a relatively young and intensely fertile land. It is named after the Sumerian *tell* of al'Ubaid; its creators accomplished the heavy but rewarding labour of draining

and irrigating this valley bottom where fertility was annual-
ly renewed by flooding as effective as that of the Nile valley,
if less regular. 'The many channels and lagoons teemed with
fish; wild fowl and game swarmed in the reed brakes; date
palms grew wild. But the exploitation of this natural paradise,
the original Eden, required intensive labour and the organized co-operation of large bodies of men.' This the Ubaidans
achieved during their long history, irrigating their farms
and developing an agriculture able to support a rapidly
growing population. Thus in time their culture became powerful enough to spread right up the valley and as far west
as the Mediterranean, everywhere overtaking and supplant-
ing the Halafian. Where these people, who can already be
called proto-Sumerians, came from is not known, but they
may well have been of mixed origin, derived in part from
farther south, in part from the Iranian highlands. Another
possible interpretation is that the Ubaid culture was born of
a fusion of Halafian and Samarran elements with an earlier
element already present in southern Mesopotamia. They had
to import nearly all the raw materials for their equipment,
such as stone for axes and hoes, and obsidian and chert for
knives and sickles. This lack of local stone stimulated the
use of a more durable substance—copper—which, although
evidently remaining rare, might be used for such substantial
implements as axes and small spear-heads. Their architecture, originally in reed, presently came to include building
in sun-dried brick. It was the earliest Ubaidans who founded
the original settlement at Eridu, establishing a modest little
temple there that was to be enlarged again and again by
successive generations until it became the great temple of
Enki in the first royal city of the Sumerians. Thus their story
is already the prologue of history. With the spread of
Ubaidan culture round about 4000 B C the full achievement
of the Neolithic revolution, which is the proper subject of
this chapter, was brought to a close.

The story of the introduction of the Neolithic way of life
in Egypt can be made simpler and more coherent than is
possible for south-west Asia. Partly this is because it is now
almost certain that it was introduced when already some way
advanced, partly because of the far greater geographical unity of ancient Egypt. This unity can be exaggerated, for
while Lower Egypt was always accessible from the Mediterranean, Upper Egypt was sometimes penetrated from the
Red Sea. Nevertheless, when compared with the broken and
scattered lands we have been considering, Egypt was compact and culturally already far more uniform.

The arguments against stock-raising and the cultivation of cereals having been initiated in Egypt are put forward in the chapter on the origin of the domestic species of plants and animals. The likelihood of mixed farming having been introduced from south-west Asia is clearly very great in the light of what has already been said concerning that area. Probable Asian elements will be noticed in the early Egyptian farming communities to be described, particularly in those of Lower Egypt. On the other hand there must have been a large native element in the population that would have maintained its own cultural traditions. There is no sign of any inheritance from the poor and unoriginal Sebilian culture of Mesolithic times, but the fine bi-facial pressure-flaked flint implements that already formed part of certain of the Egyptian Neolithic cultures and were developed with superb skill during the later pre-Dynastic period, may well have grown out of the north African Aterian culture or the Stillbay of east Africa. This powerful native element from the first helped to give Egyptian civilization its own distinctive character—what has been called its 'cultural form'. In it we can see the origin of the Hamitic vein in Egyptian language and ethnical stock.

At the beginning of Neolithic times the lands bordering the Nile valley were very much less arid than today, when there is virtually no rainfall south of Cairo. In late glacial times, as has been shown (p. 74), the high plateaux were grasslands, while the *wadis* running down into the main valley were full of vegetation and abounding with wild animals, including giraffe and lion. Well on into historical times the Egyptians were able to go out hunting such game, as is vividly recorded on the walls of tombs. As for Libya, it remained a fertile land rich in vineyards, olive orchards and cattle to the end of the second millennium B C. Nevertheless, progressive desiccation marked the period from perhaps 7000 B C onwards, turning the plateaux from grassland into steppe and ultimately into desert, while making the swampy valley itself more habitable. If this was true of the Tigris-Euphrates valley, it was far more dramatically so in Egypt, where the early farming settlements away from the valley bottom had to be abandoned, often after long struggles with encroaching sand.[2]

The Early Neolithic cultures can from the first be divided into two series between Upper and Lower Egypt, but always, as will be seen, there is much in common between them, not only in the general way of life of self-contained peasant communities practising mixed farming, but also in

more particular cultural traits. It is generally held that the
Upper Egyptian Tasian is the oldest Neolithic culture yet
to have been recognized in Egypt, and from it an unbroken
sequence of developing cultures can be followed up to the
beginning of Dynastic times. In the Delta region (including
the Fayum) the record is less complete, partly because desiccation led to the early abandonment of the earliest settlements, more because the constantly changing course of the
waterways and the accumulating silt must have swept away
or buried countless other sites. There is thus good reason
for beginning not with the Tasian settlement, but with those
of Lower Egypt. In view of what has already been said it
seems highly probable that the first farming communities
were in fact established there, having spread by the coastal
routes from Palestine. The Natufian site at Helwan (with an
Early Neolithic settlement close by) is of significance in this
connection. Again, it satisfies geographical propriety to work
up the river, and, more important, having thus reached the
Tasian settlement it will be easy to follow through the rest
of the Neolithic history of Upper Egypt and close the section within sight of Pharaonic times.

The Fayum depression lies to the west of the Nile some
distance south of the Delta; it still holds a considerable lake,
but in the fifth millennium B C the water stood 180 feet
higher than at present, and the Neolithic settlement was
ranged along the edge of it. The huts must have been flimsy,
for no trace of them remained except sunken hearths and
the storage pits, lined with straw matting, where the households kept their grain. From the first these peasants had the
full complement of Neolithic culture; they grew emmer
wheat and barley, kept domestic cattle, sheep or goats, and
pigs, grew flax and wove it into linen, made plain pottery
and excellent coiled basketry. Their reaping knives were
straight with serrated flint edges—very like the Natufian except that the haft was of wood—and they had the characteristic Neolithic axes with ground edges, some of flint,
some roughly made from pebbles. Like the Asian early farming peoples we have been discussing, the Fayumis still hunted
and fished. Hippopotami were among their game. Their
arrow-heads were already very elegant with long slender
barbs and they used maces weighted with a discoidal head
of ground stone; their barbed fish-spears, like their sickles,
recall Natufian forms.

Palettes used for grinding materials (later usually malachite) for painting the eyes are a characteristic part of Egyp-

tian equipment that in Dynastic times were often most beautiful objects, superbly shaped and carved. The practice of eye-painting was evidently already known to the Fayum peasantry, who made their palettes of alabaster in a simple rectangular shape. As so often in Neolithic communities, personal ornaments were the only item in the economy to be imported. As well as strings of ostrich-shell disk beads (like those worn earlier by the Capsians), the Fayumis decked themselves with shells brought from the Mediterranean, Red Sea and even perhaps from the Indian Ocean. They also imported the decorative amazonite either from the central Sahara or the eastern desert. No burials were found anywhere among the Fayum settlements, which suggests that there must have been cemeteries well beyond the edge of the houses.

Radio carbon dates for two pits belonging to the oldest Fayum settlement are 4145 ± 250 B C and 4437 ± 180 B C. It seems likely that it was already flourishing during the first half of the fifth millennium, at about the same time that the Halaf culture was spreading in Iraq.

Another site that represents this Neolithic culture of Lower Egypt, probably in a later phase, is at Merimde on a sandy spur by the western edge of the Delta. Here again at first the shelters must have been of the flimsiest, but later the villagers made huts with wooden posts supporting matting, and later again used beaten mud—possibly to get better shelter from the sand storms with which they were increasingly plagued. The hut of each household seems to have stood in its own garden or yard, aligned in rows that probably mark the course of village lanes. The practice of farming was almost identical with that in the Fayum except that in the later period the grain was stored in large jars. Though showing variations, most of their pottery, tools and weapons and personal possessions had much in common both with the Fayum and also to a lesser extent with Tasa. It is noticeable that their mace-heads were an Asian form, in place of the Egyptian disk type. The dead were buried among the huts, lying in the crouched position and generally facing towards the sunrise; they were not provided with food or any other grave furniture. In another village at El Omari near Helwan (the one known Natufian site in Egypt), in almost every other way similar to that at Merimde, the dead were all laid to face westward and one of the graves contained a carved wooden baton said to resemble the *ames* sceptre, that in the historical period was among the insignia of Lower Egyptian kingship. It seems to suggest that at least some of these early villages may already have been ruled by chiefs.

In spite of some weakness in the chronological framework, it is reasonably sure that while in the north the Fayum culture developed into the Merimdian, in Upper Egypt there was a succession of three cultures, the Tasian, Badarian and Amratian, all of them purely Neolithic, and all showing something of the distinctively African character that was to crystallize in Egyptian civilization.

The encampments on desert spurs at Tasa near Badari are usually recognized as representing the oldest farming communities in Egypt. Certainly they were the most primitive. Yet already they cultivated emmer wheat and barley, and ground the grain on large saddle querns. They seem also to have had herds of sheep or goats. It has been thought that these people may have lived like the Hadendoa, who until recent times were herdsmen in the eastern desert, but kept permanent villages near the Blue Nile where they regularly returned to raise a harvest after the annual inundation. Whether or not the Tasian encampments were summer villages of this kind, it should not be forgotten that by themselves they do not give a full picture of early farming life by the Nile. There must have been many shacks and clusters of huts on the ridges and hillocks that formed the ever-shifting and marshy valley floor. 'All traces of these settlements in the valley proper have long since disappeared; they have been not merely silted over but washed away by the changes in the river's course. This explains why we find traces of early settlement only at the edge of the valley, on the spurs of detritus at the foot of the high cliffs. We must imagine the valley, not flat and featureless as it is today, but dotted with hamlets perched on the high banks of former water-courses, and surrounded by an ever-changing maze of channels, marsh and meadow.'*

This, then, was the kind of prospect that would have lain below the Tasians as they worked at flour mill or loom, made their rough pottery or talked and idled outside their shelters. This, too, was the nature of the country they would have had to contend with when they went fishing with hooks of shell and horn, hunting water birds and swamp animals with bow and arrow, or to lead their goats in the *wadis* and to tend their plots on the alluvial spreads.

Like the Fayum people, the Tasians had alabaster palettes

*H. Frankfort, *The Birth of Civilization in the Near East*, p. 41.

for grinding and mixing eye-paint, and ornamented their persons with ivory beads and bangles and shells brought from the Red Sea. Their dead they placed in the bent or crouched position, wrapped them in skins and buried them in straw coffins; such burials are few and scattered enough to indicate how small and shifting was the population.

The Badarian culture is probably a development from the Tasian, but its known range is greater, extending from Badari itself southward as far as Armant. It was present, too, in the Wadi Hammamat. Emmer wheat and barley were still the cereals cultivated, but the Badarians began to store the grain in mud-lined pits; they kept sheep, and unlike their precursors, were also cattle-breeders. There was still plenty of game on the plateaux as well as in the tributary *wadis* and the Badarians went hunting with bows and arrows and boomerangs; for fishing they used the same shell hooks devised by the Tasians. Their huts were still simple shelters of matting like those of the Merimdians, but in all other ways their domestic equipment was greatly enriched. In particular they were potters of exquisite skill and taste, turning out a thin, burnished ware with a softly rippled surface built by hand into plain but well-proportioned shapes. Often the body of the bowl or jar was brown or warm red and the rim black, an attractive scheme due entirely to the method of firing (p. 405). Other vessels were laboriously ground from basalt, and little flasks and vases carved from ivory. Also of ivory were the charming little ladles, the handle sometimes ending in an animal carving, that presage the long line of beautiful spoons made by the Egyptians in Dynastic times. Elephants (still living on the plateaux) also provided the material for ivory beads, bracelets, rings and other ornaments and for ornamental combs that were presumably worn by the women. Nose plugs were made of stone.

The Badarians, then, were a people living some way above subsistence level, with a margin of time and materials to beautify themselves and their possessions. This is further demonstrated by their ability to maintain a small trade in luxury goods, obtaining malachite for eye-paint from Sinai or Nubia, shells from the Red Sea, semi-precious stones such as turquoise and carnelian, and, most remarkable of all, cedar and juniper wood that may have been imported from Syria. That they made simple boats for navigation on the Nile is proved by the survival of pottery models. Badarian cemeteries, though small, are yet large enough to prove a growing population; the corpses, crouched or more gently flexed and wrapped in skins according to the traditional cus-

tom of the Tasians, were laid in trench graves and provided
with pots of food and drink. Some graves were also furnished
with female statuettes of ivory or clay. Among the Badarians,
too, we seem to find the earliest examples of that ritual
burial of animals that was later to be an Egyptian peculiarity; both cattle and sheep are known to have been interred
with some ceremony.

If the culture of the Badarians already showed some style
and an economic margin that allowed for the manufacture
of luxury articles and the import of precious materials, that
of the Amratians, which appears to be directly descended
from it, is clearly approaching the threshold of civilization.
It can, in fact, be set beside the roughly contemporary but
rather later al'Ubaid culture of Sumeria as marking the close
of the Neolithic phase that is the subject of this chapter.

The economic foundations were much stronger. The
Amratians must have begun an extensive and systematic cultivation of the flood plain of the Nile, although there is no
evidence as yet for artificial irrigation. They kept cattle,
sheep and pigs, and are known to have used their cattle for
dairying as well as meat production. They had probably
domesticated the ass as a beast of burden, and had learnt
to lash bundles of papyrus stalks together to make high-
prowed boats already reminiscent of those that were to ply
the Nile from Pharaonic until recent times. Although hunting still made a necessary contribution to the food supply,
the solid economic basis to their way of life led to a great
increase in population among the Amratians; villages were
permanently occupied and cemeteries used for generation after generation, until they might contain as many as two
thousand graves. Pictures of crocodiles, scorpions and other
creatures that are neither livestock nor game animals have
sometimes been interpreted to mean that these villages were
occupied by totem clans—as is the case among the modern
Dinka on the Upper Nile, one of the Nilotic peoples who
appear to have inherited most both in culture and racial
stock from an ancient Egyptian ancestry.

The craft work of the Amratians had developed beyond
that of their Badarian forebears in everything except potting,
where there was some falling off in their black-topped, white-
painted, and incised wares. Their pressure-flaked flint work
achieved perfection for the medium both in execution and
form (Fig. 53), while their carving of ivory combs, ladles
and vases was also finely developed. For weaving they used
horizontal looms. Gold was now added to the precious substances obtained for ornaments, and native copper was used

for pins and even for harpoon-heads—cut from hammered sheets. The palettes used for preparing malachite were now often given the shape of creatures—especially fish and hippopotami.

In the form of their stone vases, in their ladles, palettes and very many other products of their skill, the Amratians were beginning to manifest, quite unmistakably, something of the style, spirit—'cultural form'—that was to distinguish the long course of Egyptian civilization. This manifestation of the shape of things to come is perhaps even more clearly evident in their burial practices and other religious forms. The graves were still no more than pits, but they were furnished in a way that was to lead without a break to the elaborate and highly characteristic funerary customs of historic Egypt. Not only were the dead provided with weapons, ornaments and goods (Palaeolithic man did as much) but also with models of women and servants evidently prototypes of the later *ushabti,* and with scenes drawn on pots and slate plaques that must have had the same purpose as the paintings of worldly possessions and joys that enriched the walls of Dynastic tombs.

The Amratians, then, were still essentially Neolithic farmers living in large villages; another culture, the Gerzean, was to intervene between theirs and that of the First Dynasty. But just as with the Ubaidans in Asia, so the Amratians must be recognized as marking an end of that primary Neolithic way of life with which we are here concerned. Having brought the history of man both in Egypt and in south-west Asia to that point when the flowering of civilization in the two great valleys is about to begin, it is time to leave these central regions where the Neolithic revolution had its beginnings and follow its gradual spread into Europe and eastern Asia.

This account of the gradual spread of farming and other traits of Neolithic culture through the Old World will generally move with the foremost edge of the spreading tide, keeping pace with the primary Neolithic conditions already described in the lands of their origin (Map VIII). Little attempt can be made to follow either the secondary waves or the countless local developments that appeared in the wake of this initial spread. Thus while the cultural level remains roughly the same, the period of time will grow later and later as we move from the ancient centres of husbandry towards the peripheries. Meanwhile, however, it must not be forgotten that just as men were already beginning to live in cities in the river valley civilizations before the Neolithic economy had spread very far, so secondary and tertiary ur-

banized regions had grown up in the east Mediterranean,
eastern Europe and India before the humblest forms of
farming life had reached lands far to the east or west. Indeed, the growth of town life, so amazingly rapid in suitable
conditions once its farming basis was firmly established, was
one of the two principal causes of the diffusion of the new
economy. As merchant traders went out from the cities to
satisfy substantial needs for materials as well as the whims
and luxurious tastes of town-dwellers, larger villages and then
small towns grew up in territories with desirable raw
materials, while the necessity for food to support the new
specialist workers and traders carried farming farther and
farther afield. The second powerful cause of such diffusion
was a much more elementary one already inherent in primitive husbandry itself. This was the exhaustion of soils—
common, before crop rotation and manuring, in all countries
other than those most fortunate valleys where nature
renewed fertility unaided. So in regions like the Danube,
peasant communities had periodically to leave their settlements and clear fresh fields in places either uninhabited or
still in the possession of hunters and food-gatherers. Commonly the cultures to be pursued across the continents will
comprise most of the traits once held to be universally characteristic of the Neolithic stage: agriculture, stock-raising,
the free use of polished stone axes and hoes, potting and
weaving. But the tally was not by any means always complete. We have seen how, contrary to the old view, in some
parts of south-west Asia and the eastern Mediterranean,
farming was being practised long before the invention of
pottery. So, too, not only were certain crafts left behind
(as weaving seems to have been in Neolithic Britain), but
also in vast if desolate stretches of north-east Europe and
northern Asia pottery and the use of ground axes were
adopted by hunters and fishers who made no change in the
way they procured their food. It should be added that this
chapter cannot be extended to include the later partial diffusion of farming into the remoter lands of northern Eurasia;
it must be limited to spreads that can still be more or less
directly linked with the initial impulse from south-west Asia
and Egypt—a decision that will fix its lower limit at not
much later than 2500 B C.

It appears that the main stepping-off point for the spread
of Neolithic cultures westward along the Mediterranean was
from the eastern end of the sea, particularly from Syria and
Cilicia. That there was also an African element from Egypt
still remains probable, but it seems that this was felt mainly

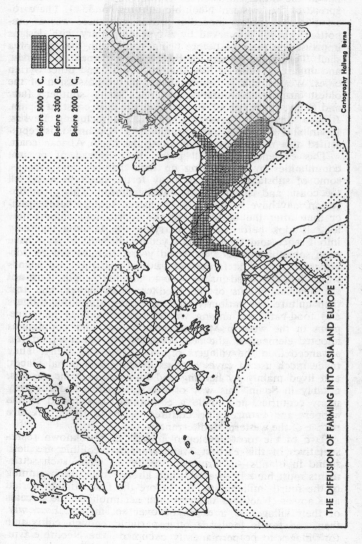

Before 5000 B. C.

Before 3300 B. C.

Before 2000 B. C,

Cartography Hallwag Berne

THE DIFFUSION OF FARMING INTO ASIA AND EUROPE

MAP VIII

not in the initial diffusion of farming but in the secondary spread of the 'western' Neolithic cultures (p. 334). The earliest diffusion (unless indeed it proves that there was a 'pre-pottery' phase) is marked by a type of pottery with designs impressed in the clay before firing, often with the edge of a shell. This is the pottery of the oldest settlement at Mersin, and apparently also of Ras Shamra, Byblos and other Syrian cities. Westward it is found, always in the possession of the oldest farming communities, in Crete, Malta, southern Italy and Sicily, the south of France and the east coast of Spain. It also occurs on several small islands including Levkas, Lipari and Elba. The same tradition, it is claimed, is represented at a number of points along the north African coast.

This evidence, then, all points to a spread of peasant communities by sea, setting up their hamlets and villages, some of substantial size, at many fertile landfalls along all the coasts and islands of the Mediterranean. This great diffusion may have begun from its eastern sources before rather than after the beginning of the fourth millennium; how long it took before it was carrying the farming economy into France and Spain is not yet established. It may have been something over a thousand years. It must not be forgotten that the first farmers, save here and there on islands which had remained inaccessible to hunting people, were not the first inhabitants of the Mediterranean shores, and that their culture was variously affected by the Mesolithic hunters and food-gatherers among whom they settled. In many regions in the western Mediterranean these older populations adopted elements of the new economy but remained far less advanced than the villagers of, say, Crete and Sicily. They made much use of caves both as dwelling and burial places, and lived mainly by herding and hunting. In some regions, notably in Spain, this way of life was maintained for very many centuries, and made a continuing background to the copper- and bronze-using cultures of the more progressive people of the western Mediterranean.

Two of the most developed as well as best known representatives of this earliest Mediterranean Neolithic are both found in islands—in Crete and Sicily. In Crete such settlements must have been established already near the beginning of the fourth millennium, for before the first Minoan period at Knossos, Neolithic villagers had accumulated the detritus of their villages to a depth of over six metres. Evidently, then, the fertile lowlands offered stable enough cultivation for villages to be permanently occupied. The Neolithic Cretans lived in houses consisting of clusters of small rooms built on stone foundations, they used flat flint axes, obtained obsidian from Melos, made good pottery, revered a Mother Goddess, practised some form of axe cult and were in general perfectly representative of the earliest farming communities of the Mediterranean.

No trace of Palaeolithic hunters has been found in the island, and probably the first cultivators may have colonized it from eastern Anatolia or Syria; thereafter its position and the chance of favourable winds and currents made Crete readily accessible from all the eastern Mediterranean, including Egypt. Hence its rise to be the home of one of the most graceful civilizations man has ever achieved.

The next step of the maritime diffusion can be studied in southern Italy, particularly in south-east Sicily and Apulia. Here, probably before 3000 B C, peasants had established substantial villages usually enclosed behind a ditch and walls. They cultivated cereals (though their crops are not known) and in addition to the usual cattle, sheep, goats and pigs, are credited with having bred buffaloes. Evidently they were very successful cultivators for their villages are thickly scattered. To supplement basalt, quartzite and other native rocks used for polished adzes and rougher tools, they imported obsidian—probably from the nearest source in the Lipari islands where traces of their culture have been detected.

It was enterprising possessors of this Stentinello culture who went from Sicily to be the first colonists of Malta. They probably settled there during the last centuries of the third millennium. They and their descendants were responsible for the magnificent Maltese temples with their unique form of megalithic architecture and extraordinary cult figures of the Mother Goddess.

The first impressive sweep of Neolithic culture along the Mediterranean was soon followed by a second which did not, however, penetrate so far. Again the source appears to have been south-west Asia, which at this time can be seen as the heart of the Old World, pumping out pulses of cultural energy through the continents. While the Neolithic pioneers had fashioned impressed pottery, their successors made fine painted wares. Their spread into the Mediterranean can be seen as a continuation of that which brought the painted-pottery makers such as those of Samarra and Tell Halaf into Syria and south-east Anatolia. There, too, they appear to have brought the earliest settlements of the impressed-pottery people to an end.

In exactly the same way painted-pottery cultures succeeded the pre-Sesklo in Greece and the Stentinello in southeast Italy, Sicily and the Aeolian islands. Beyond this the impulse evidently died out, never penetrating with any force into the west Mediterranean. Another thrust of painted-pottery peoples carried them across north of the Black Sea; we shall find them spreading through south Russia into Roumania and the Balkans (p. 251).

Meanwhile we have to consider the great overland diffusion of Neolithic culture into western Europe which was the northern, continental counterpart of the southern, maritime spread already chronicled. The relationships of the painted-pottery peasantry and their predecessors with this remarkable diffusion along the Danube which penetrated as far west as Belgium is still obscure. First something must be said of the role of Anatolia.

Anatolia has been called the 'Royal Road to the Aegean', and the natural thoroughfare across the plateau from Asia, the 'Anatolian Rails'. Asia Minor was in fact a 'promontory of Asia thrust out towards Europe' and as such a most vital bridge for the transmission of culture from one to the other. Understanding of the earlier Neolithic history of central and western Anatolia is still slight. If the 'pre-pottery' Neolithic of Thessaly proves to be really of early date, then it seems probable that such a phase existed also in Anatolia. But it has yet to be proved. A trade carrying obsidian westward from a source west of Salt lake seems to have been of some importance from the beginning. Hajilar, probably the earliest Neolithic site in the region to have been excavated, is claimed to date from the mid-sixth millennium, roughly contemporary with the proto-Sesklo culture of Greece. Kum Tepe, in the Troad, dates from well back into the fourth millennium. In the first settlements at both Hissarlik (Troy) and Thermi, copper was already being worked. Both were from the first true towns, though on a small scale, and the inhabitants were certainly concerned with trade in the Aegean. The foundation of their economy, however, was prosperous mixed farming, with the cultivation of many cereals—wheats, barley, millet—probably of vegetables and fruits including the vine, and the raising of cattle, sheep, goats and pigs. As elsewhere, the fertility cult of the Mother Goddess appears to have been supreme for traders and farmers alike.

Similar Chalcolithic trading settlements sprang up throughout the Aegean, notably on the Cyclades, those islands that 'are remnants of a land bridge between Anatolia and Greece affording a passage for cultural ideas from Asia to Europe.' Generally small and barren, they had not been attractive to a peasantry devoted to the primary Neolithic way of life. To catch up once more with this, we have to move into mainland Greece, where by 5000 B C Neolithic villages were established throughout Thessaly and central Greece. These Sesklo folk seem to have been wholly peaceful; they used the sling for hunting, but relied on a form of mixed farming very much the same as that prevailing in Anatolia. There may have been seasonal movements with flocks and herds, but agriculture was sufficiently productive to allow villages to be occupied for long periods of time. Although very largely self-contained, these Greek villages imported obsidian.

In Macedonia natural conditions were very different, for the country was thickly forested and knew bitter winter weather. This may partly account for the fact that cultural developments here tended to lag behind those in the Aegean and to show a distinctively continental European complexion. The earliest known village in the region, on the Haliakmon, was evidently an outpost of the Sesklo people, but this element seems soon to have been absorbed into another, represented by the so-called Vardar-Morava culture. This culture is of the utmost importance for any understanding of the spread of farming peoples through inland Europe, for it extended right up to the Middle Danube and beyond to the Banat and Transylvania, and it is very likely that its creators introduced mixed farming to the Danubian region. If so they were in part responsible for the later extraordinary diffusion that carried it along the river valley and the surrounding loess lands until it reached western Europe. The Vardar-Morava cultivators, who may have played this vital role of transmitting the Neolithic way of life from the Aegean to the Danube, lived in wattle and daub or mudbrick houses, sometimes warmed by clay ovens. Their farming was very much like that already described; wheat and millet were grown and fig orchards planted, while livestock included the usual cattle, sheep and pigs. It has been suggested that although, as among the Sesklo peasants, this husbandry supported fairly stable villages, the shepherds carried out long seasonal treks with their beasts as the modern Vlachs of the Balkans do today. Deer were abundant in the forests and hunting seems to have kept some importance in their economy. Nothing shows more clearly than their excellent pottery, some polished and fluted, some painted, the connections of the Vardar-Morava culture[3] with Greece on the one hand and the Danube on the other.

The glacial winds that laid down vast beds of loess from Serbia to Poland and westwards as far as Belgium prepared the way for Neolithic Danubian cultures, which, at least from Hungary to their western limits, were extraordinarily homogeneous. 'The loess lands north and west of the Danube were first occupied by a Neolithic population whose whole culture down to the finest details remains identical from Hungary to north Germany and from Galicia to Belgium . . . perhaps the most classically Neolithic culture in the ancient world.' Although, as has been seen, Palaeolithic man hunted mammoth across the loess (p. 143) a Mesolithic population has been detected only in the forest fringing it to the north and west. It is therefore not surprising that the peasants themselves seem to have been almost as homogeneous physically as they were in their habits and manufactures; not very many burials have been discovered, but almost all those known proved to be narrow-headed and generally of the 'Mediterranean' type.

Loess soil is very well suited to primitive agriculture, for it is naturally well drained and lightly forested and can be effectively cultivated with the hoe. In most regions, too, the water supply is abundant. The result of elementary farming methods on such light soil was a fairly rapid exhaustion of fertility. Always, however, virgin soil lay ahead, the old village could be deserted and fresh plots cleared and brought under cultivation. So the Danubian peasants thrust on and on along a broad corridor that took them through territories either uninhabited or thinly peopled by scattered tribes engaged in hunting and fishing.

In spite of considerable uniformity from end to end of this vast area of diffusion, three cultural groups have been distinguished during the earliest phase. The easternmost in the Banat and south-east Hungary had very much in common with the Macedonian Vardar-Morava people; indeed, they may simply have been a branch of this people who adapted themselves to life on the loess plains, or they may have been the descendants of an unknown Mesolithic population who had taken over the new economy. Certainly hunting with traps and bow and arrow and fishing with nets remained important to them, although they ran flocks and herds, kept pigs and practised the characteristic shifting agriculture. Their pottery, equally with the form of their cult objects, such as Mother Goddess figures and triangular altars, shows the close relationship (whatever its precise nature) with the all-important Macedonian culture. In north-eastern Hungary and Slovakia the people of the Bukk culture also continued to hunt and fish on a considerable scale, and even used caves for winter dwellings. In other respects they have very much in common with the great classic culture known to archaeology as Danubian I.

The economic basis of this culture (whose remarkable homogeneity has already been noticed) was the cultivation of cereal and other food crops, in little hand-hoed plots. Their main crops were einkorn wheat and barley, but they also grew emmer wheat, peas, beans and lentils. The numbers of cattle, sheep and pigs kept seem to have been relatively small. Unlike their eastern neighbours, the Danubian I people were a thoroughgoing peasantry, for whom hunting and fishing had ceased to have any considerable importance. It seems generally to have taken anything from a decade to a quarter of a century for all the plots within convenient reach of a village to become exhausted and a move to be made to a fresh site. Houses were very substantial rectangular buildings, sometimes as much as ninety by twenty feet, gabled, and raised on posts; perhaps migrating villagers may have carried with them some at least of the timbers for these fine dwellings. One of the best known of these characteristic Neolithic villages is at Köln-Lindenthal near Cologne, towards the north-western limits of the Danubian expansion, where there were numbers of houses protected by an entrenched palisade.

Such Danubian I communities were almost wholly self-sufficient, although hard stones for their hoes, adzes and axes might have to be transported over quite long distances. There was also a small trade in ornamental oddments, particularly in the Mediterranean mussel or spondylus shell that was carried from the Aegean or Adriatic as far west as the Rhineland. A piece of African ivory had reached a final purchaser near Worms in Germany. Lack of chiefs' houses or rich graves suggests an egalitarian society, and the Danubians are generally assumed to have been a peaceable folk (there was enough land for peaceableness) although presumably the heavy stone disk-shaped mace-heads found among them cannot always have served ceremonial purposes.[4]

Whether the Danubian I peoples were racially derived almost wholly from Anatolia or some adjacent Mediterranean region as their physical type, gourd-imitating pottery and fondness for Mediterranean shells suggest, or whether they represent a spread of the Vardar-Morava people, perhaps incorporating Mesolithic aboriginals, remains unknown. Radio carbon dating has given 4220 B C for a site in western Europe (Magdeburg in Germany). This Danubian peasantry was almost certainly the first to lead flocks and herds, to spread cultivated plots in the moist, Atlantic lands of western Europe. Yet it was not very long before they were to become neighbours to two other groups of Neolithic peoples, one to the north and the other to the south and west of them.

The latter were the western Neolithic peoples already mentioned as apparently including a considerable African element. Certainly their plain, baggy pottery has much in common with that of Egyptian Neolithic traditions. They seem to have reached the west Mediterranean (Spain and southern France, and north Italy) rather later than the impressed-pottery settlement, then to have pushed north and farther west along two routes. One from the south of France up the Rhone valley and one by sea up the Atlantic coasts of the Iberian peninsula, France and Britain.

Once beyond the Straits of Gibraltar coastal diffusion must have become more hazardous and bolder feats of navigation were called for. Undoubtedly some of the settlers along the stormy western and northern coasts of the British Isles must have been adventurous sailors. Nevertheless, even in these regions a gradual spread of settlements step by step along the coasts was quite possible, as was also the making of entries at favourable places and the steady penetration of the interior.

Among the earliest and most typical representatives of the western Neolithic cultures is that found in the Almerian province of south-east Spain. This corner of the peninsula was certainly settled by invading newcomers whose crafts and habits of life seem to have much in common with those of the Merimdians and Amratians of the Nile valley. Thus, though the line of their diffusion has not been tracked (there are hints of it on the north African coast) it seems that we have here a people of mainly African origin, perhaps mingling with the peoples whose spread along the Mediterranean had its first impulses from Asia and Anatolia.

These Almerians lived in villages of oval huts, their floors sunk into the ground and roofed with wattle and daub. They raised the usual flocks and herds and grew cereals, storing the grain in pit silos. They are the first people of the western Mediterranean known to have cultivated the olive, now so essential a part of the landscape. They also seem to have gathered wild grapes. They knew how to spin and weave, and good axes, adzes and gouges suggest they were practised workers in wood—it must be remembered that pines still cloaked what are now the stark hills of southern Spain.

Something has already been said of the western Neolithic cultures that represent the earliest arrival of farming peoples into much of western Europe. There is a good deal in the craft of their potters and in other traits to suggest that like that of the Almerians the culture of these farmers was of ultimate Egyptian inspiration. Indeed, in a rough and ready scheme of things (certainly over-simplified) the settlement of Almeria can be seen as a stage on the route from Africa into the west. In many areas this culture is met with only in relatively late local forms. There are traces of it in Provence, spreading up the east and on to the chalk downlands of the north. Even in this relatively harsh climate the defended village of oval huts with sunken floors, the mixed farming economy, are not so far removed from their counterpart at El Garcel—though the persisting Mesolithic traditions are stronger. But for the essential character of the western Neolithic way of life in an early and pure form the fullest evidence comes from western Switzerland, where the remains of lake-side villages have been wonderfully preserved. They were little clusters of wooden houses built on the marshy edges of many of the Swiss lakes. Presumably a heavy labour of forest clearance must have been undertaken with the stone axes and adzes that were stoutly mounted in antler sockets and hafted on to straight wooden handles. In the cleared land these Cortaillod peasants raised emmer, and probably also bread wheat and barley as well as peas, beans and lentils. They ate plums and apples, and although at first these may have been wild, apples were certainly later cultivated and brewed into cider. Cattle were more important to them than their pigs, sheep and goats, and these already skilful farmers collected their manure presumably for use on their field plot. Hunting was not of great importance, but people living at the water's edge were naturally fishermen, using traps, nets and perhaps also fish-spears. They grew flax and wove linen—though it seems that skins and furs still made their warmer clothing.

These Swiss villages, tucked away in their valleys near the threatening mass of the Alps, invoke a full realization of the power of the farming life, a power that carried it irresistibly into country utterly unlike that of the sunny cradlelands. One can imagine the pioneers arriving with a few beasts and bags of seed corn, clearing trees along the lake's edge and at once saving precious land and securing themselves by raising their houses above the mud.[5] Then within a few years cattle and sheep would be grazing where before there had been only wild animals, crops ripening where there had been forest, while many families would be busy with the tasks of husbandry where before no man had done more than loose a spear or an arrow, set a trap.

As has been said, western Neolithic cultures were carried on to the downlands of northern France, and indeed through many regions of France and Iberia, but they have hardly been distinguished in their primary form. A pure and early western Neolithic culture has, however, been recognized in Britain. Here once again it is evident that the first farmers arrived to find the country in the possession of Mesolithic hunters and fishers—descendants of the Sauveterrians and Maglemosians. The newcomers, known as the Windmill Hill people, must have brought cattle and livestock over with them in their boats, before settling first on the lightly forested chalk hills of southern England. They hoed plots for bread wheat and barley and kept sheep, goats and pigs, but cattle were their main concern—a rather robust, long-horned variety that may have had a mixture of the local wild aurochs. Their pots were of the plain 'leathery' type favoured by all the western Neolithic peoples; rather surprisingly there is no evidence that they practised spinning and weaving. There was hunting with bow and arrow, but it was of little importance in their economy. The Windmill Hill farmers are known sometimes to have lived in isolated rectangular houses, while a lake-dwelling in Cumberland recalls the Swiss villages; they made elaborately embanked compounds (p. 396) that seem to have been used for rounding up cattle in autumn rather than as permanent villages. Crude images of the Mother Goddess have occasionally been found in Windmill Hill encampments and tombs—marking the most westerly outposts of this far-flung cult so characteristic of the early farming peoples.

The date of the spread of the western Neolithic cultures has not yet been agreed, but quite numerous recent Carbon-14 estimations seem to show that France and the British Isles had been extensively settled before 3000 B C.

It has already been stated that after their penetration into western Europe, the Danubians later became the neighbours not only of these western farmers but also of another spread of Neolithic cultures affecting the extreme north. It had long been thought that Scandinavia remained in the undisputed possession of the Ertebølle and other Mesolithic hunters and fishermen until the arrival from the west of peoples distinguished by the megalithic architecture soon to be discussed. Now, however, it has been proved that farming peoples had advanced into both Denmark and southern

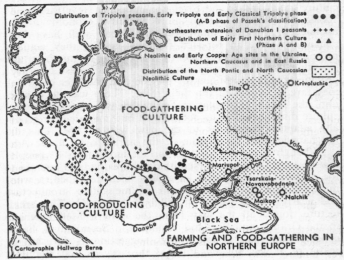

Distribution of Tripolye peasants. Early Tripolye and Early Classical Tripolye phase (A-B phase of Passek's classification)   ● ● ●
Northeastern extension of Danubian I peasants   + + + +
Distribution of Early First Northern Culture (Phase A and B)   ▲ ▲
Neolithic and Early Copper Age sites in the Ukraine, Northern Caucasus and in East Russia   ○ ○
Distribution of the North Pontic and North Caucasian Neolithic Culture

Moksna Sites   ○Krivoluchie

FOOD-GATHERING CULTURE

Elbe   Oder   Vistula   Dnieper   Dniester   Volga   Don

Mariupol   Tsarskaia-Novosvobodnaia   Maikop   Nalchik

FOOD-PRODUCING CULTURE

Danube   Black Sea

Cartographie Hallwag Berne

FARMING AND FOOD-GATHERING IN NORTHERN EUROPE

MAP IX

Sweden before that time; and that they came from a south-easterly direction (Map IX). These Trichterbecher (or First Northern Culture) people were probably earlier settled in the eastern part of their range in Thuringia and Poland but reached Denmark and Sweden when the first farmers were arriving in Britain—rather before 3000 B C. They are known sometimes to have lived in long houses that must have sheltered very many families; in east Jutland one of two such communal dwellings standing side by side was as much as 85 metres long. They practised the usual mixed farming with barley and as many as three kinds of wheat (emmer, club and einkorn). As with the Windmill Hill people, cattle were their main support, and from the first they seem to have relied very little on hunting to supplement their beef, mutton and pork. There is vivid evidence (p. 382) to show how these newcomers tackled the forests with axe and fire to open up pasture and arable land.

Nowhere has more been discovered of the impact between farming incomers and native Mesolithic peoples than in Denmark. The Trichterbecher settlers undoubtedly lived as neighbours to the Ertebølle hunter-fishers during several centuries. They were in some kind of communication with one another, for odds and ends belonging to the Neolithic culture are found in the Ertebølle middens. Nevertheless the aborigines maintained their more primitive economy almost unchanged. What is interesting—and may well have happened elsewhere in forested regions—is that they actually prospered for a time, evidently increasing in numbers and founding new settlements. Probably partial forest clearance provided better conditions for the red and roe deer on which they largely depended for their meat. There was no conflict until the farming population became dense; then the hunter culture disappeared as its people died out, migrated, or gradually adapted themselves to the new way of life. This did not happen until the middle of the northern Neolithic Age.

Although the three most important movements of peoples that brought the primary Neolithic cultures by land and sea to the extremities of Europe have now been described, a word must be said about the spread of megalithic architecture and nearly related forms of building[6] (Map X). This architecture, found all the way from the eastern Mediterranean to the Orkney and Shetland Islands and Scandinavia, has a conspicuously coastal distribution, suggesting its diffusion by seafarers. It was not a feature of the very earliest Neolithic cultures; nevertheless, in much of western and northern Europe it was adopted into these cultures at a relatively early stage and by the end of the third millennium was already their most striking achievement. Furthermore, it is interesting in a history of culture in providing a primitive example of the spread of religious ideas in contrast with the actual movement of people that we have been concerned with hitherto.

It is an architecture that is principally funerary (though later other forms emerged, such as the temples of Malta and the sanctuaries and alignments of Brittany and Britain); but as evidently it went with a cult of the dead that had wider religious significance, it can be regarded as more than a mere building of tombs. Probably it came to be associated with the fertility religions of the Mother Goddess—whose image or symbols are reproduced in the tombs in more than one region—and that the earth-fast or rock-cut chamber embodied the idea of the return of the dead to the Mother for rebirth.

It is impossible to analyse in any detail the great variety of plans and modes of construction used in these tombs or to discuss their relative dates. Certain very widely distributed peculiarities, such as small circular doorways, portals and forecourts designed for ritual use, serve to give a kind

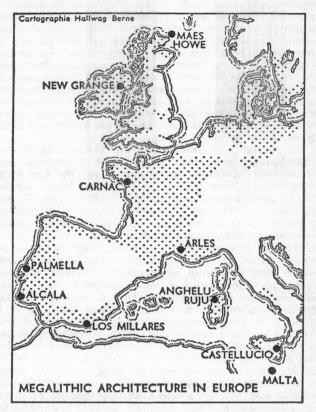

Cartographie Hallwag Berne

MAES HOWE

NEW GRANGE

CARNAC

ARLES

PALMELLA

ALCALA

ANGHELU RUJU

LOS MILLARES

CASTELLUCIO

MALTA

MEGALITHIC ARCHITECTURE IN EUROPE

MAP X

of unity to them all, while on the other hand certain consistent differences (particularly of plan) suggest a division into sects. Close parallels can be found in the various church plans characteristic of different sections of the Christian Church.

The beehive-shaped tholoi of the Cyclades and Crete make the most easterly representatives of the tradition, unless the Egyptian mastabas (which are *not* communal tombs) be included: probably they are an element in its genesis. Very

similar tombs occur in Sicily, and they must lie behind the
particular form that was to produce the most imposing of all
megalithic tombs: the passage-grave. These were chambers,
commonly roundish, approached by a narrower passage and
often covered by a large, round or long mound to make them
earth-fast and dark. They were built across southern Spain
and Portugal, in Brittany, Wales, Ireland, Scotland and the
Northern Isles, in Denmark and Sweden. Though the Iberian
examples are striking enough, none is more magnificent
than the great passage-graves, enriched with carving, of central Ireland, or those still standing in the remote and stormy
Orkney Islands.

The second most distinctive form is the long, narrow,
parallel-gallery grave, that was favoured in south-east Italy,
all the west Mediterranean islands, along the line of the
Pyrenees, in north-east France and Brittany, Wales, northern
Ireland and south-west Scotland and (very late) in Denmark
and Sweden. The gallery-grave includes such strangely
specialized forms as the Giants' Graves of Sardinia and the
enormously massive *navetas* of Minorca.

Although here and there throughout their range the possessions buried with the dead in these great communal tombs
suggest that they were introduced by invaders, far more
often they were adopted as an innovation by local peoples
and made part of their culture. Thus it seems all the more
legitimate to suppose that their adoption was due to the
spread of religious ideas and practices; their coastal distribution and the occurrence of particularly magnificent examples
in remote places suggest that the inspiration and knowledge
that went into their building may have been carried by missionaries, few in numbers but great in power. In any attempt
to reconstruct the spread of the new way of life from the
civilized east to the barbarous west the picture of humble
peasant communities pushing slowly forward in quest of land
must be set beside this contrasting picture of individuals,
perhaps often of superior culture, voyaging as bearers of
ideas that fired the mind and imagination of native peoples
in many lands, changing their customs and spurring them to
great achievements.

Having now followed the main streams of Neolithic culture
from Anatolia and the Aegean westward, it is time to seek
their oriental counterparts. Here, however, the spread will
be as much more discontinuous and spasmodic as the
distances are greater. Furthermore while Europe, and especially western and northern Europe, has been more intensively studied archaeologically than any other region in the

world, in much of eastern Europe and Asia the surface of the subject has hardly been scratched.

The first region, and one directly affected by the same Aegean and Balkan sources that lay behind the Danubian diffusion, is the Black Earth country lying between the Carpathians and the Dnieper. This is rich land and in its western parts in the region of the Lower Danube, the Neolithic farmers, with a culture that evidently owed even more to the Vardar-Morava people (p. 331) than did that of the Danubians, were stable cultivators able to maintain permanent villages. In southern Roumania and north-east and southern Bulgaria there are numbers of mounds, or *tells*, marking the sites of these long-lived hamlets. Some, such as the large mound of Karanovo, in Nova Zagra, show a series of occupations all by peasants dependent on mixed farming and living in rectangular houses furnished with clay ovens, querns and sometimes grain storage pits, but with differences, particularly in the pottery, strong enough to suggest the introduction of a new culture. By the time we reach the better known Boian culture, copper was already in use for trinkets. However, essentially it was still a Neolithic economy largely dependent on the cultivation of wheat and millet, though hunting remained an important source of meat. The villagers lived in solid rectangular houses built of split logs. Near neighbours of the Boians, settled in Transylvania and called Oltenians after the river Olt, are best known from their large village of Erosd. They lived in porched houses of the megaron type (p. 391), furnished with domed clay ovens and their roof gables embellished with ornate finials. They deserve special mention for the magnificence of their painted pottery (p. 438), among the finest of all the painted wares of eastern Europe and south Russia, and indeed among the finest products of Neolithic decorative art. Yet these beautiful spiral ornamented stands, bowls, jars were not the product of professional potters, but seem always to have been made by every family for itself, each working with its own kiln.

This Oltenian was an early forerunner of the much more extensive Tripolye culture, representing a really substantial diffusion of peasants towards the east, where in time they expanded over the plains to the north of the Black Sea to as far as the Dnieper. In this great spread agriculture was shifting and did not allow the villages to be permanently occupied. Nevertheless some were probably lived in for two generations at least, longer than was possible among the Danubians. In fertile country, villages were thickly scattered and the population must have been quite dense. Clay models of Tripolye houses suggest homely interiors (Fig. 36); the living room, sheltered, as in all houses of the megaron plan, by an ante-room or porch, was furnished with a large conical oven, raised hearth and a row of fat jars for storing grain. In one corner lay the saddle quern with its heavy rubbing-stone, and the model shows the Neolithic housewife kneeling at it, busy with what must surely have been her most wearisome task—grinding flour for her family.

The Tripolye people in fact grew three varieties of wheat (bread, club and einkorn) as well as barley, millet and rye; they were cattle-breeders and kept some sheep or goats and pigs. Despite this broadly based farming economy, wild game continued to make an important contribution to their diet, hunters coming home with elk, red deer, boar, beaver and duck. This people also netted fish, gathered shell-fish, and even acorns.

They were quite as fine potters as the Oltenians, making a great variety of graceful shapes, often painted in subtle spiral designs to produce a charming combination of black, white and soft reds. Spiral patterns were also incised on the female figurines that show the Tripolye people to have adhered to the usual Neolithic cult of the Mother Goddess.

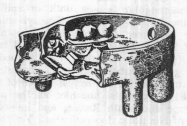

FIG. 36. *Neolithic house of Tripolye culture. Pottery model, Popudnia, Ukraine (after Singer).*

The Tripolye culture can be taken as the most easterly extension of the primary Neolithic way of life directly inspired from the same sources that gave rise to the Danubian spread to the west. Beyond it in the Pontic region, where the population of the Mesolithic Age had been considerable, the old hunting and fishing economy persisted, so it seems, until influences began to reach it not from the west but directly from the ancient oriental civilizations of Iraq and

Persia. A great communal grave on the Sea of Azov and another in central Cis-Caucasia each contained over ten dozen interments, numbers that suggest the support of a food-producing economy, although there is no positive evidence for agriculture or livestock. Grave goods accompanying these mass burials show signs of trade contacts with Iraq, but such contacts become much more obvious in the earliest culture of the Kuban, known mainly from richly furnished graves covered by enormous mounds. It has been said that 'these remarkable tombs may well illustrate the conversion of autochthonous food-gatherers to food production by agents of Oriental civilizations seeking in this metalliferous region copper, gold and silver to satisfy the demand of Mesopotamian cities'. Here again, although farming has been inferred by some authorities, there is no proof of it, and the old economy must still at least have helped to support a people who were buying copper tools and weapons and gold and silver vessels from the Orient, and had chiefs whose state was proclaimed by canopies enriched with gold and silver mounts. Although some authorities hold them to be much later, it is probable that the early Kuban barrows were of much the same age as the great communal burials, having perhaps been raised rather before 2000 B C.

Related to these Pontic cultures, but undeniably based on farming, was the Fatyanovo culture that first brought grain-growing and stock-raising into the forest zone of central Russia. It is best known in the basin of the Oka and Upper Volga and the surrounding uplands, and it has been supposed that its creators were warlike folk given to cattle-raiding as much as to cattle-raising. Formerly it was believed that this earliest penetration of the Neolithic way of life into the fringes of the vast Eurasiatic forests was inspired from the west by way of central and eastern Europe. A later view is that the Fatyanovo people were pushed up towards central Russia by the pressure of the Tripolye expansion eastward to the Dnieper.[7] Certainly there was at least a trade contact with the Pontic peoples. Whatever the source of the husbandry and other Neolithic elements, there is no doubt that these people were basically descended from the old Mesolithic hunter-fishers and maintained something of their ancient tradition.[8]

This is the moment to make a parenthesis in this survey of the diffusion of the primary Neolithic economy in order to treat an historical matter of prime importance for the later cultural history of the Old World: the origin of the Indo-

European peoples. The Fatyanovo people, like the Pontic, lavished skill and labour on the manufacture of beautifully shaped axes that are assumed to have been instruments of war: battle-axes. Similar weapons were made by many other people, including the creators of the early Northern culture (p. 421) who first introduced farming from Poland to Denmark and Sweden. Recently there has been a move to extend the range of the battle-axe cultures by including among them the Michelsberg of Bohemia, Germany and Switzerland, hitherto regarded as belonging to the western Neolithic tradition. By the time of their greatest extent at the beginning of the second millennium they occupied very large areas between the Volga and the North Sea. On no subject have authorities differed so completely or with greater lack of objectivity than on the origins of these cultures. The reason for this partisanship lies in the one thing the authorities are agreed upon—that the battle-axe cultures represent the roots of the Indo-European speaking peoples whose tremendous migrations were to have so great an influence on world history. Thus there have been schools that would make their cradle in northern Europe whence they pressed triumphantly eastward, and schools that would reverse this movement; there is a school that would believe they developed without any migration as a result of the influence of the Danubian farming economy upon hunting societies.

It is not at present possible to come to any final conclusion. It may be that the very recent recognition of an early basic Neolithic culture underlying the local developments of battle-axe cultures from Scandinavia to Poland and perhaps beyond may lead to clearer understanding—and it must be remembered that the present evidence favours the derivation of this basic tradition from the east, perhaps from south Russia. Nevertheless the claim of the Danubians to have played some part cannot be ignored. What can be said with some certainty is that the battle-axe peoples had a large ethnic, social and cultural inheritance from the hunter-fishers of the forest cultures such as the Maglemosian and Kunda[9] (p. 156). Whether these primitive folk simply took over a Neolithic economy from their neighbours, or whether they were raised up to it by a ruling class coming from the Pontic or Danubian peoples, this common inheritance gave them a rough kind of unity and a character distinguishing them sharply alike from Danubian, Mediterranean and western Neolithic peoples. Though it may not always or everywhere have been so, this character came in time to be dominantly pastoral, patriarchal, warlike and expansive.

It remains to consider the earliest spread of farming directly eastward from its cradlelands in south-west Asia. In the survey of these lands we went as far to the east as Persian Sialk; north-east from here there are a number of important settlements round the south-east corner of the Caspian Sea (such as Tepe Hissar), Anau in Russian Turkestan and the easternmost site of importance, Namasga Tepe. These small towns and villages date well back into the fourth millennium and probably much beyond. From here farming communities penetrated more or less slowly eastward towards Baluchistan and the Indus region. *Tells* mark their settlements along either side of the central desert, on the north along and beyond the valleys of the Elburz range, on the south through Fars and Makran. There were cultural differences between the northern and southern peoples that still persisted when they converged upon Baluchistan. Here the villages of the farmers clustered thickly on the uplands west of the Indus. At a place near Quetta there is evidence for a pre-pottery Neolithic occupation, and at another in the Zhob valley the earliest encampment seems to have been of a semi-nomadic people with horses, donkeys, humped cattle (zebu) and sheep. But at most sites the finely painted wares made a link between these Indian farmers and those of Iran and Iraq. As might be expected, particularly close relationships exist with eastern Iran, most notably with Hissar.

Nevertheless the local element was strong and shows not only in arts and crafts but also in domestic animals and plants. Although not a great deal is yet known about the species raised by the Indian villagers, the very early appearance of the zebu, a breed long peculiar to India, shows that there must have been a domestication of indigenous beasts. The zebu can be compared with its 'opposite number' the British cattle at the western extremity of primary Neolithic diffusion, with their admixture of the native wild species. There seems no doubt that these upland villages were the source of the great urban cultures of the Indus valley just as several thousand years before and a thousand miles farther west the original villages of cultivators in the hills lay behind the valley civilizations of the Tigris and Euphrates. If many of them were already thriving by 3000 B C, they certainly lasted to have the humble trading connections with Harappā that hill communities have usually enjoyed with the wealthier, softer citizens living below them. The upland villages can be recognized as antecedent to the high Indus culture, and we can imagine pioneers from among them who led groups of followers down to settle the wide and jungle-encumbered plain. The ruins of villages and small towns probably founded by struggling colonists of this kind are beginning to be recognized on the Indus plain. One of them, Kot Diji, some twenty-five miles east of Mohenjo-daro itself, with a strongly fortified citadel, is probably typical of these pre-Indus settlements. The ground having been prepared by the adventurous hillmen, some successful, others defeated by flood, by jungle fevers, by the unaccustomed difficulties of irrigation, then the *idea* of advanced, urban, literate civilization, already far advanced in Iraq, could germinate here with such rapidity that it has been possible to say that 'the Indus civilization appears to spring into being fully grown'.

There is little sign of any primary Neolithic cultures in other parts of India than its north-west corner.[10] In general it seems (as has already been suggested, p. 256) that archaic food-gathering cultures with microlithic flints incorporating such generally 'Neolithic' forms as the polished axe last very late indeed.

Knowledge of the spread of the Neolithic way of life eastward beyond India is slight, and anything said about it is likely to be contradicted by future discoveries. It has been thought that Chinese and other far-eastern farming with its rice, beans and pigs was an independent development. In spite of the great natural obstacles to diffusion, and the need for farmers to adapt their routines to a climate of dry winters and wet summers, this does not appear to be true. A trickle of colonists seems gradually to have penetrated every barrier and to have brought the arts of agriculture and stock-raising from south-western to south-eastern Asia. There was probably an extensive diffusion of the new economy during the second half of the third millennium B C. The main cereal crop first cultivated in China was millet, already encountered as a subsidiary to wheat in the west. The history of rice is still obscure, but it is thought originally to have been domesticated in India and to have been carried thence to China by way of the Yangtze, where it would have arrived not earlier than 2000 B C. Wherever its cultivation was adopted, this grain with its immensely heavy yield made possible a far denser peasant population than any other cereal could support.

There are sites which can be described as Neolithic scattered in many regions of China and Manchuria, but their age and affinities are little understood. The most numerous and best-known at present are in the Yellow Earth lands of Kansu, Shensi, Shansi and Honan. This central plain was, indeed, the cradle of Chinese civilization. Here the Ts'i-kia-p'ing culture of Kansu, whose creators made plain, thin strap-handled jars and beakers, may have been in being by the middle of the third millennium, but surer ground is reached with the well-known Yang-shao culture that spread in and around the middle course of the Yellow River. These peasants lived in pit-dwellings in villages protected by mud walls, raising millet by hoe cultivation and keeping pigs. At Pan-p'o in Shensi province a Yang-shao village of both round and rectangular houses possessed one large rectangular building which must either have belonged to a chief or have served some communal purpose. Their greatest achievement was magnificent pottery, best seen in their tall-necked fat jars—usually with a red ground enriched with painting. Spiral and checker patterns, and designs derived from the cowrie, as well as many bold curvilinear compositions were all simultaneously popular. Although this painted pottery of the Yang-shao peasants has a character all its own, it is usually assumed to show some indirect relationship with the painted-pottery-making people of south-west Asia. It is interesting to find that there was one highly distinctive pot form, the tri-pod vessel with legs like pendant breasts, presumably used for mulling an alcoholic drink, that appeared in the earliest Neolithic and survived to be imitated in bronze as the *Hu,* a well-known ceremonial vessel of the Chinese Bronze Age. This culture was flourishing in the third millennium B C, but how much sooner it began is quite uncertain. It lasted until at least 1500 B C. Another Neolithic culture, apparently rather later in date, carried farming into eastern China and particularly into the Shantung Peninsula and the coasts on either side of it. This is the Lung Shan culture whose creators lived in much the same way as those of the Yang-shao, but made a glossy black pottery of distinctive angular forms.

The spread of the primary Neolithic farming economy in the Old World has now been followed to its farthest extent westward, northward and eastward from its sources in south-west Asia and north Africa. In the succeeding Bronze and Iron Ages farming was of course to be spread very much more widely round these primary regions, but many great stretches of country remained in the possession of hunting and food-gathering peoples until modern times. At the point we have reached, and where this chapter must close, about 2000 B C, the enormous tracts of central and northern Eurasia were still inhabited only by scattered tribes of hunter-fishers. They had generally acquired pottery and the use of polished stone axes from Neolithic sources, but maintained their old way of life as wandering hunters, or as more settled fisher-folk. Some of the most highly developed of these people lived in the extreme eastern districts of Amour and Primorie. Here, indeed, a hunting station on the coast by the mouth of the Tetioukhe was a large permanent village with substantial houses and club rooms, and its inhabitants evidently ground grain of some kind as well as importing rich ornaments in chalcedony and jasper from China, Japan and Korea. Indeed this and the Amour region show kinship with the Jomon (comb pottery) culture of Japan, which was also created by prosperous hunter-fishers. A geographical link between the two is provided by Sakhalin Island, whose inhabitants at this time had much in common with those of Amour and of Japan. Their culture also shows Eskimoid traits, and it has been suggested that they may be racially ancestral to the Eskimo. Similarly, some authorities believe the makers of the Jomon culture to have been the forebears of the Japanese Ainu.

The other main groups of hunter-fishers to have been distinguished are those of the Baikal, probably ancestors of the modern Tungus, the related semi-settled fisher-folk of Yakoutie (some of whom had a naturalistic art), the reindeer hunters of the northern forests, and the fishers of the tundra zone. In western Siberia, particularly round the basin of the Obi, settled fishers living in clusters of large communal houses are considered to be ancestral to the Ugrians. Farming was to be introduced relatively early into this region with the establishment of the copper-using Afanasievo culture at the beginning of the second millennium.

Before leaving these northern territories where harsh conditions and remoteness from the centres of change allowed primitive ways to survive for so long, attention should perhaps be called to the remarkable uniformity of the culture of the vast forest zone stretching across northern Asia and Europe. The forest-dwellers, usually brought together under the name of the comb-pottery people, had a kind of loose unity throughout their range. They form the background to the progressive movements to the south of them as much in Scandinavia, Finland and north-eastern Europe as in northern Russia. Although, as we have seen, there were local groupings and variations due in part to differences of opportunity offered by the environment, there seems to have been trade and an elementary continuity of association between them. It is believed by some historians that there was not only trade between tribe and tribe but an actual percolation of people, perhaps 'traders, warlike adventurers and slaves', and that it was this slow infiltration towards the west that brought Mongoloid stock into north-eastern Europe.[11]

To complete the world picture, something should be said of the origins of a Neolithic way of life in the American continent.

It is possible that the general *idea* of agriculture may have reached the New World from the Old, just as the idea of literate urban civilization reached the Indus valley from Iraq. Even this, however, is by no means a necessary assumption as peoples long skilled in the collection of wild vegetable foods as were the creators of the Palaeo-western cultures (p. 151) may well have taken the step to cultivation independently. Certainly the materials and methods of agriculture had to be independently discovered and invented in America. All the plant species were native, or (in the case of the squashes) naturally introduced by sea currents.

It has been assumed until recently that all cultivation began in the lowland areas of South America where wild pod-corn was to be found as well as manioc, beans and sweet potatoes. New discoveries have modified this opinion. The detection of maize pollen grains in a boring 200 feet below Mexico City shows that wild maize, probably the pod-corn form thought to be the wild ancestor of cultivated *Zea mays,* was growing in the Valley of Mexico during the last interglacial, at least sixty thousand years ago. Furthermore tiny cobs representing a form of corn very near the beginning of its cultivation have been excavated from Bat Cave, New Mexico. An associated projectile point suggests they may be contemporary with the Cochise culture, while not quite unambiguous Carbon-14 readings have assigned them a date of about 3600 B C. Even if this age is too great, there can be no doubt that men started to cultivate maize in the south-west of the United States and that it was a very long time ago. In the La Perra cave in Mexico maize dated to about 2500 B C was almost equally primitive but of a distinctive type. Probably, then, maize was separately cultivated in a number of different centres, but it is too soon to say whether the idea itself originated in North, Central or South America. On present evidence South America appears to have the weakest claim.

Although maize was destined to be the most important foodstuff of pre-Columban America, it is unlikely to have been the first to be cultivated. A cave near Ocampo in Mexico has recently yielded cultivated varieties of gourds, lima beans and squashes which have been dated to about

6500 B C. There was certainly pre-maize cultivation in some Andean regions and along the west coast of South America.

Farming peoples seem to have been living along the coast of Peru and Chile by the middle of the third millennium B C. They are best known from middens left in the Chicama and Viru valleys in Peru. Hunting and sea fishing were still important to them, but they also raised squashes, gourds, beans and chiles; maize was unknown among them. They had not mastered potting, but grew cotton and used it for weaving fabrics, nets and bags. Their huts were usually oval, sunk in the ground, lined with cobbles and roofed over at ground-level with rafters of wood or whalebone.

The Andeans at some time also domesticated the llama for pack carrying and meat, the alpaca for wool, and the guinea pig for a tender meat. They had dogs, which indeed must have been introduced quite early in the settlement of the Americas. Neither the llama nor the alpaca was brought to the state of domestication at which it could be milked.

The more important of the South American domestic animals were not kept north of Panama. The Central and North American farmer seems to have possessed only the dog, the turkey—and the bee. Not very much is as yet known of the Neolithic communities who had undoubtedly been farming in Mexico for millennia before the rise of the higher civilizations. The La Perra cave shows that maize was being cultivated as early as the third millennium B C. It is worth noting that while Bat Cave was occupied by some of the most ancient cultivators of the region, the Pueblo Indians were still living there with what might be called a 'painted-pottery Neolithic' culture at the time of the Spanish conquest.

This chapter ends at a date much later than the opening of the second part of the volume. This is because it provides the modest setting for the brilliant lights of civilization with which that part is concerned. Ways of life become simpler, our knowledge of them generally more shadowy, as we move outwards from those river valleys where man first created high civilization. It is right at this point to give some recognition to a part of mankind that was to contribute little to the cultural progress to be chronicled in this history, yet who continued to lead human lives sometimes with achievements in arts, crafts and oral literature worthy of high admiration. For all we know, some of them may have greatness still lying in the future.

NOTES TO CHAPTER VIII

1. Professors Koppers and Pericot García point out that agriculture, and ceramics as well, might have originated independently in America, but this has never been proved. These questions are definitely still open. In this respect R. Heine-Geldern's recent papers indicate the need for care and caution. See R. Heine-Geldern, 'Herkunft und Ausbreitung der Hochkulturen', Oesterreichische Akademie der Wissenschaften, *Almanach*, 105 (1956), pp. 252–67; 'The Origin of Ancient Civilization and Toynbee's Theories', *Diogenes*, 13 (Spring, 1956), pp. 81–99.

2. Professor J. A. Wilson points out that it is increasingly difficult to find informed climatologists or geologists who follow the extremes of climatic determinism of the older archaeologists.

3. For Professor Neustupný the term 'Vardar-Morava Culture' has nowadays been generally superseded by more precise terms such as Starcewo I or II culture, Bubanj culture and Vinča culture; these designate various phases or groups of the Neolithic, which advanced northwards from Greece through the Vardar and Morava valley from approximately 3500 B C onwards. See V. Milojčič, *Chronologie der jüngeren Steinzeit Mittel- und Südosteuropas* (Berlin, 1949).

4. According to C. S. Coon the so-called stone clubs may also be digging-stick weights.

5. During the past few years most scholars have radically changed their views concerning the appearance of the prehistoric lake-dwellings in the Alpine region. The old theory, advanced in 1845 by the Zürich antiquarian Ferdinand Keller, was that they were pile structures built over the water. The problem as it stands today can be put as follows: (1) Are these the remains of 'lake-dwellings' (i.e. settlements constructed over the water), or lakeshore villages on dry land? (2) If the latter is the case, are the individual dwellings ground-level or pile structures? Excavations made at several small Swiss lakes during the past few years show that finds which had formerly been thought to be pile structures can now definitely be identified as remains of lakeshore villages on dry land with ground-level structures (see W. U. Guyan, ed. *Das Pfahlbauproblem* (Basel, 1955)). But for the time being these findings can only be generalized in so far as the old idea of pile construction in the water has to be dropped completely. On the other hand, it is not yet clear whether in view of fluctuations in the water level the individual dwellings in lake villages on the margin of larger lakes were not raised above the ground after all, in order to counter the risk of flooding.

6. Dr P. Bosch-Gimpera stresses that not all scholars are agreed in using 'megalithic' as a collective term for such completely different monuments as, for example, the 'navetas' and 'talayots' on the Balearic Islands, the 'tombe dei giganti' (giants' graves), the Bronze Age 'nuraghe' in Sardinia, and the 'mastabas' in Egypt. It may be that the 'tholos' architecture of the Aegean exercised an influence upon the development of megalith-building in the West, particularly as regards orthostats and false domes. There may also exist affinities between Sicilian tomb-types and artificial rock-cut tombs in Portugal (Palmella).

But before knowledge of orthostats and false domes spread to the West the megalithic architecture found there (dolmens, passage-graves or chambers, and gallery-graves) must have constituted an independent group not influenced by the East. The proponents of this theory, however, are inclined to accept the view that the spread of a Neolithic megalithic religion took place parallel to the spread of peasant agriculture from the Orient. But the ideas that reached the West in this way seem to have produced very different reactions among different European peoples, although it is not easy to trace these from the development of megalithic architecture. From time to time during the Aeneolithic Age the various European peoples apparently maintained close contact with one another, so that certain megalithic forms and techniques spread from the Iberian peninsula across France (especially Brittany) to the British Isles, with offshoots reaching as far as Scandinavia. But there are also more archaic forms of sepulchral architecture dating from the time before such contacts became intensive during the Aeneolithic; their origin and their development in their respective localities are problems that have as yet only been partially solved. Some other problems connected with megalithic architecture should also be mentioned here: e.g. the question raised by G. V. Childe, whether the early megalithic types in northern Europe originally developed independently, and were only reached by the western European influences at a later date; the so-called 'dolmens' in Asia Minor and the Caucasus which bear a resemblance to the large stone cists of later date in the West; and the 'dolmens' in north Africa, which are not really megalithic monuments, but appear to be very late derivatives of the 'bassina' characteristic of this area. Dr Bosch-Gimpera maintains that new excavations at Alemtejo (Portugal) confirm that there is a Megalithic culture of the Neolithic Age older than the Mesolithic 'tholoi'. In Reguengos de Moseraz 'tholoi' appear as secondary intrusions in the same tumulus of older passage-graves.

7. According to M. Gimbutas ['The Prehistory of Eastern Europe', Peabody Museum, American School of Prehistoric Research, Harvard University, *Bulletin* No. 20 (Cambridge, Mass., 1956)], it is rather a matter of the pressure of the battle-axe peoples that prevented a further expansion of the Tripolye culture; the Fatyanovo culture is regarded as the 'eastern wing' of the battle-axe cultures.

8. Professor G. F. Debetz feels that mention should be made of the mixed farming communities of the ancient tribes of the pit-graves and catacomb cultures in the south Russian steppes. In this connection the Copper Age towns in Armenia are of considerable interest. They have been discovered in many places on Shengavit Hill near Yerevan, on Shresh Blur and Kyul-tapa near Echmiadzin (Vagarshapat). The towns in the lowlands are typical tepes, i.e. mounds growing larger towards the top and formed of wrecked clay dwellings, on the ruins of which new dwellings were erected. Some of them date back to the third millennium B C.

The ruins of round dwellings made of raw brick with quadrangular structures attached have been discovered in Shengavit. In the middle of the dwellings were clay hearths. The floors are sometimes gravelled and covered with brick. Vessels found in these dwellings contained grains of wheat and barley of various species related to the wild species of the Transcaucasus. Bones of domesticated animals and clay figures of cattle testify to the raising of various cattle. Exceedingly original vessels were discovered there— the outside surface black, the inside reddish and highly polished.

Sickles with flint blades were used to reap the crops. Most of the tools were made of stone, but copper tools were found, too. Judging from the bones of game animals, hunting played an important part in the economy.

Similar towns have been discovered in other parts of Transcaucasia, in Georgia and Azerbaijan. Clearly the region inhabited by tribes engaged in crop cultivation and stock-raising and already beginning, in the third millennium B C, to use metals cannot, as is so often done, be limited to Mesopotamia, Egypt and the eastern Mediterranean, but must be extended north, east and west of the Caspian Sea. And still farther north, in the steppes of the lower reaches of the Volga and the Don, the inhabitants began to engage in a productive economy—crop cultivation and stock-raising—and soon began to use metals (between 3000 and 2000 B C). Grains of barley, indicating crop cultivation, have been found in the burials of the pit-graves and catacomb cultures which covered a huge region in the eastern section of the south Russian steppes. Pieces of meat (bones of cows and sheep or goats) laid beside the dead indicate cattle-raising. Small copper objects, such as four-faceted awls and temporal rings, have been found in some burials of the early pit-graves and catacomb cultures (the pit-grave stage).

9. Professor C. A. Nordman rejects the idea that the battle-axe culture was dependent on Maglemose and Kunda, and takes the view that the complex of battle-axe and cord-ornamented pottery cultures came to Europe from the East together with the expansion of the Indo-Europeans. See M. Gimbutas, 'The Prehistory of Eastern Europe', Peabody Museum, American School of Prehistoric Research, Harvard University, *Bulletin* No. 20 (Cambridge, Mass., 1956).

10. Professor H. D. Sankalia notes that recent research has shown that in fact also the entire south-east of the Indian peninsula seems to have been the home of Neolithic cultures. See B. Subbarao, *Stone Age Cultures of Bellary* (Poona, 1948); V. D. Krishnaswami, 'Progress in Prehistory', *Ancient India*, 9 (1953), pp. 53–79.

11. In this connection it is worth drawing attention to the Woodland culture in America and its affinities with the Neolithic in Siberia. See P. Tolstoy, 'Some Amerasian Pottery Traits in North Asian Prehistory', *American Antiquity*, XIX (1953), pp. 25–39.

CHAPTER IX

SOCIETY

THE Neolithic peasant's experience of life must have been quite unlike that of his hunting forebears of Late Pleistocene times. Probably in many fundamental ways the difference was greater than between the experiences of a modern peasant in, say, the west of Ireland or India, and his Neolithic predecessor. More than to anything else this contrast was due to the domestic and social revolution that went with living in more or less settled homestead, hamlet or village. It might be said that for the individual the revolutionary psychological change was the substitution of routine and hard work for excitement and uncertainty, while the social counterpart was a new stability demanding greater discipline and more government. The hunters' foresight in making tools and setting traps was as nothing when compared with that asked of the peasant when he fed animals in order to have their young and their milk, or kept seed corn for harvest a year later.

It has been shown that the Neolithic way of life was typically one of mixed farming with both agriculture and stock-raising. There are signs here and there, as at Belt Cave, of very primitive herdsmen wandering with flocks of goats; under harsh climatic conditions, as in the Orkney Islands, there were settled cattle-men who raised no crops. Also there were wide variations in the relative importance of crops and livestock and in the extent to which hunting remained a significant part of the economy. Nevertheless, by and large the Neolithic farmer was tied to the land. He had invested his seed corn and must wait for the dividend. On the other hand he could be reasonably certain of enjoying it and of having sufficient food supplies for the winter. It was man's first sacrifice of liberty for the sake of security.

Obviously the new bond with (or bondage to) the soil made its ownership a matter of great social importance. The rather loose forms of possession sufficient for hunting grounds would not do for cultivated fields. Forms of land ownership must always escape archaeological detection, and they have to be inferred from those of present-day primitive farmers and from those that were prevailing when written records began. These comparisons make it appear very likely that arable fields belonged to the village community and might either be worked communally or assigned to individual clans or families for cultivation. If the second custom prevailed, then the fields might be re-allotted each year, or one family's holding might be widely scattered, in order to avoid an unfair distribution of the best land. Pasture was presumably generally held in common, but possibly some peoples may have come nearer to the true nomadic pastoralism and owned their livestock communally. Not infrequently among modern peoples all uncultivated land is expressly recognized as belonging to the clan; if it is cleared and worked, it becomes the property of the family responsible but reverts to the clan should the family die out.

It has been said above that land might be assigned to clan or family, and the distinction is an important one. There is good reason to suppose that the family or genealogically related kinship group was strengthened at the expense of the clan by the change to farming. It is probably one of the social changes that came about slowly with the adoption of the new economy. Thus today the owning group is often a small or joint family or other kinship group and not a classificatory clan. On the other hand there are signs that in the past ownership may have been vested in the clan; for example, very often, although the land and its products belong to a family, all other members of the clan are allowed to ask for the use of them and are never refused. This historical change, which seems very likely to have begun with the Neolithic way of life, has been summed up from a study of modern primitives as follows, 'Behind the definite regulations concerning ownership by these smaller [kinship] groups there is often the tradition of ownership by the clan, and it seems probable that there was at one time common ownership by clan or moiety which has been replaced, at any rate in practice, by ownership in which the common rights rest on kinship'.

Such a trend is to be expected, for there is surely something to encourage exclusiveness and sense of possession in hard labour in the closed field, the family hut, just as there is much to encourage collaboration and communal sharing in the hunt and the domestic life of the cave. Irrigation calls for a special kind of common social effort and social control in a farming community. It has been shown that the opportunity offered by their oasis may have helped to raise the people of Jericho to their extraordinarily high level of social development; the channelling and distribution of water was also practised in Persia at Sialk; but generally elaborate irrigation works belong not to the primary Neolithic culture but to civilization.

Family ownership was a very genuine form of communal possession, for quite numerous parents, brothers, sisters, cousins might all have equal claim to the land and its produce. Nevertheless it may have been inclined to lead on to more strictly individual possession for it already points to a much narrower sense of rights and the direct reward of labour (to each according to his deserts) than does any form of clan holding. Individual possession of land is rare among primitives, but there are many instances of particular things such as fruit trees being owned by individuals. A man may not only own a tree on land not in his possession but may even plant one there and hand it on in perpetuity to his children. It has been supposed that this kind of personal ownership has usually arisen when one people has mingled with another, particularly when a patrilineal people has permeated a native matrilineal society. If it existed at all in Neolithic times, it is likely to have been due to comparable causes—and for this reason is much more probable for the succeeding phases when infiltration and conquest were taking place in many regions of the Old World.

The trend away from clan ownership is of great significance for it would almost certainly coincide with a weakening of matrilineal inheritance and of women's whole social status. A social anthropologist has written that 'there are facts pointing definitely to the close connexion between communal ownership and mother-right on the one hand, and individual ownership and father-right on the other hand'. Now it has already been said that traces of matrilineal descent and even of matriarchy survive in the forms of Egyptian and Cretan civilization, but in general the growth of urban life everywhere brought it to an end. Again, outside the early centres of urban life it was probably extensively reduced by the Early Bronze Age upheavals just referred to and may also have been weakened when land came to be in short supply. But there is every reason to suppose that under the conditions of the primary Neolithic way of life mother-right and the clan system were still dominant, and land would generally have descended through the female line. Indeed, it is tempting to be convinced that the earliest Neolithic societies throughout their range in time and space gave woman the highest status she has ever known. The way of life and its values, the skills demanded, were ideally suited to her.

Whether, where it persisted, the clan system was still totemic it is impossible to judge. Totemism is found among primitive farmers today, and it is possible to interpret the nomes and the related animal cults of Dynastic Egypt as survivals of a prehistoric totemism. Yet there is less positive evidence for its existence among Neolithic peoples than for their hunting forebears. We may guess that the system of social organization outlasted the religious inspiration of totemism—an inspiration likely to be deadened by the settled life of field and village.

Possessions other than land can be assumed to have belonged to the small family unit or to individuals. It is true that among modern primitives things made by communal effort, such, for example, as canoes, sometimes remain as common possessions. But even this is by no means universally true. Houses, often built by a group, normally belong exclusively to the occupants, and it seems reasonably certain that the small village houses of the various forms that we have seen spreading through the Old World with the expansion of the Neolithic economy were the property of the families who lived in them. On the other hand we have seen how here and there large communal houses were still preferred.

As for the small possessions now becoming so much more abundant, they must have been individually owned. Not only weapons, tools and ornaments, but also all the attractive products of the new crafts of potting and weaving would surely have been the absolute and treasured property of the men, women and children who made or were given them. With greater skills, more leisure and a settled home, a mild acquisitiveness could now take its place among human desires.

Life in villages and little towns must have brought to birth a feeling of neighbourliness. Just because the privately owned and occupied house gave families a conscious apartness, it also gave a sense of being neighbours impossible to a hunting community that lived so much as a single group. In large villages and small towns such as those of pre-Dynastic Egypt and south-east Asia and even here and there in Neolithic Europe, there must have been some faint beginning of the life of the streets, of going out to see who was about and forgathering for talk at recognized popular meeting places. Presumably the sun must have made as much difference to social habits as it does today. The peoples who carried farming to the chillier, wetter parts of Europe and Asia must have had to pass far more time in their houses than did the more fortunate villagers in its warm cradlelands.

The primary Neolithic way of life seems generally to have been a peaceful one not given to warlike adventure. None of the Danubian villages, for instance, had defences, and although in many regions Neolithic settlements were ditched and fenced, it was usually on a scale more appropriate to protection against marauding animals than against human enemies. The walls and tower at Jericho, on the other hand, show that exceptional wealth in a countryside where there were many less settled peoples already in very early times led to the defence of the rich town-dweller against the poor, hardy raider so familiar in historic times.

The general absence of weapons of war among the grave furniture of Neolithic burials provides even more convincing proof of the absence of martial ideals in the hearts of the new peasantry. A striking contrast is provided in Late Neolithic and Early Bronze Age times when from the Caspian and the Russian steppes to Scandinavia and Britain, battle-axes, daggers and other arms appear in the grave of every adult male. Although it is rash to push economic explanations too far—many peoples have loved to fight their neighbours without any need for *Lebensraum*—it seems probable that the fact that good land was to be had for the taking and each succeeding generation could find a good living did partly account for the peacefulness of early Neolithic communities. And similarly that the more warlike ideals of the succeeding phase were partly due to mounting populations and the shortage of new land to feed them.

The Neolithic economy demanded greater specialization of labours and skills than had existed in hunting societies. But it was still slight in the primary Neolithic phase, increasing only with the approach of urban conditions. It consisted chiefly in a sharpening of the division of tasks between the sexes. It is generally accepted that owing to her ancient role as the gatherer of vegetable foods, woman was responsible for the invention and development of agriculture. Modern analogies indicate that so long as the ground was prepared by hoeing and not by ploughing, woman remained the cultivator. She probably also invented potting, spinning and weaving and kept these crafts in her hands.[1] The men's main preoccupation must have been with raising and managing the livestock, and among societies where it remained an important source of food, with hunting. It seems probable that they would also have undertaken the labour of grinding stone axes, hoes and other heavy tools. When virgin land was being opened up, tree-felling made strenuous work that presumably fell to the men, while they may also have been the carpenters where such existed.

There is practically no evidence for full-time specialists in ordinary village life. Every family seems to have undertaken all forms of labour and craftwork for itself. Even in cultures where the finest painted pottery was made, each household may have been capable of making its own (p. 404). Probably individuals gifted in particular crafts were occasionally employed by their neighbours and paid for their trouble in grain or other food, but full-time craftsmen seem to have emerged only with an urban economy.

There may, however, have been a few specialized workers outside the village community. In several parts of western Europe, for instance, flint mining and stone quarrying to get raw materials for the manufacture of axes were carried out in a remarkably elaborate fashion, and it has always been held probable that the followers of so strange and even uncanny an occupation may have formed special groups—as blacksmiths did until recently among some African peoples. Perhaps, too, there may have been odd individuals who specialized in trade, going from one community to another with shells or other sought-after raw materials, usually decorative stuff for personal ornaments. There is, however, no real evidence for the existence of such itinerant pedlars— goods such as the spondylus may well have been traded from village to adjacent village over great distances.

Another quite different type of division of function has to be considered. That is the purchase of wild game or raw materials by farming peoples from hunters surviving in their neighbourhood. This state of affairs with cultivators and food-gatherers living intermingled is fairly common today and was probably far more frequent in prehistoric times than is generally supposed—for it can only be detected where archaeological method is far advanced. It is known that the Ertebølle people of Mesolithic tradition flourished for a considerable time after the arrival of the earliest farmers in Scandinavia, and the contacts known to have existed between them may well have included an exchange of corn for fish and wild fowl. In Britain there seems to have been a comparable survival of hunting folk (though their culture may have been more profoundly affected by the newcomers), and there is evidence to suggest that they may have been in part responsible for a carrying trade in flint and stone axes. That peoples maintaining a more nomadic way of life should sometimes have acted as carriers between settled communities seems likely enough, and may have been widespread.

Neolithic villagers certainly did acquire luxury objects from afar, and sometimes more basic raw materials from outside their own immediate countryside. Yet fundamentally the Neolithic economy is characterized by small, self-sufficient communities. All the pioneering groups whose diffusion through the Old World was described in Chapter VIII could have lived their lives without any contact with the outside world. From Britain to Kansu, from the Obi to the Upper Nile, in excessive heat and cold, in arid lands and in lands where there was too much rain, the Neolithic farmers in their hamlets and villages adapted themselves to the local environment and used it as fully as they could. Generally the original settlers brought their livestock and seed corn with them (although even here we have seen how local species were sometimes domesticated or hybridized), but in most other ways their culture became closely keyed to local conditions and opportunities. That is why, apart from the basic similarity of the economy, there is such a vast number of small pieces in the mosaic of Neolithic cultures —far more than of the relatively large blocks to be distinguished in the Palaeolithic Age. A peaceful sedentary life combined with isolation leads inevitably to a multiplication of local cultures.

Forms of leadership and authority among Neolithic communities are almost as difficult to infer from archaeological evidence as are forms of ownership. It is obvious enough, however, that the possession of land, livestock and greatly increased domestic equipment would lead to more disputes and a need for greater social control. Where irrigation was practised, this need would be increased still further: disputes about water are among the oldest causes of litigation. On the other hand the various kinds of communal property-holding that we have supposed to have been general in Neolithic times are less likely to give rise to trouble than private ownership.

We can be sure that the concept of law, as opposed to custom, had not yet been consciously formulated. All that was said in Chapter V about the force of tabu, crimes against the spirits and their punishment is equally applicable to the new society. In more than one modern primitive society the private ownership of trees on common land is protected by special tabus. When disputes about land and other

evidently secular matters had to be settled they probably
came before councils—perhaps of the whole village, perhaps
of recognized elders. Decision would probably be reached
by the indefinable but readily comprehensible means of 'common consent'. It has been said of their counterparts
among modern primitives, 'In these councils there are none
of the formal means of reaching decisions by voting or other means which are customary among ourselves. At a certain stage of the discussion it seems to be recognized by
some sort of common sense . . . that the group has reached
agreement. The conclusion which has been reached is in-
tuitively known to all, and the meeting passes on to the next
business. There is . . . a group sentiment which makes unnecessary any definite social machinery for the exertion of
authority. . . .'

The fact that in true primary Neolithic cultures there are
almost never any large houses or richly furnished burials of
chiefly kind is fairly strong evidence in favour of this kind
of communal government. In an agricultural society the authority of elders with their experience and knowledge of custom and lore is perhaps likely to have been greater than
among hunting peoples where physical prowess counted for
so much. Probably, too, there were more elders to offer
their counsel—for the expectation of life, though still brief
by present standards, was certainly greater than in Palaeolithic times.

While government by custom, council and common consent seems perfectly appropriate to the type of community
represented, for example, by the Danubians, the Swiss lake-
dwellers, the people of Jarmo or the pig-keepers of the Yellow River and many other societies between these geographical extremes, archaeological evidence suggests that it
was not universal. The extravagantly rich burials of the
Kuban (p. 343) with their vessels of gold and silver, their
ornamental canopies, evidently belonged to barbarous chief-
tains. But then as we have seen this Pontic culture was not
of the true primary Neolithic type, but engendered by the
direct influence of high civilization on a hunting society.
But we must also allow for the beginning of forms of chieftainship among true Neolithic communities that were becoming socially more complex as part of their advance towards civilization. It will be recalled that at El Omari in
Lower Egypt, a village seemingly belonging to the Neolithic
Merimde culture, a man had been buried with a carved wood-
en baton comparable to the Ames sceptre, included in the
royal insignia of Lower Egypt. Perhaps a chief of this kind

may have ruled over a group of villages. An anthropologist
has described a modern African society as follows, 'The
social organization is essentially that of a number of villages united into a single community under a common
chief. . . . But throughout this form of political grouping
it is generally possible to discover a unifying influence aris-
ing from a sense of kinship and therefore the possession
of a common religious cult. . . .' This was quoted and
commented upon by an Egyptologist as follows: 'How well
this description fits predynastic Egypt becomes clear when
we view the modesty of the remains of predynastic villages;
the homogeneity of the contents of thousands of predynastic
graves; the division of Egypt, in later times, into nomes
or provinces which go back, in the main, to communities
formed in early times; the ease with which these provinces
became independent under their own local chiefs whenever
the central power weakened; their representation by standards or emblems connected with a local cult. . . . There
can be no doubt that our quotation from modern conditions applies fully to those prevailing before the time of
Menes.'*

This, then, may be the kind of structure that began to be
established in Neolithic society in regions that were advancing towards civilization. As they must to some extent have
been prototypes of the divine rulers of Dynastic times, it
can be assumed that these chiefs of prehistoric village groups,
or nomes, would have been sacred rather than secular
rulers. Almost certainly, too, although the chiefs themselves
were men, inheritance would pass through the female line,
as it is known to have done for the chiefs of the nomes in
historic times. Indeed, matrilineal descent was prevalent
throughout Egyptian society, and manifested itself in a peculiar form in the marriage of Pharaoh to his sister as the
heiress to the kingdom or at least to the sacred throne.

The existence of priests and priestesses among the leaders
of Neolithic communities is as difficult to demonstrate archaeologically as other social forms. In the simplest societies
of the primary Neolithic diffusion and those that remained
at this stage of social evolution, what was said (p. 190) of
Palaeolithic shamans and medicine men would probably still
be applicable. There is no longer, however, any reason to
connect such individuals with the practice of an inspired

*H. Frankfort in *Kingship and the Gods* quoting C. G. Seligman in
The Races of Africa.

magico-religious art. At higher levels of social development
such as we have been considering in the Merimdians, and
such as are vouched for by the temples at Jericho and
Eridu, more clearly defined priesthoods would probably be
emerging in relation with divine, or divinely inspired, rulers.
That there would have been female as well as male priesthoods seems sure enough. They emerge with history in Egypt
and Crete; they must surely have been pre-eminent in Malta
with its tremendous obsession with the Great Mother. Groups
of priestesses, some attendant on the Moon Goddess, others
on the Maize Mother, appear to go back far into pre-Inca
times in South America.

At humbler levels of Neolithic society, the cultures that
incorporated the building of megalithic tombs have a peculiar
interest. It has been shown (p. 340) that this form of architecture and its attendant cult were probably spread by
missionaries who must have acquired special power within
the local communities. If this interpretation is a correct one,
then all the far-flung western coastal peoples who adopted
these religious forms must have had sacred leaders with at
least enough social power to inspire the expenditure of un-
precedented labour. How much purely secular authority
would have fallen to them cannot even be guessed. Indeed
there is no agreement as to whether the great tombs themselves, used for successive burials over considerable periods
of time, were truly communal in the sense that they were
used for all the dead of the community, or whether burial
in them was the privilege of a ruling line. Here and there
a close family likeness has been detected between all the
bodies interred—and in western and northern Europe the
numbers are not usually very great. These facts argue in
favour of megalithic tombs standing for the persistence of a
sacred chieftainship of some kind. On the other hand in some
regions, notably Sicily, vast numbers of people were buried
in them, suggesting a genuinely communal rite.

If the social implications of megalithic architecture demand special discussion, so also do those of certain exceptional sites, notably Jericho. There seems no doubt at all
that this close-packed eight-acre town behind strong defences
and furnished with a temple must have had the social
structure of true urban civilization. That is to say there are
quite likely to have been specialists not normally engaged
in food production, even more surely an organized admin-
istration probably with a ruler and priests. Yet this was some
nine thousand years ago and before the adoption of the pot-

ter's craft. It has already been admitted that it is too soon to see Jericho in historical perspective in relation to the growth of urban life in the river valleys. In purely social history it has a clear meaning for us here. It emphasizes what is already apparent: that the forms of social organization we have been discussing are very much a matter of stages of development, fluctuating freely with the chances of local environment and of historical contacts. In exceptional circumstances such as those offered by the perennial spring at Jericho (now watering seventy thousand Arab refugees in addition to the native inhabitants) a community could be readily stimulated into creating a social organization far in advance of what was generally prevalent even in that very progressive region of the world.

Though Jericho had unique architectural features, subsequent discoveries are beginning to show that other settlements only a little less ancient were as large or even larger. Catal Hüyük in southern Anatolia, flourishing in the seventh millennium B C, covered twice the area of the later prepottery Jericho, while at its height Khirokitia in Cyprus is thought to have contained nearly a thousand houses.

This survey of the social aspects of the Neolithic way of life as it spread from its ancient centres between eight and four thousand years ago is largely based on supposition and inference, yet results in a consistent overall picture. The common basis was formed by varieties of village or group communism with appropriate forms of customary government by village council or groups of elders. The clan organization surviving from earlier times was probably gradually weakened in favour of kinship groups. Here and there as in the Pontic lands or in regions affected by religious missionaries, special forms of chieftainship and divine leadership may have been established. In south-west Asia and the Nile valley before the end of their Neolithic phase, village communities began to develop towards the great theocracies that were to emerge in Dynastic times. They need not, however, have gone very far towards it, for the old systems must have been profoundly altered by the conquests and the imposition of hegemonies that had to take place before civilized states were formed. These events, equally with the greater specialization of crafts and professions, caused the formation of the complex, stratified societies of the Bronze Age civilizations. Even in regions beyond these civilizations similar events, due to growing land shortage and the migrations of warlike peoples, led to other forms of stratified society, far more barbaric but also in strong contrast with the simple social structure characteristic of Neolithic life.

NOTE TO CHAPTER IX

1. Professor R. M. Berndt feels that the womenfolk *may* have largely been involved in the discovery and development of agriculture, pottery, weaving, etc., although there is no concrete evidence that this is so.

CHAPTER X

FARMING

IT has been made abundantly clear that the typical Neolithic economy rested on mixed farming with both agriculture and stock-raising. The relative importance might vary from one type of country to another and one cultural tradition to another, but generally speaking a fairly even balance was maintained. Because the cultivation of plants had a stronger effect on the way of life (by tying man to the soil) this subject can be granted first place.

CULTIVATION OF PLANTS

Although some consideration will have to be given to other plants early cultivated by man, cereal crops are of quite overwhelming economic importance in both the Old World and the New.[1] Wheat, barley and millet in Asia, Africa and Europe, maize in the Americas, made the solid foundation for the agriculture of our Neolithic forebears.[2] A general sketch of the spread of farmers and their crops has been drawn in Chapter VIII, but it remains to give a more detailed picture of the origin and distribution of the various botanical species involved. Precise facts about the first steps in the cultivation of the wild ancestors of the cereals are still very few, but their subsequent agricultural history is sufficiently well established.

One very significant difference between the ancestral wild grasses (and it is true also of quite other plants, such as beans) and the man-bred forms is that the former shed their seeds as soon as they are ripe. When, then, women were gathering wild seeds they had to beat them into skins or baskets and were liable to lose a large part of the yield. True reaping could only be invented after this natural method of propagation had been checked by selective sowing. 'Now and then a wild plant puts forth a suicidal mutation in which its head or pod lacks the ability to open. Ordinarily such a plant eventually falls and its seed rots. However, if a human being gathers it and opens its head or pod artificially, he can sow the seed next season and the mutation survives.' He, or rather she, can then reap the field with a sickle without loss, and take her time over threshing and winnowing.

It is likely that there were many centuries during which the food-gatherers of Mesolithic tradition were trying out different species, before the crops on which so much of the future history of mankind was to depend became selected, improved and stabilized. Who at that time could say which was certain to be a domestic plant, which a 'weed'? Even at a much later date, rye, which had been carried as a weed in soft wheat, mutated, was cultivated, and soon began to be extensively grown in the northern latitudes where wheat could not thrive. We have absolutely no tangible evidence for this period of tentative transition. But ears of wheat found at Jarmo in the Old World and cobs of maize at Bat Cave in the New were alike at a primitive and as yet unstabilized stage of development.

It is a rather surprising fact that throughout the early centres of cultivation in the Old World wheat and barley are almost invariably found together; no Neolithic culture is known to have been based on one alone. At that stage, however, wheat seems usually to have been the more important of the two.

Wheat

The cultivated wheats fall into three groups: the diploid, represented by einkorn or small spelt; the tetraploid, by emmer, macaroni and rivet; and the hexaploid represented by the bread and club wheats and by spelt. This classification based on chromosome structure is cut across by another division: einkorn, emmer and spelt are all glume wheats in which the grains are not released from their covering by threshing, while the other varieties are all naked wheats in which the grain is readily released from the glume.

Emmer (*Triticum dicoccum*) has been found more abundantly than any other wheat on all ancient sites (with the exception of some Danubian villages) from Egypt to Britain and Scandinavia. All the great wheat deposits to have been preserved in Egypt from Neolithic to Roman times are of this species. Emmer is remarkably like its wild ancestor, now known to be *T. dicoccoides,* which grows wild from

Syria and Palestine to Iraq and Persia. The discovery that
this was undoubtedly the ancestral form has finally disproved
one theory that would make Abyssinia the home of emmer
wheat. The wheat found at Jarmo and dating from about
5000 BC is of very irregular type, some ears being coarse
and loose (comparable to *T. dicoccoides*) while others are
compact and already close to the fully cultivated form of
emmer. As the wild grass is at home in relatively high
country, it is possible that bringing it to lower levels for
field cultivation helped to cause rapid mutation. From its
homelands in south-west Asia this wheat seems to have been
diffused along two routes, dividing at the eastern end of the
Mediterranean; one took it southward into Egypt, the other
into Europe, where it was grown by the Danubians, the
Swiss lake-dwellers, the Windmill Hill people of Britain and
the first farmers of Scandinavia. Indeed, in the conditions
offered by the sub-boreal climate it was able to do better
in these northern lands than it would today.

No wild form of hexaploid wheat is known, and it is
thought that bread wheat (*T. vulgare*) and club wheat (*T.
compactum*) came into being as mutational changes from
emmer—changes that may have taken place in the Trans-
caucasian region. An alternative theory sees the hexaploids
as the result of hybridization between emmer and einkorn,
among which they often occur sporadically. No Neolithic
culture is known to have relied principally on these naked
wheats, but *T. compactum* is known from El Omari in Egypt,
on Danubian sites and in Denmark; it was rather more
freely grown in later Neolithic times by the Swiss lakeside-
dwellers, spread widely during the Bronze Age and largely
took the place of emmer during the Iron Age. It was
grown in historic times in the Indus valley at Harappā. Spelt
and bread wheat were hardly established before the Bronze
and Iron Ages respectively.

Of all the cultivated wheats, only einkorn (*T. monococ-
cum*) is unrelated to the wild *T. dicoccoides* and instead is
descended from *T. aegilopoides,* wild varieties of which are
at home in the Balkans and (another group) from Asia Minor
to Palestine and Persia. It owes its name to the characteristic
of having only one grain instead of two in each spikelet.
Einkorn is not abundant at any of the really early sites in
south-west Asia though it occurs occasionally, even at Jarmo.
It evidently often grew as a weed in fields of emmer. Curiously enough it was very popular with the early Danubians
who grew more of it than they did of emmer; this may
have been due to traditional preference deriving from the

Balkans and Asia Minor where the European Danubian culture was rooted.

Barley

There are two principal kinds of cultivated barley, the two-row (*Hordeum distichum*) and the six-row. The latter is further subdivided into a dense-eared variety with hexagonal cross-section (*H. hexastichum*) and a lax-eared with rectangular cross-section (*H. tetrastichum*) sometimes known as four-row barley. All these forms occur with either glumes or naked grains.

The wild ancestor of two-row barley (*H. spontaneum*) is a native of Palestine, Arabia, Asia Minor, Transcaucasia, Persia and Afghanistan; of recent years a wild six-row species (*H. agriocrithon*) has been identified in eastern Tibet, and it is now generally held that the two barleys came from these two centres, one in western and the other in eastern Asia.

The very earliest find of barley is, like that of wheat, from Jarmo. It is of the two-row variety and, again like the emmer, is evidently intermediate between the wild form, *H. spontaneum*, and the cultivated, and proves the direct relationship between them. Two-row in the fully cultivated state was also found at the Early Neolithic site of Matarrah, at Halaf and Anau, and in Egypt in the Fayum. It also reached Switzerland in Neolithic times. This western spread of the *H. distichum* and its absence in the Far East is to be expected. So is a fairly early evolutionary development of six-row in China. What is more surprising is to find an extensive cultivation of six-row, particularly the dense-eared variety, in Neolithic Europe. The lax-eared variety turns up at the Fayum and at Badarian sites in Egypt. If, then, the six-row barley really originated far to the east, it was very much more successful in colonizing the west than two-row was in extending its range eastward.

Millet

The millets include plants belonging to different genera of which the most important in early times were true millet or panic grass (*Panicum miliaceum*) and the Italian millet (*Setaria italica*). Panic grass was early cultivated in India and central Asia and formed the basis of the economy of the early Chinese farmers. It seems to have spread westward by way of the Ukraine, Thrace and the Danube to Switzerland, Germany and France. Italian *Setaria* is a descendant of *S. viridis* that grows wild in western Asia, along the Mediterranean and in other parts of Europe. It is a moderate-warmth-loving species. Indeed, the millets, now largely displaced in temperate lands by wheats and barleys, are still of great importance in tropical countries where wheat will not thrive.

Rye and Oats

During Neolithic times these cereals were present in the fields, if at all, only as weeds. Their cultivation was not of economic importance much before the last millennium B C.

Maize

The origins and early history of maize have been studied so intensively of late that opinions have been rapidly changing. One basic conviction which has survived all attempts to challenge it is that this most productive cereal originated in the Americas and was not known in the Old World in pre-Columban times.

The view which has been most clearly and consistently developed and which has gained most support from recent archaeological and palaeobotanical discoveries is that maize developed from a wild ancestor which was at once a popcorn (hard-seeded) and a pod-corn—in which each kernel is enclosed in its own glumes or chaff. In the fully evolved maize (*Zea mays*) there are no glumes, the kernels being attached to a rigid cob and enclosed in a tight-fitting leaf-sheath or shuck. Such a form could never survive in nature as (a boon to the farmer) the seeds are non-dispersable and can only be sown artificially. In the primitive pod-corn the seed probably grew on slender rachises (in place of cobs) which easily broke when shaken by wind or by birds, so scattering the seed (Fig. 37 A and B).

Endorsement of the view that the wild ancestor was a maize and not, as others have argued, teosinte (*Zea mexicana*) or *Tripsacum* was provided by the discovery two hundred feet below Mexico City, in a geological context dating it to at least sixty thousand years ago, of unmistakable maize pollen grains. That it was also of pod-corn type is supported archaeologically—both by the finding of ancient and primitive cobs and by portrayal in prehistoric ceramics. The cobs found in the oldest level in Bat Cave, New Mexico, and a little uncertainly dated by Carbon-14 to about 3600

B C, certainly had the glumes and fragile rachis of the supposed primitive pod-corn. The same is true of the second most ancient specimens, the cobs from La Perra Cave, Tamaulipas, Mexico, which are some one thousand years more recent. As for ceramic evidence, various pots from Central and South America, particularly a funerary urn with a maize god from the Mexican Zapotec culture, look very

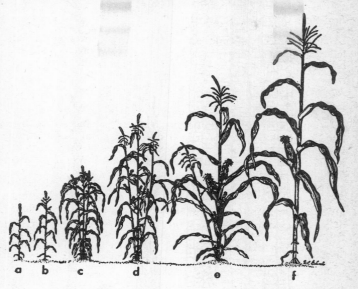

FIG. 37A. *The development of maize in America. Evolution of the maize plant:* (a) *wild pod-popcorn;* (b), (c) *improved cultivation;* (d) *after loss of pod-corn gene;* (e) *increased distance of male flower;* (f) *modern dent corn from the US corn belt.*
(Courtesy of Dr Paul C. Mangelsdorf, Harvard University.)

much like pod-corn. The Zapotec specimen also tends to confirm an interesting result obtained by a most ingenious method of regressive selective breeding. This breeding back towards the primitive suggested that in the early form the male flower, which in modern maize grows separately at the top of the stem, was immediately above the female flow-

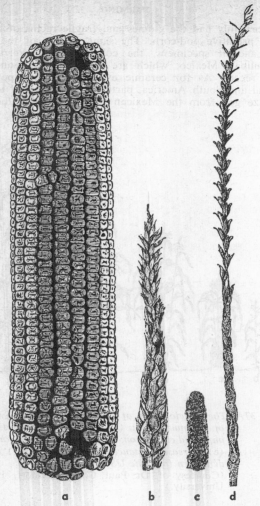

FIG. 37B. *The development of maize in America. Evolution of the maize cob:* (a) *modern dent corn;* (b) *the ancestral form of pod-popcorn;* (c) *an actual prehistoric cob from La Perra Cave.* (d) *Tripsacum, a wild relative of corn. Both* (b) *and* (d) *show the adjacent spike of the male flower. On* (c) *it has been broken off.*
(Courtesy of Dr Paul C. Mangelsdorf, Harvard University.)

er and therefore the ear. The ear held by the Zapotec god is crowned with plumes like a helmet. Almost certainly they represent the plumy male flower. This having been observed, re-examination of the Bat Cave cobs showed them to be topped by stumps which can only be the base of the male spike.

The view that *Zea mays* is descended from a wild maize of pod-corn type is, then, seemingly confirmed from many directions. With it is associated the further belief that teosinte, so far from being the ancestor of maize, was in fact the result of a natural hybridization between an already cultivated maize and *Tripsacum*. On the other hand after this hybridization maize seems often to have recrossed with its offspring, so that probably nearly all the many modern variations of corn contain an element of teosinte. In favour of this interpretation is the fact that in the borings below Mexico City while both maize and *Tripsacum* pollen occurred at two hundred feet, teosinte appeared only in the superficial deposits. Again, at Bat Cave, while the tiny primitive pods from the oldest occupation appear to be a pure *Zea mays* strain, in higher levels there is a conspicuous teosinte element. Where and when did the cultivation of maize begin? Until recently it was assumed that the wild ancestor was a native of the South American lowlands (where varieties of pod-corn still flourish) and that it was first fully cultivated in the Andes. Bat Cave, however, has very much shaken this opinion: the oldest cobs there, about the size of a woman's finger-nail, are undoubtedly very primitive and probably near the beginning stages of cultivation. If the Carbon-14 date of 3600 B C is correct—and it is not unambiguous—this is the most ancient corn known. The Mexican La Perra cobs are also primitive but they differ from those of the North American site in several botanical features. Although no such early specimens have as yet been found in the Andean highlands their absence cannot be held to dismiss the earlier arguments in favour of a South American origin. The most likely interpretation is that here again we can think of an *idea* spreading and being developed more or less independently in separate centres. It is too soon as yet to say whether South, Central or the south-west of North America can claim to have taken the lead.

Root Vegetables

Wild roots had long formed an important element in human diet, but their early cultivation is exceedingly difficult to trace. The only one to have been detected in a Neolithic context is the carrot, known from Switzerland and Germany. As it is descended from the hybridization of two wild species *Daucus carota* and *Daucus maxima* it must have originated in the region where the natural ranges of these overlap: the Mediterranean. Radishes were intensively cultivated in Old Kingdom Egypt and must have been eaten there in prehistoric times.

Fruit, Nut and Oil-seed-bearing Trees

Like roots, wild fruits have always been gathered by men —although, indeed, they were of even greater importance to his tree-dwelling ancestors. Cultivation, however, did not rapidly produce fruits that can be distinguished from their wild forms, so that the early history of orchard-culture cannot easily be followed. The apples eaten by the Danubians were small crabs of a kind that grows wild in Germany. In some of the later Neolithic Swiss lake-villages the inhabitants seem to have enjoyed a larger apple, probably derived from the cultivation of another European wild crab, *Malus sylvestris*. Pears were also eaten by these villagers, together with little plums, and cherries—possibly wild ones. It is thought (without sufficient evidence for proof) that the Danubians brought the cherry-plum into central Europe, where it became crossed with the sloe, producing the stock of the cultivated plum.

Walnuts grew wild as forest trees from Greece through Asia Minor, Persia and the Himalayas to China, and the nuts were doubtless harvested. They have been found in a Neolithic context only in Europe, where their shells survive in some of the later lake-dwellings of Switzerland and Germany; as the tree does not naturally grow north of the Alps, it looks as though it must have been brought in and cultivated by the lake-dwellers. Pistachio nuts, still so popular in the Middle East, were already enjoyed at Jarmo.

It has already been recorded (p. 334) that the first known instance of the cultivation of the olive was among the Neolithic people of El Garcel in south-east Spain. The origins of this tree, now so important in the economy of southern Europe, are uncertain; they may be Asiatic, and be traced to the wild species, *Olea chrysophylla*, which is native south of the Sahara, in Afghanistan, Baluchistan and western India. In early historic times it was certainly being grown at the eastern end of the Mediterranean, for the oil was imported into the Egyptian Old Kingdom from Palestine and

Syria. It was probably never of importance in either Iraq or the Indus region, for here by historic times sesame was the usual source of oil.

Beans, peas and other leguminous seeds have been an invaluable stand-by as a human food. They are easily dried and stored and have a high protein content. The field pea, and by mutation the garden species, are probably derived from the wild *Pisum elatius* that grows across the Old World from the Mediterranean to Tibet. Peas and lentils were eaten at Jarmo. Wild peas have been found among the grain at Merimde (p. 321), but this vegetable does not seem to have been much cultivated in Egypt. It was, however, cultivated by the Danubians who brought it into central Europe; before the end of Neolithic times it was being grown in Switzerland and southern Germany. Beans were of immense importance to ancient man in the Americas, where meat was scarce or absent. In fact several of our present-day garden beans have an American ancestry. Different wild species were cultivated in the Andean region on the one hand and the central American on the other. The tepary bean (*Phaseolus acutifolius*) of Mexico is unknown in the south, while the Mexican lima bean (*Phaseolus microsperma*) is a distinct variety. Both *Phaseolus vulgaris* and *Phaseolus multiflorus* are common to both regions, but the important yellow waxy types are peculiar to the south.

There is no archaeological evidence of the first cultivation of the soya (*Glycine max*) of such immense dietetic importance in China and Japan, nor of the Indian grams (*Phaseolus mungo* and *Phaseolus aureus*). In prehistoric Europe the usual variety was the broad bean (*Vicia faba*) which appears to have been introduced along two lines of diffusion. It is thought to have been derived from a wild bean native to north Africa (*Vicia pliniana*). It is therefore not surprising to find it introduced into Spain during the Neolithic period; its cultivation spread rapidly northward to the Channel Islands and south-east France. In addition to this southern line of entry direct from Africa, the broad bean was also carried into Europe by the earliest Danubians—which suggests that it was possibly already being cultivated in the Balkans and Asia Minor.

Squashes and Gourds

Though they formed a much less vital element in the diet of the early American cultivators than either maize or beans, squashes were extensively cultivated among them. As with the beans, there is a sharp division of species between the Andean varieties and those cultivated farther north. In Peru the squash most favoured was *Cucurbita maxima,* which was unknown in the Central American-Mexican region, while the reverse is true of *Cucurbita mixta.*

The bottle gourd (*Lagenaria siceraria*) has two distinctions. It is the only plant cultivated exclusively for making vessels and the only plant of any importance to link the cultivators of the Old and New Worlds in pre-Columban days. It was undoubtedly a native of the tropical regions of the Old World and was carried to America by ocean currents.

Comment has already been made on the fact that its imitation in pottery by the Danubians of Hungary in a region where it cannot grow is evidence of the southern, and particularly Anatolian, inspiration of their culture.

Flax

Varieties of flax were early grown both for their oil-seeds and for fibre. The Neolithic Egyptians grew *Linum usitatissimum* (Badari and Fayum), and it has been found at Alishar in central Anatolia at a level dating from about 3000 B C. Various species of *Linum* are natives of Europe, and doubtless provided the source of the ancient cultivated form *Linum bienne.* This plant was grown by the Danubians in south-eastern Europe, and they probably stimulated its spread to the west and north; it was cultivated by the earliest inhabitants of Swiss lake-dwellings and had reached Scandinavia before the end of Neolithic times.

THE DOMESTICATION OF ANIMALS

How the first stages of the domestication of wild goats, sheep, cattle and pigs were achieved is not known, and is never likely to be fully understood. There are, however, a number of theories. The least acceptable is that the step was taken directly from hunting practices, and in particular by the capture and taming of animals for use as decoys. It is just conceivable that this may have been true of reindeer.[3] Another and contrary view depends upon the womenfolk having already made enough progress with agriculture for some extra food to be available to tempt hungry animals. Again it has been suggested that in the conditions of post-glacial desiccation (p. 75) the wild flocks and herds became more and more concentrated in the neighbourhood of water, and more and more open to human influence and control. The last two explanations are compatible and can well be combined. 'It happens that just in those regions of Hither Asia where ancestors of wheat and barley grew spontaneously, there lived also wild sheep, goats, cattle and pigs. Now the hunters whose wives were cultivators had something to offer some of the beasts they had hunted—the stubble on grain plots and the husks of the grain. As suitable animals became increasingly hemmed in to the oases by the desert, men might study their habits and, instead of killing them offhand, might tame them and make them dependent.'*

One authority has put forward a theoretical time-sequence for the domestication of the different groups. First the scavengers, such as the dog; second nomadic animals such as the reindeer, goat and sheep; third beasts for which a settled life is essential—cattle and pigs; finally animals that can be used for transport including the horse, the ass and the llama. While the dog was certainly domesticated in Mesolithic times, and the horse not until after the Primary Neolithic period, the validity of the distinction between the other two classes is very dubious. However, it will be remembered that at the Belt Cave in northern Iran domesticated sheep and goats were found in the earliest, pre-pottery, Neolithic occupation dated by Carbon-14 to the first half of the sixth millennium, while pigs (the earliest known in the world) and cattle did not appear until the later Neolithic occupation dated to the second half of the same millennium.

This evidence supports the priority of sheep and goats in order of domestication. Nevertheless it may be a purely local state of affairs, and not too much weight should be given to it. It has already been suggested in discussing the origins of the Neolithic way of life in general that it is wrong to look for a single precisely limited centre. Once the idea of taking partial charge of certain animals had got about, trials, some of them successful, are likely to have been made in a number of regions and by divers methods.

The biological aspects of domestication must be briefly considered. The beasts composing the early flocks and herds in the cradlelands of farming, and those later led into Europe, were usually much smaller than their wild counterparts. The cattle in particular (*Bos longifrons*) were as diminutive as the modern Kerry. The usually accepted explanation is that wherever possible men selected the occasional dwarf from among the wild stock, and continued to

* V. Gordon Childe, *New Light on the Most Ancient East.*

be best able to keep and to breed from the smaller, weaker and more docile animals. It was only much later when domestication was complete and irreversible that their human masters could afford to reintroduce a strain from the larger wild breeds and to select for size and weight. Most bodily changes that have taken place in domestic animals have been due to selective breeding—for example the increased woolliness of sheep. On the other hand there does seem some tendency at least in dogs and pigs (though see below) to become progressively shorter in the muzzle, and for their coats to lose their natural protective shading and assume bright colours and piebald markings.

Sheep and Goats

In spite of a human inclination to estimate sheep and goats very differently, it is in fact difficult to distinguish between these two members of the sub-family *Caprinae* by their skeletal remains alone, very slight differences in the cannon bones and in the bones round the eye being almost the only reliable indication. It is already apparent from Chapter VIII that in practice it has very often proved impossible to determine whether particular Neolithic peoples kept goats, sheep, or both together.

All modern domestic sheep appear to be descended from three existing types of wild *Ovis*. The most important, because it was probably the species originally domesticated by the pioneer herdsmen of south-west Asia, is the urial (*Ovis vignei*) which has a vast Asiatic range from the Elburz mountains to Tibet. It has a fawny brown coat with a darker band along the back; this is hairy on top but conceals wool below. The ram has large horns curving outwards and backwards, the ewe small prick horns like a goat. If this was the breed first tamed in regions south of the Elburz (and represented by those very early animals found in the Belt Cave), it was certainly also the one first to be carried westward with the farming economy into Europe, for it is represented by *O. aries palustris,* the famous 'Turbary' sheep of the earliest Swiss lake-dwellers. It was, indeed, the breed raised by most of the Early Neolithic farmers of Europe.

Another type of wild sheep with domestic offspring is the mouflon (*Ovis musimon*) with a rather more westerly range than the Urial; today varieties live in southern Europe (Sicily, Corsica and Sardinia) where they must originally have had a more extensive territory. It is also found in Cyprus; its area of distribution extends eastward from central Anatolia to northern Iran. It is rather like the urial in appearance although with a somewhat darker, more reddish brown, coat; the ewes are hornless. It is not known where the Mouflon was first domesticated, but it undoubtedly was introduced into Europe at a later date than the Turbary—for it does not appear among the Swiss lake-villages until the very end of their Neolithic occupation.

A third wild species that has contributed to our modern stock is the Argali (*Ovis ammon*) at home in the highlands of central Asia. It is very large, and bears long horns making a forward turning coil. It is possible that such a powerful animal would not have found favour among the early domesticators. Its earliest recorded presence seems to be as a cross with urial at Anau at the end of the Neolithic occupation there. Argali elements certainly spread westward and are dominant in the Merino breed. A beast apparently representing a pure argali variety was found in deposits in the English Thames dating from Bronze Age times.

It is still impossible to give any coherent account of the domestication of what was probably man's first milk-giver —the goat. It is likely, however, that the Bezoar goat of Turkestan and Afghanistan was the most important ancestral species.

The Big Horn is the wild sheep native to the New World. It was never domesticated, sheep not having been kept by the pre-Columban peoples of America.

Cattle

All humpless breeds of cattle are believed to be descendants of the wild *Bos primigenius,* or aurochs, which was a native of the plains from southern Russia to the Altais. The bull of this species is huge and carries wide, outspreading horns. Yet the cow (as is well shown among the Lascaux cave-paintings) has a much lighter build and more sharply curved little horns, and altogether looks less unlike the small, short-horned *Bos longifrons* (or *Bos brachyceros*) that composed the herds of most Neolithic farmers alike in the primary areas of south-west Asia, in Egypt and in Europe. At present, then, we have to accept the view that these little cattle were obtained by giving preference to dwarfs and weaklings. Here and there, as in Britain, re-admixture with the wild aurochs evidently took place even in these early times. That it took place subsequently in many areas is shown clearly enough in the heavy long-horned oxen that still pull carts and ploughs in so many quarters of the Old

World. Breeds in which the *Bos primigenius* element is even stronger are found surviving in small pockets in remote places—as, for example, the highland cattle of Scotland.

It is very interesting to find the humped zebu (*Bos indicus*) already fully developed in one of the earliest of the upland sites in Baluchistan, supposedly founded as much as five hundred years earlier than the Indus civilization itself. This was at Rana Ghundai in the Zhob valley, where the bones lay among the remains of the oldest occupation—apparently a camp of partly nomadic herders. The zebu is also depicted in a highly stylized fashion on the pottery of some of these early upland village sites. No wild humped species is known, and it seems likely that this development, apparently a method of storing extra fat comparable to that of the fat-tailed sheep, must have arisen with domestication.

Pigs

Although in the theoretical classification of domestic animals quoted above the pig is put with cattle as demanding a life of settled farming, it may first have been attracted to human settlements as a scavenger. It seems very likely that two wild breeds were severally domesticated, though crossed in later times. The common wild boar (portrayed in all its savagery by many Palaeolithic painters) is native right across Europe, north Africa and central Asia as far as Siberia. This is *Sus scrofa,* undoubtedly the ancestor of the oldest known domestic pigs, those whose remains were left in the Belt Cave over seven thousand years ago, and of most of the pigs found on Neolithic sites throughout south-west Asia, Egypt and Europe. The Turbary pig of the Swiss lake-villages is sometimes distinguished as *Sus scrofa palustris.* The second ancestor is *Sus vittatus,* a wild pig with a much shorter snout at home in south-east Asia. This species is the prototype of the pigs kept by the first Chinese farmers (p. 346).

Llama and Alpaca

Very little is known of the domestication of these two species (both related to the camel) which were the only large domestic animals of the New World. As has been said, they were limited to the highlands of South America. The llama is undoubtedly descended from the wild guanaco, and it is interesting to find that its coat shows just the same tendency to strong colour and piebald marking found in the domestic

animals of the Old World. The wild ancestor of the alpaca
seems to have died out—unless indeed this animal was the
result of a cross between the guanaco and the vicuna. It
can be argued that the llama was only partially domesticated,
in ancient times as today, for it probably often found its
own food and shelter and calved away from human surroundings. Neither it nor the alpaca has ever been brought
to the stage of domestication at which it could be milked.

Horses and Camels

Horse bones have occasionally been found on the Neolithic sites in both Europe and Asia. The camel was very dubi-
ously reported at certain Tripolye sites. Both occurred in the
same early level at Rana Ghundai in Baluchistan that yielded
the remains of zebu. There is little question that the story
of the domestication of these transport animals belongs in
great part to a later phase of human history.

FARMING METHODS

The definitive basis of the primary Neolithic economy was
small-scale cultivation with hoe or digging-stick from villages or hamlets, and the pasturing of flocks and herds on
surrounding uncultivated pastures. The greater part of this
early farming was developed on light upland soils or on such
spreads of light soil as the loess and the yellow earth. In
Egypt the Neolithic farmers were certainly raising crops on
the changing flood plains of the Nile and as the deserts
parched they must have come to rely more and more on
the *wadis* for pasture. With the more systematic cultivation
of the flood plains both in Egypt and Iraq (by the Amratians
and al'Ubaid people) the true primary Neolithic period is
coming to an end. Simple diversion of river- or spring-water
for agriculture may have been used by these peoples as also,
earlier, by the inhabitants of Jericho and other dwellers beside oases. But systematic irrigation, like the use of the
plough, belongs to the next stage of man's agricultural progress. Chapter VIII has shown that while one of the
prime reasons for the diffusion of farming eastward, and
more particularly westward, was soil exhaustion and the
need to clear fresh land, in the early centres in south-west
Asia and south-east Europe villages were inhabited for generation after generation until their rubbish and disintegrated
houses accumulated into mounds. How this was possible in

upland regions with none of the natural soil renewal of the great river valleys is an issue that has been very generally avoided. It seems that these farmers must have learnt how to use manure, perhaps by folding animals on the stubble, or else were organized for the rotation of crops. There is as yet no evidence for either of these methods. Only in the Swiss lake-villages (which would appear to have been more stable than most western Neolithic settlements) have signs been observed of the collection of manure.

On the expanding frontiers of farming the normal procedure was for exhausted plots and the villages from which they had been worked to be deserted and new land cleared. Remarkable indications of the clearance and reversion of land have been detected in Denmark by means of pollen analysis. Here the first farmers had to tackle clearance of a kind that seems always to have been too much for the loess-loving Danubians: the clearance of deciduous forest. Studies were made in Danish bogs and 'it was found that at several places on the border between Atlantic and sub-Boreal times there was a sudden change in the country's vegetation. The forest trees (oak, ash, elm and lime) receded rapidly relatively to the herbaceous plants, indicating that clearances had been made in the once all-dominating forests. At this same time horizon layers of charcoal were observed in the bog and the first discovery was made of the pollen of cultivated cereals and of weeds normally found only in the vicinity of farmers and their dwellings. . . . These clearances were made at slightly different times in the various areas studied. The subsequent recovery of the forest can also be traced in the peat; after a local destruction of this kind the quick-growing birch returned first, then the other trees in the same sequence as in a corresponding process today.'* On one bog it even proved possible to record several superimposed clearance horizons, 'first somewhat faint, then more vigorous and, evidently, much more durable'. It has been insisted that the forests were fought by fire and axe as much to win pasture and fodder for the livestock as to get soil for crops. Thus it was definitely not fire-clearance farming such as that still practised in the conifer forests of Carelia. These horizons date from the earlier Neolithic phase in Denmark, though not from the very first known farming immigration. They gave a marvellously convincing picture of the conditions of the Neolithic farming frontier in forest coun-

* C. J. Becker, 'The Introduction of Farming into Northern Europe'. Paper contributed for the *Journal of World History*, February 1955.

try. Pollen grains invisible to the naked eye have brought
back a forgotten pioneering world.

The storage of grain both for seed and for winter consumption was of immense economic importance to the Neolithic peasant communities. Here, indeed, was the chief
factor making possible the increase in numbers that everywhere accompanied the adoption of farming. In a dry
country such as Egypt, storage pits lined with basketry could
be sunk into the ground as they were in the Fayum (p. 412),
while baskets and large pottery jars were also used. The
Danubians (and probably many other Neolithic agriculturalists in countries with a considerable rainfall) took great trouble over the construction of stilted granaries. Presumably
threshing was everywhere done on floors in or near the villages, and the straw kept for fodder and bedding.

Theoretically it seems that there must have been an early
period when livestock were kept for meat, skins and perhaps hair and wool, and not for milk. Unfortunately nothing
is known as to when milking, cheese-making and other dairy
work began, or whether they were already practised by
Neolithic farmers during their spread into Europe.

NOTES TO CHAPTER X

1. Professor S. Mizuno points out that it is nevertheless worth noting
   that in south-east Asia tuberous plants such as the yam and taro
   have always played an important part and may perhaps be associated
   with the first stages in the planting of crops.
2. According to Professor S. Mizuno rice was undoubtedly cultivated
   during the Neolithic era in northern China. Also in southern China
   there are plenty of rice remains from the Neolithic sites.
3. Both Professor K. Birket-Smith and C. A. Nordman point out that
   many scholars hold a view contrary to that of H. Pohlhausen (*Das
   Wanderhirtentum und seine Vorstufen* [Brunswick, 1954]), and date
   the beginning of the domestication of the reindeer to a relatively late
   period [see K. Jettmar, 'Zu den Anfängen der Rentierzucht', *Anthropos*, 47 (1952), pp. 737–66].

CHAPTER XI

MATERIAL CULTURE

JUST as the habits of Palaeolithic man as a hunter and food-gatherer had harmonized with those of the natural world, so, too, his dwellings had made little or no difference to the prospects of nature. Caves and rock-shelters, low and shapeless huts, were hardly more conspicuously artificial than birds' nests or warrens. But with man's entry into the Neolithic phase he began fairly rapidly to assert himself, even though for the most part his building still lacked the formal qualities of true architecture. In many parts of the world villages grew up with houses that in one way or another asserted man's imaginative power and new control of materials; here and there before the end of the period he had raised temples and monumental tombs.

Needless to say caves were still inhabited. In very many lands, and those not all uncivilized, they are still lived in today. But the great increase in population, and still more the need for agriculturalists to live where there was no natural shelter, necessitated extensive domestic building that was bound in time to develop into domestic architecture.

DOMESTIC BUILDING

In the Neolithic stage of economy, houses were everywhere built of local materials. These always played a considerable part in determining the plan and construction of the building. Thus although a change from, say, a round to a rectangular house plan is likely to mean a break in cultural tradition if it takes place within one region, such a contrast between one region and another may have little cultural significance. The use of large timbers on the one hand and of reed or matting screens on the other is very likely to result in a rectangular plan; any form of weaving (as in wattle and daub) round saplings or flexible poles favours a circular one. Stone, mud-brick and most other forms of pisé can be used equally well for either. Pit-dwellings tend to range from roughly round to sub-rectangular because exact shapes and straight lines are not easily produced by digging into the ground with primitive picks and spades. At the Yang-shao village of Pan-p'o (p. 347) the houses were both round and rectangular.

Climate is, of course, another natural factor strongly affecting domestic building. Whereas in warm countries flimsy modes of construction might go with reasonable domestic conditions, solid wind- and rain-proof houses were essential in many parts of Europe and Asia. Cold, and more particularly windy, climates encouraged the sinking of house floors below ground level and the screening of the entrance to the living-room with a porch or anteroom. Again, the sun-dried brick or other pisé construction, so popular, because so easily made, in south-west Asia, China and Africa, were out of the question in more temperate lands where rain was frequent and the sun lacked the necessary hardening power.

Pisé typically consists of soil (with as high a clay content as is available) tempered with chopped straw or dung, mixed with water and well trodden. It can be raised into solid walls between plank caissons, but the usual method in Neolithic times and afterwards was to make it into rough blocks, or moulded bricks. These, having been either patted up on a flat surface or pushed into a rectangular mould, were put out to dry in the sun—and turned from time to time until fully hardened. As the sun could effect no chemical change such as takes place when a brick is kiln-fired, the pisé blocks were liable to dissolve or crumble. A house built from them might not stand for more than two generations. As, however, it disintegrated without leaving any awkward and intractable rubble, a new one could easily be built on top of it. This relatively rapid replacement of pisé and other mud buildings is the chief explanation for the accumulation of mounds (*tells* and *tepes*) on permanent settlement sites. Although they were slight compared with the vast accumulations that formed below the later cities, even Neolithic villages could (as we have seen) accumulate a considerable thickness of layers. At Jericho the Neolithic levels were 44 feet thick.

The oldest-known farmers' houses are those of Jericho and Jarmo, and in both stone as well as pisé had been employed. The Jericho houses appear to have been close packed inside the walls very much as in the poorer quarters of modern towns where mud-brick is still in use. The oldest dwellings, those belonging to the older of the two pre-pottery Neolithic settlements, were rounded in plan and approached through a projecting porch with steps or a short ramp leading down to a sunk floor level. Although mainly of sun-dried brick of plano-convex, hog-backed form, some stone was used in the walls. At least in some the brick walls seem to have been carried up into domed roofs. The second pre-pottery Neolithic people of Tahunian culture brought with them a sharply contrasting type of domestic architecture. Their houses were rectangular and much more complex in plan, with a series of well-proportioned living-rooms. These were approached through a courtyard which also gave access to storage rooms and other outbuildings. More remarkable still was the careful interior decoration of the living-rooms. The walls were lined with lime plaster and sometimes painted. The floors were also plastered, burnished with

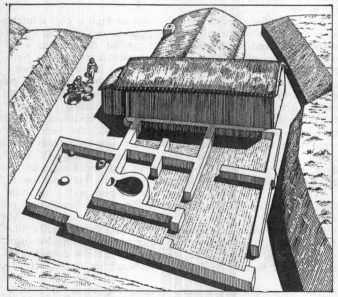

FIG. 38A. *Plan of Neolithic house in Iraq: Jarmo (after Braid-wood, courtesy of the Oriental Institute, University of Chicago).*

smooth stones to obtain a high polish, and furnished with circular mats of plaited rush. The door frames were of wood, but probably closed with skin curtains rather than by doors. The bricks used for these later houses were also different from the earlier, and highly distinctive. They were shaped like flattened cigars and their makers had used their

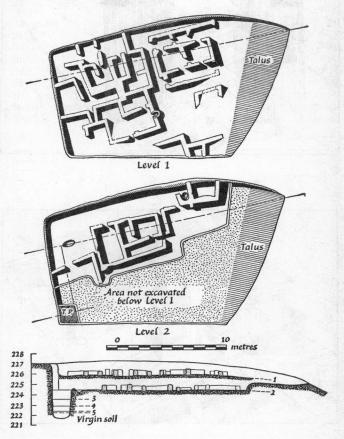

FIG. 38B. *Plan of Neolithic house in Iraq: Matarrah (after Braidwood, courtesy of the Oriental Institute, University of Chicago).*

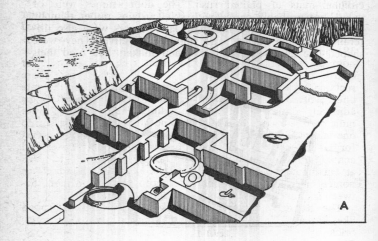

FIG. 39. *Neolithic house at Hassuna. A: remains as found; B: reconstruction (after Singer).*

thumbs to impress a herringbone pattern on the upper surface.

At Jarmo the houses consisted of several rectangular rooms built of pisé on a stone footing; they were furnished with ovens and basins sunk in the floors. At Hassuna (Fig. 39) the development is striking; immediately overlying the nomadic squatting place, the earliest true houses were of coarse rammed or kneaded clay, some round, some more rectangular, but generally lacking in formal plan; the late ones evolved towards a rectangular house of several rooms adjoining a courtyard with outbuildings. Here the walls were built of pisé blocks and had become completely merged into one another. Storage space was made by sunk jars (the oldest form) and by pits sometimes lined with gypsum plaster and coated with bitumen. The Jericho houses and these later ones at Hassuna give the best idea of the relatively commodious homes enjoyed by the most prosperous of the farmers between six and eight thousand years ago.

The houses at Cypriote Khirokitia were beehive-shaped like those of the early period at Jericho. Walls of mud-brick or pisé, well smoothed, rose from stone foundations. They were entered through wooden-framed doors, and floors, sunk slightly below ground level, were furnished with central clay hearths. A remarkable feature in several of these houses was a partial upper floor below the domed roof supported on square limestone pillars. Niches and cupboards might be let into these pillars. Some prosperous households at Khirokitia lived in compounds with a kitchen and workshops grouped round the main dwelling house.

Other comparable Neolithic sites have nothing very remarkable to add. In the Syro-Cilician region stone foundations and traces of wattle and daub as well as pisé walls have been found. Away to the north at the oasis site of Sialk where reeds were available these were used by the earliest settlers, but were later given up in favour of pisé. The al'Ubaid people who first settled the Euphrates delta lands, where there must have been vast stretches of reed beds, developed a much more elaborate reed architecture in which closely tied bundles were used as framework and the walls thickly plastered with mud.

Special mention should perhaps be made here of the domed, tholos-like rooms discovered in the Halafian occupation at Arpachiyah near Nineveh, and thought to be household 'chapels' or shrines rather than living-rooms. They were of mud-brick on a stone foundation. It seems very probable that stone-founded circular constructions found at another

Halafian site, Yunus, and identified as 'kilns', were in fact similar ceremonial rooms and that this architectural peculiarity was characteristic of the Halafians. Many authorities believe it to have inspired the tholos tombs of the central Mediterranean and through them the megalithic passage-grave architecture of western and northern Europe.

In Egypt, rainless and warm, the pre-Dynastic villagers found no great need for substantial houses. In the lake-side settlements of the Fayum the huts were too flimsy to leave any trace beyond their fire-holes and basket-lined grain storage pits; so, too, were the first dwellings at Merimde. Later on, however, shelters seem to have been built from reed mats fastened to posts, and later again (perhaps as protection against the worsening sand storms) the Merimdians learnt how to build dome-shaped huts of rammed mud. To judge from Merimde, Egyptian villages may have been rather more spacious than the huddled ones of south-west Asia, for here the huts were ranged in rows, each in a garden or spacious yard, giving access to what must have been village lanes. Up river at Badari, families lived in matting huts very much like those of the second period at Merimde.

In north-west India the domestic builders probably followed the same general methods as those of Iraq and Iran. At the pre-Indus upland village site of Rana-Ghundai the houses were built on footings of boulders, but little seems to have been recorded as to their plan.

A great deal is known about the houses of the Neolithic farmers who spread westward through Europe. Here stone and wood were usual along the Mediterranean, and substantial wooden construction in the forested zones. The Neolithic houses of Crete were made of rather planless groups of little rectangular rooms raised on stone foundations. The El Garcel villagers (probably of African origin) preferred oval pit-dwellings for their hill-top settlements. The Vardar-Morava people to some extent represent an outpost of Asiatic tradition in that in addition to wattle and daub they sometimes built mud-brick houses. The related Boians, however, as we have seen (p. 341), lived in stout houses of split logs, while their neighbours, the Oltenians, already built the rectangular type of house with an anteroom or porch, known as the megaron, that was to have a long and distinguished development among the Greeks. The Oltenians were also responsible for a very early exercise of fantasy in domestic architecture, for the people of Erosd crowned their gables with elaborate spiral-shaped clay finials. Enough has already been said of the comfortable porched houses of the prosperous peasants of the Black Earth lands of the Ukraine.

The dwellings of the Neolithic Danubians seem to have evolved through three styles. The first (until recently believed to have been barns) were very imposing, long, rectangular houses sometimes as much as 32 metres in length. The central ridge of the steeply pitched roof was supported on a line of posts, flanked by a further line on each side that presumably helped to support the sloping rafters. These long houses were divided into two parts, one end having a raised floor and walls of split logs sunk into the sub-soil, the other lighter walling of wattle and daub. Perhaps the timbered end only was used for human living, the rest being handed over to the animals or used for stores. From these first houses, among the finest built in Neolithic Europe, the later Danubians seem to have changed to a smaller, two-roomed megaron type of house, and then to a still smaller one-roomed form. Some of the second type were built on marshy ground on the Federsee in Württemberg, supported on a framework of beams and floored with a substantial platform of timber (Fig. 41). Typically each house was rectangular and had two rooms—an anteroom and an inner chamber. The roof was gabled and the walls were of split sapling and wattle. In the anteroom, a beam with mortise holes for two uprights lay before the open hearth; it was probably part of a drying frame. In the inner room, in the right-hand corner were supports for a raised couch or bench, and a hearth lay against the partition. It is thought that the food and materials were prepared in the outer room, where there was normally a clay oven for baking bread. In front of each house was a planked forecourt, presumably a place for working and sitting. These Aichbuhl houses are a little later than our primary Neolithic diffusion, but the simple peasant interior that they suggest probably offers a fair picture of great numbers of Neolithic homes in central Europe. They, their larger predecessors, and indeed most of the wooden houses of Neolithic Europe, demanded much labour and not inconsiderable carpentering skill. Probably the long-handled adze was the principal wood-working tool used by the Danubian house-builders.

In spite of the preservation of so many of the perishable possessions of the Cortaillod people of Switzerland, the exact plan of their dwellings is uncertain—though perhaps generally rectangular. They stood in small groups on the damp or boggy margins of the lakes. Although it is now the prevalent view that they did not stand on raised piles, there is

no question that in many instances piles were driven into the
soft soil beneath them to discourage sinking. Some had
wooden floors supported on sticks or timbers resting directly
on the wet ground. Others utilized long sheets of bark to
keep out the damp, while others again had clay floors. Clay
hearths were a common feature, and often they had to be
renewed again and again as they sank into the soft soil beneath. Nothing is known of the plan of the only Neolithic
lake-dwelling to have been recognized in Britain, at Ehenside
Tarn, Cumberland.

Not very much is known, either, of other forms of domestic architecture among the Windmill Hill people of Britain.
They certainly camped at least seasonally in their hill-top
enclosures (p. 396). Hearths and rubbish pits have been found
in the interior, and considerable quantities of domestic rubbish in the ditches. One oval hut was found inside the entrance of a camp in Devon, otherwise true house remains
are unknown in them.

Another Windmill Hill house has been found at Haldon,
also in Devon; it was a small rectangular building about
6 metres long with stone footings that probably supported
wattle-and-daub walls; it may have had a screened-off anteroom, and an inner living-room with a hearth in one corner.

In Denmark we are once more in country where long
houses in wood were apparently the usual form of Early
Neolithic domestic building. It will be remembered that at
Barkaer in east Jutland the earliest Trichterbecher farmers
seem to have lived many families together in two immensely
long houses (one was 85 by 65 metres) divided into a number of rooms about 3 metres across. These were not of solid
timber construction but were built of poles with branches
plaited between them. Such communal long-houses recall
those of the north-west coast Indians of America. Fine
wooden houses, belonging to a rather later phase of the Danish Neolithic, are those of the village of Troldebjerg where
there was a long row of rectangular buildings, at least two
of which were houses about 30 metres long. They may be
compared with the lovely farm-houses still characteristic of
the Black Forest country of Germany, in that their gabled
roofs sloped right down to the ground on one side and
covered both the family living-room and the stalls of the
beasts.

One other site in the extreme north of Europe deserves
description here, even although it falls a little later in time
than the primary Neolithic phase. This is the village of
Skara Brae in the Orkney Islands that was built by a com-

munity of stock-breeders directly descended from the native Mesolithic population of Britain. Probably by the time they were making their homes in these bleak and remote islands bronze was already coming into use in England, but their own economy remained fully Neolithic. The compact little village was built in a hollow among sand-dunes, and the excellent pasture of the treeless (because gale-swept) countryside made possible a settled economy; Skara Brae was continuously inhabited for many generations. The houses were squarish though with rounded corners, measuring up to 20 by 18 feet and with substantial stone-built walls. The roofs were partly corbelled but the central opening may have been closed with whale-bone rafters. Each was entered through a very narrow entrance only 4 feet high closed by

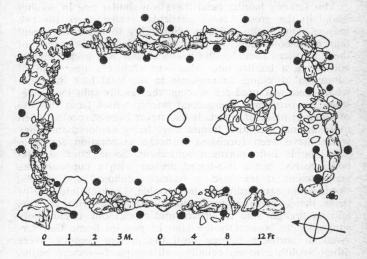

FIG. 40. *Plan of Neolithic house at Knockadoon, Limerick, Ireland (after O'Riordain). Black spots mark postholes.*

a door, presumably of stone, which could be fastened by a bar of stone or whale-bone. In the centre was a square hearth on which a peat fire burned (with a stone seat beside it). On either side were beds, enclosed by stone slabs, once containing a mattress of heather and covered with a canopy of skins supported by stone bed posts. Shelves in the walls above the beds served to store personal possessions. Small

boxes of thin slabs with carefully luted joints let into the
floor seem to have been intended to hold liquids. A two-
shelved dresser of stone stood against the back wall. One
to three small cells opened off each hut; some may have
been used as storerooms, others as privies, since they are
drained. The huts were grouped into regular clusters connected by paved alleys. In its final form Skara Brae comprised
six or seven dwellings and one 'industrial hut' (probably
used communally) that lacked the usual beds and dresser
but was provided with a kiln and had been used as a workshop by a chert-knapper. The alleys connecting the houses
were all roofed over and the whole complex buried in sand,
refuse and ash. Skara Brae was drained by a system of
stone-lined sewers running under the huts.

This Orkney hamlet (and there is a similar one in another
island in the group) is of particular interest here for two
reasons. One is the extreme adaptability to the environment
that it demonstrates. In response to the tireless winds of
these northern latitudes the whole cluster was under shelter,
converting a hamlet into what was almost a new kind of
communal dwelling. In response to the total lack of wood,
whale-bone was used for roofing, the readily split local flag-
stone for furniture. The second interest arises from this use
of stone in place of wood. It had never been suspected when
more normal Neolithic homes were being explored that they
would have been furnished with the elaboration found in
this humble little northern settlement. Some kind of box-
bed possibly, but a two-tiered dresser with a cupboard-like
arrangement at the base, a bedside cupboard and closets,
would seem extraordinarily improbable. Looking into one of
these living-rooms and imagining the place with its furs
and its firelight and its ornamental crocks one could easily
suppose it to be exactly the kind of peasant home that survived in northern Europe until the present century. Were
other Neolithic homes equally well equipped—indeed better,
as would befit the larger houses and richer communities to
be found in easier lands? It can hardly be doubted that they
were. Indeed, reflecting again on these interiors where the
furnishings have been, as it were, petrified into survival, it
appears that just as farmers were from the first dependent
on the same cattle and sheep, wheat, barley and maize that
are still the basis of our lives today, so, too, almost from
the first they found how to satisfy the essential needs of a
simple peasant life in a manner that was to endure for many
thousands of years: the hearth and the fireside seat, the
comfortable bed and the dresser with its utensils.

Before leaving Neolithic dwellings we should perhaps look across to what is almost the opposite limit of our range from the far north-western Orkney Islands. The Yang-shao pig-keepers of China sheltered themselves in roughly rounded pit-dwellings, and enclosed their villages within mud-built walls.

At the village of Pan-p'o, Shensi province (p. 347), the rectangular houses were from 4 to 6 metres long with rounded corners and floors sunk up to a metre below ground. The walls were of clay containing grass, and the roofs of the same mixture above rafters supported on central posts. Most of the round houses were built on the ground surface without sunken floors. In construction they were similar to the rectangular ones except that inside the clay walls were reinforced by a ring of small posts or poles.

The houses of the pre-pottery farmers in the Andes were usually roughly oval, with floors sunk into the ground and lined with cobbles. The roofs did not rise much above ground-level and were supported on wooden or whale-bone rafters.

VILLAGES AND ROADS

When we come to consider the characteristics of Neolithic settlements as a whole, it is evident that they vary with local circumstances even more than do individual houses. It would be true to generalize to the extent of saying that in the earlier phases defences were usually absent or slight owing to the pacific temper of primary Neolithic economies. A ditch and palisade against wild animals or straying cattle was frequent enough, but anything on a scale to be called military

FIG. 41. *Neolithic village of the Danubian culture: Federsee, Germany* [reconstruction (after Coon)].

works very exceptional. Yet we at once have to recognize
the great exception presented by Jericho. Jarmo and other
early villages in south-west Asia seem to have been entirely
open. Yet the earliest Jericho had masonry walls of massive
mortared stone that still stand to a height of 12 feet. An
internal drum tower had a long flight of steps running down
from its summit, through its solid core to street level. (Pl.
9, b). Tanks seem to have been built against it for water
storage. Thus nine thousand years ago there were already
men living in surroundings not at all unlike those of a small
mediaeval town.

At the typical Danubian village of Köln-Lindenthal (Fig.
42) the first houses were unprotected for a while, then later
fenced against animals. It was only after the site had been
deserted by these shifting agriculturalists and reoccupied at
a time when land shortage was beginning to make itself felt
that a part of the village was strongly entrenched. The 'interrupted ditch camps' of the Windmill Hill people of southern
England were curious structures. Usually built round hill-
tops, there were two or more concentric rings of earthworks;
the banks appear to have been continuous, but the ditches
from which they were dug were no more than intermittent,
thus forming a chain of long pits. The banks were sometimes
reinforced by palisades. As we have seen (p. 336) these places
were probably seasonally occupied camps rather than true
villages. Rather similar entrenchments were dug by the
Michelsberg people in south-west Germany. Stone or earth
walls and embankments seem often to have been raised
round hill-top settlements by the western Neolithic peoples of
France. The Camp de Chassey, Le Campigny, Fort Harrouard and the Camp de Catnoy are all possible examples,
but the exact period in their history at which they were
fortified is uncertain. Undoubtedly, however, these hill-top
settlements look defensive, and the possibility that the western
farmers felt a need for protection against indigenous peoples
of Mesolithic tradition cannot be ignored.

The internal structure of the villages would have varied
with the architecture. In many of the Asiatic villages where
the houses were close-set rectangular buildings the roads between them would have been narrow, crooked alley-ways;
at Arpachiyah the alleys were cobbled. At Khirokitia a paved
'high street' ran through the settlement, with stone ramps
leading down to the individual houses. In Egypt, Merimde
gives evidence for straighter, more open lanes running between the fences of gardens or yards. In most European

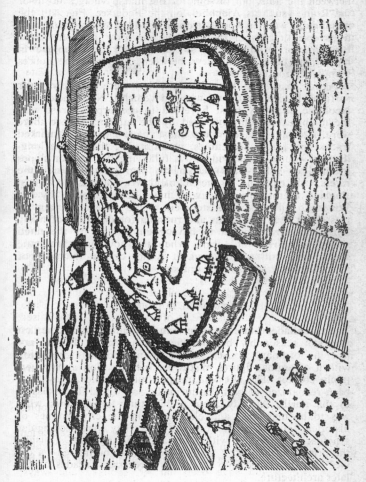

FIG. 42. *Neolithic village of the Danubian culture: Köln-Lindenthal [reconstruction].*

villages there were presumably simply stony or muddy paths between the huts, but in some of the marsh villages north of the Rhine (such as Aichbhul, on the Federsee, Fig. 41) the rectangular wooden houses fronted roads carefully made with transverse timbers in the regular 'corduroy' fashion. Skara Brae in the Orkneys was, so far as is known, unique in having the little paved alleys between the few stone houses completely roofed over.

As for roads outside settlements, they were probably never surfaced before the use of wheeled vehicles. Nevertheless the Neolithic economy must have led to a sharp contrast with the unobtrusive pathways used by the hunters. Where there were sizeable villages there must have been well-marked tracks and fords. Sometimes, undoubtedly, there were long-distance routes, either ridgeways following the tops or slopes of hills, or valley-ways keeping to firm ground beside the rivers. An example is the Icknield Way across south-east England that seems already to have been followed by the Windmill Hill folk. The stone-cut tracks of Malta, pairs of ruts about 4½ feet across and running for distances of many miles, are now thought to have been formed by the tilted sledge or *travois,* at a time when the now bare limestone slopes were still soil-covered. It is not certain that any of them date back to Neolithic times.

CEREMONIAL BUILDINGS

The colonnaded building at Jericho is unquestionably the first that can reasonably be identified as a temple. It was not like the ordinary houses in the town, and the association with it of animal figures makes the identification almost certainly correct. The al'Ubaid people built temples: they have been recognized at both Eridu in the south and Tepe Gawra in the north. Already their architecture foreshadows what was to be magnified and elaborated in the city temples of historical times. Founded on platforms, they were rectangular sanctuaries furnished with altar and offering-table. Outside, the prismatic mud-brick walls were heavily buttressed—a device that developed into the striking recessed façades of the later architecture.

Jericho and the al'Ubaid villages show that when communities were beginning to lose their simple rural character and develop towards little towns, special buildings might be communally instituted as places of worship—and perhaps served by a small priesthood. But this was not the usual pattern for primary Neolithic societies. Mention has already been made of the circular domed shrines at Arpachiyah. The latest and largest of them was as much as 30 feet across, and approached by an anteroom 60 feet long. Images of the Mother Goddess were associated with one of them. But such sanctuaries were exceptional; usually the Neolithic folk kept their cult objects in their own huts and houses and had not thought of combining to build places of public worship.

Something must be said of what might be taken as striking exceptions to this pattern: the great temples of Malta. These were built by villagers living in a genuinely Neolithic cultural stage; on the other hand this island population was certainly retarded, remaining long without metal and developing striking local peculiarities in isolation. The temples, like the megalithic tombs with which they have affinities, were in part inspired from the centres of civilization. In this sense they are not truly a part of primary Neolithic culture, yet they, like the tombs, show what Neolithic communities could do under the stimulus of a religious idea. The temples, such as the two finest examples of Hagiar Kim and Mnaijdra, are composed of double apsidal chambers, the apse roofed by corbelling (Pl. II). The entrance-ways, communicating doorways and certain recesses are made of enormous blocks of stone, some of the doorways are closed by slabs perforated to make a small round opening. The walls are sometimes formed by stone slabs set alternately flat and edgeways on, the edges projecting a little beyond the flats. These sanctuaries have been many times altered or remodelled, and it appears that the latest refinements were made well into the second millennium B C. In these later stages at least, if not before, the blocks of masonry have been accurately shaped with stone hammers, sometimes given a kind of ornamental rustication, and enriched with spiral designs and processions of men and animals. The presence in these strange buildings of many cult objects, mostly evidently related to the Mother Goddess, prove them to have been religious in purpose and therefore legitimately to be described as temples. Certain buildings in the Balearic Islands may be related, although they belong to a full Bronze Age; while they have some features in common with the Maltese buildings, they are particularly distinguished by pillars supporting large flat slabs and so resembling gigantic pedestal tables. It has been suggested that these *taulas* are merely roof-trees, but it is more probable that they have some cultic significance.

There is no question that in their origins the Maltese temples have some relationship with the megalithic and related funerary architecture of the western Mediterranean and Atlantic coast lands (p. 340). In these tombs, too, we are again dealing with a trait derived ultimately from a higher culture that was grafted on to local cultures still in a Neolithic stage of development. Enough has already been said of the history and general forms of this remarkable architecture—certainly among the greatest and most imaginative achievements ever made by peoples dependent on a primitive rural economy. It would, however, be appropriate here to say a little more about the building methods employed. Both the passage-grave and gallery forms might sometimes be cut into limestone, chalk or other soft rocks, sometimes built in the true megalithic style with huge blocks weighing many tons. Again, particularly with passage-graves, small drystone building might be favoured, or, very commonly, the drystone technique be used in conjunction with megaliths. Often the large blocks are unshaped or only roughly dressed and the building therefore of a very crude though monumental kind. On the other hand where, as in the enormous passage-grave of Maes Howe in the Orkney Islands, the local stone is laminated and readily splits into regular shapes, an extraordinarily exact and narrow-jointed masonry was obtained. The corbelling of the roofs of the main chambers of passage-graves was often executed skilfully and on a massive scale. The apex of the roof of the richly carved New Grange in Ireland is nearly 20 feet above the floor, that of Maes Howe originally about 15 feet. In their total length chamber and passage may be over 65 feet, while the covering mounds are frequently large enough to support small churches built on them by Christians anxious to counteract the influence of lingering pagan customs. The galleries, though generally smaller than the passage-graves, are often very roomy; an example in Scandinavia, walled with huge orthostats, is as much as seven feet high throughout. In very many types of tomb strong architectural emphasis was put upon the portal, both at the outer entrance and at the openings to inner chambers. Sometimes, dummies were made, either to conceal the real entrance or to serve as a purely ceremonial feature. These monumental trilithon portals must be related to those dominating the Maltese temples, and may conceivably lie at the back of the trilithon construction at the great Bronze Age temple of Stonehenge in southern England.

It is appropriate here to mention the Late Neolithic sanctuary that has been proved to underlie the Bronze Age monument at Stonehenge. It was a circular embanked area with a ring of ritual pits inside the bank and numbers of cremated burials. There is no evidence for any settlement in the immediate neighbourhood. This earliest sanctuary at Stonehenge is chiefly of value in warning us that although places for public worship or ritual may not be found in Neolithic settlements, it does not follow they never existed. Sometimes, and particularly among the more highly pastoral and therefore less settled Neolithic societies, there may have been ritual meeting-places raised and used by scattered communities ranging over wide territories.

Our ignorance of the Early Neolithic scene is still much greater than our knowledge. The passage of thousands of years and the activities of hundreds of later generations have allowed little enough to survive of the handiwork of the pioneer farmers. Yet the last two chapters have shown that these humble founders of a way of life that was to be the basis of all the human achievements still lying in the future were already beginning to change the face of the earth. By 4000 B C in the cradlelands of farming, by 2000 B C in regions of its primary diffusion to the west and east, large tracts of land in Asia, Africa and Europe had become man-made landscapes. In one countryside it might be a numerous scatter of clustered mud-brick villages; in another a straggle of matted huts; in a third, groups of high-roofed wooden longhouses. Here the surroundings might be open or even semi-desert; there dense forest might enfold the settlements or marshes or water stretch round them. But everywhere in the favoured regions there were human habitations surrounded by cultivated fields and well-cropped pastures. And everywhere there were increasing numbers of men, women and children endowed with the energy and the powerful, if hardly conscious, will that was to strengthen their control and extend it more and more widely.

POTTING AND POTTERY

It was long held to be axiomatic that true Neolithic cultures included the craft of potting among their skills. Very soon after agriculture made a settled home both possible and necessary, woman invented the processes of shaping and firing clay. An added incentive was provided by the need for watertight containers and cooking-vessels to contain cereal foods and, perhaps, dairy produce. So the argument went. It remains true up to a point, but we now know that farming and a settled life had been established, at any rate in south-west Asia and the eastern Mediterranean, thousands

of years before the invention of fired pottery. As we have
seen at both Jericho and Jarmo (pp. 308-11) there was a long
period of occupation before pottery came into use. At Jericho the first pots can be dated to about the middle of the
sixth millennium B C, while the settlement goes back towards
or into the eighth millennium. There was a clearly defined
pre-ceramic phase in Peru, when the farming and fishing
communities of the coast made free use of gourds. Although
the introduction of pottery among them has not been closely
dated, it may have taken place by 1200 B C. Villagers in
the Valley of Mexico were making good pottery as early as
1500 B C.

When potting reached Jericho and Jarmo, the craft had
evidently progressed beyond the experimental stage. Nowhere
in south-west Asia have the first tentative efforts at the firing
of clay vessels been recognized. It is an invention of a kind
that could easily be made in a number of different centres, for
the structural change that takes place in clay when the chemi-
cally combined water is expelled at between 450° and 700° C
can be observed in various fortuitous ways. If baskets lined
with moist clay to make them watertight fall into the fire
then a partially hardened vessel may result; fires lit on
clay-daubed hearths or cooking-pits can easily cause them
to become fully fired.

The craft was almost certainly independently invented in
America,[1] and there is no reason why it should not have had
more than one home in the Old World. On the other hand,
it is an invention that can be spread simply as an idea by
word of mouth. For instance, the Basket Maker Indians in
the south-west of the United States seem to have got hold
of the general idea from southern neighbours, but they had
to work out all the processes for themselves. It is not impossible that the same thing may have happened among the
Ertebølle people when they first adopted potting.

The raw materials for the making of pots are widespread
throughout the world. Clay is the product of the decomposi-
tion of rocks, particularly the granites and gneisses that are
largely made up of feldspar. The chemical breakdown of
feldspar is caused by the action of carbon dioxide and water
on rock surfaces in areas where air is excluded by bogs or
other natural blankets; the resulting clay minerals are hy-
drated aluminium silicates with small admixtures of such
constituents as alkalis and iron oxides. Kaolin is the most
important of the primary clays formed in this way; its deposits
are fairly well marked by the present-day distribution of
famous china manufactures: they lie in south-west England

and Brittany, round Limoges and by the Pyrenees; in Saxony, Czechoslovakia and the Ukraine, China and the southern United States.

This is the substance that, if suitably compounded and raised to a high enough temperature, will vitrify into porcelain. Practically all the clays used for ordinary earthenware, however, are secondary clays that have been carried from their original beds by water, wind or ice, and redeposited mixed with various impurities. These secondary clays are found in almost every kind of territory except on sandy deserts and coral islands. Locally, however, they occur only sporadically, and in upland country are usually limited to the beds of lakes and rivers. Thus in a primitive culture woman potters must often make short expeditions to collect their raw material.

Natural clay is highly plastic when worked with water, but may become too sticky to handle. Partly to counteract this stickiness and partly to obtain a greater porosity that prevents cracking and warping when the pots are being fired, it is commonly tempered with such things as powdered quartz, flint, sand or shell; occasionally old potsherds may be pounded up and used for this levigation—or even chopped grass or straw. The work of mixing the clay, water and tempering material is heavy and not unskilled. If a large quantity was to be mixed, it may sometimes have been done by trampling underfoot, but an ordinary Neolithic potter working for her family would probably have kneaded it by hand—a manipulation very similar to that of pastry-making but carried out with a force that would produce a leaden pie-crust. For very fine and thin wares the clay might first have to be dried out, pounded and sieved.

Once the clay had been prepared, there were several ways in which the Neolithic potters may have proceeded to build up their vessels.

The wheel, the use of which is responsible for so many of the features that we regard as characteristic of pot forms, was nowhere used in the primary Neolithic phase. The simplest method, feasible for simple dishes or bowls, was to take a ball of clay, push the thumbs into the centre and then gradually lift and thin the walls by pressing them between thumb and fingers. No great size or height can be obtained in this way, and the primitive potter is likely to use either the coiled or the ring technique for her more ambitious vessels. In the first a continuous roll of clay is used spirally, each turn of the spiral being pinched on to the one below; in the second the procedure is similar except that separate rings are built one above the other. When the pot has been roughly put together in either of these fashions, the walls have to be thinned and the shape perfected. The thinning may be done simply between the fingers, one hand working inside the pot, the other out, or some convex surface such as that of a pebble may be held inside while the outer surface is either patted with the flat of the hand or with a specially made wooden bat. The more thoroughly the thinning and shaping are done, the more completely will the coils or rings be united into one piece; in the coarser prehistoric wares the lines of junction often show when the pot is broken, but in the finer fabrics they cannot be detected.

Whatever method is employed, the gradual thinning and symmetrical shaping of a pot requires that it shall be turned round and round—a need that was bound in the end to be met by the invention of the spun wheel. Although the Neolithic potters had not advanced so far, they probably used simple devices to facilitate turning—one of which would be building the pot in a large curved potsherd that would readily turn on a hard floor. When two women worked together the vessel could of course be made to revolve if it were fixed to any solid base as a turn-table.

Having been fully shaped the pot must be left to dry in the air. When the water content is reduced to about 8–15 per cent it is in the 'leather hard' state and is ready for trimming, decorating with impressed designs (some of these are more likely to be made when it is still fully wet) and above all for burnishing. This rubbing of the walls, with or without a slip coating of finer clay, not only gives an agreeably glossy surface but helps to make the fabric less porous and therefore more watertight. A smooth pebble is the most usual burnishing tool. The pot is now further air-dried (and at this stage a strong sun is an advantage) until the water content is down to about 3 per cent, and it is ready for firing.

Many primitive potters fire without the use of a kiln, and as very few remains of Early Neolithic kilns have been discovered, it is probable that they were seldom used. On the other hand, it will be remembered that even Palaeolithic hunters (pp. 201, 230) used a kiln-like structure for hardening animal figurines, so that it would not be surprising to find this method of firing in use among even the earliest potters. If firing is to be done without a kiln, the batch of air-dried pots is piled, often in a hollow, with fuels such as brushwood, grass, straw or dung placed below, among and over them. With a hot fuel such as brushwood this process may take as little as an hour, but the uneven distribution of heat is likely to make many wasters. Better results are obtained if a method akin to charcoal burning is used, the pot stack and its burning fuel being damped down with a covering of green-stuff or earth, which may maintain a steady heat for several days. Cooling-off must be equally gradual. It is said that a temperature of up to 800° C can be created in an effective smother fire of this kind—well above the minimum required to drive off the combined water.

Firing has a great effect on the colour of the finished pot. The factors involved are complex and must vary with the constituents in the clay, but the most general rule is that if the firing is carried to a fairly high temperature with a plenti-ful oxygen supply the clay will fire red (especially if it has a considerable iron content) while if the oxygen is kept away the colour will be grey or black. A well-known demonstration of this is provided by the Badarian and Amratian Egyptian pottery in which the body of the pot was red and the top part black (Fig. 43). This attractive bicolour was secured by standing the inverted pot in ashes that prevented the access of oxygen to the buried portion while the rest of the vessel was exposed.

The Pueblo Indians of New Mexico who make poly-chrome pottery quite as fine as the Neolithic painted wares of Eurasia fire it successfully without a kiln. On the other hand if it is true, as had been claimed (p. 315), that the Halafians fired their fine pottery at temperatures up to 1,200° C, they must have used kilns. These are likely to have been either cylindrical or beehive-shaped with a furnace either just outside, or directly below a perforated clay floor. In a famous fourth-millennium example from Sialk, however, the fuel appears to have been inside the firing-chamber. Many little family kilns of beehive shape were in use among the Oltenian people of Erosd. Surprisingly enough rough kilns of turf and stone have been found at Late Neolithic sites on the Hebrides off the coast of Scotland. Possibly their use reflects the Mediterranean contacts represented by megalithic tombs. Kilns have two disadvantages to the primitive potter. They demand quantities of good faggots or charcoal as fuel, and it is difficult to make them large enough to hold anything like the number of pots that can be dealt with in an open or smother fire.

Of the factors determining the preferred pot shapes, cul-tural tradition, function and material are obviously the most important. Material plays no great part, save that if only poor or coarse clay is available subtle forms are out of range. As for function, such determination of form as the plate for

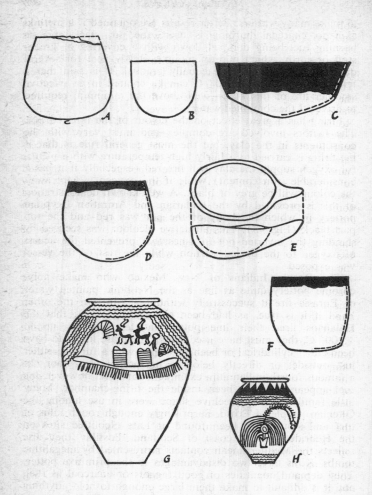

FIG. 43. *Neolithic Egyptian pottery. A and B: pots from Merimde; C, D, E, F: Badarian pottery; G, H: Gerzean decorated pottery (after Vandier).*

solid food, the bowl for slops, the beaker for liquid drinks and the constricted-necked jar for water or other storage is obvious enough. Special ritual usages determined a number of early forms such as the stand for offerings. Very many Early Neolithic vessels have round or mildly pointed bases. These are somewhat easier to make, for the thickening of the foot ring may give trouble on firing: they are also less liable to break if heated directly over an open cooking-fire. Round bases have no serious disadvantage if domestic conditions are such that they will generally be stood on yielding surfaces. Conversely, the use of tables or dressers would certainly favour the development of flat bases. On the other hand, clay rings on more elaborate supports may be devised to prevent the tipping of round-bottomed pots. The really pointed base such as that favoured by the Ertebølle, and some of the pit-comb northerners, must usually have been intended to be pushed into earth or sand.

Of far greater historical interest is the determination of shapes by cultural tradition. In primitive communities these are quite often based on the imitation of vessels made of materials other than clay—supposedly materials that were in use before the adoption of potting. We have seen that the Danubians often imitated the natural shapes of gourds, and this particular skeuomorphic development is found also in the prehistoric wares of Central and South America. Baskets sometimes served as models, as they did for the Egyptian Tasians and Amratians. On the other hand, leather prototypes (and we have assumed leather to have been used for containers in Palaeolithic times) seem to have inspired many of the plain Egyptian forms, such as those made by the people of the Fayum, Merimde and Badari. It is even more easy to detect the influence of leather containers (including the use of withy hoops for stretching) in the related plain wares of the western Neolithic cultures. The elaborate painted wares of eastern Europe, south-west Asia, Baluchistan and China, on the other hand, do not show any skeuomorphic forms; in them the craft had advanced to a stage at which form followed the best opportunities allowed by the medium (Fig. 44, E, F).

As primitive man happily is seldom satisfied by the purely functional, the tempting surfaces of pots from the first often attracted decoration and the use of colour. Patterns were either impressed, incised, gouged out, plastically applied or painted; incisions might be filled with red or white clay for contrast, or even filled with other substances (birch-bark was used in Neolithic Switzerland). Sometimes impressions were

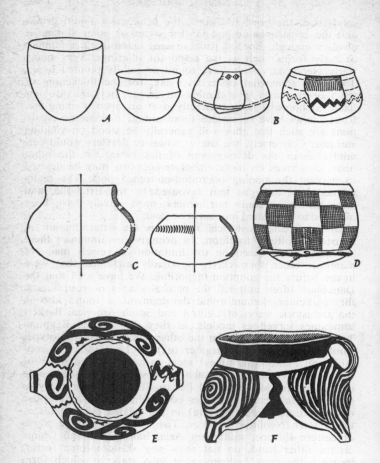

FIG. 44. *Neolithic pottery. A: Windmill Hill culture, England (after Piggott); B: incised wares, Stentinello culture, Italy (after Brea); C: Mersin, Anatolia, levels XXVII-XXVI (after Garstang); D: incised ware, Xemxija, Malta (after J. Evans); E and F: Late Yang-shao, China (after Cheng te-k'un).*

made with natural objects such as bird bones, or with pointed or cylindrical sticks; in western and northern Europe Neolithic potters often favoured cord impressions of various kinds, or used combs to obtain dotted lines. A similar dotted effect could be obtained by the use of a shell with a toothed edge such as the cockle; this cardium decoration was very popular among the earliest Neolithic settlers along the central and western Mediterranean.

The basket-shaped Tasian and Amratian pots also imitate basketry in the weave-like pattern of their white-filled incised decoration following the lines of weaving. Various kinds of incised and gouged ornamentation are found throughout Europe. One of the most characteristic manifestations is the curvilinear ribbon patterns incised on the early Danubian pottery (Bandkeramic). Round the Mediterranean (and often associated with impressed cardium wares) incised patterns were popular with some of the earliest farming communities. The designs are often rectilinear, sometimes curvilinear, and range in execution from fine scratches to broad excised channels. Such decoration is found on the Neolithic wares of Crete, in south Italy, Sicily and most of the other Mediterranean islands as well as in Iberia outside Almeria. Comparable wares are found in many parts of France and Atlantic-coast Britain. In Scandinavia, although the very earliest Neolithic pottery is lightly ornamented, during later phases of the period most elaborate and richly ornate forms of incised wares are characteristic (especially the 'Grand Style', contemporary with the megalithic passage-graves).

It has already been seen that certain elementary colouring effects can be obtained by firing alone. But for more elaborate decoration painting is essential. This was usually done after the pots had been air-dried but before firing. Often the ground colour might be simply the red or buff, brown or black, of the fired clay. But in south-west Asia an all-over slip was often used particularly to obtain a white surface. The use of slips presupposes a great refinement in the preparation of clay, for they are normally made by dipping the vessel in a solution of the finest particles. Slips may be burnished and left plain, but their advantages as a background for painted designs are very great.

The mineral pigments used by the early potters have been little studied; they were probably the various oxides of iron, with manganese for black, already used by the Palaeolithic cave-painters. Changes of colour with firing had to be allowed for.

The decorative art of the vase paintings will be considered

elsewhere (p. 438); here it is only appropriate to consider meanings and techniques. Certain of the stylized animal forms found in Asia are thought to have been inspired from copying the angular representations inevitable in basketry, and are to that extent skeuomorphic. Whether painted designs were imitative or proper to the potter's craft, their application was a matter of extreme skill. As far as is known the Neolithic potters (like the modern Pueblo) made no preliminary marking out of their designs but brushed them in free-hand—a difficult feat on the full contours of a pot. From this point of view no Neolithic wares show greater accomplishment than the large, handsome jars of the Yang-shao people of China, with their bold, strong designs covering the entire surface.

Finally it must be insisted that very many designs, whether painted or incised, and whether geometric, or semi-naturalistic, probably had symbolic meanings and magical purposes. In decorating a vessel a woman would be at once showing her skill (there is usually considerable friendly rivalry between potters), making her possession more beautiful, and serving some such end as the falling of rain, the growth of plants or the well-being of all and sundry.

VESSELS OF STONE, WOOD AND IVORY

As the Palaeolithic hunters shaped stone lamps, it is hardly surprising to find that stone was used for containers from the earliest Neolithic phase. At both Jericho and Jarmo although the first inhabitants had no pottery they were carving excellent stone bowls; those from the Palestinian site were made of calcite, while the Jarmo specimens are of variegated stones, some of them quite decorative. The Cypriotes at Khirokitia made fine vessels of polished stone, sometimes using tough volcanic andesite. They liked to enrich them with geometric patterns, possibly deriving the designs from basketry. The al'Ubaidans made some elaborate ritual vessels of stone and were even able to work obsidian for the purpose. In Egypt, where alabaster and other stone vessels were so abundant and beautiful in Dynastic times, the tradition was already represented by basalt vases at El Omari and among the Badarians. The Amratians used alabaster.

Wherever wood was abundant it is likely to have been hollowed into containers, but they have seldom survived. The Swiss lake-dwellers had good solidly made bowls and handled ladles, seemingly hewed out of the piece with an adze and then polished. These ladles may not be unconnected with those that the Badarians of Egypt cut out of ivory; these had both round and rectangular bowls, and handles decorated with animal figures. The Badarians also made little flasks and cylindrical vases out of ivory.

BASKETRY

Before the beginning of loom weaving, it is difficult to make a theoretical dividing line between basketry and matting on the one hand, and textile weaving on the other. Yet for the Early Neolithic period in the Old World it is usually possible to do so in practice; only in the Swiss lake-side dwellings have specimens been found that might almost equally well be assigned to either craft. The best touchstone for distinguishing between them, though it is not infallible, is that textiles are nearly always made from spun or twisted threads, while basketry and matting are commonly made from threads, bast, withies and the like that have not been spun and are quite often in more or less their natural state.

As spinning was itself an invention of some complexity, it appears likely that basketry would have been made before textiles. Probably it was, although the evidence for it remains slight. The coiled rush-mats which left their impressions on the floor of the houses of the second Neolithic period at Jericho must have been made during the seventh millennium B C if the Carbon-14 dating is correct. On the other hand, there may possibly have been textiles in Jericho at this time, as holed stones which could be spindle whorls have been found there. Again, some of the Mesolithic peoples of northern Europe had nets and plaited eel-traps and no textiles—but in absolute age these were no older than true textiles farther south. So in the Old World the case for the precedence of basketry is not proven. In the New we shall find it to be much stronger.

There seems little question that like so many other things in the Old World, basketry was first developed in Iraq, Iran, Palestine and Egypt. Probably the second oldest instance after Jericho comes from Jarmo—and again it is represented only by mud impressions. Here the villagers had made woven matting. They had employed the plain weave technique by which either reeds form the woof on a warp of cords, or reed strips are simply interlaced.

For the earliest known survivals of actual specimens of basketry we have to turn to Egypt. In the lake-side settle-

ments of the Fayum the grain storage pits were lined with
basketry of a type most unlike the woven matting of Jarmo
(Fig. 45). They had been built up by the coiled technique—
which may be said to have more in common with potting
than with weaving. This method depends on the use of a
fairly bulky core, made up of a continuous bundle of whatever material is being used and a wrapping or sewing strip
of the same or another substance. The core is then coiled
spirally into whatever shape is wanted, each turn being
stitched on to its neighbour; sometimes the sewing strip may
be wrapped round the core between each stitch. The Fayum
bins were made of corn straw, and were mostly 3 or 4 feet
across and up to 2 feet deep. In addition to these large containers there were straw mats, coiled basketry lids or platters
and one fine boat-shaped basket in which man's irresistible
urge to decorate is already displayed. Here the core was of
grass and the wrapping thread of flax bast, and the whole was
given life by coloured vertical strands interwoven into the
walls. At Badari there were more specimens of the coiled
technique. Reeds were the preferred material. There were
also reed mats made in two manners. One was the simple
twine, in which reeds, or slender bundles of reed, are laid
side by side and interlaced by two threads that twine between
them. The other, the only specimen of this kind of work
known for the period, was made by the wrapped technique.
In this the sewing thread is wrapped round the reed bundles,
going over two and under one.

FIG. 45. *Basket-lined grain storage pit, Fayum, Egypt. Diameter
110 cm. (after Singer).*

The coiled basketry already predominant at the primary
Neolithic settlements of Fayum and Badari remained very
popular in Egypt and was used for some splendid ornamental
work in Dynastic times.

Looking outside the cradlelands of Neolithic culture, it
appears that the Yang-shao people of China were probably

both weavers and basket-makers, but unhappily the only traces of their work are impressions on the base of their pots, and from these it is impossible to distinguish the method used—or even to be sure whether the soft clay had been placed on coarse cloth, matting or basket work. However, there is no reason to doubt that both textile and basket-making went with the general spread of the Neolithic way of life through Asia; coiled basketry was being made at Mohenjo-daro.

Turning now to the west, it is to be expected that our best evidence should come from the Swiss lake-side dwellers. The villagers were, in fact, highly skilled at basketry, favouring both the coiled and twined techniques, commonly in flax, though also in bast and rush. Twining was used mainly for bags and was therefore done spirally. An unexpected development in some of the twined material was the introduction of a fleecy nap of fibrous flax; it is not known whether this was intended for mats or for the stuff of thick cloaks. Some coiled twine pieces were padded and the nap was so thick that it has been suggested they came from cushions. Plain interlace rush mats were also made by these domestically well-provided villagers.

In Spain we find the influence of a new material. Here in a very dry cave in Andalusia, people of the Neolithic cave culture, probably rather later in time than the primary Neolithic peoples of the peninsula, had used esparto grass for bags and baskets. This fine material (of a variety that now grows only in north Africa) made very neat and elegant upright baskets; they are thought to have inspired the pottery beakers of the Early Bronze Age.

In Britain and Scandinavia we have as yet no certain evidence for basketry in the primary Neolithic phase—and it will be remembered that the Windmill Hill people do not seem to have made textiles. On the other hand, at a period probably not much later than Skara Brae, the Orkney islanders were making a coarse coiled basketry and twined sedge matting.

It is generally assumed that the basketry of the New World was, like most other American crafts, an independent invention. Indeed, the evidence from Danger Cave, Utah, has led to the claim that twined basketry of quite an advanced technique was already being made in the area by 7000 B C. If this early dating can be confirmed, then it looks as though basketry was invented in America earlier than anywhere else; knowledge of it may even have been diffused westward into Asia. We are on more certain ground for South America.

In the dry lower valleys and coasts of Peru conditions are most suitable for preservation, and so we have ample evidence of the excellence of the craftsmen. Basketry was to spread throughout the continent, and be brought to a very high pitch in both form and design; indeed, few would dispute that the most beautiful baskets in the world have been made by the American Indians. The pre-pottery farmers of Peru used sedge, reed and leaf-bast to make mats and baskets. The matting was sometimes twined, sometimes woven with reeds on a cord warp, approximately as at Jarmo. In one type of basket, twined walls were built on to a cross-framed base—a very unusual combination. One of these coastal sites has been dated by Carbon-14 to near the beginning of the second millennium BC.

Potting has been revolutionized by the wheel, moulding and other mass production methods. But basket-making remains little changed. It is one of the small but moving reminders of the continuity of our history that nowadays little girls in kindergartens, ladies laying tables in genteel cafés, are handling just the same coiled mats and woven baskets as those made many thousand years ago beside the Nile, by the first hill farmers of Asia and the valley dwellers of the Andes.

SPINNING AND WEAVING

'Spinning is the forming of threads by drawing out and twisting fibres. The thread has also to be wound, but this is always a separate process, while drawing and twisting are sometimes separate and sometimes simultaneous. Drawing consists in pulling out the fibres lengthwise, which arranges them in more or less parallel order. Twisting is the important factor in spinning.'*

It is possible that this very tricky skill, that had to be mastered before textile weaving became a possibility, had already been tentatively tried in Palaeolithic times. It is true we have no examples of it before the Mesolithic fishing-nets, but conceivably twisted fibres may have been used for bow-strings, sewing skins, or fixing dart-heads, among those Palaeolithic hunters who lived in regions where vegetable fibres were available. However, even if these hunters did make cords, true spinning is most unlikely to have been known to them, and the rapid development of the processes

* Grace Crowfoot, *History of Technology,* Vol. I, p. 424.

of textile making is one of the most remarkable instances of the great spurt in craft skills that went with the more settled life of Neolithic times.

Spinning must have begun by twisting threads between the hands or against the thigh without the help of any implement, but archaeologically this stage is very hard to detect. The spindle weighted with a whorl was widely used in Early Neolithic times. It was probably arrived at by using a stick on which to wind the twisted thread, which might then be used to do the twisting by attaching the fibres and rolling it on the thigh; this primitive method is still in use. The next and most important stage was reached when it was discovered that the spindle could be rotated, then allowed to drop and continued spinning in the air; the duration of the spin could be increased by weighting the spindle with a whorl. These whorls of clay or stone, commonly disk-shaped, conical or spherical, and perforated for the reception of the spindle shaft, are found in use among almost all the Neolithic peoples described in Chapter VIII. It is interesting to find that whorls were never employed by the excellent weavers of the Chicama valley in Peru; some Peruvian Indians still spin with a small, unweighted stick. The Danubians and the Windmill Hill people of Britain do not seem to have made textiles at all. There is no certain evidence for the craft, either, among the peoples of Jarmo and Jericho.

Weaving at its simplest can be accomplished without a framed loom. With stiff materials it can be carried out with the fingers with no kind of bar, but this must usually be regarded as resulting in matting rather than fabric. True textiles can be woven on warps stretched between, say, a tree and the weaver's waist. But the most effective of the very primitive devices, and one that was used among the Badarians and probably other Early Neolithic villagers in Egypt, consisted simply of two bars pegged out horizontally on the ground with the warp threads held taut between them. The woof threads would at first be darned in by hand, but later perhaps first the shed rod would be devised to raise one set of the warps, then the idea of the heddle for raising the other set would have been hit upon. In addition to this horizontal loom, the upright loom with two beams may have been in use (it has been suspected among the Amratians of Egypt), but all our evidence is for another type of upright loom in which instead of a second beam to hold the warp at the bottom, large weights were used to make the necessary tension. This weighted loom (which has almost disappeared but long survived in Iceland) caused the weaver to work at the top of the frame instead of at the bottom as in the double-beam form. Loom weights, usually made of large perforated lumps of clay, are sporadic but widespread among Neolithic cultures. They occur for example at the earliest settlement at Hissarlik (with thousands of spindle whorls), in the Boian culture and then far to the west among the western Neolithic farmers of northern France (Fort Harrouard).

The textile material most often used in Early Neolithic times in Egypt, Asia and Europe was flax. It must have required a period of experiment to work out the processes of retting, beating and scraping—far more complicated than the simple teasing out of wool and cotton. No finds of woollen fabrics have been made for the Early Neolithic phase, but they are extremely perishable and may simply have failed to survive. The Egyptians regarded woollens as unclean for garments, but it is hard to believe that sheep-herding peoples in colder climates failed to make them even if their sheep were not as yet heavily fleeced. Cotton was already being used in early days at Mohenjo-daro, but there is as yet no evidence for it in pre-urban times in Baluchistan. It was known to the pre-ceramic farmers of Peru.

The earliest actual textile remains come from Egypt, and from the same villages that yielded the oldest baskets. A torn scrap of linen was found in one of the Fayum granaries; the weaving is even and the two-ply threads are up to 25 by 30 to the square inch. Many more specimens are from graves at Badari; they were formerly believed to be linen, but are now thought to be of some other, unidentified, plant fibre. One piece has a true selvedge, proving that the woof thread was of considerable length. Both the Fayum and Badarian linen show the simple plain weave with a regular alternation of warp and woof threads. All the fine Egyptian linen was in this plain weave until Old Kingdom times. Traces of linen were detected (through contact with copper) in the oldest settlement at Susa and at Sialk in Iran.

In the west, once again the evidence comes from the Swiss lake-side dwellings. Here some of the napped fabrics described under basketry might equally well be claimed as textiles. The ordinary linen is like the Egyptian, a two-ply plain weave; it was even, and the gauge went up to 48 by 37 threads to the inch. These villagers knew many weaving tricks; they made borders woven at right angles to the main run of the cloth, fancy fringes, ribbed bands and a striped effect obtained by jumping woof threads over two warps ('floats'). Unfortunately we know nothing of the contrasting colours that may perhaps have formed part of these ambitious schemes. It is difficult not to regard the inhabitants of the Swiss lakes as particularly skilful and industrious among the Neolithic peoples of Europe; but in fact this impression is probably entirely due to the chances of preservation.

In the New World, the people of the Chicama valley and the coast of Peru were as active at weaving textiles as they were at basketry (Fig. 47); cotton was their usual material, but it was often mixed with a plant fibre; they used plain weave, but almost always combined it with insertions or borders of twined work. They were able to make simple patterns by the use of 'floats'.

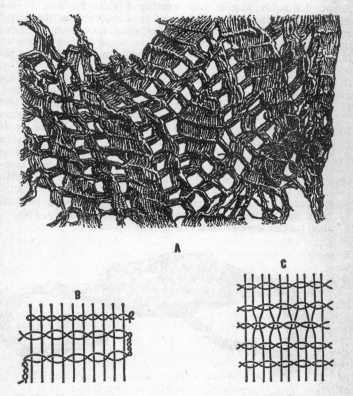

FIG. 46. *Early textiles from Peru. A: patterned cotton from Rio Seco; B and C: two forms of weaving.*

CLOTHES

While vast numbers of personal ornaments have survived from primary Neolithic times, evidence of style of dress is surprisingly slight. Presumably in all the cultures in which weaving was known, linen might be used for clothes. Probably both the peoples of Lower Egypt and the al'Ubaid people had already started the distinctive types of loin cloth and skirt later to be the usual modes in the two river valley civilizations. At Sialk, in western Iran, too, the man shown on the sickle handle was wearing a skirt fastened at the back. The Badarians still dressed in skins, but must have had linen garments as well. The Amratian men seem to have worn very little; they are depicted on some of their pots with feathered head-dresses and penis sheaths. The women favoured linen aprons.

In southern Europe the inhabitants of the Cueva de los Murcielagos, Andalusia, wore woven tunics of esparto grass. North of the Mediterranean lands, clothes of leather and furs must presumably have been used in winter in addition to linen garments. It will be remembered that in the Swiss lake-side dwellings fragments of weaving with a thick flaxen pile may have come from warm cloaks. Until evidence is found to the contrary, it must be accepted that the Danubians, the Windmill Hill people and the first Scandinavian settlers had no textile garments but relied entirely on skins. Buttons were already made for fastening clothing particularly by Mediterranean peoples; in Britain neatly finished shell toggles were probably used as belt-fasteners.

FIG. 47. *Early basketry from Peru: sling from site of Asia (Department of Lima, Province of Cañete).*

FOOD, COOKING AND OTHER DOMESTIC ARTS

Greater variety of foodstuffs and a wider range of methods for cooking them were among the immediate advantages of man's adoption of the Neolithic economy. It is true that the Palaeolithic hunters had been able, in favourable regions, to collect roots, fruits and seeds, but these relatively small and strictly seasonal supplies could not compare with having a corn store, a safe supply of tender meat and, among some peoples at least, one's own fruit trees and vegetables. Throughout the Old World mixed farming, supplemented to a widely varying extent by hunting and fishing, provided a well-balanced diet. In America, where domestic animals were lacking or of less importance, the protein supplied by the cultivated bean must have been of nutritional importance. Unfortunately we do not as yet know whether flocks and herds were milked during Early Neolithic times; it seems quite likely that the goat was the first milk-giver.

The essential cooking equipment of the Neolithic house was the hearth, and the quern for corn-grinding; in many houses, as has been seen in Chapter VIII, a domed clay oven was also installed. In any megaron or other two-roomed type of house the hearth was usually in the inner room, the oven in the outer anteroom. The hearth might be surrounded by stones or neatly enclosed by slabs as at Skara Brae. Such arrangements would make it easier to support pots being used to boil and simmer. Presumably the fire-proof pots now available were used both for meat stews and for various kinds of porridge and other cereal concoction. Primitive peoples usually make good use of various herbal flavourings, and we can assume that Neolithic man was taking the first steps towards an established herb garden. Salt must usually have been kept in store. The ovens are likely to have been mainly used for baking unleavened bread, but conceivably also for roasting meat. At least there was now for the first time the possibility of a distinction between roast and grilled flesh.

Querns, at which Neolithic housewives must have spent so many hours on their knees, were among the earliest items of their domestic equipment. They were in use already in the earliest settlements at Jericho and Jarmo. Throughout Egypt, south-west Asia and eastern Europe the type known as the saddle quern was employed from the first. This is characteristically a fairly large flattish slab which the friction of the

FIG. 48. *Saddle quern in use.*
Egyptian statuette,
Fifth Dynasty (after
J. G. D. Clark).

upper stone, pushed steadily up and down upon it, has worn to a gently concave surface. It may be set at a slight slope, so that as the miller grinds away the rough flour can fall downwards (Fig. 48). In America a similar type still persists in the Indians' *metates.* In some parts of Europe, however (notably among the Windmill Hill people of Britain), a seemingly less efficient quern was in use in Neolithic times. The upper stone was smaller, almost bun-like, and instead of being pushed up and down with a long stroke, must have been moved with a shorter, circular action, for the nether stone shows a well-defined saucer depression at the centre.

There is no definite evidence for the fermentation of drinks in primary Neolithic societies, but as all mankind at every level from savagery to decadent civilization has always been dissatisfied with his state of consciousness and sought to change it by the use of alcoholic drinks (or other drugs), it is most unlikely that the first farmers were an exception. With a regular supply of grain, beer must surely have been brewed. It was certainly already being made on quite a large scale in pre-Dynastic Egypt.

TOOLS AND WEAPONS

Ground and Polished Stone Tools

Axes, adzes and hammers partly or completely smoothed by grinding are characteristic of primary Neolithic cultures over their entire range (Fig. 49). Very occasionally they may be unaccountably absent, as at Anau. They were of the utmost importance in the new economy for forest clearance and for tilling the soil, as well as for carpentry and other specialized skills. So important were they, indeed, that the nearest approach to industrial and commercial enterprise of the period was undertaken to obtain the best possible raw materials for their manufacture (p. 431). We have seen that tools were being ground and even perforated by Mesolithic hunters (p. 221) but now that sites such as Jericho are pushing back the beginning of the Neolithic techniques in south-west Asia, it cannot be claimed that these (c. 6000 B C) were more ancient than the first use of polished tools among farming communities.

Patient labour was involved in their manufacture. First the flint and tough igneous rock which were the preferred materials were percussion flaked or pecked into roughly the correct shape; then either the cutting-edge or (more usually) the whole implement was ground down and smoothed by rubbing it on a suitable rock such as sandstone, probably always with the addition of an abrasive. If, as was not very common, the tool was to be perforated for the reception of the handle, this was at first done by the crude method of drilling from both sides, probably with a bow-drill and an abrasive; it was only in later Neolithic cultures that some kind of cylindrical drill was devised to get a clean, straight shaft-hole. Such straight perforations are found in the equipment of the 'battle-axe' peoples, whose beautiful weapons brought the whole technique of the polished stone tool to its greatest perfection.

The two tools that most concern us here are the axe and the adze—both of which, but more particularly the adze, were probably often used also as hoes. The axe, of course, was set with its cutting-edge parallel to the haft, the adze with it at right angles. The axe was symmetrical, usually oval, in cross-section, and thick enough to stand vigorous use against tree-trunks; the adze was normally asymmetrical, probably D-shaped in section and might be much more slen-

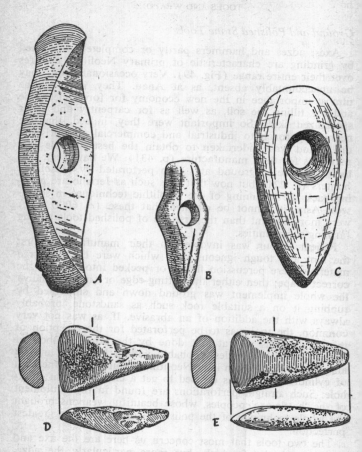

FIG. 49. *Neolithic polished stone implements. A, B, C: double-edged axes and hammer axe from France; scale 1/3 (after Déchelette); D, E: stone axes from Brahmagiri, India; scale 3/8 (after S. Wheeler).*

der. There was a difference, too, in the mode of their hafting; it was normal for the axe to be fitted into a straight wooden haft (often thickened at the upper end for its reception) while the adze had to be bound into an elbowed handle.

These polished axes and adzes are everywhere so similar that it is seldom useful to try to distinguish between one region or culture and another. Perhaps there is some general tendency for the northern forest-dwellers to make larger and rather finer axes; in later Neolithic times in Scandinavia a square-sided form that was probably derived from metal prototypes was sometimes of gigantic size—up to 30 inches in length. The Danubian culture is characterized by a rather special form that used to be called the 'shoe-last celt'. Essentially it is an adze with a pronounced D section; there is no question that it often served as a carpenter's adze, but it probably also served these agriculturalists for their hoe; in both uses it would have been set in an elbowed handle.

In some later Neolithic cultures specialized tools such as carpenter's gouges and chisels were added to the range of tools in polished stone.

Hoes and Digging-Sticks

Although it has been shown that both adze and axe blades were used as hoes by the early farmers, more specialized versions of this essential implement of small-scale cultivation were also made in a few places. The best-known come from Hassuna (p. 313). They are rather clumsy, flaked from quartzite and sandstone and unpolished; the broad cutting-edge may measure about 15 centimetres across. All taper from this broad edge to a point at the other end, but while some are triangular, others are more pear-shaped; they are moderately thin and sometimes curved between butt and edge. They were hafted with the help of bitumen. Comparable to these Hassuna hoes are some flaked stone hoe-adzes from Sialk; these, too, are normally unpolished although rarely the edge may be ground.

The digging-stick, which was probably already in use in Palaeolithic times for getting roots, must have continued in use beside more advanced implements. Digging-sticks can only be detected archaeologically when perforated stones were used to weight them. It is worth noticing that such stones have been found at Jarmo.

Sickles

The other all-important agricultural tool used by the early farmers was the sickle. The Mesolithic Natufian sickles in

which small, blunted-back blades were set in the edge of a
rib-bone haft have been described (p. 255 and Fig. 50).
This type of construction remained popular among the earliest farmers of south-west Asia and Egypt. It already seems
to have been in use at Jarmo. There were also more elaborate
forms prevalent in the more westerly parts of the region in
and round Palestine in which the cutting-edge of each flint
was denticulated; sometimes coarsely, as at Abu Usba, Byblos,
and in the Yarmukian of Palestine; sometimes more finely
as in the early Amouq culture and at Jericho. Simple blades
were used at Hassuna, and at Sialk long ribbon-like blades
were set in ribs with carved handles extraordinarily like the
Natufian hafts.

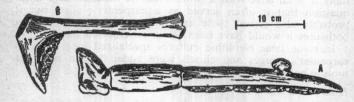

FIG. 50. *Mesolithic and Neolithic sickles. A: Natufian bone
       sickle with animal's head handle and flint teeth (re-
       stored), Mount Carmel, Palestine; B: flint sickle, with
       antler haft [reconstructed, Denmark (after Singer)].*

The same straight, composite form was also used by the
early farming peoples of the Nile valley; but here the hafts
seem often to have been made of wood. The little blades
from them are immensely common at Merimde, rather less
so at Badari. At the Fayum the denticulated variety reappears
—set in a wooden haft. Roughly the same kind of implement
was used in Anatolia and south-east Europe. It is interesting
to find the denticulated variety identical with that characteristic of the Fayum in use among the people of El Garcel—
whose African origin is generally accepted.

The early history of the sickle in western and northern
Europe is not clearly established. Probably the oldest known
type is that used by the first Cortaillod people of Switzerland.
The wooden handle was pointed and the blade was formed
by a single flint flake set about half-way up the handle and
projecting obliquely upwards. Evidently the haft was tapered
on beyond the blade so that it could be turned and used for
gathering together the stalks before cutting. Later in Cortaillod times this curious form was improved. The wooden point

was now still more slender and curved sideways for gathering, while the flint (or flints) were slotted into the side of the shaft at right-angles to the hook. While this evolved form was undoubtedly more efficient, it still demanded two quite separate movements of the reaper; one to gather, the other to cut.

By the end of Neolithic times an implement in which a single flint was set in wood or antler is thought to have been in use in Scandinavia. This crooked form (Fig. 50, B) was near the true sickle shape. For in truth the straight type that served to reap man's earliest crops should not properly be called a sickle but a reaping knife. With its straight edge it did nothing to gather and hold the stalks; the reaper must have had to grasp them firmly in quite small bundles and saw away at them—probably close below the ears. The single, slightly crescentic blade set in an antler in such a way that the tine continued the curve was an approximation to the jaw-shaped sickle which by that time had long been in use in Egypt and Asia. In Britain another variant has been rather doubtfully reconstructed. This again is in one piece, a carefully flaked blade with a curved tip, and it has been thought that it was set at right-angles at the end of a straight shaft. This arrangement would certainly serve to gather the heads, but the cutting-edge would still be wrongly placed. In China and adjacent regions the Neolithic farmers used both reaping knives and sickles made from potsherds and large shells.

One other implement of the true sickle form deserves mention as an impressive example of Neolithic adaptability to local materials. The al'Ubaid people of the lower Tigris-Euphrates had no native stone suitable for making blades. They therefore made sickles of clay, and fired them at a high enough temperature to obtain partial vitrification and a reasonably keen and tough cutting-edge. They probably were not very efficient, but they were easily made and so could be easily discarded when blunt.

Weapons and Other Flint and Stone Work

The generally pacific temper of societies in a primary Neolithic phase of culture has been insisted upon. It is therefore not unexpected to find no great development of lethal weapons. Furthermore, it is sometimes impossible to distinguish between weapons of war and of the chase, and even between the peaceful digging-stick weight or spindle whorl and the mace-head.

The bow and arrow (Figs. 51 and 52) probably remained

the most important and effective weapon—intended primarily for hunting but doubtless sometimes directed against enemies. Many of the old types of arrow-head used by the latest Palaeolithic and Mesolithic hunters remained in use: the transverse edge so useful for fowling, the triangular and the simple tanged forms. There were, however, some improvements, principally in the delicate flaking of barbs to hold the arrow in the wound. The finest of the barbed arrow-heads were those made by the Egyptians of the Fayum, Merimde and Badari; they had no central tang, but long slender wings projecting almost straight backward in line with the shaft. Heads with both tangs and barbs were popular in western Europe, but (an interesting example of how cultural traditions can control such matters) the Windmill Hill people of Britain kept rigidly to a simple leaf-shaped form, and the tanged and barbed arrow came into the island only with the Bronze Age.

A hint has already been provided in Chapter VIII of a special cultural significance in the use of the sling (usually with clay pellets as missiles) in south-west Asia. These forerunners of the weapon of David were perhaps the one total innovation in weapons made by the Neolithic peoples. It was made in south-west Asia and was not adopted by the early Egyptian farmers. Slings appear to have been the only weapon employed by the first settled population at Hassuna; they were widely prevalent in northern Iraq and Iran. Round the eastern end of the Mediterranean, on the other hand, bows and arrows or darts seem to have remained in favour. It was the spread of the Halafian culture that brought the sling over the divide to Syria and Cilicia. From here it seems to have spread westward to be adopted in Anatolia, in Greece

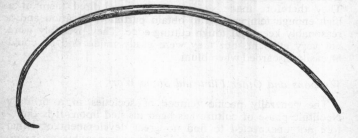

FIG. 51. *Neolithic bow from Sutz, Switzerland (about 145 cm.).*

and Macedonia, southern Italy and then gradually farther west. The Balearic Islands were to get their name from the

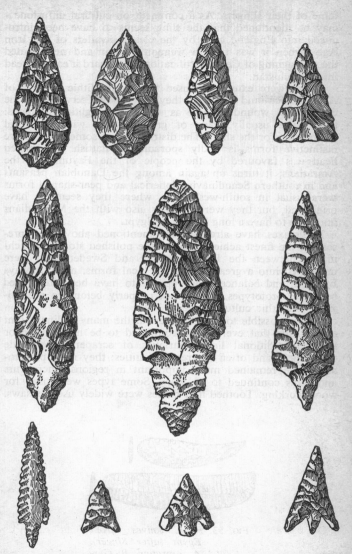

FIG. 52. *Flint arrow-heads from France: scale 1/1 (after Déchelette).*

fame of their slingers. As a comment on cultural diffusion, it
may be mentioned that the sling seems to have been introduced into England only by the Celtic invaders of the Iron
Age—when it was fully a weapon of war and necessitated
the redesigning of Celtic fortifications. Eastward it early spread
into Baluchistan.

Maces were extensively used by the Neolithic peoples of
Asia, Africa and Europe; they may have served for the
despatch of wounded game as well as for fighting weapons.
They were usually made of ground stone with a central
perforation for the shaft. The distribution of some of the more
distinctive forms is oddly sporadic. A flattish disk-shaped
head was favoured by the people of the Fayum and the
Amratians; it turns up again among the Danubian peasants
and in southern Scandinavia. Spherical and pear-shaped forms
were usual in south-west Asia, where they seem to have
originated, but they were popular also with the Merimdians
and were to have a long history in Egypt.

Battle-axes have already been mentioned above as representing the finest achievement of the polished stone-axe technique. Between the Pontic steppes and Sweden they were
developed into a great number of local forms, nearly always
of grace and balance. They appear to have been influenced
by metal prototypes and do not properly belong to the primary Neolithic cultures (see p. 342).

It is impossible to discuss in detail the many ordinary flint
implements that everywhere continued to be made more or
less on traditional lines. Varieties of scraper were made
everywhere and often in great quantities; they must presumably have remained more important in regions where furs
and skins continued to be worn. Some types were used for
wood-working. Toothed flint blades were widely used as saws.

FIG. 53. *Flint knives from
Egypt (after Singer).
A: Amratian; B: Ger-
zean: 1/5.*

Something should perhaps be said of the best flint-work executed by the Amratians of Egypt, for it offers an astonishing demonstration of what the pressure-flaking technique can do at its most skilful—although it was carried to an even further degree of refinement by the Gerzeans. The Amratians already made slender, slightly curved knives of astonishing thinness and long lozenge-shaped blades; also a fish-tailed blade reputed to have been used for ham-stringing animals. These exquisite Egyptian implements can be seen as perpetuating the ancient African tradition for bifacial points (Fig. 53 and Pl. 10, a).

PERSONAL ORNAMENT

There was no very striking change in the kind of ornaments men and women wore to beautify themselves and display their wealth. Necklaces, bracelets and anklets remained popular, and they seem hardly to have been better designed or more elaborate than the kind of thing already being worn by the Natufians. On the other hand there was inevitably a considerable increase in the sophistication of individual beads, pendants and the like and the materials from which they were made. There is some contrast here between the ancient centres of farming and the rest, for whereas in south-west Asia, Egypt and adjoining regions such articles were generally artificially carved, often from rare and precious substances, the more primitive folk in Europe, although they, too, had a variety of carved beads, still made free use of natural objects and particularly shells. Even the Danubians, it will be remembered, maintained their liking for spondylus. There was naturally a great decline in the popularity of teeth as ornamental objects, for the successful hunting of big game no longer brought such high prestige. Nevertheless boars' tusks were fashionable as far apart as Egypt (Merimde), the Swiss lakes and Scandinavia.

Another change is in the prevalence of amulets as pendants. A widespread axe-cult (p. 447) seems to account for axiform amulets, commonly representing the ordinary 'polished axe'. They were worn at Merimde, by the Neolithic Cretans, in Malta, Sardinia and round the Atlantic coast—although in this more westerly part of their range they seem to have been fashionable at about the time of the megalithic diffusion rather than among the primary Neolithic settlers. Another kind of pendant very popular in France among western Neolithic peoples is a perforated stone arc—possibly derived from a boar's tusk. Somewhat macabre amulets, made from the skull-bone disks resulting from trephining, were worn in the south of France and by the Cortaillod Swiss.

The natives of any region that had an attractive local material might exploit it for beads. Along the Nile ivory was much sought after. In Brittany the bright green caläis was popular and widely traded—but this was in Late Neolithic times; more important here is the famous Danish amber, found so abundantly on the coasts of western and northern Jutland. This was later to supply one of the most important trades of prehistoric Europe, but already the Neolithic farmers were evidently not merely gathering it individually but hawking beads in the local market. Hoards of up to thirteen thousand have been found in the northern bogs.

At the Fayum and Badari and among the Amratians disk beads cut from ostrich shell like those made by the Capsians (p. 235) remained in fashion. As emerged in Chapter VIII, many of the peoples in both Egypt and south-west Asia who were still in a Neolithic stage of culture used copper, probably always native copper, for beads and other trinkets. Another small Neolithic innovation was the wearing of ornamental combs in the hair; the Badarians and Amratians were able to cut theirs from ivory, while in the Swiss lake-side villages they made do with wood. The Amratian women may have worn them in wigs. The Badarians wore stone nose plugs, and comparable objects found in south-west Asia may have been worn in an equally uncomfortable manner.

In addition to trinkets, we have to consider make-up as a universal form of self-ornamentation among mankind. The only evidence for it that we have among truly Neolithic societies comes from Egypt. The Badarians were already importing malachite for eye-paint from Sinai or Nubia and grinding it on simple palettes. Among the Amratians these palettes were already being given decorative forms (animals were most popular) that would lead up to the superb artistic productions of the pre-Dynastic Age. Malachite (copper carbonate) was undoubtedly first sought as a protection against eye diseases—the name for the palettes is associated with protection—but equally surely the alluring effect of green eye-shadow was early appreciated.

It is not easy to sum up so scattered and locally particular a subject as this, but it is possible to distinguish two principal themes. One is that in the Neolithic economy personal ornaments and make-up, or the material for them, were the main items of long-distance trade. Then as now people liked exotic material for their necklaces and bracelets and by one means or another contrived to get them. Thus gold, copper, ivory, turquoise, carnelian, amber, caläis and many other substances attractive for their colour or glitter were being hawked about the Old World before the end of Neolithic times.

The second theme is that throughout the Neolithic cultures of the Old World the advance from the very first primary Neolithic stage to the next (which, of course, took place at widely different dates) saw a rapid increase in sophistication in these matters. The Ubaidans and Amratians on the one hand, the peoples of the full megalithic period in Iberia, France and Scandinavia on the other, were far more richly and elaborately decked and arrayed than their predecessors. In this as in more important matters they were already developing towards the full flowering of their respective ages of Bronze.

MINING, TRADE AND TRANSPORT

Because the heavy axe, usually polished, was the most important tool essential to the Neolithic economy, exceptional effort was directed towards its production and distribution. Most remarkable among these activities were the quarrying and mining of the necessary raw materials: hard (usually igneous) rocks and flint. Our knowledge of mining and quarrying, the first undertaking by man that can properly be called industrial, comes very largely from Europe. The most highly specialized of these industries was flint mining by means of deep shafts sunk through the chalk to reach the flint nodules layered within it. Nodules obtained in this way were not only larger but fresher and more readily worked than surface flint. Mines have been recognized in Sicily, Portugal, France, Belgium, England, Denmark, Sweden, Poland and Bohemia.

Where it has been possible to recognize a chronological sequence, the earliest shafts have been simple pits, while later the miners learnt how to drive galleries along the seams, leaving columns of chalk to support the roof in lieu of pit-props. The shafts might be as much as 12 metres deep; sump holes were sometimes sunk near their foot to collect rain-water, and occasionally there were even such conveniences as wooden steps. The miners had their own kit bags; the commonest tools were picks made from the shaft and brow tine of red-deer antlers, shovels made from shoulder-blades (ox, deer and pig), and wedges from antler tines. Flint axes were also used, and at Spiennes in Belgium rough flint picks. Antlers with tines left to make two-prong rakes were used for drawing back the rubble. The dark galleries were lighted by chalk-cut lamps, and the nodules seem sometimes to have been bagged and then drawn to the surface with ropes. At some sites, such as the famous Grime's Graves in eastern England, there were hundreds of shafts, and each shaft involved shifting up to five thousand cubic feet of chalk. In short, this was a skilled and specialized industry.

Once mined, the flint implements were roughed out on the spot. Usually axes were flaked to approximately their final form, only the grinding and polishing being left to the purchasers; this reduced the weight and bulk of the goods to be transported. Occasionally (notably in Denmark) the working-up was not carried so far, and flint was traded in the form of shapeless bars.

In some areas, such as the island of Rugen and in Denmark, excellent flint lay on the surface and workshops developed to exploit it. This method of working is exactly paralleled by the known factories for stone axes, several of which have been identified in western Britain (Wales, Cumberland and northern Ireland). Here again the axes were brought up to the state at which only grinding and polishing was needed. Generally the workers do not seem to have undertaken any actual quarrying for their raw materials but used scree or flakes struck from boulders. In Cumberland there is some evidence for the existence of 'middlemen' working away from the quarries, who polished the axes before they were traded farther afield.

As has already appeared in Chapter IX, it is impossible to be sure of the social background to this specialized trade and industry. It is hard to believe that the workers of the more elaborate flint mines were not specialists, even full-time specialists. On the other hand it is not impossible that members of agricultural communities went to the mines in off-seasons to dig their supplies for the year. Really large hoards of axes such as would represent a professional merchant's stock have been found in Denmark and northern Sweden. In Britain there is evidence that the transport of the stone axes was in the hands of the native, pre-Windmill Hill people, who were not fully settled agriculturalists. Undoubtedly, however it was effected, the axes travelled far within the British Isles and beyond. Specimens from North Wales have been found in the Channel Islands, from northern Ireland and Cumberland in considerable quantities in southern England.

Attention has been concentrated on the axe trade, because it is typical of the Neolithic economy. Other flint forms were rarely involved in specialized industry, for small tools could always be made by every family for itself. At Grand Pressigny in central France, however, a readily worked and pleasingly honey-coloured flint was shaped locally into long, elegant flakes that were exported widely in western Europe. This trade began only towards the end of Neolithic times and reached its height as part of the expanding trade of the Bronze Age.

Nowhere else has Neolithic trade and industry been so exactly studied as in these western extremities of the farming economy. Much less is known about sources of raw materials elsewhere. The Danubians were largely self-sufficing, but they too had sometimes to depend on foreign materials. For example the green schist used for the familiar hoe-adzes at Köln-Lindenthal had been brought over sixty miles; lava for querns was imported into Belgium from Mayen in Germany; Russian flint from the Valdai region was exported to Finland; implements of green schist from Carelia to western Finland and Estonia. Egypt was well supplied with excellent flint, but in various parts of the Mediterranean and over south-west Asia there was a network of trade in obsidian; it was already being imported by the villagers at Jarmo.

Thus although our knowledge of the processes of trade are sketchy, we can see that the basic self-supporting economy of each Neolithic community was already being broken by an import of tools, or raw materials for them, superior to what was available locally. No community (before the settling of the lower Euphrates) was wholly dependent on such imports. If for any reason supplies failed, they could get on very well without them.

The luxury trade in precious and decorative substances, usually for ornaments, has already been discussed (p. 429).

Transport

It has been made clear that ridgeways and valley tracks must have existed in Neolithic times though we know practically nothing of them. Similarly there must have been simple vehicles both for transporting produce about the farm and for travelling longer distances, even although man's, and more particularly woman's, back no doubt still bore most of the burdens. Before the invention of the wheel the simple two-pole *travois*, developing into the hardly more complex slide car, was the vehicle most likely to have been devised. Slide cars still go bumping down the hillsides of northern Italy and along the Irish lanes. No evidence for their existence (unless it is the Maltese tracks, p. 398) has come down to us, yet it can hardly be doubted. In the northern forest lands the use of the sledge continued (p. 253) and the sledges themselves were improved. Skis also came into use, doubtless mainly for hunting expeditions. In Egypt the Amratians were probably already using the donkey as a pack animal.

By far the easiest, least exhausting highways were offered to primitive man by water—rivers, large lakes and navigable coastlines. There is abundant proof of water traffic in primary Neolithic times, yet few boats survive. The Nile must have been the first river in the world to carry much traffic. Probably rafts made of bound reeds came first, but already the Badarians had boats that had been developed beyond the raft stage, and the Amratians made a very buoyant and practical craft out of long bundles of papyrus lashed together. They were large enough to support two cabins amidships and might be rowed by up to eight pairs of oars. On the Euphrates the men of the al'Ubaid culture were probably the first regular navigators of the river, and by the end of the period had already adopted sail. A model found in a late al'Ubaid grave at Eridu represents the oldest sailing boat known in the world.

Traffic had become considerable in the Mediterranean in Early Neolithic times; we have already noticed the peopling of many islands at this time and evidence for shore-line contacts of all kinds. Obsidian must have been carried by boat. Probably these sea-going vessels were wooden—as some undoubtedly were in the more northerly and westerly part of Europe. Here the dug-out canoe, already thought to have been in free use in Mesolithic times, was the usual form. They have survived in German marsh sites such as Federsee, in Danish bogs (notably Aamosen), in Finland and in the Swiss lakes. Already the dug-outs from Aamosen and Federsee show a careful streamlining of the prow.

Unhappily we have practically no knowledge at all of the use of a quite different type of vessel that must almost surely have played an important part in water traffic in Neolithic times. Boats of one kind and another made of skins stretched over wooden or wicker frameworks survive over much of the Old World. The only scrap of archaeological evidence comes from northern Norway, where rock carvings appear to depict this coracle (*curagh*) type of boat. In north-west Ireland the fishermen still use a kind of high-prowed coracle that can ride heavy Atlantic seas. Probably boats of this coracle type would have been more suitable than dug-outs for the long and dangerous voyages that must have been made to settle the Hebrides, Orkneys and Shetlands; they may also have had some share in the traffic along the Atlantic coasts from Portugal to Scandinavia.

NOTE TO CHAPTER XI

1. See p. 351, note 1.

CHAPTER XII

ART AND RELIGION

ART

IN no department of life is there a more complete break between the Palaeolithic and Neolithic traditions than in artistic creation. It is true that schematic drawing and geometric design were beginning to emerge at the end of the Palaeolithic Age in Europe and were continued in the very undistinguished decorations of the Mesolithic peoples, but if what is best and most characteristic of the two traditions be compared they are utterly unalike. The hunters created pictures of an inspired realism, the Early Neolithic peoples decorated surfaces with geometric patterns or highly formal or schematic renderings of natural forms. One art is expressive and full of emotion, the other abstract and decorative.

In only one important manifestation was there continuity between them. That was in the models and sculptures of the Mother Goddess, the form in both traditions that was most cultic and religious. Even in these figures there was characteristic difference. The best of the Upper Palaeolithic examples, in spite of their stylization, still show a sensuous response to the female body; the Neolithic figurines have lost this sensuousness, and either show a formal plastic design derived from the female form or are mere grotesques.

The leading reasons for the break must be historical change, unique and unpredictable, and the revolution in man's way of life that divides the two periods economically. That the end of naturalistic art was in part due to the mysterious workings of history, as particular and unrepeatable an event as the decline and death of any great artistic tradition, must be accepted. At the same time it is evident that the rise of the new abstract art was in part due to the conditions of the more rhythmic, settled farming life.

The only primary Neolithic achievement that is first-class even within the limitations of a purely decorative art is ceramic. In both shape and decoration the best of the Asiatic

and Egyptian pottery is as good as any that has been produced since. The only other medium in which work of any
real merit was produced was that of rock engraving—and
even this does not belong to the primary Neolithic phase.
The best of the geometric enrichments carved on the slabs
of megalithic tombs in Brittany and Ireland are powerfully
impressive and can inspire some aesthetic response, while the
sculpture of the Maltese temples is very effective indeed.
Some of the Mother Goddess figurines in the Neolithic tradition have considerable formal beauty; in their contrasting
ways the huge masses of the Maltese Goddess (Fig. 55B)
and the bare austerity of the best of the Cycladic examples
can be admired (Pl. 7, b). But even less than the stone engravings do these belong to the primary Neolithic cultures of
their areas. Certain of the Amratian types with arms up-
raised in a manner suggestive of a barbaric ancestress of
the famous Minoan Goddess have tautness and vigour. So,
too, have some al'Ubaid figures.

Only an occasional little carving might be seen as giving
promise of the revival of a representational art with the rise
of the great river valley civilizations. And here it is perhaps
significant that Egypt has much more to show than south-
west Asia, as though presaging the superiority of her naturalistic artists in Dynastic times. Some of the small carvings
of birds and beasts that ornament the tops of Badarian and
Amratian combs and ladles, as well as their theriomorphic
slate palettes and amulets, give a faint hint of what was to
come. In Asia the little peasant from Sialk is the only work
that can aptly be compared with them (Pl. 10, b).

It remains to consider the unique phenomenon of the clay-
modelled skulls from the second Neolithic settlement at Jericho (Pl. 9, a). A few of these have the fleshy part of the
face built upon the bone with some feeling as well as deft-
ness; the rest are no more than barbaric daubs. Great artistic importance has been claimed for these curious relics, but
it can hardly be substantiated. Their magico-religious interest is very much greater.

Ceramics, then, have the chief claim to attention among
the artistic creations of Early Neolithic peoples. This in itself
presents a striking difference from the Palaeolithic Age: it
has never been doubted that cave art was created by men,
while the pottery was both shaped and decorated by wom-
en. One authority, indeed, has claimed that it is entirely
expressive of the sex: for him it is 'a strictly limited mode
of art, but within its limits healthy and efficient, pleasing
by reason of the industry displayed and its external decora-

tiveness—the expression of the female spirit in art'.* This
is very largely nonsense. Almost exactly the same decorative
merits are found in the La Tène art of the Celtic Iron Age
in Europe, a virile art in a warlike society. Nevertheless the
fact that the artistic crown does pass briefly to women in
this period is clearly expressive of the fact, already established on other grounds, that the phase of primary farming
gave women a great part to play and a high status.

It is not necessary to make a detailed analysis of ceramic
styles; they can be more tellingly revealed by photographs.
Potters of the Nile never had much talent for decoration;
the virtue of their best work lies in a fine mastery of form.
This is true, in a humbler way, of all European pottery which
had any virtue at all. Only in the megalithic phase did the
Scandinavian potters achieve an incised decoration that has
great formal strength in spite of its rigidity (the 'Grand Style'
of the passage-grave phase). Among the painted pottery, in
which Asia excelled, the Tripolye, Oltenian, Yang-shao,
Halafian and al'Ubaid are all of high merit. Some of the
Baluchistan upland village designs are also excellent, but one
is doubtful which can properly be included in the primary
Neolithic phase (Pl. 8, a). It is a rather curious fact of
distribution to find that while the Halafian, al'Ubaid and also
the Baluchistan pottery painters nearly always built up their
designs in panels, often strictly framed panels, those at the
two geographical extremities, the Tripolye and Oltenian cultures in the west, the Yang-shao in the east, shared an
ability to cover the whole vessel with continuous pattern.
They also have in common a fondness for bold spirals. The
Yang-shao peasants probably commanded the greatest range
of designs; in a single grave in Kansu there were jars with
straight geometrical panel designs, curvilinear medallion
composition, repetitive motives in bands and the dynamic
all-over spiral forms already described. The pot shapes, on
the other hand, are of limited range (Pl. 8, b).

The use of the spiral in Neolithic decorative art demands
special mention, particularly as it occurs both on pottery
and in stone carving. It was not new, for it had already
appeared, though very exceptionally, in Magdalenian times
(p. 282). The Yang-shao manifestation lies in total isolation,
but the use of the motif by the peoples of the Black Earth
(Oltenian and Tripolye) is part of a wider cultural tradition,
shared between them and the Morava-Danubian peoples
and by others (rather later) round the Aegean (Fig. 54). It

* Hoernes in *Urgeschichte der bildenden Kunst Europa*, p. 40.

was to have a superb flowering in this region among the Minoans. The Danubian peasantry carried the spiral and meander designs (engraved on their gourd-inspired pottery) right across Europe. Meanwhile from the Mediterranean focus it can be assumed to have spread to Malta, where it appears in magnificent strength on temple walls (Pl. 11, a). It was carried westward apparently with the megalithic movement; it is not by any means universally associated with this architecture, but finds what is certainly its most striking manifestation in Ireland. Here a number of tombs (outstanding among them the passage-grave of New Grange, Meath) have spiral designs incised on their stones. The great spiral-covered stone lying before the entrance to the New Grange tomb is a handsome and even awe-inspiring monument (Pl. 12).

Although potters may have employed the spiral with only confused ideas about its meaning, the conspicuous use of the motif in temples, tombs and grave furniture (Yang-shao) confirms the general probability that it had a symbolic meaning. It is easy enough to derive it from plant tendrils or coiled basketry, and these may have contributed to its origins. Yet undoubtedly it came to have meaning as a symbol, and the meaning is likely to be that of endlessness—of eternity.

This raises the general question of the possibility of symbolic meaning in the decorative art of Neolithic times. A sharp distinction has often been made between the secular art of the Neolithic potter and the sacred art of the tombs and idols. One authority has claimed that 'with the separation of sacred and profane art, artistic activity in the Neolithic age probably passed into the hands of two different groups'.* This is not likely to be any more true than it was of the 'cave' and 'home' art of the Palaeolithic hunters. Undoubtedly the spirals would have been carved on tombs and temples, and painted on vessels intended for interment with the great dead, with more solemnity of purpose than a woman would have given to the decoration of pots soon to be broken in the kitchen. Yet, as the spiral serves to show, the two could be united, and it is very likely indeed that many of the standard motifs found on such formal wares as those of Halaf and al'Ubaid had their exact meanings and served to bind the household utensils into the general pattern of cultural life of their owners. This is certainly true of the

* Hauser, *The Social History of Art*, p. 40.

FIG. 54. *Neolithic painted pottery from Europe. A: Ērosd; B:
Cucuteni; C: Tripolye A (after C. F. C. Hawkes); D:
Sesklo; E: Dimini (after Childe); F: Stentinello culture,
Megara, Hyblea, Sicily; G: Aeolian Neolithic II, from
Lipari, Sicily.*

aesthetically comparable, and equally non-representational, ceramic art of the Pueblo Indians of New Mexico.

It would be an excellent thing to be able to draw together all the clues that have by now been discovered and make a statement as to why the Early Neolithic peoples had the artistic traditions they did and why they were so unlike those of their hunting ancestors. But cultural traits, and particularly art forms, are not amenable to such logical analysis, nor are they fully determined by economics or social structure. The most one can say is that the peasants had lost the excitement, the intense sensuous observation of nature, the immediate magical urges and the religious wonder at animal life that inspired the hunters. Perhaps, too, their unconscious mind was less often stirred in their quieter, more routine way of life and so was less able to inspire high imaginative art. One can say also that a perfectly successful but unambitious decorative art, showing tremendous talent but little individual genius, might well be expected in peasant cultures in which women (or the feminine principle) were powerful. Clearer understanding of artistic motifs may come from a consideration of the religious forms of the Neolithic peoples.

RELIGION

In writing about religious beliefs known only from material remains, Scylla and Charybdis lie before one. One may either imagine too much of the emotions and ideas involved in the beliefs, or one may be wrecked on the meaningless description of objects. In the Neolithic period in particular, there is the added difficulty of trying to reconcile such evidence as has been discovered with the religious beliefs and divine pantheons that emerge in the dawn of history. This, as will be shown, is a very real difficulty, for there seems in fact to be a deep difference between the two, due, one can only suppose, to the new conceptions that rose with great ruling dynasties and priesthoods. It might almost be said that there appears to be more continuity with the preceding religious ideas of the hunting peoples than with those of the succeeding urban societies: the exact reverse of what has just been observed in artistic relationships. It would in fact be going too far to say this, yet there is enough truth in it to counteract any easy assumption of economic determinism. The adoption of farming life must from the first have modified religion in changing man's greatest desires, but it made no complete break.

First of all, what was said in Chapter VII about the daimonic view of the universe, and about the roots of myth, magic and religion, is applicable also to Neolithic times. It is sometimes claimed that the Palaeolithic hunters were entirely devoted to magic and that true religion came only with the adoption of farming. This cannot be justified. Modern hunting communities, though they may not often recognize high gods, know powerful religious emotion, and, as has been shown, there is good reason to believe that similar feelings possessed our Palaeolithic forerunners. It can, however, be agreed that the life of the husbandman strengthened particular religious tendencies. The hunter's desire for good hunting was both active and immediate; the farmer consigning grain to the earth had to wait long and passively for his harvest. Such helpless patience was bound to heighten the attitude of dependent supplication. Also the regular cycle of the seasons may not only have changed the pattern and objectives of the ritual year but also have encouraged a belief in powerful divinities as the originators and controllers of such a mighty order. Certainly, too, agriculture roused an altogether new interest in the sun, rain and earth.

What in fact provided the strongest and most definite bond between the Palaeolithic and Neolithic religious impulses sprang from their common desire for fertility. It has been seen that although Palaeolithic religion may have been very much bound up with totemistic animal cults and hunt-

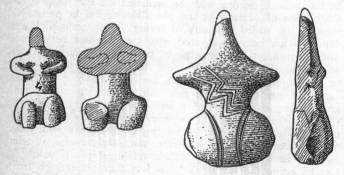

Fig. 55A. *Neolithic Mother Goddess figurines from Knossos (after J. Evans).*

ing magic, the most developed and clearly defined cult objects to have survived are the Mother Goddess figures and carved phalli. In the primary Neolithic cultures these two fertility symbols are still absolutely dominant. An axe cult

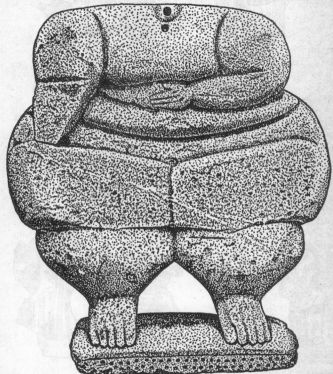

FIG. 55B. *Limestone figurine of the Mother Goddess, Hagiar Kim, Malta. Height 20 ins.*

and a more highly developed cult of the dead have been added, but these were not unconnected with the idea of fertility. Even totemism and animal cults left some lingering inheritance among the new farmers.

However much is uncertain, nothing can shake the mute evidence of hundreds upon hundreds of little clay, bone and stone effigies of the Mother Goddess (Fig. 55). They are present in the second pre-pottery Neolithic settlement at Jericho; they are present in almost every cultural province

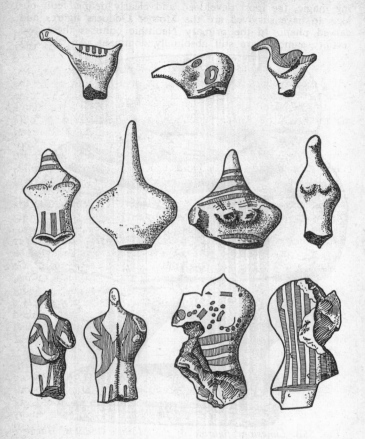

FIG 55C. *Clay figurines from Arpachiyah, Iraq (after Mallowan).*

between Sialk and Britain and from Persia to Badari. Their presence has been repeatedly mentioned in the account of the rise and spread of the primary farming cultures (Chapter VIII). The few cultures that have not as yet been proved to have possessed these figurines do not seem to have any special significance—unless it is the earliest northern farming culture of the Trichterbecher people. These northerners are not known to have made such figurines nor any other symbols of the goddess, although they evidently shared in some form of the axe cult. Conceivably this absence may have meaning if it can be linked with the later emergence of a male sky deity among the northern battle-axe peoples. At Arpachiyah it is thought that a male counterpart to the Mother Goddess (herself well represented by figurines, some steatopygous and tattooed) was symbolized for the Halafians by the bull. They made pendants with bulls' heads and hoofs and frequently painted patterns derived from the bull's head on their pottery. The figurines of the goddess were also sometimes accompanied by models of a dove. There seems no doubt that all these cult symbols (together with domed buildings) were later carried directly to the Mediterranean, and particularly to Crete.

The cult of the goddess must have been brought to its highest, purest and most fantastically elaborated form among the conservative Maltese peasantry. In their megalithic temples they kept many limestone carvings of the lady, larger than the usual effigies and always portraying her with a magnificent obesity worthy of the Venus of Willensdorf. She is not only shown in the usual standing and sitting positions, but also lying on her side on a couch, her huge hip rising mountainously into the air. Associated with her are betyls and other cult objects. If these Maltese figures are linked with the spirals that ornament the temple walls, a great deal of the meaning of the feminine principle is proclaimed: eternal continuance through fecundity.

The Maltese temples were related to the megalithic funerary cult, and megalithic tombs very often (though by no means everywhere) show the presiding presence of the goddess. Her figurines were buried in the rock-cut tombs of Sardinia, and stylized symbols representing her took many forms in the grave furniture of megalithic and rock-cut tombs in Iberia. In Brittany some of the 'scutiform' carvings certainly represent her, and one megalithic tomb (Tressé, Ile-et-Villaine) displays two pairs of her breasts on its entrance slab. She looks down, somewhat faintly it is true, from the roof of a passage-grave in the Channel Isles. Nowhere does she rule more conspicuously than over the megalithic and chalk-cut gallery tombs of northern France (mainly in the Seine, Oise and Marne departments). Here carvings representing her face, and sometimes breasts, in a highly stylized manner dominate the narrow entrance to the tomb itself. A number of these curious carvings show the

Fig. 56. *Stone carvings from France. A: tomb, Petit Morin, Marne; B: menhir, Gard (after Childe); C: slab from megalithic tomb, Garvinis, Brittany.*

goddess with an axe, one of the links connecting the two cults (Fig. 56, A).

In the megaliths of Britain and Scandinavia she is less in evidence, but some of the designs on the Irish tombs, and some of the patterns (occuli and other motifs) on Scottish and Scandinavian funerary pots almost certainly represent her.

It is possible to see these tombs themselves as representing the womb, and the crouched position of many of the burials contained in them as the foetal position in which the dead must await rebirth. However this may be, there is no question that the tombs, always kept dark and earth-fast however great the labour involved, do in some sense represent the chthonic ideas behind the Earth Mother; there is very little doubt, either, that the idea of rebirth was associated with burial in them. In this there was a contrast with the fertility ideas of the hunters. For clearly the divinity so universally honoured by the Early Neolithic farming communities was identified with the earth where the dead seed is buried and lives again. In this the religion of the first farmers is like that of most simple agriculturalists at all times. How far their Mother Goddess can be identified with the various historical goddesses with son-lovers who die, are lamented and are reborn with the corn must be considered later.

Some idea of the distribution of the axe cult has already been given in describing the little amulets that are one of its most frequent manifestations. That it was in truth probably sexual in meaning and associated with the goddess has already been suggested. The evidence already given is supported by the frequent engraving of axes on megalithic tombs in Brittany, and by the discovery there of a long greenstone axe of an obviously ceremonial magnificence buried with its pointed end towards a stone ring. In Denmark axes have evidently been placed in the bogs as votive offerings, and in one particularly interesting instance on Langeland one had been stood upright before a small earthenware cup. Another bog find was of a flint axe with a very short wooden handle evidently designed to be attached to a stand and quite useless for any practical purpose. Large axes carved in amber, found in Denmark, must also have a religious purpose. In fact this symbol provided by the most characteristic tool of Neolithic culture, may be seen as a fresh embodiment of the bison horn held by the goddess in the famous Palaeolithic reliefs at Laussel. The double-axe already made by the Halafians at Arpachiyah and elsewhere must have had a different connotation. It makes another of the religious symbols linking this culture with Crete.

It has been shown that the Neolithic goddess, though with a new earthy connotation, is directly descended from her Palaeolithic ancestress. What evidence is there for a comparable survival of totemistic ideas and animal cults? Many authorities think that the Amratian villages were occupied each by a totemic clan like Dinka villages on the Upper Nile. The representation on vases of crocodiles, scorpions, and other noisome creatures would be intelligible if they were totems, and some Amratian symbols reappear in historic times as emblems of nomes. This survival of totemistic ideas in social organization seems most likely, but how far they would still command strong religious emotion cannot be known. No doubt there would have been proper observances among the members of the nome, but there would hardly have been any strong emotional belief in the common origin of man and animal, no impassioned dancing and miming of the great spirit ancestors. The Nile-side villagers would have become both too domestic and too anthropocentric.

As for animal cults of other kinds, it is very interesting that they should appear to have existed at those two ancient Neolithic settlements: Jericho and Jarmo. It will be recalled that rough little clay models of animals were found near the colonnaded building at Jericho presumed to be a primitive temple. Similarly the villagers of Jarmo had modelled animals in clay, although here there was no association with a sacred building. It seems, then, that there might at first have been some transference of the religious feeling formerly directed towards wild animals to the beasts tamed and reshaped by man.

Something must now be said about burial rites and evidence for any cult of the dead and of ancestral spirits. Characteristically the earliest communities buried their dead carefully, often with food pots and other simple grave goods but with no funerary elaboration. Nearly always they were placed in a bent, crouched or tightly flexed position (as was also usual in Palaeolithic burials) in single graves either among the houses in the village or outside in small cemeteries. This was true of the Tasians (who used straw coffins), the Badarians (who preferred skin shrouds), the Amratians, Samarrans and Halafians. The al'Ubaidans were exceptional only in interring their corpses in an extended position. The most famous of the Yang-shao burials in China showed a gently flexed skeleton surrounded by a ring of magnificent funeral jars. In Europe the Black Earth peoples (of Tripolye and their neighbours) do not appear to have taken great care of their dead, nor do the Danubians—though few of their graves have come to light. Of the early western Neolithic peoples, those of El Garcel buried in caves or round cists, nothing is known of the Cortaillod rite, while the earliest Windmill Hill settlers in Britain were as lacking in ceremony as the Danubians, often making rough graves for their dead among the embankments of their causewayed camps. From all this evidence it emerges beyond dispute that the primary Neolithic peasantries did not at first practise either the large-scale communal burial nor yet the imposing funerary architecture and rituals that accompanied the spread of the 'megalithic missionaries'. On the other hand they everywhere readily embraced the new forms, and the recognition of the Mother Goddess, common to the early phase and to the age of megaliths, proves some continuity of religious impulse between them. The megaliths not only suggest more advanced ideas about death and rebirth, but also rituals that may have been in the service of ancestral spirits. The semi-circular forecourts, sometimes extended into complete circles, built before the entrance of certain tombs look as though they have been used for ceremonial dances. Gifts of food and drink placed at the entrances suggest the propitiation of spirits or the nourishment of those awaiting rebirth, while the small 'porthole' openings found in so many of the tombs may have been intended for the passage of spirits. The megalithic movement along the Mediterranean and up the Atlantic coasts seems likely to have been ultimately inspired by the far more elaborate funerary customs which by that time had grown up among the civilized peoples, and particularly among the Egyptians.

It is impossible to know how to fit the Jericho skull-heads into this general picture of Neolithic funerary observances. They can hardly have been trophies as the Mesolithic Ofnet skulls probably were, for they had not, like them, been rudely hacked from their bodies—indeed the bodies themselves had been given careful burial. Again, they had been more or less carefully built up to resemble the living face, and had been buried in or among the houses of the living. The chances are, then, that the original owners of these unique relics had belonged to the Jericho community and that the skulls were guarded by their descendants in the hope of winning their spiritual support.

This is the best point to mention a somewhat astonishing practice that was known to some primary Neolithic peoples as well as in Bronze Age times: the trephining of skulls. Equipped with nothing better than flint instruments, the operators chiselled round and round on the head until they had detached a neat disk of bone. Whether this feat was always performed on living subjects is not known but certainly it sometimes was—for they continued to live and the bone edges calcified. The disks were perforated and worn as amulets. This performance—one hardly knows whether to call it rite or operation—was already practised by the Cortaillod people. It may indicate the existence among them of semi-religious 'curing societies'; they may have conjured mad spirits, or harmful things the spirits had intruded, out through the hole.

A good deal has by now been said about the continuance of religious practices and concepts from Palaeolithic into Neolithic cultures. What can be inferred of the links between the religions of the earliest peasants and those that emerge in historic times? Above all, is it possible to see the primitive Mother Goddess living in any recognizable way in the female deities of the historic pantheons?

The answer, vague and uncertain as it must in any case be, seems to fall into two parts. First it is possible that the primitive goddess may be continued in certain very elementary female deities that can roughly be said to represent the beginning or basic nourishment of things. In historic Egypt the creative deity in myths of the beginning of the world were male, but Hathor, a goddess who is usually seen as a cow, but also has a role as the 'throne' or mother of Horus, represents a figure of this type. Drawings on Amratian pots seem to represent a cow-headed female and this, together with the similarity of the general conception of the Cow Goddess, suggests that she perpetuated some aspects of the older idea. On the other hand, because the Egyptians, after the unification of the Two Lands and the recognition of Pharaoh as a god, had exalted the male principle and left the female merely the reproductive and supporting role, Hathor had none of the pre-eminence that the Mother Goddess evidently enjoyed among the simple Neolithic peasants of the Nile valley.

In south-west Asia the position was almost reversed. For the Sumerians, as will appear more clearly in the next part, 'the universe was conceived rather than begotten: the source of life is female. In the epic of Creation, Tiamat, primeval chaos, is called the mother of the deep who fashions all things'.* This view was common to most of the other Asiatic civilizations.

This brings us to the other half of our answer. It concerns the seasonal aspect of the Great Goddess. So far more emphasis has been laid on the simple idea of fertility that the Neolithic peasants shared with their hunting precursors. But there is no doubt that as the peasant societies developed, the idea of the rhythmical cycle of the agricultural seasons grew upon them, an idea naturally quite alien to any hunting society. The seasonal rhythm was associated with the burial of the dead seed and its rebirth in the green blade; it has already been suggested how the 'megalithic religion' may have incorporated this conception. As this grew, the old Mother Goddess was rivalled in importance by a son, a male divinity, whose loss she must lament but who may beget upon her his own rebirth. 'For if the female principle is taken seriously as the First Cause, the male principle must of necessity derive from it, and the god is, in this view, the child of the goddess.'

With the usual kaleidoscopic behaviour of divinities within and between pantheons, the elemental, cow or primeval chaos type of Mother Goddess might merge into this rather more poetic idea of the mother of the dying god. On the other hand they were not always identical, as is shown by Isis and Hathor in Egypt. These two were often identified, Isis even borrowed Hathor's horns, yet in relation to the dying god Osiris, Isis was quite distinct. A similar dualism can perhaps be seen in Tiamat and Ishtar. Thus we seem to see the very ancient fertility aspect of the Mother Goddess continuing as something just perceptibly distinct from the Mother Goddess of the dying god, a divinity proper to a fully agricultural people. The beginning of the emergence of the second out of the first must have taken place among the simple Neolithic peasants with whom we have been concerned.

Urban life, the strengthening of intellectual powers and of individuality and self-consciousness, male rulers and priests, military conquests, were to combine to lower the status of the goddess in all her manifestations in the centres of ancient civilization. In much of Europe (though later in time) her power seems to have been at least temporarily overthrown by the conquest of the battle-axe invaders. A warrior people, their pantheon was dominated by a sky or

* Frankfort, *Kingship and the Gods*, p. 284.

sun god, in all probability the deity who was served at Stonehenge. Only round the Mediterranean, and most brilliantly among the Cretans, did the Mother Goddess maintain her sway. In large part she does so still.

Finally, is it possible to detect among our Neolithic societies the germ of the great public deities who made up the pantheons of the civilized states and who lacked the deep roots in the past attributed to the Mother Goddess? The al'Ubaid people not only built a simple temple at Eridu on the site where the later city temples were to stand, but it seems they also worshipped there the same god who was to be the presiding deity of the city state. '. . . it is likely that at Eridu there was continuity not only of architectural development, but of worship. In the absence of inscriptions this cannot be proved. But the god worshipped there in historical times was called Enki—lord of the earth but also god of the sweet waters. He is depicted surrounded by waters . . . and fishes sport in the streams which spring from his shoulders. Now a discovery made during the excavation of the al'Ubaid temples suggests that the same god was adored in them. At one stage the offering table and sanctuary were covered with a layer of fish bones six inches deep, remains, no doubt, of an offering to the god of whom it is said "When Enki rose, the fishes rose and adored him".'*

So in the history of Neolithic religion we can see the survival of Palaeolithic elements, the establishment of a Mother Goddess with a seasonal and earthy aspect proper to a primitive peasantry, and at last the first glimpse of the gods who were to come to power in the great urban civilizations of the Bronze Age.

* Frankfort, *The Birth of Civilization in the Near East*, p. 47.

CONCLUSION

THE Palaeolithic hunting era and the first spread of husbandry saw the peopling of our world. That must be recognized as the basic historical achievement of this vast span of time. From an inconspicuous and not very numerous family at the beginning of the Pleistocene Age, mankind, now a single species, had spread to cover the greater part of the land surface of the earth by the end of the primary Neolithic phase. There were still great territories round the Pacific not yet penetrated by our kind, still many inhospitable regions in all the continents that had been avoided, but vast regions in Africa, Asia, Europe and the Americas had been populated.

At the point about four thousand years ago to which our account of the diffusion of the primary Neolithic cultures has been brought, that world population varied widely in density and in modes of life. Not so widely, indeed, as it does today, but all the same to a comparable degree. The pattern of living and of density was clearly zoned. From the Indus to south-eastern Europe and the Nile valley lay the urban centre whose full history is about to be told, round about it from China to Britain and from central Russia to the Sudan was the ring of farming peoples living in villages and hamlets, some more dependent on their crops, others on their flocks and herds. Beyond them again, in the vast northern ranges of Europe and Asia, and in the greater part of Africa, the hunting cultures survived, some affected, some quite unaffected, by the revolution in their midst. In America, while there were still as yet no truly urban civilizations, there was a zoning between the farming centres in the northern Andes and Central America and the hunting and food-gathering peoples to the north and south of them.

This, in roughest outline, is the final picture, but here we have to look back over the slow stages by which it was composed.

It has been agreed to recognize as men the beings who first started to use their hands and brains to make tools. The mastery of the animals' fear of fire was a bold step of early humanity. The hunting band gathered round its hearth is already far removed from the beasts. Yet it is very doubtful if even those of us most devoted to the fellowship of man could have felt very close to the *Pithecanthropi* or yet to those seemingly more variable and promising races who created the hand-axe cultures. We should certainly still have felt ill at ease with the Neanderthalers, even if they already knew of intimations of immortality. It is only with the Upper Palaeolithic hunters that we can begin to imagine a fellow feeling. Perhaps the survival of works of art, the only fully effective bond between one age and another, the living and the dead, has made this sympathy come too abruptly; perhaps for the whole of Upper Pleistocene times some at least of our forebears would have been hardly more mentally inaccessible to us than the more primitive hunters surviving into the modern age. Yet certainly that stage of human development that saw the rapid growth of imaginative expression through the arts, perhaps a great access in the power of language, and a new purposiveness in devising material equipment to meet the challenge of nature, does come suddenly into focus for modern eyes.

We have, then, to think of the achievements of this Upper Palaeolithic Age, most of them still incorporated far down in the foundations of our modern cultures. From the past the hunters inherited bodies and brains potentially as effective as our own, but which had as yet provided them with no more than a very modest beginning in material culture. Fire, the use of cave-dwellings, wooden spears, stone tools roughly shaped for thrusting, hacking, and the scraping of skins, skin clothing—this, so far as we know, was the sum of their material inheritance. They greatly enhanced it, equally for domestic life and for the arts of the chase on which all well-being depended.

The greatest contribution to domestic life was the development of the roofed house. The best examples come from eastern Europe and from a late phase of Upper Palaeolithic culture, but it is likely enough that they were being used much more widely and at an earlier date. The possession of such artificial shelter certainly helped to extend the human range, and in particular to enable the hunters to move northward and occupy the lands released by the retreating ice. Furthermore, one does not have to be a building society operator to feel that man is not quite man without at least the possibility of an artificial roof over his head.

The great development of working in bone and antler led to better equipment for both home and hunt. While detachable harpoon-heads and barbed spear-heads made of these materials were important additions to hunting gear, the spatulae, awls and, finally, needles must have greatly increased the women's capacity as leather-workers. Thus by the end of the period the inhabitants of northern latitudes were dressed in fitted garments that could do much more than a mere wrapping of skins to defeat frost and penetrating winds. So the satisfaction of man's two basic needs in a cold climate, for clothes and shelter, were simultaneously advanced. It is likely, too, that the ability to stitch seams enabled the women to improve the bags and other leather vessels, in many regions the only effective domestic containers.

The rapid development of manufactures in bone and antler was itself made possible by the increasing specialization in stone tools that was so important a part of the cultural acceleration of Upper Palaeolithic cultures. Gouges, chisels, saw-edged blades, awls (and possibly drills for turning them), all of them tools which later would be made in bronze, iron and steel, lay behind the new techniques. It must be supposed that in forested country they were used to improve carpentering skills, but of that we have no evidence before Mesolithic times. The new blade technique also provided the first efficient knives.

While better harpoons, spear- and dart-heads undoubtedly increased man's effectiveness as a hunter, they were much less important than the two inventions that enabled him to kill at a distance. The spear-thrower, followed by the bow and arrow, must have meant that every hunter or hunting party could expect to bring back far more game than ever before. Fleet animals could more often be hit before they were out of range, dangerous ones before they had time to finish their charge.

So while houses and better clothes enabled the progressive blade cultures to extend their geographical range into colder lands, more deadly missiles increased the food supply and hence the possible density of population. It is therefore not surprising to find a great expansion of these progressive cultures, particularly into eastern Asia, where poor and conservative cultures had long been stagnating, and into the American continent, where our species had never before set foot. They were also carried into Africa, where they affected the various cultures of hand-axe ancestry, which, though they were more advanced than those of eastern Asia, had nevertheless also tended to stagnate.

The Mesolithic cultures away from the region where they gave rise to the new farming economy are generally adaptations to the new climatic conditions of post-glacial times and the resulting spread of forest. Their interest here lies mainly in the speed and success with which they met this challenge. The standard hunting equipment was modified for killing different, and usually smaller, game; nets, traps and hooks were invented or developed to exploit the sea- and fresh-water fish that had now become accessible and abundant. Fishing must also have been the main reason for the invention of the dug-out canoe and bladed paddle, in themselves considerable works of carpentry. This use of wood, representing both the threat and the new resources of the age, introduces the greatest innovation—the axe capable of felling trees. If the Lyngby antler version was the first true axe devised by man, the heavy, transverse-edged flint axe of the northern forest cultures was probably as effective an implement as could be made by flaking flint. The carpenter's kit-bag was further reinforced with the pick and the adze. Thus the Mesolithic cultures show man equally able to overcome fresh difficulties and to take advantage of fresh opportunities. When this mastery of the changing environment is compared with the forced migrations that seem to have been accepted in Lower and Middle Pleistocene times, we can see how much more flexible and purposive cultural forms had become even before the end of the hunting era.

The advances made in the non-material aspects of culture in the late glacial and early post-glacial period are likely to have been at least as great as in the material; unhappily it is impossible for us to know as much about them. We have inferred the growth of complex kinship systems, possibly totemic, and the sexual regulation that would have been a part of them. We have inferred, too, the ordering of communal societies by custom enforced by common consent and magico-religious sanctions. It has been assumed that although these societies may have been matrilineal and have allowed women a high status, their leaders would have been the most successful hunters and men with imaginative and other psychological gifts that enabled them to become shamans, medicine men and artists. There may have been no fully personified gods; but men's view of the universe about them being as much alive, as fully infused with spirit as themselves, was the expression of a religious emotion. So far as we can judge from the art, this emotion was largely directed towards the game animals with which they lived in such close relationship. Men certainly impersonated these beasts, and probably venerated common spirit ancestors. The most unexpected expression of a religious intuition was in the Mother Goddess, who seems already to have been established from western Europe to Siberia. Whether this personification of fertility came from an inherited image in the psyche or from the common emotional experience of all mankind, she has certainly, in her various manifestations, proved to be one of the most powerful and indestructible of all the great religious symbols.

As for the art that has told us most of what we know of the magico-religious life of the latest Palaeolithic cultures, it showed such an astonishing flowering of imaginative expression, such varied technical skills, that the incredulity with which the earliest discoveries were received can be understood and forgiven. No one could have supposed that the first known manifestation of man's creative powers as an artist could have risen at once to such heights. The purely technical aspect of this development is of particular interest here as it represents a new kind of cultural flexibility. If such inventions as axes and fishing gear show man's new ability to meet an external and material challenge, the devising and mastery of painting, engraving, carving and modelling show his ability to find the techniques to meet an inner, mental compulsion.

So by the close of Pleistocene times mankind had gone far towards building up the cultural foundations of future power. In material equipment our ancestors had already become the most deadly hunters among all the carnivores. They undoubtedly played a large part in the extermination of some of the old animal species. They had also devised cultural means for extending the climatic range in which they could exist. In magic they had found a means of reinforcing their material equipment by giving themselves confidence, psychological reassurance, in a hostile and difficult world. Socially they were organized for living together in an orderly fashion in spite of stresses quite unlike those present in animal groups, and by such disciplines as sexual regulation were probably already damming up vital energy and diverting it to turn the wheels of culture. And, by no means least important, they had built up religious rituals and beliefs that made it possible for the mind with its conscious summits and unconscious but potent depths to bring itself into harmony with the world in which it found itself. Without such religious manifestations the burden and strain of consciousness, the problems of the quickening psyche, might have been too much for our kind in spite of its success in creating a material culture.

As our knowledge of the earliest farming peoples carries us farther and farther back in time, we are beginning to be able to see Neolithic merging with Mesolithic traditions. Indeed at Jericho, where early in Boreal times the first farming population had tools closely related to those of the Natufians, the union can be said to have taken place. Belt Cave, too, although there is no continuity between the Mesolithic and Neolithic occupation there, gives us new understanding of a very early group of herders. Yet what we know of the beginning of farming is still so slight, so dependent on the chances of excavation sites, that we cannot be sure it is not seriously distorted.

Again, although Jarmo has taught us a good deal about the early selection and stabilization of cultivated varieties of wheat and barley, and Bat Cave in New Mexico about the cultivation of maize in the Americas, we still know little about the similar processes in the domestication of animals. The domestic forms of cattle and sheep or goats and pigs appear before us 'ready-made'. Once they had been established, it is remarkable with what uniformity the cereal crops and the domestic species that were to remain the foundation of all later cultural development were spread throughout the areas of primary farming. For this reason, and because domestic building and crafts improved so rapidly with the adoption of husbandry, we find the Neolithic communities from western Europe to China living lives remarkably close to those of all the subsequent peasantries that have supported the civilizations of mankind. Although metal tools, the plough, improvements in grain and livestock raised the output of food, there can have been little essential difference in way of life and outlook between these pioneers and their inheritors down to a century ago. Early progressiveness and later conservatism are equally striking.

There is no need to say much more about the tremendous effect the new Neolithic economy had on the size of populations. If advances achieved in the Upper Palaeolithic cultures made a considerable increase in population possible, farming and the storage of produce multiplied it many-fold. Indeed we have seen how in favourable conditions a community of three thousand souls could live in a compact little town even before the invention of the potter's craft.

This vast increase in the number of human beings who could find a livelihood on earth, together with the tendency to exhaust soils, led to the colonization of a number of localities, including many islands, that had never before been inhabited. On the other hand the limits that climatic extremes of heat, cold and aridity set on the possible range of husbandry coupled with geographical isolation from progressive movements, left many parts of the world still occupied exclusively by hunters, fishers and food-gatherers.

The domestic standards of the Neolithic populations were raised by the crafts developed by the women. Together with pottery, weaving and basketry, personal appearance and home amenities were greatly improved. Socially the villagers had to deal with questions of property and ownership much more difficult than those confronting any hunting society. We have assumed that generally the Neolithic village maintained communal ownership, and that government was by common consent interpreted by a council of elders or leaders. No doubt in the progressive cultures that were to attain civilization a more complex order of private and public ownership was beginning to establish itself in preparation for what was to come.

The underlying uniformity of the primary Neolithic village cultures, whether they were represented by the wooden houses of Europe, the matted huts of Egypt, or the mud-walled buildings of south-west Asia, is reflected also in their religious forms. These show no abrupt break with the past. The Palaeolithic Mother Goddess persisted and held sway over almost the whole range of primary Neolithic cultures; the concept of an embodiment of fertility was the same as of old, but now her aspect as the Earth Mother came to the fore. Rituals were adjusted to the cycle of the farming year, and the idea of death and rebirth assumed a deeper and wider significance. The dead were buried with some provision for a future life of the spirit, but in the absence of princely chiefs and aristocracies these preparations were normally simple enough. The furnishing of the grave with food and the weapons, tools and ornaments formerly possessed by the dead, can, indeed, be likened to Palaeolithic practice. The intense religious preoccupation with animals hardly survived in Neolithic cultures, although it is significant to find evidence for a cult of animals in two of the oldest known farming communities. Here and there animal cults may have been maintained to emerge in historical times, but more generally man's new mastery over his fellow creatures must have meant the loss of the old sense of relationship and of religious veneration for them, and the beginning of the belief that the beasts had been made for the

benefit of man. The emergence of the high gods and pantheons whose power was to become so enormous in the
ancient civilizations does not appear to have gone far before the end of our period.

Thus below the great diversity of local cultures that we
have seen to be characteristic of Neolithic times there was
also a strong underlying uniformity, based on the farming
village community with its domestic and economic preoc-
cupations and religious urges. There was, however, one important distinction between the villages of those parts of
the world where civilization was to be born and those of
other regions. They were permanent. Neolithic settlements
in south-west Asia, the Indus valley, Egypt and south-east
Europe were inhabited for generation after generation. Such
outlying cultures as those of the Mediterranean incised
wares, the western Neolithic, the Danubian, the Trichterbecher, and the Yang-shao never achieved this stability.
Climate, soil, vegetation, failures in agricultural techniques,
and historical chance worked against the long occupation of
settlements. They might be lived in for decades, but not for
centuries. The permanent village was the necessary prelude
to the city. Once such villages could be established in the
great river valleys with their ever-fertile flood plains, man's
achievement of urban civilization was in sight.

The Palaeolithic and Neolithic cultures, in their slow but
continuous improvement of material equipment, had incorporated a number of scientific principles and processes. In
making fire, in cooking, brewing alcoholic drinks and potting
they made use of chemical change. The spear-thrower was
based on the principle of the lever, the bow and arrow and
spinning on that of stored energy, the boat on those of
density and of displacement. Domestication of plants and
animals involved them with botany, zoology and genetics.
Such empirical discoveries are sometimes written of with en-
thusiasm as representing the beginning of science. But this,
surely, is a mistaken approach. If science is to have any
real meaning, it must refer to a method derived from a
mode of thought. Prehistoric men and women, it is true,
possessed that part of scientific method that depends on observation. They saw the force behind a bent bough or what
happened when a piece of clay lay in the fire, and individuals of genius made use of what they observed. But they
understood neither the processes involved nor how to make
the controlled experiments that would explain them. They
did not follow up lines of thought. Furthermore they would

not expect their 'scientific' knowledge to be effective without the help of magic and religion.

It can only detract from the later development of a genuinely scientific attitude if we try to recognize it too soon. Therefore in this account of Palaeolithic and Neolithic cultures no attempt has been made to disengage a strand of 'science' from the whole cultural fabric. This must be studied in one piece as representing early man's energetic and intelligent, but essentially unscientific, struggle to control the natural world about him.

SELECTED BIBLIOGRAPHY
FOR VOLUME I, PART I

* Signifies articles requested by Jacquetta Hawkes in connection with the preparation of this volume and published in the *Journal of World History* issued by the International Commission for a History of the Scientific and Cultural Development of Mankind.

PHYSICAL ENVIRONMENT AND RACES OF MAN

W. C. BOYD, *Genetics and the Races of Man* (London, 1951).

C. S. COON, *The Races of Europe* (New York, 1939).

R. A. DALY, *The Changing World of the Ice Age* (New Haven, 1934).

R. F. FLINT, *Glacial Geology and the Pleistocene Epoch* (4th ed., New York, 1953).

F. E. ZEUNER, *Dating the Past* (3rd ed., London, 1958).

F. E. ZEUNER, *The Pleistocene Period, its Climate, Chronology and Faunal Succession* (London, 1959).

PHYSICAL AND MENTAL EVOLUTION OF MAN

M. BOULE and H. V. VALLOIS, *Fossil Men* (London, 1957).

W. E. LE GROS CLARK, *The Fossil Evidence of Human Evolution* (Chicago, 1955).

W. E. LE GROS CLARK, *History of the Primates* [6th ed., Brit. Mus. (Nat. Hist.), London, 1958].

C. R. DARWIN, *Descent of Man* (10th ed., London, 1930).

C. G. JUNG, *Collected Works*, VIII, *The Structure and Dynamics of the Psyche* (London, 1960).

W. KÖHLER, *The Mentality of Apes* (2nd ed., New York, 1927).

T. D. MCCOWN and A. KEITH, *The Stone Age of Mount Carmel*, II (Oxford, 1939).

E. NEUMANN, *The Origins and History of Consciousness* (London, 1954).

A. S. ROMER, *Man and the Vertebrates* (Chicago, 1941).

P. TEILHARD DE CHARDIN, *Le Phenomène Humain* (Paris, 1955) (and *The Phenomenon of Man*, London, 1959).

ARCHAEOLOGY OF THE PALAEOLITHIC AND NEOLITHIC AGES

W. ALBRIGHT, *The Archaeology of Palestine* (Harmondsworth, Middlesex, 1949).

V. G. CHILDE, *New Light on the Most Ancient East* (4th ed., London, 1952).

J. D. CLARK, *The Prehistory of Southern Africa* (London, 1959).

J. G. D. CLARK, *The Mesolithic Settlement of Northern Europe* (Cambridge, 1936).

S. COLE, *The Prehistory of East Africa* (Harmondsworth, Middlesex, 1954).

C. S. COON, *The History of Man* (London, 1955).

C. S. COON, *Seven Caves* (London, 1957).

G. DANIEL, *The Megalith Builders of Western Europe* (London, 1958).

H. FRANKFORT, *The Birth of Civilization in the Near East* (London, 1951).

*D. A. E. GARROD, 'Relations between SW Asia and Europe in the Later Palaeolithic Age', *Journal of World History,* I, 1 (Paris, 1953), p. 13.

D. A. E. GARROD and D. M. BATE, *The Stone Age of Mount Carmel,* I (Oxford, 1937).

*M. GIMBUTAS, 'The Stone Age of North-Eastern Europe', *Journal of World History,* III, 2 (Paris, 1956), p. 409.

E. A. GOLONSHTOK, 'The Old Stone Age in European Russia', American Philosophical Society, *Transactions,* XXIX, 2 (1938).

K. KENYON, *Digging up Jericho* (London, 1957).

*B. B. LAL, 'Prehistoric Lithic Industries of the Indian sub-Continent', *Journal of World History,* I, 3 (Paris, 1954), p. 505.

L. S. B. LEAKEY, *Adam's Ancestors* (4th ed., London, 1953).

SETON LLOYD, *Early Anatolia* (Harmondsworth, Middlesex, 1956).

C. B. M. MCBURNEY, *The Stone Age of Northern Africa* (Harmondsworth, Middlesex, 1960).

J. MELLAART, 'Roots in the Soil', *Dawn of Civilization* (London, 1961), p. 42.

*H. A. L. MOVIUS, 'Palaeolithic Archaeology in Southern and Eastern Asia', *Journal of World History,* II, 2 (Paris, 1954), p. 257.

H. A. L. MOVIUS, 'Radio-Carbon Dates and Upper Palaeolithic Archaeology', *Current Anthropology* (1960), p. 355.

K. P. OAKLEY, *Man the Toolmaker* [4th ed., Brit. Mus. (Nat. Hist.), London, 1958].

A. OKLADNIKOV, 'Palaeolithic and Neolithic in the USSR', *Materialy i Issledovaniya po Arkheologiyi SSSR* (1959).

*A. OKLADNIKOV, 'Le Néolithique en Sibérie', *Journal of World History*, VI, 3 (Paris, 1961), p. 476.

S. PIGGOTT, *Prehistoric India* (Harmondsworth, Middlesex, 1950).

S. PIGGOTT, *Neolithic Cultures of the British Isles* (Cambridge, 1954).

*F. H. H. ROBERTS, 'Earliest Men in America', *Journal of World History*, I, 2 (Paris, 1953), p. 255.

CHÊNG TE-K'UN, *Prehistoric China* (Cambridge, 1959).

H. M. WORMINGTON, *Ancient Man in North America* (4th ed., Denver, 1957).

F. E. ZEUNER, *Dating the Past*, (3rd ed., London, 1958).

SPEECH AND LANGUAGE

A. GARDINER, *The Theory of Speech and Language* (2nd ed., Oxford, 1951).

C. D. HOCKETT, 'Origins of Speech', *Scientific American* (September, 1960).

O. JESPERSEN, *Language, its Nature, Development and Origin* (London, 1922).

R. A. PAGET, *Human Speech* (London, 1930).

*R. A. PAGET, 'The Origin of Language with Special Reference to the Palaeolithic Age', *Journal of World History*, I, 2 (Paris, 1953), p. 399.

G. RÉVÉSZ, *Urspung und Vorgeschichte der Sprache* (Bern, 1946).

A. SOMMERFELT, 'Speech and Language', *History of Technology*, ed. C. J. Singer, 4 (Oxford, 1954), p. 85.

*A. SOMMERFELT, 'The Origin of Language: Theories and Hypotheses', *Journal of World History*, I, 4 (Paris, 1954), p. 885.

SOCIETY

R. BENEDICT, *Patterns of Culture* (New York, 1935).

V. G. CHILDE, 'Early Forms of Society', *History of Technology*, ed. C. J. Singer, I (Oxford, 1954), p. 38.

J. G. D. CLARK, *Prehistoric Europe: the Economic Basis* (London, 1952).

C. D. FORDE, *Habitat, Economy and Society* (London, 1945).

R. H. LOWIE, *Primitive Society* (New York, 1920).

M. D. SAKLINS, 'The Origin of Society', *Scientific American* (September, 1960).

S. ZUCKERMAN, *The Social Life of Monkeys and Apes* (New York, 1932).

MATERIAL CULTURE

K. and F. BERTSCH, *Geschichte unserer Kulturpflanzen* (Stuttgart, 1947).

H. H. BOBART, *Basketwork through the Ages* (Oxford, 1936).

V. G. CHILDE, *Man Makes Himself* (4th ed., Oxford, 1941).

*V. G. CHILDE, 'Documents in the Prehistory of Science', *Journal of World History*, II, 1 (Paris, 1954), p. 9.

R. J. FORBES, *Studies in Ancient Technology* (Leiden, 1955).

L. FRANCHET, *La Céramique Primitive* (Paris, 1911).

J. L. KELSO and J. P. THORLEY, 'Study on Ancient Potting Techniques', *Annual of the American School of Oriental Research*, 21-2 (1943).

F. H. S. KNOWLES, *Stone-worker's Progress* [Oxford (Pitt-Rivers Museum), 1953].

K. P. OAKLEY, *Man the Toolmaker* [4th ed., Brit. Mus. (Nat. Hist.), London, 1958].

C. O. SAUER, *Agricultural Origins and Dispersals*. American Geological Series (New York, 1952).

R. U. SAYCE, *Primitive Arts and Crafts* (Cambridge, 1933).

C. J. SINGER, E. J. HOLMGARD and A. R. HALL (eds.), *A History of Technology*, I (Oxford, 1954).

R. THEVENIN, *Origine des Animaux Domestiques* (Paris, 1947).

G. D. WU, *Prehistoric Pottery in China* (London, 1938).

ART AND RELIGION

H. G. BANDI and J. MARINGER, *Art in the Ice Age* (Basel-London, 1953).

H. BREUIL, *Four Hundred Centuries of Cave Art* (London, 1952).

J. CAMPBELL, *The Masks of God: Primitive Mythology* (London, 1960).

O. G. S. CRAWFORD, *The Eye Goddess* (London, 1957).

J. G. FRAZER, *The Worship of Nature* (London, 1926).

P. GRAZIOSI, *L'Arte dell'Antica Età della Pietra* (Rome, 1956) and *Palaeolithic Art* (London, 1960).

J. HARRISON, *Ancient Art and Ritual* (London, 1918).

E. O. JAMES, *Prehistoric Religion* (London, 1957).

A. LAMING, *The Lascaux Cave Paintings* (London, 1949).

G. R. LEVY, *The Gate of Horn* (London, 1948).

G. H. LUQUET, *L'Art et la Religion des Hommes Fossiles* (Paris, 1926).

L. PERICOT GARCÍA, *El Arte Rupestre Español* (Barcelona, 1950).

R. SUMMERS (ed.), *Prehistoric Rock Art of Rhodesia and Nyasaland* (London, 1959).

INDEX

Abbevillian culture, 117, 119, 122, 124, 128, 132–3, 211–2, 236–7

Abyssinia, 71, 134

Acheulian culture, 117, 118, 122, 129–33, 181–2, 199, 206, 207, 211, 215–6, 236–7

Addavra Cave (Sicily) 277

adzes, 309, 329, 334, 421–3: *see also* axes

aesthetic sense, development of, 167, 187, 265

Afalou bou Rummel, 104

Afanasievo culture, 348

Africa, 67; Almerian cultures and, 335; Australopithecines, 87–90; Capsian culture, 147; cave paintings and rock art, 147–8, 264–5, 278–9; Dabba culture, 145–7; origin of desert areas, 76, 77–9; fossil finds, 89–91, 98–104, 130, 135; lake formations, 71; Levalloisian culture, 133; Mesolithic cultures, 257–8; Middle Stone Age cultures, 246; Negroids, 107; Oranian culture, 145; pebble-tools, 122; pre-*sapiens* and earliest emergence of *Homo sapiens*, 49, 83, 92–3, 102–5; oldest tool finds, 117–24, 129, 130, 132, 134: *see also* Bantu tribes; Bushmen; Hottentots; Pygmies; and entries for individual countries and sites

after-life, beliefs in, 182, 288

agriculture, 74, 303–50 *passim*, 366–83

Ahrensburg culture, 156, 251

alabaster, 321, 322, 409

Alaska, 153, 183

Algeria, 147

Almerian cultures, 334–5

alpaca (animal), 380

Alps, first folding of the, 62–3; ice-sheet, 68

Altamira paintings, 263, 265, 276

al' Ubaid: *see* Ubaid, al'

America, 63; agriculture, 349–50; basketry and weaving, 413–4; cave-dwellers, 197; deities, 363; desert areas, 76, 79; dwellings, 188–9, 395; hunting, 65; lake formations, 72; man's arrival in, 50, 70, 105–6, 148–50; Mesolithic cultures, 154; Neolithic cultures, 349; population densities, 183; Post-Pleistocene cultures; pottery, 402, 403, 405; priests, 363; racial types, 106, 108–10; spirit cults, 295; textiles, 416–7; tools, 153–4; tribal system, 183; vegetables, 375, 376; vegetation, 65: *see also* North American Indians

Amratian culture, 324–5, 381, 405, 407, 410, 418, 428, 434, 448, 450

Anatolia, 329–31, 364

ancestor worship, 192, 294, 448

Andaman Islands, 108

Andes Mountains, first folding of, 62; ice-sheets, 71

Angles-sur-l'Anglin (France), 232, 267, 277–8

animal cults, 233, 289, 293, 448: *see also* totemism

animals, 63–5, 73, 77, 79, 81, 143; in art, 157, 265, 270, 276, 277, 280, 315; domestication of, 64, 324, 345, 350, 376–80; as food, 153, 207–8: *see also* animal

An **NAL** Hardcover Book

A must for business executives—
and for men on their way up
MANAGERS FOR TOMORROW

BY THE STAFF OF Rohrer, Hibler & Replogle
Charles D. Flory, EDITOR
WITH Paul J. Brouwer, Thomas B. Blackwell,
AND Howard D. Smith, ASSOCIATE EDITORS
INTRODUCTION BY Clarence B. Randall

For men at the top in the business community, this comprehensive new guide by leading psychological consultants to management analyzes the increasingly complicated role of today's executive, and provides new insight into the problems of recruiting, training, and holding men destined for future business leadership.

For the young businessman, the authors' analysis of what motivates success, of what criteria are used to select and develop executives, will help him to realize his business goals more constructively and effectively.

If you want to learn how to increase career potential in yourself or in others, you may purchase MANAGERS FOR TOMORROW at your local bookstore, or use the coupon below to place your order for this book. You will find it an indispensable addition to your business library.

NEW AMERICAN LIBRARY,
501 Madison Avenue, New York, N. Y. 10022

Please send.......copies of MANAGERS FOR TOMORROW
(H0023). Enclosed is my check for..............($5.95 plus 15¢
per copy to cover mailing)*

NAME_____

ADDRESS_____

CITY_____STATE_____ZIP____
* New York City residents add 4% for City Sales Tax.